Stoddard Martin is an editor, journalist and lecturer. Currently he teaches writing and literature at Harvard University. He attended Stanford University and University College, London, where he received his Ph.D. He is the author of three novellas, two screenplays and three critical books: *Wagner to "The Waste Land"*, *California Writers* and *Art, Messianism and Crime*.

ORTHODOX HERESY

Orthodox Heresy

The Rise of 'Magic' as Religion and its Relation to Literature

Stoddard Martin

St. Martin's Press   New York

First published in the United States of America in 1989

Printed in Hong Kong

ISBN 0–312–02389–8

Library of Congress Cataloging-in-Publication Data
Martin, Stoddard, 1948–
  Orthodox heresy.
  Bibliography: p.
  Includes index.
  1. Magic—Religious aspects.   2. Cults.   I. Title.
BL65.M2M37 1989   299   88–15863
ISBN 0–312–02389–8

BL
65
.M2
M37
1989

In memory of my mother

(1912–85)

*who had little time for religious
'nonsense' in her life but, as she
died, seemed to begin to wish that
one might look forward to something
more*

Contents

Acknowledgements

Of the many people who assisted with this book, special thanks are due to Deirdre Toomey, whose knowledge of Yeats – and through Yeats of Theosophy, the Golden Dawn and Aleister Crowley – was always engagingly offered, and who made useful suggestions on the text; also John Symonds, who authorised quotation of Crowley materials originally in his possession, and Anna Haycraft (Alice Thomas Ellis), who read the typescript on completion and in some ways helped to guide me to the subject in the first place.

Others whose inspiration and support were essential include the Rodney Beard family of Stanford, California, especially Julie for providing exposure to Scientology over the years, Philip for contact with Steinerism and other things German, and – as ever – Edin, who listened and encouraged. I am grateful too to Christine Salmon, Geoffrey Layton, William and Lynne Wilkins and not least Vince Whelan for moral support.

Finally, thanks are also due to the staff of the British Library and the Warburg Institute and to my editor, Frances Arnold, whose enthusiasm has made author–publisher relations a consistent pleasure; also to Valery Rose and Graham Eyre, who have seen the work through production with faithful attention, and to Virginia Smyers of Harvard University, who helped me prepare the index.

1

Introductory: 'Magic' as Word and Idea

I DEFINITIONS

At least since the advent of the written word, the problem of 'magic'[1] has given rise to prolix and unruly discussion; and any author approaching it in the present day might begin by admonishing himself to proceed with simplicity. To simplify 'magic' may involve making generalizations, which in turn may give rise to objections from those who fancy themselves 'adept'. If so, so be it. This author is no adept and can claim only vast ignorance in an area of all-embracing knowledge. Still, it seems imperative that any author seeking to gain a comprehensive view of modern literature and thought should at some stage try to come to grips with this elusive yet pervasive motif.

To begin with, he must have a lexicon. In 'magical' texts from the Bible to works of Aleister Crowley, we come up against the idea of a generative *Logos*. 'In the beginning was the Word.' The word in this case is 'magic', and it has been bandied around so loosely as to seem opaque – as opaque as 'love', which indeed it may be, if not more so. *The Oxford English Dictionary*, for instance, describes it as 'the pretended art of influencing the course of events by compelling the energy of spiritual beings or by bringing into operation some occult controlling principle of nature; sorcery or witchcraft'. This is daunting. What is meant in the context by 'energy', 'spiritual beings', 'occult', 'sorcery', 'witchcraft'? If the 'compelling' of 'energy' is a part of 'magic', then does 'magic' include the processes of the internal combustion engine; or, more daunting still, the nuclear bomb?

'Energy' is defined by the same dictionary as '1. Force or vigour of expression. . . . 2. Exercise of power, operation, activity. . . . 3. The capacity and habit of strenuous exertion. . . . 4. Power actively

1

and efficiently exerted. . . . 5. Ability or capacity to produce an effect. . . .' This may be helpful. From it we might construe, with a little reflection, that, while many forms of 'energy' do not involve 'magic', at least not in an important sense as we use these terms, no form of 'magic' can fail to involve 'energy', in at least one of the forms described.

'Spiritual beings'? 'Energy' is a fairly concrete term: 'masculine', having to do with force. 'Spirit', however, introduces abstraction. What is this nebula? The same dictionary animadverts on '1. The vital principle in man. . . . 2. The soul of a person, as commended to God, on passing out of the body in the moment of death'; or, more obscurely still, at least to the garden-variety materialist, '3. A supernatural, incorporeal, rational being or personality, usually regarded as imperceptible at ordinary times to the human senses, but capable of becoming visible at pleasure, and freq. conceived as troublesome, terrifying, or hostile to mankind.' This last is no doubt what the *OED* dictionary has in mind by 'spiritual beings' when defining 'magic'; and with it we might rest for the moment without trying to take in the compilers' observations about the relation of 'spirit' to 'the deity', man or medieval alchemists.

'Occult' introduces different elements of obscurity. It is described as '1. Hidden, concealed. . . . 2. Secret; communicated only to the initiated. . . . 4. Of the nature of or pertaining to those sciences involving the knowledge or use of the supernatural (as magic, alchemy, astrology, theosophy, and the like). . . .' Here we begin to confront the maddening quality of dictionaries to define one term by reference to another, which in turn is defined by the term from which we have been referred. Our trusty tome also fails to be precise about *what* is 'hidden', 'concealed' and 'secreted' behind the term 'occult'. From other sources, we might construe this to be the discarded fragments of old religions and mythologies. Thus a person who is said to 'dabble in the occult' (and the occult, by its nature, is best given to 'dabbling') occupies himself in gathering odd bits of lore – 'fragments shored against my ruins', as T. S. Eliot put it[2] – in order to develop some new, eclectic, idiosyncratic and therefore usually obscurantist system.

'Sorcery' and 'witchcraft'? But the author, if not the reader, is beginning to weary of rushing to the shelf to pin down each term. And 'sorcery' and 'witchcraft' do not seem as germane to 'magic' for him as for the lexicographer.[3] Both refer to traditions of the occult primarily devoted to doing mischief – even evil, perhaps –

and traditionally associated with a turning-upside-down, or reversal, of orthodox ritual – specifically that of the Catholic Church in the Middle Ages. 'Magic', however, constitutes for this author a concept so elastic as to allow inclusion of Catholic mysticism and humanistic Cabalism[4] as well as their negating opposites.

As one historian of the tradition has written, 'Side by side with those strayed seekers into the mysterious who had deliberately chosen the path of evil, there were many possessors of occult secrets and magic formulas who lived, like the sorcerers, on the fringe of everyday life, but put or claimed to put their knowledge at the service of good.'[5] These the historian designates as 'magicians' proper. Returning to the dictionary once more, we might add that this designation, as well as its root, derives from the word 'mage' or 'magus', which refers to 'a member of the Persian priestly class' and comes down via Greek, Latin and early French, gathering accretions of meaning from each of these cultures as it passed through.

Thus 'magic' must refer to the doings of not only 'sorcerers' and 'witches' but also, more significantly, 'priestly' inquirers. It includes the 'white' as well as the 'black' (*magie noire* is a term the French began to use widely in the eighteenth century to describe pursuit of 'powers' for anti-social aggrandizement, rather than for personal or general well-being[6]). 'Magic' in this sense is related to 'science' and 'wisdom' as much as to 'power'. As concept, it is moving in the direction of 'religion' – which, in its turn, is variously defined as 'A bond between man and the gods . . . 1. A state of life bound by monastic vows. . . . 2. A particular monastic or religious order or rule. . . . 3. Action or conduct indicating a belief in, reverence for, and desire to please, a divine ruling power. . . . 5. Recognition on the part of man of some higher unseen power as having control of his destiny, and as being entitled to obedience, reverence and worship; the general mental and moral attitude resulting from this belief, with ref. to its effect upon the individual or community; personal or general acceptance of this feeling as a standard of spiritual and practical life.'

Of course there is a second definition of 'magic', one which small children will no doubt think of first. This is the *unpretended* art of creating illusions, or 'conjuring': the 'magic' of the sideshow –

sawing the girl in half, pulling the rabbit out of the hat – which
has to do mostly with concentrating spectators' attention *away*
from the real action taking place. This sub-set of the *Logos* is
not one we are principally concerned with. That Uri Geller can
apparently bend spoons without grasping them is remarkable, but
it has little or no *moral* significance; and 'magic' historically may
have more to do with the study of morals than any other discipline
– to wit, its origins among priests of the oldest civilisation known
to have priests,[7] and its frequent association in popular estimation
with 'anti-moralists' (witches and sorcerers) of so many traditions.

In this light, the 'white' *versus* 'black' dichotomy is of central
importance. The Persian religion of Zoroaster, of which the 'magi'
were priests, posited a war for universal dominance between the
opposed principles of Ahura Mazda, representing the light and
the good, and Ahriman, lord of darkness and evil. The 'magi'
were supposed to be able to play one of these forces off against
the other; and in traditions of 'magic' which have followed –
certainly those of the Middle Ages – a war of angels and demons,
forces of good and evil, has been prominent. With its relegation
of the devil to a status inferior to God, the orthodox Church
was not disposed to favour any such dualism. Thus those who
perpetuated a Persian sort of moral split – Manichaeans, Gnostics
and others – were condemned as 'heretics'. In fact, they were
really rival 'white' magicians of a different order of belief.

In the eyes of the Church, such 'heretics' were no less dangerous
– perhaps even more so – than those who conscientiously sought
to turn dogma on its head and celebrate their 'sabbath' on the
bare Brocken hill. Along with these, the tag 'heretic' was also
applied to those who persisted in believing in pre-Christian dieties,
whether of Egyptian, Greek, Roman, Celtic or Nordic origins.
Equally proscribed, all heresies went 'underground', there to
commingle, so that doctrines of one, formerly distinct, became
mixed up with symbols of another. Then too came motifs from
rival monotheisms beyond Rome (Judaism, Islam) and even from
'non-believing' polytheistic disciplines further afield (Buddhism,
Hinduism, and so on), as well as traditions which these had
supplanted, such as Chaldean astrology.

Thus a homogenising trend in Western heresy began, and its
progress is fascinating. It takes us beyond our immediate subject,
however, which remains this protean word and its definition.
Thinking about it, looking at it and referring once more to the

dictionary, we might see how 'magic' suggests sibling concepts. 'Image' is one. 'Imaginary', 'imagination' – Theodore Ziolkowski makes much out of this linguistic connection in his book *Disenchanted Images*;[8] and for us it is valuable as an indication of how 'magic' relates to *inward vision*, as the forces and spirits which the 'magician' is supposed to be able to conjure do not always come out of heaven or hell directly. Indeed, more often – particularly in the modern period, and particularly in that most inward of the arts, psychological fiction – they come from within the 'magician' himself, either through some 'medium' or via a form of ritual meditation.

One of our definitions – that to do with 'spiritual beings' – brought in the word 'soul'. I have just mentioned 'psychology'. 'Psyche' is Greek for 'soul'; and 'magic', in both its Gnostic 'white' and Mephistophelean 'black' phases, has always been involved with the situation of that least definable aspect of live beings. 'Conjuring with souls' is a face of 'magic' which, if brought out of poetic nomenclature into the 'scientific' jargon of today's world, would present itself as 'psychology': literally, the study of the 'soul'. Thus it would follow, as several modern 'magicians' have argued,[9] that Freud, Jung and the rest are only more rational, systematic and clinical versions of crystal-ball-gazing charlatans in silk dressing-gowns who decorated courts of the superstitious in more picturesque centuries.

To this we shall return. Meanwhile, no definition of 'magic' would be complete were it not to attend to at least one more tricky term: this too quite intimate with the matter of 'soul' and journeys of the 'psyche'. I mean 'mysticism', which the dictionary describes as 'belief in the possibility of union with the Divine nature by means of ecstatic contemplation' and 'reliance on spiritual intuition as the means of acquiring knowledge of mysteries inaccessible to understanding'. This may be practised by the Christian or the 'black' adept – anyone, in short, whose 'soul' or 'psyche' is so disposed. Nor is it likely that an aspirant 'magician' could afford not to practise it in one form or another. This is because 'magic' is, as we have indicated – at least on one level – the science of the Unknown; and, being such a vast, uncharted space of light and darkness, it requires individuals of more than usual self-knowledge and control to explore, with any success, and gain even the 'pretended' arts, let alone actual 'powers', which the dictionary touches on.

In the past, these journeyers have tended, in eschewing received
religion, to depend on various occult doctrines: necromancy, or the
art of resurrecting dead souls; Cabala, or the micro-macrocosmic
transcendental 'system' of medieval Jews; the Tarot, or 'game'
of personalities and forces derived (perhaps) from gypsy lore;
astrology, or science of celestial determinism; metoposcopy, or
science of frontal lines; physiognomy, or study of the face; cheiromancy, or palm-reading; cartomancy, which, like the Tarot,
involves fortune-telling from cards; divination, which uses 'magically' charged objects; rhabdomancy, which is related, being the
art of using a divining-rod; the study and interpretation of dreams;
clairvoyance; 'astral projection', which has to do with unrestricted
travel by the body's incorporeal 'shadow' or 'double'; use of talismans; alchemy, or the hermetic 'science' of turning base metal
into gold – the 'secret doctrine'; and so on.[10]

Some of these pursuits must seem today entirely daft. Most of
them have lent themselves to charlatans of one degree or other.
All, however, are manifestly methods of approaching the
Unknown: of trying to discover the motive forces behind all, the
true natures of ourselves and others, the course of destiny through
the future. As sub-headings of 'magic', they may be helpful in
defining the term. Provisionally, we might now describe it as *the
study of first principles, both without and within, and of how to control
them*. This the reader may find similar to his impression of
'science'. But, as he will have discerned, the 'magician', unlike the
'scientist', is by no means concerned to confine his attention to
'powers' which can ultimately be quantified or explained ration-
ally. 'Religion', 'the occult' and 'mysticism' are equally of 'magic's'
sphere. Nor should it be forgotten that, in an age in which 'science'
has become orthodox, all these imponderables have become
'heresy', much as 'science' itself was during the heyday of a
proscriptive Church.[11]

Now we have ransacked the dictionary for understanding of the
Logos and touched on some of the guises it has taken in the past.
Still, defining it for the present is no elementary job. As stated,
the ascendancy of 'science' since at least the eighteenth century
has made most practitioners of what once might have been called
'magic' reluctant to describe themselves by means of the now-
suspect term. Nor might many of them even recognise the identity

of their pursuits with 'magic' as historical concept. But 'magick includes all acts whatsoever', wrote Aleister Crowley, one of the few educated men of this century to have dared present himself as a 'magician'.[12] 'Anything', he adds, 'may serve as a magical weapon.'

But what does this mean? Everything is everything, as a recent 'hip' phrase puts it? Or, as James Joyce witticised in *Ulysses*, 'Nothing is anything'?[13] So we might construe Crowley's universalising declaration; and, with it, all effort to encircle 'magic' in sure definition might seem to be dispersed. Indeed, this may in part be what the 'magician' wants; for chaos in a world ruled by the order of 'science' might be seen as a proper 'magical' goal – a phase leading toward greater final good. ('The magician creates a commotion by disturbing the balance of power.'[14]) All the same, sheer nihilism is by no means the meaning of 'magic' in our century, even to a 'magician' ostracised as 'the wickedest man in the world'.

Elsewhere Crowley describes 'magick' as 'a direct means of coming into contact with reality'.[15] This might seem incongruous when one considers the elaborate symbolism and ritual involved in so many of his acts. But then 'magick' for Crowley was not limited to his performances: they were merely particular, and for him particularly amusing, forms of it. The concept at large was as inclusive as creation: 'A magical operation may be defined as any event in Nature which is brought to pass by will.'[16] Expatiating with uncharacteristic appreciation of the mundane, he adds, 'We must not exclude potato-growing or banking from our definition.'

The significant word in this twentieth-century definition is 'will'; and in Crowley's system a repeated word and concept is 'will's' actualising concomitant, 'concentration'. When Crowley states that 'the Law of the New Aeon shall be "Do what thou wilt. . . . Love under will" '[17], he is signifying that no understanding, scientific discovery or act of intercourse with a 'spiritual being' is going to gain a 'magician' power or control, whether for good or evil, unless he is able and prepared to exercise 'will' as well.[18] Indeed, it is unlikely that power or understanding can come to him at all unless he is able to exercise 'will', both within and without. In fact, the principal ordering force, both within and without, may finally be revealed as 'will' itself, rather as Schopenhauer had argued.

The 'magician', it would follow, in this era post-Nietzsche might be described as, among other things, one who is gifted in the exercise of 'will'. Nor would this be incompatible with the dictionary definition which describes 'magic' as 'compelling the energy'. To 'energy', 'will' is logically related; and, as one of Crowley's disciples, Kenneth Grant, has said,[19] 'magic' might be defined as 'the summoning of energy in one form or another' or – more specifically echoing Crowley's remark about causing 'a commotion by disturbing the balance of power' – as 'energy tending to change'.

'Will', 'energy', 'change' – these are broad terms with connotations likely to make careful minds squirm. How can one talk about concepts so vast? so little ready to be hemmed in by definition? Is there not a kind of hubris, arrogance, intellectual cheek in trying to describe the world – man and the cosmos or whatever – with such inflationary, deductive 'signs'? Indeed there is. And this surely is part of the point about 'magic', and part of the reason why it has been looked on as heretical in the past and crankish in the present. The *Logos* begins by universalising and ends by declaring that, in the midst of the dualities and multiplicities of an infinitely complicated world, there is a final unity: a unity perhaps even knowable by the sanctioned 'happy few'.[20]

God, the *primum mobile*, grand architect of the universe, force which governs the 'interdependence of things' – 'magic', in whatever form, ortho- or heterodox, has behind it, explicitly or implicitly, an impression of a 'system' governing all. Some 'magicians' have contended that their powers come from nothing more than perfect attention to and understanding of Nature. Others claim full knowledge of the *micro* (man) as the key to understanding of the *macro*. Others still (those of the theistic bent) claim authority on the basis of special knowledge of the moral absolutes of the 'outer', God. But, in whichever form, the 'magician' – as opposed to, say, the sorcerer or conventional priest – has been and remains in the practice of proposing to embrace and know not part but *All*.

To unify, to universalise, is both the point and the justification of his acts. The 'One' is almost always the declared end, even while raging dualism exists immediately beneath the surface. Thus the affinity of 'magic' with hierarchical socio-political systems, the predilection for a single ordering principle at the top and therefore – in recent eras – a kind of complicity, either direct or indirect, with the fascist formula of dictatorship over anarchy. This of course brings us to a further boundary of the subject and has little to do with our initial quest for the *Logos*, which we might now try again – still provisionally, but with benefit of one or two more insights this time – to define as *the summoning of energy, whether of a spiritual or scientific nature, in an attempt to gain power over the unknown, whether within or without, and influence the motion of that energy for good or evil, depending on the magician's perception of the universal moral balance.*

To this we might add that any classification of 'magic' as 'white' or 'black' has more to do with the classifier than with the 'magician' himself. For, given the universality of its claimed sphere, 'magic' embraces both good and evil; and the deployment of the one or the other depends entirely on an intuition of what force *needs* to be invoked. Thus the 'magician' who feels that the governing unity of the moment is prejudicial to himself, his kind or the 'energy' he is trying to evoke, may feel obliged to unleash 'dark forces'. To him, this will appear to be in service of the 'white' end of better universal balance. By such logic, 'destruction' can become a 'good' magical act: Hitler destroying Jews and socialists in order to 'purify' Europe of his day;[21] a mother battering her child in order to inculcate a needful sense of discipline; and so forth. 'Magic' is not mere satanism or witchcraft. On the other hand, even the 'whitest' Christian orthodoxy would acknowledge that 'the devil' is a necessary component in 'God's' overall moral scheme.

II YEATS VERSUS ELIOT

This 'sympathy for the devil' which seems to surface in 'magic' is what makes conventional souls hold the subject at arm's length, or insist on viewing it only as the innocent child's play of the illusionist. But such responses suggest lack of moral daring on the part of the viewer more than lack of moral sensitivity in 'magic'.[22] As stated, the evocation of angels, or good forces, has traditionally been central to 'magical' practice. Moreover, at times when the universal balance seems excessively 'black', this generally becomes apparent. Consider, for instance, the responses of 'magicians' in disciplines from physics to psychology to religion to an overcharge of 'black' forces in the Nazi period. Surely the activities of Einstein,

Jung and Teilhard de Chardin must seem 'white' in the eyes of the norm. Nor would any of these sages have denied the identity of his developed 'powers' with what in previous ages had been called 'magic'.

However, we have now listened to what the dictionary has to say and begun to define the basic, protean term. Thus it would appear a good time to turn to the second part of the overall subject, the relation of these matters to literature, and hear what some careful thinkers have had to contribute. Yeats is an obvious choice. At the beginning of the century he wrote,

> I believe in the practice and philosophy of what we have agreed to call magic, in what I must call the evocation of spirits, though I do not know what they are, in the power of creating magical illusions, in the visions of truth in the depths of the mind when the eyes are closed; and I believe in three doctrines, which have, as I think, been handed down from early times, and been the foundation of nearly all magical practices. These doctrines are –
>
> (1) That the borders of our minds are ever shifting, and that many minds can flow into one another, as it were, and create or reveal a single mind, a single energy.
> (2) That the borders of our memories are as shifting, and that our memories are a part of one great memory, the memory of Nature herself.
> (3) That this great mind and great memory can be evoked by symbols.
>
> I often think I would put this belief in magic from me if I could, for I have come to see or to imagine, in men and women, in houses, in handicrafts, in nearly all sights and sounds, a certain evil, a certain ugliness, that comes from the slow perishing through the centuries of a quality of mind that made this belief and its evidence common over the world.[23]

This remarkable statement, couched in the language of a religious creed, confirms with the sensuality of a poetic view what we have already discovered from dry lexicology: that 'magic' has first to do with 'evocation of spirits' and second with creating 'illusions'. Significantly, however, Yeats does not suggest 'pretence' as the dictionary does. Moreover, he adds a third primary meaning which the dictionary ignores: the matter of 'truth in dreams'. Here the writer reveals himself as of the era of Freud; and his 'three doctrines' – 'universal unconscious', 'memory of Nature' and summoning of energy by 'symbol' – are remarkably like the programme set down by Freud's great disciple and disputant, Jung.[24] This all underlines the identity already noted of 'magic' in this century with 'psychology'. But Yeats, one realises, is concerned with more than just what occurs in the mind. His 'magic' embraces external forces as well: in nature, history and other men, women and objects which cast shadows over individual lives.

The subject causes him apparent unease. He claims that he would, if he could, 'put this belief in magic from me', and conveys some nostalgia for the conventional world, where such emanations are less notable. The province of 'magic', as he describes it, is definitely on the 'fringe', to use a word come across earlier:[25] outside the pale of comfortable, even healthy, life; redolent of an order which knows little of material progress and would perhaps curse it if it came to the door. 'Magic' for Yeats is old, of 'early times', linked to the past more than the future, raddled, 'ugly', ripening into decay, and perhaps (here is the morally charged term) even 'evil'.[26] Thus it is no surprise that he presents himself as approaching with trepidation, nervously self-protective, clutching fast to his identity as an outsider, not a true participant – surely not a 'magician', hardly even an adept.

And yet. . . . For all his reassuring circumspection, Yeats is powerfully attracted. Indeed, his unease at his own diffidence seems part of what attracts him so much. If the realm of 'magic' is disturbing – even if it is *wrong* – still it promises to be more sure, more potent, than his own personality, somnambulistic as he makes that appear. Indeed, as the essay unfolds, we find him contrasting the character he secretly aspires to be with the one he initially presents: 'Certainly all imaginative men, must be for ever casting forth enchantments, glamours, illusions; and all men, especially tranquil men who have no powerful egotistical life, must be continually passing under their power' (p. 49). The 'magician', it appears then, might be defined for Yeats as any 'imaginative' Being with a 'powerful egotistical life'. Thus 'magic' in this world constitutes the spell these embodiments of energy and will are able to cast over less strong personalities, whether for good or ill.

Of the myriad guises such embodiments might take, it turns out that one may be 'the poet' himself: he who can 'cast glamour', as Yeats glamorously puts it,[27] on characters of ancient times, rewrite histories and summon the imaginations of others through neglected or forgotten symbols. Thus meek approachers, diffident *tabulae rasae*, may take hope: even they may be transformed into 'great magicians'. In company with other aesthetes of his era,[28] Yeats goes on to add, 'The poet, the musician and the artist are the half-conscious successors to the masters of magic' (p. 64). Thus inflated to a status of world-historic (if not cosmic) significance, the mere author need no longer appear so nervous and negligible in his own eyes; and so, in drawing back from the 'disturbing' topic, he may bow to bourgeois sensibility with a new ambiguousness:

> I have now described that belief in magic which has set me all but unwilling among those lean and fierce minds who are at war with their time, who cannot accept the days as they pass, simply and gladly; and I look at what I have written with some alarm, for I have told more of the ancient secret than many among my fellow-students think it right to tell. I have come to believe so many strange things because of experience, that I see little reason to doubt the truth of many things that are beyond my experience; and it may be that there are beings who watch over that ancient secret, as all tradition affirms, and resent, and perhaps avenge, too fluent speech.   (p. 66)

This is a remarkable piece of manipulation – perhaps of author as much as of audience. Pity the poor chap who has somehow been forced to study that which disturbs him and, by implication, should disturb us as well. Admire, on the other hand, those 'lean and fierce minds' which you otherwise might deplore because of the brave poet's reluctant, yet inevitable, recognition of his identity with them. Believe what he has told you, for he has – even 'unwilling' – undergone 'experiences' which you have not. Thank him, in fact, for he – at once more generous and more foolish than most – has dared to reveal 'secrets' which others cling to selfishly. He may indeed be punished for his indiscretion. Thus you, reader – 'mon semblable, mon frère',[29] philistine bourgeois though you may be – must really like, trust, even *love* this young man. Hasn't he, after all, defied the Unseen, just as surely as Lucifer did God or Prometheus Jupiter, in order – for mankind's sake – to bring 'fire' down from heaven?

If ever prose were to be reckoned a 'magical' art, this piece of studied lack of candour must surely qualify; and indeed most writing on 'magic', as we shall discover, is at least as opaque, if rarely as beautiful. This last notwithstanding, there is a certain moral 'ugliness' – 'evil' even – in Yeats's circuitous mode of expression. His slightly archaic sentence-structure and words suggest, no doubt deliberately, a sense of things olden and brilliantly obscure. Nor does the rest of his essay shed much light on his subject, dealing as it does with the poet's experiences of drawing-room 'games' of the time – séances for evocation of spirits; identification of 'past lives'; moments of synchronicity implying powers of suggestion and so forth. The reader should not get bogged down in these, however. The main value of the essay is in communicating an overall fascination; and in this the serpentine muddiness of the prose may paradoxically be a help. It contributes to one's more (or less) than purely rational appreciation of a pervasive idealistic drive, propelling vision upward, toward Eden, that 'walled garden upon a high mountain', which is a traditional symbol of the destination of 'white' magic;[30] toward 'remaking the world' using reformulated forces out of 'that Great Mind . . . that Great Memory'; and toward the dawning of a new day of 'poetry, romance [and] intellectual beauty' which will constitute 'the only signal that the supreme Enchanter, or some one in His councils, is speaking of what has been, and shall be again, in the consummation of time' (p. 68).

The notion of 'hidden masters', or even single 'supreme Enchanter' moving behind and within the activities of magically charged souls, comes out strongly toward the end of Yeats's essay. Elsewhere in his writing – in 'The Body of Father Christian Rosenkreuz',[31] for instance – he speaks with less feyness about the duty of these souls to remake consciousness: to replace the Age of Reason, that false (for him) 'Enlightenment', with its faith in science and criticism. He speaks about the unnaturalness of contemporary city life, with its 'dissociation of sensibility', and looks forward to a time when 'the winds of heaven' may blow again through 'our souls that were once naked and now are thickly clad'. In specific, he calls for a new 'age of imagination', in which 'belief in a suprasensual world' will once more be at hand and mankind will be driven by strong emotions and these unseen 'magical' forces, as it was in a more barbaric past. 'We will learn again', he says, 'that the great Passions are angels of God.'

Yeats in this vein of course disturbed T. S. Eliot, the great literary defender of Reason and Christianity during the contemporary period; and it is useful to view the Irish poet's invocations in the light of the Anglo-American's equally manipulative and circuitous counter-arguments.[32] These are put forward most forcefully in *After Strange Gods*, a series of lectures Eliot delivered at the University of Virginia in 1932 – that is, a third of a century after Yeats had written his essay and thus a time by which some of the 'new consciousness' Yeats was trying to invoke had begun to manifest itself.

Eliot does not speak of 'magic' directly. The word and concept no doubt struck him as 'unsound' and best rarely spoken about. The 'unknown' at large does not appear to him as a proper study for lay minds. In defence against the kind of moral aberration he sees arising from such study, he proselytises in favour of two protective concepts: (1) 'tradition', which he defines as 'a way of feeling and acting which characterises a group throughout generations' and which 'must largely be, or . . . many elements of it must be, unconscious'; and (2) 'orthodoxy', which means 'that element of agreed upon moral intelligence growing out of tradition which organises the best of tradition in such a way as to make it a standard by which to value the present'.[33] The past is a 'good' to Eliot as to Yeats. He too disdains 'tired' conventional liberalism and inclines toward romantic glorification of 'race'. Beyond this, however, the two have little in common.

'Novelty and originality' are false values, Eliot believes. Province and class represent positive forces which may help inhibit pernicious modern tendencies to universalise, unify and posit moral relativity. These tendencies are themselves the result of an era of 'the decay of protestant agnosticism' [p. 38]. New gospels and old doctrines neglected since the fall of Atlantis, or resurrected via the example of primitive peoples, have produced a rash of new messiahs. But 'no messiah can last for more than a generation', since 'an uncritical public tends to move from one new programme to another, viewing all as equally valuable "experiences" ' (p. 34). Furthermore, ancient or Eastern or primitive belief systems, however fashionable, are not practical in the long run: they cannot be understood by the Western mind as Christianity can. Christianity remains necessary because 'without certain doctrines like that of Original Sin, neither Hell nor Heaven [terms favoured by Yeats after his "heretical" precursors, Blake and Swedenborg[34]] have dignity' (p. 40).

Eliot criticises his friend Ezra Pound for creating an *inferno* in his *Cantos*, where money-lust is the only real sin, and for creating a heaven peopled by 'individuals, heretics, and libertarians of his own stripe' where 'the pleasures of the senses' are by no means excluded (p. 42). This is 'perfectly comfortable for the modern mind to contemplate', Eliot remarks disparagingly, and perhaps inaccurately. 'Horrors' as found in Baudelaire, or in the Jesuit lecture on hell in Joyce's *Portrait of the Artist as a Young Man*, are preferable: they acknowledge the hegemony of Christian myth even while reacting against it. Yeats, Eliot concedes, is a 'powerful unfolder of symbols' but Yeats's preference for the occult as subject matter and for the rhythmic trance as method confine him to an area of 'lower mythology' (p. 46). Indeed, Yeats only becomes 'admirable' in Eliot's view when, in his later period, he begins to slough off 'this wrong supernatural world', which is 'not a world of spiritual significance . . . real Good and Evil, holiness and sin', but a corpus of fragments of 'extreme self-consciousness' designed to 'supply the fading pulse of poetry'.

Where Yeats comes to identify himself with 'those lean and fierce minds who are at war with their time', Eliot reacts in favour of a well-fed and collective establishment determined not to let the future pull it out of its comfortable past. His argument with the present is precisely *against* those impulses leading toward an 'age of imagination' and 'passion' for which Yeats has called. 'The most fruitful operations of the Evil Spirit today' are not, Eliot says, signalled by blasphemy so much as by these impulses in literature. In England, the rot began with George Eliot, who was a 'fine moralist' but began to breed heresy by espousing morals which were not those of the community and Church but of her own individual *personality* (p. 54). This development was carried further by Thomas Hardy, who detached himself from 'submission to any objective beliefs' – even a desire to 'please the public' – and came to glorify expression which veered toward passion, or 'extreme emotionalism': that 'symptom of decadence' which opens the door for 'intrusion of the *diabolic*' (p. 56). D. H. Lawrence, however, is where the tendency has surfaced in its most disturbing form; and the Lawrence syndrome is held up as what is most wrong-headed in modern life and thought.

For Lawrence, Eliot argues, any form of spirituality seems good, while only 'the absence of spirituality' seems to constitute evil (p. 59). This bias leads to cults of 'sexual morbidity', the 'inner light' and 'belief in Life which almost inevitably ends in belief in Death' and makes Lawrence a 'blind servant' to Evil and a 'fatal leader'. The aberration has grown because Lawrence began with 'an untrained mind'. His background and education created 'a soul destitute of humility and filled with self-righteousness'. In him, one can see clearly where Yeats's 'magical' longing for renewal of passion and natural forces might lead: toward a 'cult of personality' in which the individual is inflated by whatever heterodox 'magic' he may choose to invoke, without reference to social or spiritual good or evil. 'To be oneself, as the era conceives,' Eliot concludes, 'is to be that kind of personality which fascinates in art, partly self-deceived and partly irresponsible, and because of its freedom, terribly *limited* by prejudice and self-conceit, capable of much good or great mischief according to the natural goodness or impurity of the man; and we are all, naturally, impure' (p. 63).

That Eliot begins his lecture by lauding the essentially fixed, agrarian, backward-looking, racist order of the American South of his day demonstrates the narrowness of his 'magic', if we may call it that. His intent is to discriminate, not to universalise. In terms Crowley uses in his novel *Moonchild* (and which I discuss at some length in *Art, Messianism and Crime*) Eliot is pursuing a 'black-magical' path in this; for one of the purposes of 'magic', as Crowley describes it, is to recognise one's identity with the whole of the cosmos. Of course, Eliot would never have regarded himself as of 'the black brotherhood'; nor, in light of the terms set out a few pages back, should we press the designation too far, as Eliot was surely (and unambiguously to himself) pursuing what he saw as a 'white' end. All the same, in his very reactiveness, divisiveness, parochialism and distaste for identification with the broadening current of modern life, Eliot seems painfully out of step – indeed, much more so than Yeats – and the fact puts his arguments for orthodoxy and tradition, in both religion and social structures, into question.

The truth seems to be that the values Eliot wished to remain ascendant were being eroded seriously in his day and have continued to be ever since. The 'free thinking' which he regards as 'undesirable', whether among Jews (whom he specifically cites – p. 20) or among these 'messianic' literary apostates, has in fact become a norm in the West, if not throughout the world. 'Tradition' as a value matters less now than self-realisation. Nor is 'orthodoxy' a highly tenable ideal amid increasingly mixed social orders. Christianity may retain some respect, though probably more for its inherent universality than for any religiosity of an 'elect' such as Eliot seems to have favoured. Moreover, the 'liberalism' he deplores so roundly had been revealed increasingly in subsequent decades as the most viable, life-preserving and truly Christian 'tradition' – or 'orthodoxy' – amid warring conservatisms.

Values of province, class, race and traditional education such as Eliot advances can lead, inasmuch as they are anti-universalising, to a new barbarism: an era of perpetual struggle, which is surely not what Eliot would have desired, with his distaste for emotion, passion and spirit. But indeed, to the extent to which the present era does reflect Eliot's values, struggle and passion have become an unhappy norm. On the other hand, inasmuch as it reflects Yeats's opposed values, they have become an increasingly tolerable norm. Which brings us at last to the point of suggesting that 'magic' provides a more *positive* explanation for the forces at work in our period than any Eliotic brand of socio-religious conservatism. The very universalizing thrust of it is more appropriate to 'one world', and its habit of constructing eclectic moralities out of the occult makes it compatible with the need to fashion one morality for everyman out of a myriad of conflicting belief-systems. The idea that the 'wisdom of the East' should be considered in the West is not only proper, to confute Eliot, but necessary; and 'magic' has been weaving Oriental strands into Western thought for centuries. Meanwhile, the idea that everyman should have the potential to become his own 'magician' – perhaps God, even[35] – is, whether desirable or not, simply inevitable in an age when old imposed systems break down and the ideology of 'life liberty and the *pursuit of happiness*' seems triumphant.

Morality as it has been known in previous centuries persists only in part today. Christ may remain an example of importance to some, but 'stranger gods' are increasingly influential. Satan, the god of ruthless pursuit of self-interest in defiance of imposed moral systems, is not nearly so 'evil' to our age: in fact, some American soap-operas seem to promote his kind of behaviour as exemplary.[36] Venus, the goddess of sex and the power which comes with it, is now openly revered. So too, nearly as overtly, is Mammon, the spirit of money and greed. Nor is Proteus without his trendy following: the principle of ever-changing, ever-shifting personality; opportunism; 'chameleonism'.[37] Eliot and establishmentarians of his ilk might wish to dismiss such emanations as 'unsound'. Nevertheless, a time-traveller from the past would not have to visit any modern metropolis for long before concluding that this is what our pantheon contains, thus that the 'heresy' of the Christian era has become significantly 'orthodox' and that 'magic' in various guises has come to seem the best method of deploying the spirit.

III THIS BOOK

The reader may recognize the phenomenon being discussed here in many areas of contemporary life: 'power of positive thinking' cults in America and elsewhere, faith in medicine and science, the 'spiritualism' allegedly pursued by Prince Charles, contemporary ideas about vitamins and diet, the cult of will of the early Margaret Thatcher – indeed, the generally self-interested 'world-view' of the dominant 'new person' of the 1980s, sometimes called the 'yuppie'. For me, interest in the subject grows out of not only these but also previous studies. My first critical book was on Wagner, whose opus is often seen to be steeped in 'magic' and Western heresy. My second, *California Writers*, explores the literary growth of a locale sometimes known as the international haven of eccentric 'spiritual' disciplines. My third book, *Art, Messianism and Crime*, pursues the course of destructive urges within and without the arts in the West, both Europe and America, since the French Revolution, and touches on this matter of 'magic' in relation to Yeats, Crowley, Hitler, Indo-European mysticism, the 'hippy' movement, drug cults of the 1960s, rock music and the so-called 'counter-culture'.

These books are about literary art and thought teetering, as it were, on the 'edge of the abyss'.[38] In the third, I try to confront the final question raised by the first two: to what extent can a kind of literature lead toward 'answers' which, if arrived at in life, may be as destructive as (if not more destructive than) they are beneficial. In Wilde, Baudelaire and even Yeats, as I argue, formal brilliance may mask moral disintegration. *The Picture of Dorian Gray*, *Les Fleurs du mal* and 'The Second Coming' are all testaments that 'orthodoxy' and 'tradition' have become a 'rubble heap', a 'waste land'. So too are Jack Kerouac's picture of his generation in *Desolation Angels* and, in their own ways, the 'real life' excesses of frustrated 'artists', Hitler and Charles Manson. All are symptoms of a vast moral groping and need for some positive new direction. And here, as in similar periods of crisis throughout history, is where 'magic' and the occult enter; for it is in new doctrines of quasi-religious import, or out of the discarded fragments of old, that men who fear they are losing their way are bound to start searching for 'the light'.

This is why, in the first paragraphs of this chapter, I comment that, if the student of literature (let alone modern thought and cultural progress) is to understand his subject in the fullest context, he must eventually deal with that body of ephemeral writing, action and thought which exists out on the fringe of the subject proper. He must have some idea, for instance, why a great literatus such as Yeats spent much of his youth and dotage chasing 'magical' visions; what those visions amounted to; and why, on the other hand, an aspirant great literatus such as Crowley should have turned to 'magic' as the superior 'art'. What were they after? What in literature was (or is) lacking? Or, to put it more hopefully for the *aficionado* of literary arts and believer in the desirability of their continuance, what new spiritual values had (or have) to be found and digested to give the writing of these times full power and value for readers likewise suffering the effects of crumbling 'tradition' and trying to find their way towards a new 'orthodoxy'?

I trust this makes clear that, as has been stated, I take on this subject primarily in its relation to literature and for literary students to consider. The book will be introductory – that is, a rough guide for those who wish to know something but have neither time nor inclination to wade through the innumerable tomes and hack works which weigh down library shelves. As the project has grown out of literary studies, particularly of the Romantic period and its modernist offshoots, so its trajectory is back to literature, of the same period as well as now. We have already touched on the opposed points of view of Yeats and Eliot. As we progress, the reader will note how the topic connects with works of Goethe, Balzac, Huysmans, Bulwer-Lytton, Browning, Mann, Hesse, the Symbolists, and writers of science fiction and 'magical realism'. Meanwhile, before going on in the next chapter to sketch a background of the main strands (at least some of them) of the 'tradition' in the West since classical times, I should add a few words about texts.

Perhaps the most formidable and authoritative source-work in modern English is Lynn Thorndike's six-volume *History of Magic and Experimental Science*, published between the world wars. More influential, and more than specifically about 'magic', are Frazer's *The Golden Bough* from the Yeats–Eliot era and Joseph Campbell's *Masks of God* from our own recent past. Among the many books of the 'magical revival' of the 1960s and early 1970s, Frances Yates's studies on Hermeticism and Rosicrucianism are the most distinguished from a historical–literary point of view, while Pauwels' and Bergier's *Morning of the Magicians* is one of the more provocative mass-market books. For an overview, one might turn to Gareth Knight's *History of White Magic*, Colin Wilson's *The Occult* or works of Francis King and James Webb. The facts contained in these might be supplemented by Georges Chevalier's *The Sacred Magician: A Ceremonial Diary* for insight into the 'adept's' psychology, and by Kenneth Grant's books, especially *Cults of the Shadow*, on how the tradition attaches to the perverse.

Works on specific 'magicians' and movements discussed will be noted in their proper places. Meanwhile, about my selection I should add that, by concentrating on the modern period (that is, since the French Revolution), I have hoped to reduce a vast and unruly topic to dimensions easily comprehensible by contemporary minds. Likewise, in choosing subjects, I have tried to concentrate on those worth discussing both because there is sufficient documentation and because they have had significant cultural impact. My choice includes the principal and most representative instances of what we are after. Some dispute may arise about whether they all deserve to be considered under the general term 'magic'. Undeniably, there is a wide divergence in approach and objective between, say, Steiner and Crowley. But that too is a matter best discussed in individual chapters – and in light of the scope of the *Logos* itself, which has already been indicated.

2

From Egypt to Freemasonry

I THE INITIATE AS 'ASS'

A first function of 'magic' is to create an effective type of personality. Jungian psychology makes a distinction between archetypes of the hero and archetypes of the initiate.[1] Potentials for both must be embraced in the full 'magical' worldview, but the second, paradoxically, may be stronger than the first; and on it 'magic' has ever put great emphasis. The trajectory of the hero begins with a rise from humble origins, through early proofs of strength; continues with accession to 'power', struggle with 'evil', return to 'home'; and ends with a fall through hubris or self-sacrifice. This, one can see readily, is a model for action in the world of affairs and requires an instinct for moral discrimination, even prejudice, more than philosophical appreciation of the forces moving behind things. The hero attempts to dominate destiny, achieves glory through exercising his will, and falls through lack of full knowledge. He is Wagner's Siegfried rather than Parsifal. The latter is an initiate. His type achieves integration and power through submission to fate and reverence for natural and cosmic laws acquired through symbolic experiences of death: circumcision, outcastness, imprisonment, unwilling *ensorcellement*, or other forms of subjection of the ego.

The initiate, a Jungian or Wagnerian would say, is made wise through sympathy:[2] a sympathy which originates in waiting, watching and suffering. He must make contact and peace with his inner *daemon*, soul or 'self'; also with his *anima* – female aspect of his nature, impulse to 'das Ewig-Weibliche' or vision of the 'Holy Grail' – in a kind of 'alchemical marriage'. The hero does not have time for such things. In early primitive form, he may be the 'trickster', a figure of blithe anarchy. Later he might appear as the 'culture-bearer', Prometheus, whose virtue remains the opposite of submission: defiant, daring theft of fire from the Gods. Self-initiation might turn this type into a 'man–god', a type represented by the Buddha. More likely, however, is transformation into a version of the 'twins' – Castor and Pollux, Romulus and Remus – whose capacity for exuberant deeds spills over into plunder. The initiate, by contrast, whether introduced into the ecstatic cult of Dionysus, the pastoral of Orpheus or the beatific of Christ, is tempering his potential with a superior outer principle. He is becoming something larger than himself, while the hero – even when sacrificing his life for his tribe – by nature remains bound to a superior individual (and ultimately solitary and tragic) identity.

The 'magician', as priest, must begin by being an initiate; thus the 'magical' message regarding personality is nearly always couched in terms of initiation. Typically this is portrayed as a journey, either inward or outward with obvious inward reson-ances. The archetype of the journey may well be traced back (as Jung indicates[3]) to cults of Isis and Osiris and the programme for transcendence of the souls of the dead in the *prisca theologia* of Egypt. In this the 'candidate' presents himself at the portal of the Temple of Isis, has his heart weighed by Anubis, the dog-headed 'opener of the ways', and Horus, the lord of the underworld, against a feather supplied from the plumage of Maat, goddess of law and order. The result is recorded by Thoth, the ibis-headed lord of magic and learning, patron god of writers and early incar-nation of Hermes. If it is satisfactory, the 'candidate' passes on to the table set for the Devourer of Souls. If not stopped there, he may ultimately arrive at the foot of the throne of Osiris, the original man–god once murdered by the satanic Set but resurrected necromantically by his consort Isis, the original Great Mother and overarching presence above all the gods, through whom in turn Osiris has fathered Horus.[4]

In this mystical progress can be found the motifs of supernatu-ralism, terror, mercy, power, powerlessness, love, decay, regener-ation and above all mysticism which have characterised initiations throughout the centuries. Though the 'experience' may be symbolic, there is nothing 'unreal' about the commitment necessary to carry through to admission and 'grace'. Nor may the process initially be perceived as solemn. Indeed, initiation as such may not even be perceived as taking place until the 'candidate' in in the middle of his journey. So much Aleister Crowley tells us in his twentieth-century novel of initiation, *Diary of a Drug Fiend*.[5] So much is also apparent in what Crowley and others claim as the prototype of novels on 'magical' themes, *The Golden Ass* by Lucius Apuleius, a Roman citizen who lived in the period of religious crisis of the second century AD and, in the words of Frances Yates, 'is a striking example of one of those men, highly educated in the general culture of the Graeco-Roman world who, weary of the stale teachings of the schools, sought for salvation in the occult, and particularly in the Egyptian type of the occult'.[6]

In his picaresque narrative, Apuleius presents himself as a naïve and lusty young man, rather thoughtless but of pleasing high spirits, who gets himself transformed into an ass by trying to imitate a witch who is able to change herself into an owl at night to torment an uninterested beloved. Apuleius's transformation is the culmination of a serious of intemperate, if exuberant, acts on his part – seductions, apparent murders – and is described as a penance for them, as for his 'unprosperous curiositie'.[7] In 'assy' form he becomes subject to maltreatment by various masters, mostly thieves, and can only return to his 'pristine' shape by eating roses. As it is winter, this is no easy task; and the bulk of *The Golden Ass* is taken up with dark months of trial of the man-as-animal. Eventually discovered to have remarkably human appetites, the ass is put on show as a freak by his masters. In this capacity, he is scheduled to fornicate with a whore and murderess at a spring fertility festival presided over by somewhat debased and vicious versions of the Roman goddesses Juno, Minerva and Venus. Confronted with this, the ass (who all the while has retained Apuleius's human intellect) revolts.

Escaping out to the beach, he sleeps at the edge of the tide and – in the moonlight – prays to the great mother goddess, Ceres, who appears to him in resplendent guise suggesting the 'powers' of the natural world:

Shee had a great abundance of haire, dispersed and scattered about her neck, on the crowne of her head she bare many garlands enterlaced with floures, in the middle of her forehead was a compasse in fashion of a glasse, or resembling the light of the Moone, in one of her hands she bare serpents, in the other, blades of corne, her vestiment was of fine silke yeelding divers colours, sometime yellow, sometime rosie, sometime flamy, and sometime (which troubled my spirit sore) dark and obscure, covered with a black robe in manner of a shield, and pleated in most subtill fashion at the skirts of her garments, the welts appeared comely, whereas here and there the starres glimpsed, and in the middle of them was placed the Moone, which shone like a flame of fire, round about the robe was a coronet or garland made with flowers and fruits.[8]

Ceres reveals herself to contain all the important female deities who have even been, from Persephone to the presiding goddess of Eleusis to Hecate, but principally and first of all the one whom the 'Aegyptians' call Isis. She tells Apuleius that the next day there will be a festival in her honour in the city and that he must join the worshippers and, when the high priest arrives bearing a garland of roses, eat of them and be transformed. Following this, he must become a devotee to her. To do so will protect him from further abasements, extend his life and make easy his journey through the underworld afterwards.

Chastened by his experiences as a beast, Apuleius readily submits. He watches with reverence the procession of priests and marvels over their symbolic costumes and talismans. When the high priest appears, he eats of the roses, is retransformed and covers his nakedness with a priest's robe. Joining the celebrants, he participates in consecrating a ship to the goddess and in a rite in her temple. Later, becoming an initiate proper, he learns to 'refrain from prophane and unlawfull meates', to fast and perform holy sacrifices under the supervision of his own 'principallest Priest' or guardian–teacher Mythra. Eventually he is allowed into the 'most secret and sacred place of all the temple', where he approaches 'neere unto Hell' and sees 'the Sun shine about midnight'.[9] There he is sanctified, 'adorned like unto the Sun' himself and made the central figure in a 'feast of the nativitie'. Next he goes out into the world to preach in other cities, including Rome. Often he is in poverty. Sometimes he must sell his robes to eat. Finally, however, he returns to take orders as a 'minister of Osiris', different from yet complementary to those of a priest of Isis. Years on, he is elevated to a 'third order of religion', at which level he is directed by Osiris to become 'an Advocate in the court'. This Apuleius does, 'in great joy and with a shaven Crowne', and – thus arrived – takes his readers' leave.

II HERMETICISM

The finale of *The Golden Ass* abounds in details from cults of
Apuleius' cult-ridden times and anticipates motifs from cults of the
future. Beyond Egypt, elements might be found from Mithraism,
Dionysian and Orphic religions, the Eleusian mysteries and
perhaps early Christianity itself. What was common to all these
was a highly spiritual, essentially non-material, religious attitude,
in contrast to the materialistically oriented, hypocritically 'civilised'
and increasingly empty 'religion' of Rome. In them, we see seeds
of a 'left-hand' Western way: out of the mainstream, characterised
by supernaturalism and secrecy, opposed to established orders
and partially contemptuous of *this* world. Apuleius must rise from
animal toward godly nature. Both as an uninitiated human and
as an 'asse', he is completely subject to physical wants and 'the
blindness of fortune', which has no compunction about treating
him cruelly. The entirety of *The Golden Ass*, apart from the finale
and interpolated 'Marriage of Cupid and Psyches', is a saga of
fornication, beating, theft, murder, witchcraft and duplicity. That
the author should revel in such subject matter may suggest a
persistent this-wordly zest which belies his 'moral'. Nevertheless,
that 'moral' is spelled out clearly enough: one must purify oneself
with natural religion in order to attain a 'magical' personality in
this world, let alone true 'power' in it or any other.

The interpolated story of Cupid and Psyche reinforces the theme
by making a young woman progress through an initiation analogous to Apuleius's own. Such secondary female initiations would
also characterise subsequent 'magical' works, from *The Magic Flute*
with its Masonic overtones to (again) Crowley's pre-'hippy' *Diary
of a Drug Fiend*.[10] In Apuleius's prototypical version, the young
woman falls from the grace of her ideal marriage through doubt,
gossip, 'woman's wiles' and deception. As a result, she delivers
a malignant wound to her husband and compels herself to take a
journey through hell and other terrible places in order to find
materials to placate an angry god. The god in this case is Venus,
a classical 'older woman' jealous of Psyche's beauty and concerned
to retain power over her son. Once again we are confronted with
the unhelpfulness of the 'social', all-too-human dieties of Rome.
Neither Juno nor Minerva will assist Psyche for fear of offending
Venus; and the girl is allowed to achieve a state of grace in the
end only by the intervention of Jupiter, the great-father principle,

who – concerned to maintain order in his court – negotiates an arrangement with Venus. A Jungian might say that Psyche has come to make peace with her *animus* in this way, as Apuleius has done with his *anima* by submission to Isis. Only thus is she (whose name we should not forget means 'soul') able to secure her 'alchemical' marriage with the divine embodiment of *love* (Cupid's identity).

The Golden Ass is addressed by Apuleius to 'his Sonne, Faustinus'. This underlines, among other things, its purpose as an instruction to youth on how to attain mature 'magical' personality. What remains mystifying at the end of the 'novel' is what the personality is meant to *believe*. What really is this religion, whose 'magic' and occult rites are able to confer 'powers' on its devotees? Much has been speculated. The early Christian fathers thought that Apuleius might also have been the translator or even author of all or part of the *Corpus Hermeticum* of Hermes Trismegistus and of the *Asclepius*, which that *priscus theologus* is supposed to have addressed to his son;[11] and scholarship since the beginning of the seventeenth century has shown that these seminal 'magical' works do in fact date from Apuleius's time and place, rather than from pre-Mosaic Egypt as Renaissance 'magi' believed. Whether Apuleius himself was a Hermeticist is not clear, though his 'faith' surely has some relation to this body of thought. What is important to us is that Hermeticism, in both its philosophical and astrological (or 'astral')[12] interests, embodies elements typical of the 'magical' worldview of not only Apuleius's time but also the principal subsequent eras of religious crisis and ferment in the West.[13]

What is the doctrine of the so-called Hermes 'Thrice Greatest'?[14] Essentially, belief in the pervasive divinity of the natural and cosmic world and the unsurpassed divinity of man as *magnum miraculum*. This is propounded in forty-two books, written in Greek by anonymous authors, some no doubt 'weary of the stale teachings of the schools', others Pythagoreans, Platonists or devotees of more arcane bodies of thought.[15] Thirty-six of the books are on metaphysics, six on natural medicine. The first and most important of them is the *Pimander*, or so-called 'Egyptian Genesis', from which Moses was supposed to have taken his account of the Creation. In the beginning in the *Pimander* is also 'the Word': that is, the *Nous* or divine *mens*, which is 'the Father of all beings, being life and light'. This demiurge has created the 'Seven Governors' or known planets of the time, including in ascending order the Moon,

Mercury, Venus, Sol (the Sun), Mars, Jupiter and Saturn; also the thirty-six decans and other astrological structures and hierarchies of the heavens above; the earth and Nature below; and most important, Man, who is described as 'similar' to the *Nous*, perhaps even his 'brother', 'beautiful', reproducing the divine image and so specially loved by the Father that '[He] gave over to him all his works'.[16]

Though enjoying such an exalted – even equivalent – status to creator and creation, Man has chosen to take for himself an intimate and animating relationship with Nature:

Then Man, who had full power over the world of mortal beings and of animals, leant across the armature of the spheres, having broken through their envelopes, and showed to the Nature below the beautiful form of God. When she saw that he had in him the inexhaustible beauty and all the energy of the Governors, joined to the form of God, Nature smiled with love, for she had seen the features of that marvellously beautiful form of Man reflected in the water and his shadow on the earth. And he, having seen this form like to himself in Nature, reflected in the water, he loved her and wished to dwell with her. The moment he wished this he accomplished it and came to inhabit the irrational form. Then Nature having received her loved one, embraced him, and they were united, for they burned with love.[17]

By love, Man incarnates in Nature. By love in turn, Nature opens her secrets to Man so that he can, if he wishes, gain knowledge of sympathetic 'powers', the benefits of different plants and herbs and sources of vitality. Though Man should avail himself of these, he can and should also, being of the higher spheres, be seeking always to raise himself back toward 'light and life'; in which ascending phase he will learn to disincarnate, leaving behind at each sphere the corresponding part of his physical nature and 'the evil it contains' (as lustfulness with Venus, melancholy with Saturn and so forth). We can see from this that, though Nature is good and full of love, Man's descent to her may paradoxically attach 'evil' to him; and he must seek to purify himself from the 'irrational punishments of matter', ever transposing ignorance into knowledge, sadness into joy, incontinence into continence, concupiescence into endurance, injustice into justice, cupidity into generosity, deceit into truth and so forth.

If Man does this, he will realise his immortality and have no fear of death, which is after all 'not the destruction of the assembled elements in a body, but the breaking of their union' and transformation of matter into other elements and bodies throughout an eternity (the 'Aion') which has neither beginning nor end. If, on the other hand, Man fails to use his intellect, or divine part, he will settle increasingly into his animal nature, like Apuleius becoming an ass. In this state, he of course remains divine; for God is the One, the All, nothing and at the same time everything, inherent in matter and anti-matter alike. But, without using his *mens*, Man may cease to recognise those subtle effluvia always descending from the higher spheres onto earthly matter; and these are as important to the sustenance of his special 'powers' as the secrets vouchsafed by Nature. Through images and talismans, the intellectually alert man may invoke beneficent aspects of the stars; for in Hermetic doctrine he is not merely subject to fixed cosmic patterns, as traditional astrology would have it, but able to influence astral patterns himself. This capacity also makes him theoretically capable of invoking demons; for, as with all other forces in creation, he is 'brother' to the maleficent aspects as well – the 'bad angels', 'decan demons' and so forth – which is what made the early Church fathers, St Augustine in particular, oppose Hermetic thinking and see it as encouraging witchcraft.[18]

So it may have done on occasion in dark medieval times, with certain Gnostics and antinomian devotees; also later among those who found diabolic indications spread amid Hermetic 'secrets' in works such as Cornelius Agrippa's *De occulta philosophia*.[19] But on the whole it seems that the Hermetic impulse was positive, pantheistic and cosmic in nature – an 'optimist' *gnosis* – and has remained so through most of its metamorphoses. In one of his supposed addresses, for instance, Hermes describes his ideal 'City of Adocentyn', prototype of the City of the Sun of Tomasso Campanella and 'magical' equivalent of Augustine's City of God, in which all will be ordered after a pattern to bring the most beneficent effects out of heaven and earth onto Man. This is enlightened, enlightening 'magic'. It anticipates the spirit of More's *Utopia* or Bacon's *New Atlantis*, both of which may have derived from it, and, as Frances Yates shows, belongs to a tradition of thought tolerant to and encouraging of scientific as well as spiritual quest. Hermeticism tends to reappear with movements putting high value on study of the natural and cosmic worlds and on man as an essentially godly creature with rights and abilities to determine his own reality. Fittingly, the *Corpus Hermeticum* ends with a lament for those ages in which the 'religion of the mind' may be suppressed, its devotees persecuted and way of thinking deemed 'a capital crime'. In such ages, 'the gods will separate themselves from men' and 'only the evil angels will remain'. The world will be given up to violence, war brigandage and terror; and the secrets of Nature and her fertility will be lost until some future 'magicians' – full Hermetic men or 'fisher-kings'[20] – may reawaken them.

III RENAISSANCE MAGI AND ALCHEMY

Driven underground by the Church in the Middle Ages, Hermeticism resurfaced to become a motive force for the Renaissance and its spin-offs, the Reformation and growth of the 'new science'. In Italy, where this revival began, a kind of 'apostolic succession' of neo-Hermetic thinkers may be traced: (1) Marsilio Ficino, who translated the *Pimander*, dabbled in 'natural magic' and believed one could invoke beneficent influences by the singing of 'Orphic' songs; (2) Pico della Mirandola, who found in Cabalistic 'magic' another effective method of moving up and down the spheres and finding out the 'powers' behind the planets and hierarchies; (3) Alexander VI Borgia, who accepted Hermetic studies, Ficino's natural magic and Pico's Cabalism as useful aids to Christian inquiry; (4) the creators of Siena Cathedral, who were so taken by the vogue for Hermeticism that they had a fresco constructed over the entrance depicting Trismegistus dispensing his 'Egyptian' wisdom to Moses; and finally (5) the man who for Frances Yates appears the ideal, or at least most dramatic, Renaissance 'magus': Giordano Bruno, who fought for acceptance of a Hermetic world-view against the opposition of post-Borgia popes, narrow Protestants and anti-spiritualistic neo-classicists; invoked Hermes on the side of Copernicus and the heliocentric universe (though at the same time inveighing against the new mathematics, favouring instead what he called 'mathesis', a pseudo-science of symbolic geometry and 'magically-charged' numbers); and wandered across Europe in the restless manner of so many 'magicians' of his time and later, proselytising in favour of man's pursuit of knowledge without restriction, into the 'infinite'.

Rejected by pedants at Oxford and the Catholic cabal in Paris, Bruno found some followers in the universities of Lutheran Germany before returning to Italy in the naïve hope of soliciting patronage from a new pope, being tried by the Inquisition and burnt at the stake; and Yates speculates that these 'Giordanisti' followers may have formed a basis of the mysterious Rosicrucian Brotherhood, which first appeared in Germany in the decade after Bruno's death and, by all descriptions, believed a Hermetic doctrine similar to his.[21] Taking it a step further, Yates wonders if a similar Hermetic impulse, perhaps even deriving from Bruno's agitations in England, might not have been a basis for early Free-masonry,[22] which was first written about openly by Elias Ashmole in 1646 and (according to Eliphas Lévi) may have been created 'as a counterblast' to the 'Puritanical anarchy' let loose by Cromwell.[23] The origins of speculative Masonry remains somewhat obscure; but doubtless they have a relation to these things, as well as the agitations of the Rosicrucians in Paris in the early 1620s and controversy surrounding the last of Yates's Hermetic Renaissance 'magi', Robert Fludd, in Stuart England.[24] Common to these figures and events was an impulse, Yates argues, to develop a worldview which might replace the bloody spiritual wars being fought between Protestants and Catholics, and the intellectual war brought on by the advance of the inductive, empirical 'new science' against deductive, 'structuralist' pre-modern cosmogony. It was the era of not only the English Civil War but also, in continental Europe, the Thirty Years' War, Descartes and what T. S. Eliot would label the 'dissociation of sensibility'.

It was also the last great age of alchemy; and, before discussing the situation of 'magic' on the verge of the nineteenth century, we might say something about this as an example of a third essential aspect of the 'tradition': that is, of 'method'. We have talked in general terms about the development of the 'magical' personality and the sort of ideas in which such a personality might 'believe'. What exactly, however, is it that the 'magician' *does* apart from developing his self and espousing a universal world-view? The answer is as various as the types of 'magic'; but a repre-sentative and immensely influential *praxis* may be found in this pseudo-, or perhaps proto-, science which may have existed from Egyptian times (as suggested by an etymology of the word[25]) but in any case was carried on in shadow through the high Middle Ages and reached some kind of zenith with the Renaissance 'magi', Paracelsus most famously, just before the appearance of the Rosicrucians, breakthrough of the new science and dawn of the period to which Yates's work delivers us.

Alchemy has produced too vast and obscure a literature to facilitate any easy or comprehensive account of it.[26] The reader may be familiar with images of solitary dabblers bent over heating-flasks and strange books in ersatz laboratories or Faustian cells in darkest *Mitteleuropa*; of sudden explosions caused by these male cousins to toad-stewing witches, which animate childhood memories in works of such authors as E. T. A. Hoffmann.[27] This is the adverse typology. In theory, the alchemist was studying in detail the processes of natural matter in order to transform it to a higher state; in which discipline it was believed fervently that he simultaneously would transform himself. The essence of the pursuit was patience. The alchemist had to observe chemical transformations for years before any enlightening occurrence, either inner or outer, was likely to take place. In this, he was making himself implicitly into the supreme initiate, as opposed to hero. Watching, waiting and suffering the worldly privations inherent in his task were the conditions of his existence: a 'feminine', as it were, passivity – even receptivity – rather than 'masculine' action; no heroic leaping forward based on deductive instincts, but almost disembodied mental–spiritual concentration on inductive evidence, leading, perhaps, toward ultimate thoughts.

To begin with, the alchemist had to study old texts, written in a deliberately confusing manner.[28] Once he had mastered – or believed he had mastered – these, he would commence his operation or 'working'. He would mix, say, an ore, a metal and an acid in a mortar. After grinding these by hand for five or six months, he would heat the result in a crucible. After ten days or so, he would dissolve the substance in an acid, doing so under polarised light – perhaps that of the moon. Evaporating the liquid and recalcining the solid, he would repeat the same process perhaps thousands of times, until the moment when fatigue of matter was sufficient and terrestrial and other conditions exactly right. Eventually something extraordinary would happen. This was the event the alchemist was waiting for. Using an oxidising agent or melting his substance, he would discover *signs* on the surface of his crucible. These would alert him to remove his mixture and allow it to 'ripen' until the first days of spring. When that moment was reached, the mixture would be replaced in a transparent receptacle made of rock crystal and 'hermetically' sealed. Then it would be heated and heated again until an 'essence' or 'fluid' appeared. Called 'raven's wing' owing to its blue-blackish colour, this would constitute a new substance, hitherto unknown in nature: a synthetic chemical element man-made by the alchemist, as if God, and ready to be mixed with other elements in a similar process in order to create, eventually, synthetic precious substances exactly like what the uninitiated knew as gold, silver or what-have-you.[29]

It is thought that some of these substances may have had 'magical' properties: extremely low resistance to electricity, for instance, like the 'super-conductors' of modern science. In addition, in the process of creating these, a reddish-mauvish powder might be produced in the partially melted glass of the crucible – a powder which, when treated, formed the basis of the 'philosopher's stone'. The alchemist who had gone so far as to produce this had achieved the 'great work'. The process would have brought him 'the promise, or foretaste, experienced by a privileged being, of what awaits humanity after attaining the very limits of its knowledge of the earth and its elements: its fusion with the Supreme Being, its concentration on a fixed spiritual goal, and its junction with other centres of intelligence across the cosmic space'. Possessing thus the 'key to the mechanics of the Universe', the alchemist was now *'illuminated'*. Furthermore, it was believed that, by exposure to 'radiations emitted by nuclea undergoing changes in structure', he himself started to mutate into a being of more rarefied intelligence and capability. It was even imagined that, by drinking the 'heavy water' created by washing and rewashing the dregs in his receptacle with triply distilled water, he suffused himself with the 'universal solvent', the 'elixir of tradition that ensures longevity', the 'elixir of Faust'.

IV   FREEMASONRY

Louis Pauwels, from whom I have taken this extraordinary description, contends that alchemists successful at such a process could conceivably have become 'awakened' to a state superior to that of normal 'half-asleep' man, and that the Rosicrucian Brotherhood may have been composed of a group of such personages. This fantastic theory he offers as an explanation for the secrecy which the Brotherhood and its descendants imposed on themselves. In the first place, he suggests, popular knowledge of their exalted condition would have provoked suppressions by jealous temporal and religious powers. In the second, their 'secret doctrine' might have been used for destructive ends in the hands of those not having experienced the 'purification' imagined inherent in the interminable creative process. In the third, what possible benefit could have derived to this enlightened elect from intercourse with the non-enlightened, lesser species of ordinary men?

Pauwels' interpretation is coloured by his interest in semi-secret elitist movements of the twentieth century, notably Nazi; and there may be a degree or projection back onto the early seventeenth century of modes of thought more typical of our age of 'intelligence', 'counter-intelligence', industrial secrecy, non-proliferation of nuclear information, eugenics and 'biotechnology'. Still, it is irrefutable that the geniuses of the new science had to protect themselves from the upheavals and witch-hunts of their violent times (Descartes may have been a Rosicrucian, Newton a Freemason).[30] Furthermore, as Yates states, it was in the interests of all enlightened men to create some new, synthetic type of religio-philosophical doctrine which would bind mankind into a peaceful, harmonious collectivity – into one Man, as it were – in which they could proceed with works which seemed to them obviously of universal benefit.

The most problematic aspect of Freemasonry – its secrecy – might be taken in this light. The difficulty one has in discussing it down to this day is that, as Yates also says, nothing terribly concrete is known about it, in spite of a vast literature. To some degree, it remains a case of the phenomenon that those who have known have not told and those who have told have not known very much. Masonic writing generally has been of a historical nature, not theoretical or 'magical'.[31] In fact, the banality of many books on the subject leads one to believe that, for the most part, the movement degenerated rather quickly into a glorified 'service club', with 'help in the high street' and comradely drinking after lodge-meetings being its most notable characteristics.[32]

Masons themselves have long since learned to deny significant involvement with theology. Their vague deism is supposed to allow members to continue to practice the Catholicism, Protestan-

tism, Judaism or Mohammedanism in which they may have been
brought up; the only stricture is that a man's 'religion' should fit
into an overarching idea of one 'Great Architect of the Universe'
in whose service all 'good men and true' are working.[33] This
formula could hardly help but be attractive in an age of increasingly damaging and absurd religious controversies. But, along
with the secrecy, it would prove an Achilles' heel to Masonry
when male predominance, a paternalistic God and monotheism
altogether came under varying degrees of (perhaps partly
'magical') attack. Should there not, for instance, be priestesses of
Isis in the temples, as in ancient times, and as introduced by Götz
Friedrich into the run-down enclave of the Grail at the end of the
centenary production of Wagner's *Parsifal* at Bayreuth?

This looks ahead toward twentieth-century concerns. Meanwhile, in the eighteenth century, when Masonry was enjoying
rapid development through Europe, and contributing to the
destruction of superannuated orders through the American and
French Revolutions,[34] it must have seemed to many to augur the
dawn of a new Western orthodoxy. From its origins in medieval
craft masonry, it offered for those concerned with practical
progress a humble yet eminently reasonable doctrine of (1) regu-
lation of standards in industry, (2) spreading a moral code and (3)
imparting wisdom to the young. At the same time, for those
hungry for arcane explanations, it provided from accretions of
Renaissance thought apparently sophisticated 'keys' to 'the
mysteries', based on quasi-Egyptian rites, the 'wisdom of
Solomon', Pythagorean geometry, neo-Platonism, Palladian architecture and traditions apparently developed by Masons for
Masons, such as the legend of Hiram Abiff, supposed builder of
Solomon's temple, whose murder by three wicked apprentices
and subsequent 'resurrection' is played out in Masonic rites to this
day.[35]

The full paraphernalia of the cult is, of course, too various and
recondite to go into here; nor are Masons themselves in agreement
about all their lore. A fairly lucid description comes from Éliphas
Lévi, a 'magician' not always invoked for his clarity, as we shall
see. In his *Histoire de la magie* (1860) he writes,

Their doctrine is that of Zoroaster and of Hermes, their law is
progressive initiation, their principle is equality – regulated by
the hierarchy and universal fraternity. They are successors of

the school of Alexandria, as of all antique initiations, custodians of the secrets of the *Apocalypse* and the *Zohar*. . . . Truth is the object of their worship, and they represent truth as light; they tolerate all forms of faith, profess one philosophy, seek truth only, teach reality, and their plan is to lead all human intelligence by gradual steps into the domain of reason. The allegorical end of Freemasonry is the rebuilding of Solomon's Temple; the real end is the restoration of social unity by an alliance between reason and faith and by reverting to the principle of hierarchy, based on service and virtue, the path of initiation and its ordeals serving as steps of ascent. Nothing, it will be seen, is more beautiful, nothing greater than are such ideas and dedications; unhappily the doctrines of unity and submission to the heirarchy have not been maintained in universal Masonry. In addition to that which was orthodox there arose a dissident Masonry, and all that is worst in the calamities of the French Revolution were the result of this schism.[36]

This aptly suggests the dialectic between idealism and skulduggery which has long characterised Masonry in popular impression.[37] By others we are given conflicting 'facts'. Some Masons, for instance, contend that they derive from Nimrod, others from Augustus Caesar;[38] some English Masons have claimed Charles II as their founder, while others hark back to Athelstan; the French, meanwhile, have claimed the Knights Templar or even Charles Martel. And then there is the matter of the 'secret word'. Some say this has come down from the Towel of Babel and, in English, has been variously 'Mahabyn', 'matchpin' or 'Marrow-in-the-bone'; but one recent chronicler – seeming to get the 'word' muddled up with the names of the twin Masonic pillars, Jachin and Boaz – identifies it as 'Jabulon', the name of a synthetic Masonic deity combining the roots 'Jahweh', 'Baal' and 'Osiris' and thus indicating for enemies of the cult an undercurrent of devil-worship.[39]

Such speculative excursions lead into the murk; and, indeed, all questions as to the origins of the Masonic idea are less important than the fact that a pervasive atmosphere of universal intention was subscribed to by a large and influential group of undeclared initiates and came to dominate the West of the last three centuries via this heterodox grouping. In particular, as said, the Masonic century was the eighteenth; for, as the movement began to come together in the seventeenth, so it seems to have begun its gradual dispersion throughout the nineteenth, to be followed in the twentieth century as it was preceded in the sixteenth by a proliferation of related 'magical' ideas and cults, all concerned to one degree or another with the struggle of (Hermetic) Man (and Woman) to establish or maintain power over his (or her) inner and outer destiny in the face of an enfeebled 'orthodoxy'. Of this, ironically, Freemasonary at last became part; in which way the development sketched in the following chapters might not so fancifully be described as the 'reformation' of a new catholic order – the anti-religion of Masonry, grandaddy and prototype of all serious cults of our period – with the principal succeeding groups taking their places in the scheme as the main 'protestant' sects.

V   THE SPIRIT OF FAUST

This may be the most significant theme of this study, and the reader is encouraged to keep it in view. Meanwhile, given the influence of Masonry on culture at large, it would be surprising not to see its brand of 'magic' being reflected in literature; and the best place to look for this might be in a representative spirit of its great era. Goethe is the obvious choice. He was, after all, almost undoubtedly a Mason and probably also an early member of the related German cult, the Illuminati.[40] Expert testimony in these matters might be had from 'Germanist' scholars, of which I am not one. However, I have it on authority of Eric Harber,[41] a long-time researcher in this field, that he was once told by a distinguished lady reader in the British Museum that she once saw a letter from the young Goethe to a friend in which the poet claimed that he would not know what to do were he to not become a Mason, since that seemed 'the only way to get on'. The lady scholar, Harber continued, has since died; nor has he been able to locate Goethe's letter. The import, however, he regards as essentially true: how better to explain the mysterious goings-on in *Faust, Part II* than in relation to various inner-temple playlets and grade rituals of higher-level, speculative Masonry?

This deduction I accept more readily than the coyness of the account may seem to merit, having come to similar conclusions myself in reading and becoming mystified by Goethe's master-work; and about it, as a kind of prelude to our subject in the modern period and summation of the *Zeitgeist* out of which it flowed, it seems pertinent to say one or two things. In the first place, Faust is, obviously, a 'magician'. In the second, the type of 'magic' he practices is in large part alchemical. In the third, his philosophy is 'Hermetic',[42] as a look at his early speeches will show:

> How all things in one whole do blend,
> One in the other working, living!
> What powers celestial, lo! ascend, descend,
> Each unto each the golden pitchers giving!
> And, wafting blessings from their wings,
> From heaven through farthest earth career,
> While through the universal sphere
> One universal concord rings![43]

This is the 'faith'. Faust reminds himself of it by gazing at a macrocosmic 'sign' in one of the numerous occult texts around him. The problem for him (and from the first we may identify him with everyman and his problem with *the* problem of Hermetic Man in his day) is that he cannot find his way back to the pristine realms of 'light and life' which are his true homeland in Hermetic terms.

Having come down to Nature and dwelled in her without exercising his divine *mens* for so long, Man has ceased to be able to reascend the spheres. Indeed, he is now even poorly able to coax beneficent secrets out of Nature herself. He has, in short, substantially lost his 'magic'; his devout alchemical experiments have not brought satisfying results; and some more fantastic, desperate measure must be taken. Mephistopheles is the measure, if not the end. To him (at least at the beginning of the 'quest') Faust has the relation of initiate to fully fledged 'magician', or – in terms, say, of *The Sacred Magic of Abra-Melin the Mage*[44] – of adept to guardian angel. Mephistopheles is Faust's guru, or guide. What is shocking and disappointing, of course, is that he should also be an embodiment of chaos, dispersion, 'evil' in a traditional moral sense. But this, as Goethe presents the case, is a condition of Faust's era, in which (as said) Man has lost touch with 'magic'.

In particular, Goethe decries that institutionalised repository of 'magical' doctrine the Church, which is depicted as turning its back on 'evil' when used to gain material wealth and then self-righteously invoking arguments about 'good' in order to attract that wealth to itself.[45] This *animus* determines his selection of a Christian 'devil' to lead his Hermetic, Freemasonic 'new man' to glory. For, as Lévi elucidates,

> The Rites of Masonry are designed to transmit a memorial of the legends of initiation and to preserve them among the Brethren. Now, if Masonry is thus holy and thus sublime, we may be asked how it came to be proscribed and condemned so often by the Church. . . . Masonry is the Gnosis and the false Gnostics caused the condemnation of the true. The latter were driven into concealment, not through fear of the light, for the light is that which they desire, that which they seek and adore; but they stood in dread of the sacrilegious – that is to say, of false interpreters, calumniators, the derision of the sceptic, the enemies of all belief and morality.[46]

An anti-Christian posture is now necessary for mankind to progress. In Crowleyan terms,[47] a 'new aeon' must be brought about, by any means. But, whereas for Apuleius, in rebellion against Roman gods, an 'age of Osiris' or 'the god within' was coming to replace an 'age of Isis' or 'the gods without', for Goethe, in rebellion against Church hegemony, a moment of Set – the murderer of Osiris – is at hand: a moment which will lead on to a 'third age', an 'age of Horus' or 'the god within', which will establish a 'religion of Unity' based on 'semen and ecstasy', in place of the 'blood and agony' of Christianity and stony paganism which preceded it.

The reader may feel that he or she is confronting an obscure terminology here and ideas which overleap our subject by a century. But the fact is that the identity of Mephistopheles bears on the development of the whole 'magical' tradition from Goethe's period to the recent past. This devil of course relates to Satan; and Satan, Kenneth Grant tells us, does indeed originate in the Egyptian god Set, the shadowy fourth member of the trinity Isis–Osiris–Horus,[48] who becomes the god Shaitan of the Sumerians: the 'Black God' or 'Burnt One' whose symbols were the peacock and serpent; a 'Saturn-god'[49] worshipped perhaps by early Gnostics and still by sects in Kurdistan; a spiritual emanation who has reappeared in modern times – to Crowley, for instance, as Aiwaz, his personal 'holy guardian', the 'angel of the New Aeon', a 'tall, dark man in his thirties', Persian or Assyrian by race, reminiscent of the devil of Christian tradition but also in Crowleyan cult terms related to the Ipsissimus or 'His most selfness' of those latter-day Illuminati the A.·.A.·.. In addition to these identifications extrinsic to Goethe, Mephistopheles might also be identified in Hermetic terms with the 'decan demons' Man is able to invoke as intermediaries between him and the gods: the 'bad' angels Augustine condemned Hermeticism for countenancing, who can bring terrible power but, in the end, are not themselves able to progress through the spheres to the highest levels, because they are not, like Man, 'brother' to the primal *Nous* nor originally inhabitants of pristine realms of 'light and life'.

This would explain Mephistopheles' failure at the end of *Faust, Part II*, in contrast to Faust's own increase in independent 'magical' powers, followed by a renouncing of those powers altogether and unbroken ascent up the hierarchies. Faust indeed obtains the high Hermetic status he began by seeking, and this is revealed as not so different after all from the ideal of 'true' Christianity. The moment of Set does seem to be leading toward the dawn of a new age of Unity, which Crowleyans would describe as the 'Aeon of Horus' and Freemasons and revolutionaries of the end of the eighteenth century saw as liberation from the strictures of king and Church – strictures they would soon reimpose after their own 'democratic', yet no less hierarchical, design. Meanwhile, however, the process opened to Faust by his invocation of Mephistopheles is really more significant for 'magic' in the coming age than any impression that such 'satanic' means may be allowed to 'wither away' once grandiose ends have been achieved. About this process, we might make the following observations:

1 The exceptional man may view his development as that of Man-at-large.[50] He represents the 'brains',[51] as it were, of the human race and thus need not – in fact should not – concern himself overmuch with the effect of his necessary 'experiments' on other, lesser mortals. Consider the fate of Gretchen in *Faust, Part I* and of the old couple whose land and house are expropriated to make way for the reclamation scheme in *Part II*.

2 Following from this, he should learn to regard men and women at large, like the secrets of nature and influences of the planets, for their *usefulness* as opposed to feelings or common humanity. In the interests of the unitary Great Man, they

might be viewed as invocable forces, like chemical re-agents or Mephistopheles himself.

3 No desire should be regarded as impossible to fulfil, so long as the necessary price be paid. The Great Man should never restrict his imagination in pursuit of ultimate capabilities.

4 Personality itself is a 'power', like any other; and the Great Man should exploit the myriad personae available to him, as revealed in the demons presented on northern and classical *Walpurgisnächte*, the characters in dramas from his own imagination (masques in the Emperor's court), the 'powers' revealed to him below (the 'Mothers'[52]) and on high (angels and other celestial beings).

5 The Great Man's true mate is Beauty, as embodied in Helen of Troy: a creature rather like Apuleius's Roman goddesses: self-interested, glorious and vain. With her, he should mate in an 'alchemical marriage', which will create, for a moment, the essential, flaming, uprising spirit of Man's greatest joy, the mortally doomed yet eternal *magnum miraculum*, Euphorion.

In the end, it seems that the message of *Faust* is for the Man of the age to take power where he can find it: to storm heaven, as it were, and regain his high original place. For the Judaeo-Christian, Hermetic and even Masonic 'Word' 'In the beginning was the Word', Faust substitutes 'In the beginning was the deed!', which suggests how, in the new age Goethe was helping to inaugurate, the true 'magician' would have to be more than an Apuleian initiate with his waiting, watching and religiosity. He would have to contain aspects of the hero as well: the alchemist who comes out of his laboratory to apply his discoveries; the Parsifal who joins the Grail Order not only to temper and complete his own personality but to gain alliances and the means to set larger changes in motion, in this world and perhaps even the cosmos. Inasmuch as Freemasonry and its derivatives helped to form the framework in which mankind as a single Hermetic Man has been able to do such things, from the explosion of the French Revolution and establishment of bourgeois capitalism to the explosion of the atomic bomb and dissemination of Dionysian post-war lifestyles, it has been an essential – if ever recondite – stimulus to an epoch of pervasive and increasingly 'orthodox' 'magic'. And 'magic' in this connection we might now further define as the 'religion' of the 'third age': the age of 'man as god himself' no longer restricted by absolute, arbitrary or parochial moral principles.

3

Eliphas Lévi

I THE MYSTERIOUS COUNT

In the winter of 1913–14, Ezra Pound and W. B. Yeats shared for the first time a house, a cottage in Sussex. There the young American exponent of the 'hard and clear' and the middle-aged Irish romancer of the 'Celtic twilight' pursued their own work and assisted in each others'. Pound was editing *The Egoist* and advancing 'Imagism' into 'Vorticism', Yeats reading Lady Gregory's fairytales and writing 'Witches, Wizards and Irish Folklore' and 'Swedenborg, Mediums, and the Desolate Places'. In the evenings the two would discuss 'real' symbolism; and Pound took occasion to write to his fiancée, Dorothy Shakespear (who was, by no coincidence, daughter of Yeats's erstwhile mistress Olivia Shakespear), that this originated in the Cabala – 'genesis of symbols, rise of picture language, etc.' – and thus predated by centuries the aesthetics of Villiers de l'Isle-Adam and Arthur Symons.[1] If one wanted to understand the true origins of Symbolism, Pound continued, one might begin by reading *Le Comte de Gabalis* by the seventeenth-century Abbé de Montfaucon de Villars, go on to the *grimoire*[2] of Pope Honorius and Ennemoser's *History of Magic*, and only then return to the best of the recent French theorists, Mallarmé and Rémy de Gourmont.

Pound's programme is rather astounding in a poet who saw his destiny as being to liberate poetry (and not least Yeats's poetry) from nineteenth-century 'fog' and was later vociferous about the responsibility of Jewish culture (of which the Cabala must be seen to be part) for the 'decline of the West'. But, as James Longenbach argues in his essay 'The Secret Society of Modernism',[3] Pound at this stage was influenced by the Yeats of *The Wind among the Reeds* (1899) as the Yeats of *Responsibilities* (1914) was influenced by Pound; and, indeed, Yeats's interest in the occult may have been instrumental in helping Pound refine his modernist theories. From a *grimoire* Yeats recommended, Ludovico Sinistrari's *De daemonia-litate, et incubi, et succubis,* Pound became charmed by the idea that 'there are in existence on earth rational creatures besides man'; and from Olivia Shakespear he commissioned a translation and adaptation of the aforementioned *Comte de Gabalis* because, as Longenbach relates, it 'provide[d] a pleasant and diverting approach to the doctrine of symbolism in its profounder sense'.

Pound serialised Olivia Shakespear's 'Memoirs of a Charming Person' in issues of *The Egoist* which also carried such milestones of the new literature as Joyce's *Portrait of the Artist* and Wyndham Lewis's *Tarr*. As Shakespear's title indicates, the story embodied a kind of 'aristocratic charm' which appealed to Pound and his confederates; also 'esoteric ideas and language' and 'a rationale for an elect elite'. The gentle anti-clerical tone of *Gabalis*, typical of the era of Rosicrucians and early Freemasons, was in harmony with the intention of these modernists to 'subvert the ethnocen-tricity of Christian monotheism' in ways we have seen T. S. Eliot complaning about.[4] At the same time, the 'novel' does not substi-tute an excessively rational classicism, as would many of its successors in Yeats's despised eighteenth century. On the contrary, it points toward realms filled with 'Djinns, tribal gods, fetiches' and 'the spirits of our ancestors', to use Pound's quaint formulation. The fairytale atmosphere looks forward to that stream of French letters, tainted with the occult, which in the nineteenth century would produce de la Motte Fouqué's *Undine* and Maeter-linck's *Pélleas et Mélisande*. Radical further departures into such realms are what Pound at this juncture imagined might lead on to a new kind of literary 'power'. 'It is by them [the Djinns, etc.] that we have ruled', he writes elsewhere in *The Egoist*,[5] sounding almost more like Yeats than Yeats himself, 'and shall rule, and by their connivance that we shall mount again into our hierarchy. The aristocracy of entail and of title has decayed, the aristocracy of commerce is decaying, the aristocracy of the arts is again ready for service.'

That *Gabalis* should have appealed to post-Symbolist writers is not surprising when one considers the quote from Tertullian with which it begins: 'Quod tanto impendio absconditur etiam solum-modo demonstrare destruere est.'[6] This translates nicely into the Pound–Yeats dictum that 'to explain a symbol is to destroy its ability to embody . . . the divine or permanent world'. The story's *mise-en-scène* too could only appeal to literary scholars who favoured Faustian personae, especially Yeats in his tower-bound vein. The narrator is a Parisian student of the occult. As the tale opens, he is brooding over a rumour that a mysterious 'count' who once helped him in his studies has died for having revealed too many 'secrets'. (This was indeed the fate of the Abbé de Montfaucon de Villars, if one believes the 'author' of Sir Edward Bulwer-Lytton's nineteenth-century 'Rosicrucian' novel *Zanoni*.[7]) Rich and dazzling in dress and apparently German in origin, the Count appeared to the narrator just at the time when the latter had begun to correspond with 'an elect cabalist' in that nation of witches and Rosicrucians across the Rhine. The narrator has wished to know more about the 'philosopher's stone' and similar recondite matters being discussed in the *demi-monde* of the day. Though having arrived on the scene rather like Mephistopheles to Faust, the Count advises an approach that is more conventionally Masonic than satanic. To make himself 'worthy' for 'cabalistic knowledge', the narrator must first 'adore the All-Good, All-Great God of the sages', and second learn to 'watch, pray, hope, and be silent'.

Questioned on his identity, the Count responds modestly that he is 'the least of the sages' and 'certainly no phantom or sylph'. Later, shifting attention back onto the narrator, he declares that the young man will become 'one of the elect'. Why? Heroic ambition (which the narrator has presumably demonstrated by his curiosity) is always the mark of 'children of wisdom'. And what is 'wisdom'? comes the further question. The tradition of Plato, Pythagoras, Celsus, Porphyry, Trismegistus and others of their kind, the Count replies. Like the Renaissance magi we have seen Frances Yates describing,[8] he goes on to predict that through study of the works of such ancients, the narrator may 'learn to control all nature', so that 'the supreme intelligences will be proud to obey your wishes; the demons will not dare go where you are; and the invisible peoples who inhabit the four elements will be happy to be the ministers of your pleasures'. Concluding what can only be seen as an invitation to initiation, the Count puts to the narrator several further questions: 'Whether I wished to serve God only, and realised what it is to be a man; whether I did not object to being a slave when I was born to be a king, and so on, coming at last to the question, would I renounce all things in order to reach the heights to which I was destined.'

The reader will quickly grasp the Hermetic import here. The

Count is encouraging the narrator to become the 'Great Man': to regain his original high place above 'the armature of the spheres' as the 'brother' of God.[9]. As in *The Golden Ass*, the last stricture – worldly renunciation – is seen as essential to the task. Only through this, the Count contends, may a mere mortal gain intercourse with the elemental spirits, who are themselves more influential than God or the devil. Like the 'decan demons' of Hermetic tradition, these are 'an order of beings between God and man to whom everything can be attributed which is superhuman but less than divine.' In early times, as related in the *Pimander*,[10] they inhabited Egyptian and Jewish idols. Later, during the period when 'God had abandoned the Earth' (classical Greece), they spoke through oracles. Finally, after 'God had returned as man', they could be content to 'be quiet' and inhabit the ether, fire or water as may be in their 'magical' forms as sylphs, gnomes, salamanders or undines. Each man has his proper elemental partner, which can be determined by the stars. Intercourse between a man and an elemental provides an 'immortal soul' for the latter and deliverance from the horrors of 'the second death' for the former, otherwise condemned to damnation by a proscriptive Church.

The point of union with an 'elemental' is (to use a Crowleyan trope) to produce a 'magical child'.[11] Allegorically, this might mean any 'great work'. But biologically too, according to the Count, the idea is valid in itself. 'Ah, if only there were more of these philosophical families and none of the children of sin!' he complains. Great figures from Zoroaster to Apollonius of Tyana to Diane de Poitiers were created out of such unions, as indeed all the truly great must be. The elementals are thus 'demonic' in a good sense. Moreover, they are loved by God: it is only humans who have ever condemned them; and in the past God has helped them to escape persecution by allowing them to take the form of animals, 'mystery lovers' or even gods – thus the origin of ancient legends about the marvellous conception of heroes. Of all elementals, only gnomes have some footing with the devil, the Count contends. This is because they come from underground and harbour a natural suspicion of the light. Still, even gnomes can be brought right. They need only be preached to by a 'proper cabalist' at midnight – which practice in its turn is the origin of the myth of the 'witches sabbath'; for the first gathering of the kind came when Orpheus charmed up from the depths a group of gnomes whose eldest member was called Sabatius.

So much is the essence of the eccentric Count's message. In person, he is described as 'at once so strong and so weak; so much to be admired and yet so ridiculous'; and the tone of the narrative – fantastic, ironical, perhaps even 'mocking', as the Introduction to *Zanoni* suggests – reflects this. Taken as a whole, *Gabalis* is an excursion into the illusionistic 'alternative religion' of its day: Masonry or its near-precursors. In this, it is as playful as *Faust* would be, yet less revolutionary, more 'clair, précis, net au but'[12] in a French tradition more self-consciously mannered and tasteful than Goethe's German, which sometimes descends to the level of farting witches and similar Düreresque motifs.[13] We have mentioned the legacy of *Gabalis* in the legendary, fairy-tale stream of French 'magical' literature. In cultural history, its more immediate legacy might be seen in the behaviour of another 'count', this 'de Saint-Germain', and his presumed initiate Cagliostro, the two of whom had much to do with the rapid growth and fantastic aura of Masonry in France in the eighteenth century.[14] 'Magic' in this period came (as we have also seen via *Faust*) to have as much to do with personality as with dogma. But Saint-Germain's diamonds and obscure Eastern travels, his linguistic attainments and alleged perpetual youth, anticipate the 'modernist' magic of the era of Yeats and Pound – the peripeteia and antics of Crowley, for instance – more than the high academic theorising of the nineteenth century. For 'magic' in France after the Revolution was to have more in common with the studious context and renunciatory message of *Gabalis* and to be dominated by its most serious scholar since the Renaissance, who took the name of 'Eliphas Lévi'.

II FRENCH LITERARY FASCINATIONS

In literature, it became a theme of increasing importance in the years after Napoleon's fall. Charles Nodier's interest in fairytale kingdoms, secret societies and occult lore was enhanced by his tenure as librarian of the Bibliothèque de l'Arsenal and disseminated among the premier literati of his day at his noted 'dimanches'.[15] Attending these could be found Victor Hugo, who would later use 'spiritualist' techniques to summon kindred great authors of the past – Aeschylus, Dante, Shakespeare and Molière, notably – to brighten his exile in Jersey;[16] Dumas *père*, who was interested in any subject which might make best-selling copy and would actually publish work by Eliphas Lévi in his magazine *Le Mousquetaire;*[17] and of course Balzac, whose pet theories on Swedenborgianism and synchronistic 'sympathies' are set out in his stories 'Séraphita' and 'Le Réquisitionnaire'[18] and whose life-long belief in a *substance étherée* (related to what we shall see Lévi calling 'the astral light') is most fully laid out in his early philosophical novel *Le Peau de chagrin* (1831).

Of these figures, Balzac might be taken as the great literary bellwether of the vogue for and nature of 'magical' ideas in his generation, much as Goethe for a previous one. Romanticism had advanced, and Balzac's bias is even more radically individualistic than that of the author of *Faust*. At the same time, pre-Revolutionary idealism having been tarnished, Balzac shows little interest in Masonic paraphernalia and ideas of a 'brotherhood'. Still, his great theme develops the Faustian problem of domination through will; and, like Goethe, he shows how success in this sphere is likely to require the price of comfort, peace and ultimately life itself. Through the eyes of his Faust-like 'hero' in *Peau de chagrin*, he sets out the first part of the formula:

> The human will was a material force similar to steam-power. . . . Nothing in the mortal world could resist it when a man trained himself to concentrate it, to control the sum of it and constantly to project that fluid mass on other men's minds. . . . He who had learned the technique could modify as he pleased everything relating to mankind, even the absolute laws of nature.[19]

Elsewhere in the novel, via the vaguely Mephistophelean, Gabalis-like or wise old 'magician' character who introduces the hero to this 'key' in the first place, Balzac sets out the second part of the formula:

> Man exhausts himself by two acts. . . . The exercise of the *will* consumes us; the exercise of *power* destroys us; but the pursuit of *knowledge* leaves our infirm constitution in a state of perpetual calm. So desire or volition is dead in me. . . . And yet I have encompassed the whole wide world. My feet have trodden on the highest mountains of Asia and America. I have learnt all

human language and lived under every kind of rule. I have lent
my money to a Chinese and taken his father's body as a pledge.
I have slept under the tent of the Arab in reliance on his word,
I have signed contracts in every European capital, and without
a qualm, I have left my gold in Red Indian wigwams. In short
I have had everything I wanted because I have learned to
dispense with everything.[20]

Two things are of particular note in this speech: (1) the mix of
'knowledge', travel and experience which is central to the Rosicrucian formula for enlightenment and which we shall see cropping
up later in this study;[21] and (2) the identification of 'knowledge'
with quiescence, asceticism and renunciation, which we have
noted in *Gabalis* and of course *The Golden Ass* before it. That this
equation would characterise 'magic' over the next several decades
is indicated by the motto Lévi repeats throughout his mature
works: 'DARE, KNOW, WILL, AND BE SILENT'.[22] This harks back to
'Watch, pray, hope and be silent' in *Gabalis*; and the philosophy
of the premier 'magician' of the mid nineteenth century would
have progressively less to do with *Faust*'s 'In the beginning was the
deed!'[23] In the begining for Lévi as for Balzac's sage (as opposed
to his doomed 'hero'), is most definitely 'the Word'. 'Magic' for
him, as for the ageless Rosicrucian Mejnour in Bulwer-Lytton's
contemporary *Zanoni*, is a matter of detached contemplation,
mental travel and willing, not direct intervention on the physical
plane. Several reasons for this change in *Zeitgeist* might be
proposed; but surely one of the most important must be that the
first French Revolution and rise and fall of its youthful hero,
Napoleon, substantially satisfied 'deed'-oriented cravings,[24] while
the century of relative peace which followed created both an
atmosphere and an opportunity for quieter 'initiations'. This in
turn Lévi and his kind hoped might lead on to the reign of a
new Christianised Napoleon, or 'Paraclete', and 'rebuilding of the
temple'.[25]

Lévi forms the proper focus for study of 'magic' in the nineteenth century both because that century was a period in which
the baton was carried largely by the French and because his
magnum opus, Dogme et rituel de la haute magie (1856), became the
principal *grimoire* for writers interested in 'magical' ideas in the
following generations, as subsequent chapters will show. Major
French writers who knew Lévi and his work include Balzac, to

whose widow Lévi dedicated his 'novel' *Le Sorcier de Meudon* (1861)[26] and in whose house he was introduced to many of his admirers; Baudelaire, with whom Lévi shared the distinction of writing a poem on the Swedenborgian subject of 'correspondences',[27] an interest both men may have derived in part from Balzac; Dumas *père*, who, as stated, published Lévi and in return received flattering, if sometimes inaccurate, praise from him;[28] and Villiers de l'Isle-Adam, whose interest in the supernatural, Solomon's Temple and Rosicrucianism as exhibited in such stories as 'Occult Memories' and 'The Messenger' – and of course the influential 'play' *Axël* – appears to have been reinforced by readings from Lévi, particularly the *Dogme et rituel*, which he recommended to his fellow Wagnerophile, the poet and literary theorist Catulle Mendès, who in due course would introduce it to the Symbolist *prince des poètes*, Mallarmé.[29]

These represent only some of Lévi's literary connections. Certainly his austere, Parnassian approach encouraged a more formidable and lasting reputation among serious men of letters than that of any other occultist of his time. All the same, this reputation was not always entirely favourable. Joris-Karl Huysmans, who made perhaps the most extensive sortie into the occult of any distinguished French writer of the *fin-de-siècle*, says this of Lévi in connection with alchemy in his *roman à clef*, *Là-bas* (1891):

> Eliphas Lévi explained the symbolism of these bottled volatiles as fully as he cared to, but abstained from giving the famous recipe for the grand magisterium. He was keeping up the pleasantry of his other books, in which, beginning with an air of solemnity, he affirmed his intention of unveiling the old arcana, and, when the time came to fulfil his promise, begged the question, alleging the excuse that he would perish if he betrayed such burning secrets. The same excuse, which had done duty through the ages, served in masking the perfect ignorance of the cheap occultists of the present day.[30]

These 'cheap occultists', whom Huysmans does not neglect to castigate elsewhere, include Gérard Encausse, called 'Papus', who admired Lévi and carried on one strand of his studies in *Le Tarot des Bohémiens*;[31] the 'Marquis' de Guiata, who also was introduced to Lévi's work by Catulle Mendès, and helped to establish the aesthetic order of the Rose-Croix in Paris of the later 1880s, in which this phenomenon of 'magic' as an adjunct of personal style began to make its revival; also 'Sâr' Peladan, who brought to his own schismatic branch of the 'order' a characteristically perverse orientalism, Catholicism and taste for the 'forbidden pleasures', as reflected in his books *La Décadence latine* and *Le Vice suprême*.[32]

Huysmans himself weaves a study of the medieval mass murderer Gilles de Rais into his inquest into this contemporary scene and at the end of *Là-bas* comes to a conclusion which a number of writers on the subject, frequently Catholic and frequently French, have shared: namely, that satanism is the only form of the occult with a substantial material basis and that 'white magic' is generally a pretext for fraud:

> The others, the mages, the theosophists, the cabalists, the spiritists, the hermetics, the Rosicrucians, remind me, when they are not mere thieves, of children playing and scuffling in a cellar. And if one descend lower yet, into the hole-in-the-wall places of the pythonesses, clairvoyants, and mediums, what does one find except agencies of prostitution and gambling? All these pretended peddlars of the future are extremely nasty; that's the only thing in the occult of which one can be sure.[33]

So much may have been the case at the time Huysmans was writing and after: a time when 'magic', as well as the eye viewing it, was becoming infected with a cultural taste for 'sin', the 'ugly' and strange. So much, however, was less true in the heyday of Lévi (*c.* 1860), who, in spite of poverty and other sordid circumstances throughout his career, appears to have maintained a considerable degree of purity. But then Lévi was in essence a man of the cloth; a priest in spirit if unfrocked in fact. And this may be why the casuistical Huysmans, himself to become an active Catholic shortly after publishing *Là-bas*, exempts him from the degree of scorn he heaps on others.

III APOSTATE PRIEST

Born Alphonse Louis Constant, Lévi was the son of a shoemaker. Brought up in the old Latin Quarter of Paris, his childhood seemed on recollection 'weak and dreamy', characterised mainly by a 'need to love' and an interest in drawing.[34] Educated by priests, the boy

showed precocious intelligence and was marked out early on for
the seminary. One of his teachers, the Abbé Frère-Colonna, introduced him to Mesmerism, ideas of social justice and a semi-
Hermetic interpretation of the purpose of Original Sin, i.e. that,
having fallen from God, man's destiny was to 'return towards
Him by a process which tears him away from matter and spiritual-
ises him by degrees'. Abbé Frère subscribed to a view of history
as the 'three ages'.[35] In his formulation these were (1) the Age of
Penitence, characterised by Cain and the Deluge; (2) the Age of
Faith, thus of Abraham, Moses and Christ; and (3) the Age of the
Holy Spirit, which would include a return to a new Eden. The
Abbé's mix of utopianism and conventional religion filled the
young Constant with a love of 'ancient Catholicism'; and the
kindly man's eventual dismissal by Church authorities started the
youth on a path of disillusionment which would result ultimately
in his adult attitude that the Church was rather like a beautiful
maiden waiting to be rescued out of profane hands.

Lost illusions increased after his admission to the theological
college at Saint-Sulpice. (The bell-tower of the cathedral there
is, incidentally, the venue for most of the important religious
discussions in *Là-bas*.) Constant attended the college at around the
same time as his more orthodox and celebrated contemporary,
Renan, and left under not dissimilar circumstances. Passionless
scholasticism in clerical instruction annoyed him almost as much
as Oxford pedantry had Giordano Bruno.[36] 'At Saint-Suplice one
learns ignorance slowly and with difficulty', he would remember.
His comrades were 'dirty' and given to 'spying' on one another.[37]
As a result, the budding heresiarch felt forced to pursue spiritual
development in increasing solitude, concentrating on singing and
song-writing and finding in *The Golden Verses of Pythagoras* 'a
magical view of the universe' and 'network of hidden forces
"binding together" the elements of the invisible world and capable
of being controlled by the adept'. A 'unitary vision' from this
time dominated his religious imaginings. The 'seemingly insoluble
problem of evil' was resolved with contempt for 'the Manichaean
and dualistic fiction', which the Church hypocritically kept up.
'God was one. Love was one. Mankind was one.' The role of the
truly religious should be 'reintegrating the individual into the
whole and the whole into oneness of divine love'.

Following his departure from the seminary came many ardent,
turbulent years. He gave up the Church altogether, then returned

to it, then gave it up again. He wrote *La Bible de la liberté* (1841), which was banned and landed him in jail. On release, he was forgiven and became a sub-priest. Then he wrote *La Mère de Dieu* (1844), fell out with the Church again and went to jail again. In the 1830s, among interesting characters he had fallen in with was Flora Tristan, a 'bewitching creature' who was a blue-stocking and a journalist, the grandmother of Gauguin, friend of the socialist–anarchist Proudhon, and founder of her own fringe religious movement. Affected deeply by her death in the early 1840s, Constant collected her socialist and feminist writings as *L'Emancipation de la femme, ou testament de la pariah* (1846). Meanwhile, emboldened, he carried on as a poverty-stricken radical and political idealist, writing tracts against famine, contributing to *Le Tribun de peuple* and finally publishing on the eve of the Third Revolution *La Testament de la liberté* (1848), which yoked socialism to his fermenting 'religion' in a utopian vision of a reign of Love brought on by the Holy Spirit as breathed through the fervours of heretics and revolutionaries.

Constant looked to the events of 1848 to rekindle religious sentiment. He himself sought to contribute 'a synthesis and rational explanation of symbols', out of which might come 'the true Catholic Church or the universal association of all men'. A first result of this was his *Dictionnaire de la littérature chrétien* (1851). It was the last work to be published under his given name; for during the early 1850s, rather like another disillusioned participant in the 1848, his exact contemporary and philosophically kindred spirit, Wagner, Lévi went through a moral crisis which led on to full realisation of his mature identity and meaning of his subsequent life-work. Part of this was a result of his reading: not Schopenhauer, like Wagner at the same period, but Renaissance magi and post-Renaissance 'Illuminati', especially Knorr von Rosenroth and his *Kabbala denudata*. Another part was the result of his meeting the aged Polish *émigré* Hoene Wronski, an extreme eccentric whose great work, *Messianisme, ou réforme absolue de savoir humaine* (1847) had advocated a new union of philosophy with religion to produce (1) truth on earth, (2) paracletism, (3) definitive science, (4) history explained on the basis of liberty, (5) states designed to stop political torment, (6) a fixed purpose for mankind derived by reason, and (7) a 'revelation of the destinies of nations'.

Much of this ideology was absorbed into Lévi's next published book, the seminal *Dogme et rituel*. But a third and perhaps most important impulse for his changes of identity and direction arises out of the fact that his young wife, formerly a socialist comrade-in-arms, became bored with his arcane pursuits and (according to his undoubtedly biased intimations[38]) jealous of his growing reputation (she herself was an aspirant painter) and left him for Wronski's brother-in-law. Desolate, Lévi threw more energy into *Dogme at rituel* than into any other work of his, before or after; and with its publication his reputation did indeed burgeon, though according to some[39] his influence would never again be so great as it had been during his feminist–radical phase. Whether or not this proved to be the case, political and sociological disappointments attending the ascent of Louis-Napoleon convinced Lévi that 'the time was not ripe to regenerate man as a whole', only to 'show individuals the way to enlightenment'. Disillusionment with public life was not sufficient to force him into exile, like the righteous Victor Hugo. He did find himself in jail again briefly for writing a poetic polemic against the Emperor, *Caligula;* but this was compensated for by an opportunistic recantation, *Anti-Caligula;* and Lévi ended by renouncing this-worldly radicalism, even to the point of decrying the Paris Commune and enunciating a vague, occult-based doctrine of France's messianic role among nations.[40]

This development is analogous to that which can be seen in other ex–1848 firebrands during the waning years of the nineteenth century, Wagner again to wit; and it locates Lévi's thought in this area in the sometimes daft and eventually ominous 'nationalist' drift which would bring down the fascist avalanche in the next century. Supporting the tendency in his rhetoric was a simultaneous drift from an egalitarian 'brotherhood of man' toward belief in the need for hierarchy. This, as we have noted, is characteristic of much occult thought, especially in groups based on 'initiation', such as Masonry. Nor is it surprising in this connection that Lévi should have joined the 'Rose of Perfect Silence' Lodge in Paris in 1861 and supported the Masonic idea in many of his later books. Always an individualist, he eventually found Freemasonry confining and broke with it rather in the manner and with the lingering regret that he had once broken with the Church. Two things in particular annoyed him: (1) that the Masons did not acknowledge him as a great elucidator of the meaning and origin of their 'secrets'; and (2) that they continued to harbour antagonism toward the Church, which was understandable in the light of

seventeenth-century persecutions but hardly appropriate in an
era when both organisations were equally 'establishment'. 'True'
Masonry and the 'true' Church shared the same goals, Lévi
believed; they just expressed them differently.[41]

Following his Masonic interlude, the aging 'magus' retired to
his rooms in Montparnasse, there to become fixed increasingly in
the public eye as a great oracle who gave out wisdom through
correspondence and private instruction and who liked to show up
the charlatanism of rival celebrities of the occult. These included
the satanists of Lyon, Vintras and Boullan, who would inspire
characters in *Là-bas;* also the Anglo-American 'spiritualist' D. D.
Home, who among other distinctions is remembered in literature
as the model for Robert Browning's 'Mr Sludge, "the Medium" '.[42]
From his cloister or cell, such as it might be viewed, Lévi produced
books extending and reinforcing doctrines laid down in *Dogme et
rituel: Histoire de la magie* (1860), *La Clef des grands mystères* (1861),
Le Sorcier de Meudon, La Science des esprits (1865), *Les Mystères de
Qabalah* and *La Grande Arcane* (both published posthumously), and
others. 'Pilgrimages' were made to him, as by the English 'Rosicrucian' Kenneth MacKenzie, who wrote an influential article on Lévi
in his final period.[43] But the most revealing account of what the
man aspired to, and perhaps achieved, comes in his own prescrip-
tion for the well-ordered life to an aristocratic disciple:

> A great calmness of spirit, a great cleanliness of body, a
> constantly even temperature, rather on the cold side than too
> hot, a dry and well-aired lodging, where nothing is incongruous
> and there is no reminder of the base needs of life (I would be
> just as ashamed to display a wash-basin in my apartment as to
> go out into the street without my trousers), well-regulated meals
> proportioned to the appetite which should be satisfied but never
> overstimulated. Simple and substantial food; stop work before
> one becomes tired; take moderate and regular exercise, never
> allow yourself to become overexcited in the evening, to ensure
> that the greatest possible calm precedes sleep.[44]

In the end, Lévi seems to have drawn toward an ideal of
Western Buddhism, though without the world-weariness and cult
of *endura* arrived at around the same time by Wagner, under the
influence of Schopenhauer's 'pessimism'. Lévi was an optimist;
holiness was his goal; he believed it could be achieved and would

lead on to glorious transcendence. Force and counterforce, idea and its negation were the principles by which this might occur: a complete commitment to *equilibrium:* balance: bringing together in unity all opposites. Thus the 'magus' could look back without self-castigation at a career full of apparent contradictions: radicalism *versus* traditionalism, rationalism *versus* the supernatural, revelation *versus* the rule of KEEP SILENCE. Finally, Lévi believed that the gap between the Known and the Unknown would continue to necessitate religion as well as science and, in spite of scars from the old battles for social justice, came to feel that, while for him, a true thinker, complete freedom of religion amid age-old speculations was a right, for most of mankind, downtrodden and potentially demoralised, imposed dogma was a necessity. Thus he ended, apparently, like Wagner and Huysmans, 'at the foot of the cross', waiting for 'Parsifal': a great 'white magician' or Gnostic representation of the 'third force' or Holy Spirit.[45]

IV CABALA GOOD AND BAD

Unlike Cagliostro before him or Crowley after, Lévi was not a practising 'magician'. His one great experience of 'practical magic', recorded in detail in *Dogme* and repeated by chroniclers as the central event in his career,[46] was an evocation of Apollonius of Tyana undertaken while on a visit to London during the critical juncture when, abandoned by his wife, he was beginning to settle down to his great work. This adventure and Lévi's account of it probably deserves to be viewed as illustrative rather than strictly factual. In any case, it served two useful purposes. In the first place, it added to Lévi's authority as as 'adept', both by the fact that he was (he alleges) led to the evocation by a high-born lady, member of a secret order and friend of Bulwer-Lytton (who, as a member of Parliament, successful novelist and aristocrat, had special standing among occultists of the day); also by the fact that the spirit appearing to him (and implicitly taking on the role of sponsor or 'guardian' for his subsequent career) should have been one of the most influential mages of classical times, a precursor any practitioner of *haut magie* might dearly have liked to invoke.[47] In the second place, it allowed Lévi to dispense with the idea of a true magus had to be practising arcane rites continually. Henceforth he might answer if challenged that – having gone through

the vitality-draining experience once and received from the oracle
the unequivocal message 'Death' – a mage would be foolish, if not
to say irreverant, to allow the specially charged instrument of his
body to be put through the same again.

Some such line of reasoning seems to have been persuasive.
Even dedicated practising 'magicians' such as MacGregor Mathers
and Crowley, both of whom would also cite the physical danger
inherent in some evocations,[48] continued to view Lévi as the great
'magician' of recent generations, in spite of what might have been
regarded as a lack of absolute personal commitment. For us, Lévi's
timidity regarding 'practical' magic simply qualifies him as a less
fascinating figure. In it lies a seed for the sometimes bloated development of his theoretical activities. Perhaps age too may be a
factor here. Both Mathers and Crowley were, as we shall see, well
on their way to full realisation of their 'magical' destinies in young
adulthood. Lévi by contrast only adopted his semi-priestly persona
after a career of politics and failed affairs had delivered him to
middle age. It is a pity that the great modern exegete of occult
'religion' could not bring to his subject the clarity and force of the
young poet, *chansonnier* and polemicist. But that is the case; and
the reader must proceed patiently in the knowledge that it is no
longer a physically robust spirit he will be dealing with.[49]

Numerical form dominates Lévi's great books, even the titles
and subjects of his chapters. In this lies a characteristic and
unifying force of his thought. He took his *nom de plume* from
Hebrew because that was the most ancient tongue of written
Western religion. From Hebrew as well he took the idea that letters
equal numbers (Hebrew letters have traditional numerical values)
and thus that the 'key to all mysteries' might be represented as a
mathematical formula. From this, it was a short step to fascination
– even obsession – with geometrical symbols; a tendency Lévi
shared with Giordano Bruno and which caused him at various
stages in his career to see his drawings as an important as his
words.[50] Here is a dual approach toward the Absolute similar
to that of another writer and draughtsman with Swedenborgian
interests, William Blake; and a profitable study might be made
(perhaps again via the often-serviceable Yeats) of the relation
between that poet's opus and 'magic'.[51] Leaving that aside for
other explorers, what is important for us here with Lévi is that a
combined interest in word and image naturally led him to suppose
that the highest expression of 'magic' might be diagrammatic.

Thus it should come as little surprise that he put an enormous importance on what we have seen Pound calling the 'genesis of symbols, rise of picture language, etc.', the Cabala, with its 'Tree of Life'.

Lévi's Cabala, T. A. Williams tells us,[52] is an elaboration on the Hermetic thesis, sometimes called the doctrine of the 'Emerald Table', that 'what is above is like that which is below'. Literally, Cabala means 'what is received', i.e. traditional knowledge. In theory, it sets out a plan for metaphysical system-building and debate, while in practice it involves 'magical' operations for ascent and descent through the spheres. The former naturally absorbed our sedentary mage the more, continuing and refining the interest in analogy and 'correspondences' set out in his poems and satisfying his need to find some synthetic spiritual mechanism which embraced not only Christian but other mystical systems. The Cabala, Hebrew traditional maintains, was taught originally by God to the angels and by them in turn to man. After the Fall, man lost direct communication with the Divine. Still, Adam was able to pass substantial fragments of the Truth on to Noah, thence to Abraham, thence to Egypt, where Moses was initiated. The Pentateuch, which the latter is supposed to have written for his people, formed a numerological and alphabetical codification of the Cabala 'in the outer'. But the first written elucidation of its meaning 'in the inner' was the early medieval *Zohar*, or 'Splendour', by Simon bar Jochai. Rediscovery of this by Moses de Léon in thirteenth-century Spain and subsequent dissemination among Christian heretics, Gnostics and Jewish mystics constitutes, after the developments of the second century AD outlined in the last chapter, the most significant event in the development of Western 'magic' up to the Renaissance.

In essence, the Cabala teaches that 'an unknowable and undefinable source' (*Ain Sof*) created through 'the Word' ten principal spiritual emanations, known collectively as the *Sephiroth*. The first ray is sent out from *Kether* or Crown (or Primordial Point, Long Face, White Head, Ancient of Days) and proceeds in a zigzag pattern down through nine other points: *Chokmah* or Wisdom, *Binah* or Understanding, *Chesed* or Mercy, *Geburah* or Severity, *Tiphereth* or Security, *Netzach* or Victory, *Hod* or Glory, *Yesod* or Foundation, and *Malkuth* or Kingdom. The 'Tree' formed by this pattern may also be interpreted in corporeal terms as 'the archetypal Adam', after whom Man was fashioned. Concentration on each point in the 'Tree' or 'body' allows the individual to identify specific qualities in himself or another, master them and thus progress on towards fuller 'magical' realisation. Connection between the points – twenty-two subordinate 'rays' – constitute 'paths' for the initiate between stages of advancement: 'ordeals', in the nomenclature of medieval quest tales, complete with their characteristic opponents (demons) and guardian spirits (angels); or, in some interpretations (including Lévi's, Cabalistic equivalents of the archetypal personae and situations necessary to encounter and master embodied in the trumps of the Tarot.

'The fundamental idea of the Qabalah,' Aleister Crowley writes,[53] 'is that the Universe may be regarded as an elaboration of numbers from 0 to 10, arranged in a certain geometrical design. . . . The problem is to acquire perfect comprehension of the essential nature of these numbers.'[54] Lévi's comprehension might be sketched briefly thus: 'One' expresses unity, the masculine creative principle and source of all existing things. 'Two' is fission, the binary Adam split into himself and Eve, Cain and Abel, good and evil, the 'Jachin' and 'Boaz' of Masonic tradition. 'Three' denotes the relationship which heals the rift, mediates and saves Being from perpetual dualism. 'Four' adds unity to the ternary and thus creates the first square, the cross, the four elements in balance, thus perfect equilibrium. 'Five' has as its magical sign the pentagram, which is 'the star of enchantment', symbolising Man's dominion over Nature by its representation of the head above four outspread limbs. 'Six' is symbolised by the 'seal of Solomon', the star made of superimposed triangles, one pointing up toward the heavens, the other down toward the depths, and thus representing the potential to ascend or descend so essential to Hermetic Man's progress. 'Seven' represents 'the full force of magical power', combining triangle with square and relating from ancient times to the seven planets, virtues, vices, colours, notes of music, sacraments, *et cetera*. 'Eight' is the filling out of the square toward the circle, finite toward infinite, or *vice versa*, thus in one of its significances the concentration into form of the 'astral light' or 'magnetic breath'. 'Nine' is the number of initiation, the months of gestation before birth, and thus suggests 'the Divine in all its abstract power' or, to the evil-minded, 'superstition and idolatory'. 'Ten', being the number of Sephiroth, denotes 'the ten emanations that mediate between the unknowable God and man' and thus represents, like 'zero', wonder and, further, a first stage toward final completion.

In *Dogme et rituel*, Lévi goes on to detail the meanings of all the twenty-two principal numbers, that total being arrived at by the number not only of rays of the Tree of Life and trumps of the Tarot but also of letters of the Hebrew alphabet, which, as said, have numerical equivalents. Space does not permit us to go into these further meanings here. The process in any case leads into the swamp of speculation and obscurity which has engulfed Cabalists since they began parsing these matters in the later Middle Ages. Suffice it to say that belief that letters have numerical values, and that numbers have metaphysical significations, leads directly to belief that words, composed of letters, may constitute 'codes' to ideas far beyond their apparent meanings. Lévi's promotion of such a belief 'in the outer' is one of the motifs which make him important to Symbolists such as Mallarmé and modernists such as Pound, who would try to bring a new, quasi-religious significance to the use of word and phrase. At the same time, his belief that the ten areas of the Sephiroth constituted 'boundless regions' of archetypal 'correspondence' is perhaps his most important legacy to the 'magicians' of the Golden Dawn, with their urge to create 'vast periodic charts', and, via that organisation, to such a thinker as Yeats, who yearned to reduce the universe and history to a predictable system, as outlined in *A Vision* (1925, 1937).

To these matters we shall return. Meanwhile, to 'equilibrate' the picture, we might also note Lévi's legacy to those 'magicians' of the mid twentieth century, who, following Crowley, advocated gaining knowledge of 'dark forces'.[55] In *Les Mystères de Qabalah*, he explains how the Sephiroth might be inverted – indeed *per*verted, as he alleges it was in ancient times by 'philosophers of decadence' still tied to the animistic idols of Egypt and Samaria rather than the one God and abstract dogma of the Hebrews.[56] The *Qliphoth*, or invisible backside of the 'Tree of Life', may be reached by passing through the mysterious eleventh, central and unconnected point of the Sephiroth, *Daath*,[57] meaning 'knowledge'. Travelling on this path constitutes descent (or ascent, if one 'transvalues' terms) through realms of chaos and evil. There, Lévi tells us using symbolic terms, Kether or 'the Crown understanding' might become an inverted pentagram or 'the star of despotism'. Chokmah, wisdom, might become *Nibbas*, 'the dog fanaticism'. Binah, active intelligence, might become *Thartac*, 'the

ass or stubborn fatality'. Gedulah, divine mercy, might become
Azima, 'the goat or obscene love'. Geburah, justice, might become
Marcolis, 'inflexibility or stone'. Tiphereth, beauty, might become
Anamelech, 'the horse symbolic of triumph of the beast'. Netzach,
victory, might become *Nergal*, 'the cock or foolish pride'. Hod,
order, might become *Succoth* or *Benoth*, the hen, representing 'fatal
maternity'. Yesod, celestial marriage, might become *Nissoch*, 'the
impure lingam'. And Malkuth, the religious world, might become
Adramelech, 'the peacock or proud world'.

V   MANIPULATING THE ASTRAL LIGHT

The reader should not be confused by designations shifting
slightly here: Tiphereth from 'security' to 'beauty', for instance.
Interpretations of the Cabala have always been varied, and Lévi
altered his designations from book to book. The point is that, in
spite of his mockery of Manichaeanism and belief that 'evil' as an
independent force was incompatible with God,[58] Lévi was aware
that this apparatus which could lead toward the light for a 'white'
adept might become a programme for uncovering the bestial in
his 'black' counterpart. Lévi regarded himself as a man of Reason
(he capitalised the word and invoked it with the gusto of an
eighteenth-century *philosophe*); thus such a programme could seem
no more than an 'evolutionary regression' to him (though he
would not have used such Darwinian terms). All the same, he
recognised the 'dark tradition' as part and parcel of 'magic' and,
in spite of his piety, devoted several chapters of *Dogme et rituel* to
it. Chapters xv and xvi of the first book are entitled respectively
'Black Magic' and 'Bewitchments'; the same numbers of the
second, 'The Sabbath of the Sorcerers' and 'Witchcraft and Spells'.
By no mistake, these numbers are the same as those of the most
'terrible' cards of the Tarot, 'The Devil' and 'The Tower struck by
lightning'. The fact underlines this central importance of 'correspondences' for Lévi. Understanding them will, according to him,
illuminate 'all allegories of India, Egypt and Judaea and the Apocalypse of St John'.

The latter is praised as a 'Kabalistic book' and analysed at length
as one of the great 'magical keys'.[59] But, along with the Cabala,
primus inter pares of the 'keys' for Lévi is the Tarot. Describing this
moves him to some of the most enthusiastic of his ever-lofty

rhetoric: '[It is] a truly philosophical machine, which keeps the mind from wandering, while leaving its initiative and liberty . . . mathematics applied to the Absolute, the alliance of the positive and the ideal, a lottery of thoughts as exact as numbers, perhaps the simplest and grandest conception of human genius', and so on.[60] The reader may look at any one of several famous decks of Tarot cards[61] to begin to understand the variety of archetypes which so fascinated this mage. In general, Lévi's system follows standard patterns, though objections have been raised to his idiosyncratic placement of 'The Fool' *et cetera*. In historical terms, it derived from the reasearches of Court de Gebelin[62] and Etteilla, two more of Lévi's many occult precursors in France from the turbulent close of the eighteenth century. According to them, the system had been discovered in the reign of Charles VI (also the era of Huysmans's Gilles de Rais and St Joan – another time of consequence in the saga of Western 'magic'[63]) from the lore of gypsies and Bohemians, who had been using it since about the time we have noted for emergence of the Cabala 'in the outer'. Like that doctrine, the Tarot is supposed to have had more ancient origins as well, in the religions of India and Egypt. Connection to the latter is one of Lévi's reasons for calling it 'The Book of Thoth' or 'Hermes'; and he makes characteristic contribution to the dicussion by adding the etymological note that 'Tarot' comes from 'rota', which means 'wheel', and reversed, as 'tora', in Hebrew means 'law'. Thus, in concept, we are encouraged to construe it to mean the 'law of the wheel' or, interchangeably, 'wheel of the law'.

This metaphor seems apt enough. For Lévi, it becomes the beginning of a typical spin-off. 'The wheel', he tells us, via Williams, 'represents the Cosmos itself in the incessant play of its phenomena and in its ultimate grounding in a unitary, unchanging source. The centre is the world navel. . . . The spokes are the creative emanations that give rise to the world of experience.' This is helpful, and it seems destined to bring Lévi's thought squarely into the realm of the 'wisdom of India'. Then he adds, 'They also form the cross, the redemptive way toward reintegration with the creator.' And so we have another characteristic synthesis: Christian symbol, the philosophy of the East, a governing 'system' from the Western occult.[64] That they all merge into one in the eyes of this 'magus' should surprise no one by now. The point of his quest is to establish a single new religion; and in the final chapter of *Dogme et rituel*, entitled 'The Book of Hermes' and devoted to the Tarot, he sums up:

> Thus in religion universal and hierarchic orthodoxy, restoration of temples in all their splendour; re-establishment of high ceremonial in its primitive pomp; hierarchic instruction of symbols, mysteries, miracles; legends for children, light for grown men who will beware of scandalising little ones in the simplicity of their faith: this religion is our whole Utopia, as it is also the desire and need of humanity.

This is the highblown spiritual trajectory of Lévi's concentration on theoretical systems such as Cabala and the Tarot: the 'Great Work', which he will describe again in his exegesis of the prophecies of Ezekiel and Revelation[65] as 'the building of the temple'. But how is mankind to accomplish the ideal mission? Initiation, Lévi says in a chapter on the subject,[66] is essential to 'restore tottering and distracted society' and to 'reawaken' in man a natural respect for the concept of 'hierarchy', which must reign in the 'microcosm' of earth as in the 'macro-' of heaven above. And how is 'initiation' to be undertaken? By the self for the rare genius; by organisations such as the Masons for an elect; or by that great repository of 'magical' lore 'in the outer', the Catholic Church, for the mass. And what will such 'initiations' entail? In whatever form, the purpose is the same: to lead the 'candidate' through 'unnumbered terrors' toward a power which 'does not surrender [but] must be seized'. Is this not just a metaphor for the self-aware life fully lived? 'The essential law of Nature', Lévi concludes, 'is that of initiation by effort and of voluntary and toilsome progress.'

As initiation of the mass should lead to utopian religion, so initiation of the individual ought to result in discovery of one's own will. Indeed, 'will' as word and idea recurs in Lévi's opus with as much frequency as in Balzac's *Peau de chagrin* or the works of Nietzsche, which would become gospel for men of letters (and others) of the Yeats–Pound generation. As Christopher McIntosh says,

> [Lévi] presented [magical systems like the Tarot and Cabala] not primarily as a means of ordering demons about or of playing with the forces of nature but as a system of drawing the will through certain channels by the use of symbols which touched

off certain basic reflections in the human make-up. 'Would you reign over yourself and others?' he wrote [echoing the question the Count asks the narrator in *Gabalis*.] 'Learn how to will. How can one will? This is the first arcanum of magical initiation.'[67]

The 'second arcanum', equally Balzacian or Nietzschean perhaps, might be to 'learn how to "equilibrate"'. For, as Lévi explains elsewhere, all Nature is 'bisexual', and 'perfect magnetism' is 'androgynous'.[68] Thus it would follow that one must learn to master 'the alternate use of contrary forces'. Indeed, he tells us, this constitutes the 'secret of perpetual motion' and thus may assure the 'permanence of power'.

'Power' belongs to the 'initiate' who has learned how to 'will' and how to 'equilibrate'. He alone may qualify as the true 'magus', poised to direct the 'great work'. But how can he do this? How may he make his 'will' serve himself and others? Here enters a final and most difficult concept in Lévi's scheme, that of the 'astral light'. This finally is the agency of applied 'magic'; all previous systems and secrets have been theory-based and preparatory to its deployment. But what is the substance? this 'ether' or 'mesmeric fluid' over which Lévi, like Balzac, spins out page after page of the most abstract, metaphoric prose? From various of his books, as well as commentators' glosses,[69] one gathers the following.

It is the 'primary matter' of the alchemists, in which may be found the forces of electricity and magnetism. It is, at the same time, what God created when he said 'let there be light.' It is the substance which mediates between spirit and matter and the origin of what in tradition has been called the 'Holy Ghost', *Spiritus Mundi*, primeval serpent and universal seducer, Lucifer, who is 'the bringer of light and shadow'. It is a 'blind, amoral, universal force that sweeps all before it in a perpetual search for equilibrium'. (One might think of what G. B. Shaw and other 'heroic vitalists' of the Yeats–Pound era would refer to as the 'life force'.[70]) It is the repository of 'all our desires, wills, intentions'; a 'physical electrolyte working even when we do not know it; a fatal power which can stir love or hate and sap energy'. Individual 'auras' are sub-divisions of it, as are emanations of imagination and dreams. The 'astral body' exists within it as an 'intermediary' between body and soul and can be made to 'project' itself through it. It is 'the incessant generator of incorporeal creatures', like the elementals of *Gabalis* and their spawn. These can be controlled by manipulation of it, but only at considerable risk to the manipulator and through unwavering will.

Spiritus Mundi is, in this way, the original 'dragon' of legend: the great irrational force a 'magician'-as-hero must triumph over to realise his destiny. As Lévi sums up in one of his many passages on the subject, chapter VI of *Rituel*, 'The Medium and Mediator',

> Two things, as we have shown, are necessary for the acquisition of magical power – the emancipation of the will from servitude and its instruction in the art of domination. . . . The whole magical work consists therefore in our liberation from the folds of the ancient serpent. . . . [This] natural medium is . . . the ever-active and ever-seducing serpent of idle wills, which we must withstand by continual subjugation. Amorous, gluttonous, passionate, or idle magicians are impossible monstrosities. . . . To will well, to will long, to will always, but never to lust after anything, such is the secret of power. . . . The man who has escaped the chain of instincts will first of all realise his omnipotence by the obedience of animals.

He will next 'realise' it by the 'obedience' of other humans, whom he may subdue by this 'phenomenon of magnetism', i.e. successful projection of the 'astral light' 'by glance, by voice, by the thumb and the palm of the hand', by music, drugs or a variety of psycho-sexual agencies. Finally, he will thus be able, as said, to control the 'elementals' – at which point in Lévi we return most importantly to the lore of *Le Comte de Gabalis*.

In chapter IV of *Rituel*, 'The Conjuration of the Four', Lévi repeats 'The Prayer of the Salamander' and other invocations from the Abbé de Montfaucon's text. In chapter V, 'The Blazing Pentagram', he goes on to describe how effective deployment of these is 'the sign of intellectual omnipotence and autocracy'. Elementals for him, as for *Gabalis*, are neither good nor evil; they are simply intermediary spirits between God and man ready and wishing to be controlled. But how now, finally, are we to interpret these 'tricksy little elves'[71] which seem to be part angel, part demon? They represent, firstly, archetypal principles in Nature, as their 'earth, air, fire and water' identities indicate; in this, they may be seen as the true originators (or at least 'suggesters') of scientific discoveries. Taking the principle a step further, they may be viewed as the originators of all ideas or actions waiting to be realised: thus the muses who lead artists to perfection or nemeses who pull criminals down. Finally, however, they seem in Lévi, as perhaps in *Gabalis* as well, to suggest a particular level of human spirit: those types more sharply defined than the mass, less liable to be affected by unsubtle manipulations yet more profitable to seek out and control; for, being unafflicted by the normal vagaries of the soul and having special capabilities owing to their super-mundane (or sub– in the case of gnomes) status, they may concentrate more readily on appropriate aspects of the 'great work' and bring innovation to them.[72]

Gabalis was metaphoric in treating these matters, and Lévi is circuitous. Still, in both cases the sub-text seems clear enough: as in *Faust*, the 'elect' man, 'Hermetic' high initiate or 'magician', will gain the ability – perhaps even duty – to 'marry' elementals and thus produce 'children' who will advance history and culture for otherwise half-asleep, unenlightened mankind-at-large. Whether these elementals eventually come to control those who summon them (as, similarly, whether Mephistopheles can win Faust's soul in the end) depends on the summoner's degree of 'magical' attainment: his power of concentration and sustained ability and desire to manipulate the 'astral light'. This finally is what requires the 'magus' to exercise caution, Lévi warns. He must always measure his ends against his capabilities and only summon or manipulate forces for effects he has a chance of bringing off. Failure will mean causing accidents to befall others and bringing down opprobrium on himself. Nor must he ever simply seek 'power' for its own sake, as some Nietzscheans of a subsequent generation would.

Having raised these qualifications, Lévi fails to go on to question the moral worth of 'magic' overall, like more strictly literary contemporaries. Take Balzac, Bulwer-Lytton and Huysmans, for instance: the three outstanding writers with interest in magic whom Lévi brushed with at the beginning, middle and end of his career. For each of them, the 'moral' of *Macbeth* prevails finally. Any mere man who has the temerity to summon 'magical' forces will find himself threatened and ultimately destroyed by them. Human energy is finite, whatever the Rosicrucians may have preached;[73] and 'power' gives way to entropy. Thus the 'hero' of *Peau de chagrin* may be able to gain all he wishes through his talisman, but he remains unable to prevent its shrinkage and so must end by 'willing' his own death. Thus Margrave, the 'natural', 'charming' yet utterly amoral villain (hero?) of *A Strange Story* (1862) – which Bulwer-Lytton wrote after a visit from Lévi[74] and which concentrates on Mesmerism and 'astral powers' – is finally exterminated by the same mysterious spirits he has so long commanded. Thus Huysmans's narrator in *Là-bas* – indeed, Huysmans himself in 'real' life apparently – becomes increasingly alarmed by the arcaneries he has sought out and wonders if the 'spirits' who have compelled him, both incarnate and otherwise, may not be modern equivalents of what the medieval Church called incubi and succubi.[75]

An 'equilibrating' conscience is at work in all these tales, providing the suggestion that true goodness may finally reside in the normal world, rather than 'magical' aspirations. Irony, sometimes even mocking as noted, provides an analogous equilibrating function in the first work of fiction taken up in this chapter, *Gabalis*, as it does in different ways in *Faust*. In Lévi's non-fiction, no such structural demand for 'equilibration' exists; thus, while warning of certain dangers for the 'magician', he at no time is forced to acknowledge the claims of a more prosaic morality. A general distinction might be drawn here, between serious literary writers and 'magical' ones. The first is ever required to return to 'reality' and take note of it, while the second always has a ready excuse to dwell entirely in the ideal. This and a single-minded pursuit of the lore of 'power' are what make Lévi's work finally seem to set out a massive, semi-obscure programme for Hitler – or, less ominously, at least such 'Cagliostros'[76] of the arts as Wagner, with his devotees at Bayreuth, or 1960s rock singers, with their drugged, mesmerised and blindly adoring 'groupies'.

Are not such phenomena logical outgrowths of this doctrine of realising one's will via 'astral' manipulation? Indeed, in spite of (or perhaps in view of) Lévi's ecstatic vision of Cabalistic or Masonic ordering of civilization by such means, does not the doctrine itself seem 'contrary to morality and religion'? To his credit, Lévi, always the exhaustive thinker, asks himself this very question in *La Clef des grands mystères* and answers thus:

A. Yes, when one abuses it.
Q. In what does the abuse of it consist?
A. In employing [the astral light] in a disordered manner, or for a disordered object.
Q. What is a disordered magnetism?

A. An unwholesome fluidic emission, made with a bad intention: for example, to know the secrets of others, or to arrive at unworthy ends.

Q. What is the result of it?

A. It puts out of order the fluidic instrument of precision, both in the case of the magnetiser and of the magnetised. To this cause one must attribute the immoralities and follies with which a great number of those who occupy themselves with magnetism are reproached.

Q. What conditions are required in order to magnetise properly?

A. Health of spirit; right intention, and discreet practice.

Q. What advantageous results can one obtain by discreet magnetism?

A. The cure of nervous diseases, the analysis of presentiments, the re-establishment of fluidic harmonies, and the rediscovery of certain secrets of Nature.[77]

4

Madame Blavatsky and the Theosophists

I ZANONI THE INSPIRER

I have mentioned the works and influence of Sir Edward-Bulwer Lytton. Lévi visited him twice, revered him throughout his 'magical' phase and is said to have belonged to a 'Miracle Club' with him.[1] The English writer's vogue with occult-minded thinkers of the latter two thirds of the nineteenth century extended to Wagner, whose first successful opera was an adaptation of one of his novels; also to MacGregor Mathers, leader of the Golden Dawn, who apparently regarded himself as an incarnation of Lytton's Byronic 'magus' Zanoni.[2] Further afield, it extended to the great female occultist of the period, creator of the Golden Dawn's immediate predecessor and rival among cults, Madame Helena Petrovna Blavatsky (*née* Hahn) of the Theosophical Society. On leaving her father's home for St Petersburg at the outset of her career, this peripatetic adventuress had a literary (or at least journalistic) success in condensing the English novelist's *Godolphin* for a contemporary Russian *Readers' Digest*.[3] On the strength of this, the magazine's editor suggested that young Helena try her hand at a novel, and she set to work on something she planned to call *The Ideal*. There is no evidence that the work was ever completed; still, the experience may have been formative. Having made her first break-out to freedom by means of writing – and a type of writing which mixed the Lyttonesque occult (*Godolphin* has an astrological episode at the centre of it) with her own characteristic spiritual exaltation – HPB (the designation she would prefer in later life) found her niche, after a career of fraud and illusion, in presenting the world with a new 'religion' via literature of a kind: *Isis Unveiled* and *The Secret Doctrine*.

Regarding Bulwer-Lytton specifically, Madame Blavatsky's most recent and exhaustive biographer informs us that he was 'one of the two main influences on [her] philosophical vision', the other being the French writer on India, Louis Jacolliot.[4] Among Lytton's books, *Zanoni* above all moved her, as it would Mathers two decades on.[5] 'Rich, handsome, ageless, and a member of the [secret] Brotherhood', Lytton's hero (whom Marion Meade identifies as 'Indian' by race[6]) was the prototype for Blavatsky's Tibetan 'Mahatmas', or 'hidden masters', Moyra and Koot Houmi. Moreover, 'HPB herself is in several important respects reminiscent of Lytton's heroine Viola, who has seen her protector in dreams since childhood but meets Zanoni in fleshly manifestation only as an adult.' Revealing her scepticism of Blavatsky's good sense (thus the intellectual underpinnings of Theosophy at large), the biographer admonishes, 'Bulwer-Lytton was of course writing fiction, but Helena believed quite seriously that he purveyed fact without knowing it.' She believed in any case that he had provided a useful model; and, as a middle-aged 'magician' in America in the 1870s, she adopted a female Zanoni persona herself. So much is apparent from the description of Theosophy's co-founder, the journalist and Mason, Colonel H. S. Olcott. After first meeting Blavatsky at a 'Spiritualist' gathering in Vermont he wrote, 'Upon her bosom she wears "the mystic jewelled emblem of an Eastern Brotherhood". She is probably the only representative in America of the secret fraternity who boast[s] of secrets of which the Philosopher's Stone [is] but the least; who [consider] themselves the heirs of all that the Chaldeans, the Magi, the Gymnosophists, and the Platonists [have] taught.'[7]

An equally sceptical biographer, John Symonds, tells us that this last phrase comes directly from *Zanoni* and is a description of its hero. Clearly the book made an imprint on the occult mind of the times even as far afield as America. What is it about exactly? We have mentioned a *mise-en-scène* in Europe around the French Revolution. The plot swings around the careers of a young English artist, Glyndon, who wants to become an 'initiate', and an unaging young 'initiate', Zanoni, who chooses to give up his 'power' for love and service in the world. Both adore the young singer Viola; but Glyndon is determined to forswear her for 'power', thus puts himself in the hands of an unaging old 'initiate' – in this case 'hierophant' – Mejnour, who embodies coolness and retreat from the world in inverse proportion to Zanoni's warmth and participation. Glyndon's ambition far exceeds his discipline; he is not able to maintain the strict asceticism Mejnour demands; as a result, he loses not only his promise as an artist and chance for true love but his integrity as a man as well. This terrible sacrifice to 'The Dweller of the Threshold' (dispersion, destruction and death) foils the even greater sacrifice of Zanoni. Unbinding himself from the sublime indifference required of 'initiates', the hero goes to the guillotine in order to protect his wife and child from the Reign of Terror and help bring down the tyrants who have set it in motion in the first place.

In historical terms, the novel thus comments on the phenomenon we have seen Lévi complaining about in relation to Freemasonry:[8] i.e. the nobility of the 'true' order as opposed to extremist fragments responsible for the 'worst excesses' of the great 'liberating' events of 1789–94. This is buttressed by various details of characterisation, such as the Jacobin dilettante Mervale's fatuous suggestion that Glyndon's painting lacks 'the great pyramidical form'[9] or 'Saint Robespierre's' pretensions in trying to establish his 'Cult of the Supreme Being'.[10] These are excrescences of the false 'brotherhood'. Against them, Zanoni's behaviour is set as an embodiment of the ethics of the 'true' order. This order is identified as 'Rosicrucian' in places. But, as Mejnour points out, 'Do you imagine that there were no mystic and solemn union of men seeking the same end through the same means, before the Arabians of Damus in 1378 taught to a wandering German the secrets which founded the institutions of the Rosicrucians?' (p.217). Indeed, the *theologia* in question is at least as *prisca* as Trismegistus, or the antique thinkers Olcott lists in his purloined description of HPB. Its object is twofold: (1) to find the great secrets from Nature; and (2) via the 'genius' of Art raise mankind toward God. The first will confer the mysterious longevity both Zanoni and Mejnour enjoy: 'All that we profess to do is but this – to find out the secrets of the human frame, to know why the parts ossify and the blood stagnates, and to apply continual preventives to the effects of Time.' The second qualifies imaginative creation as among the most exalted activities available to man: 'Yes, art was magic; and as he owned the truth of the aphorism, he could comprehend that in magic there may be religion, for religion is essential to art' (p. 125).

The distinction is important. Lytton belongs to that school of Romantics of the mid nineteenth century which believed that study of the human heart was as essential to 'magic' as the 'new science' had been in the pre-Enlightenment.[11] He advances concentration of the individual spirit beyond even the break-throughs noted in Goethe and Balzac. His prose is inward, some-times 'purple', always in pursuit of emotional 'vibrations',[12] in a way which anticipates Huysmans or Proust. Thus he looks forward to the new 'magical' discipline of the twentieth century, psychology, and obsessive programmes for self-realisation such as have emerged with it. That 'vivisection of the soul' is a motivating purpose of *Zanoni* is indicated in the Introduction, which previews the novel's development along the lines of Plato's four kinds of 'mania': the musical, the 'telestic' or mystic, the prophetic, and 'that which belongs to love' (p. 13). The point of all these, we are told, is a Hermetic one: 'to lead back the soul to its first divinity and happiness'. Thus the headings of the book's seven major divisions are (1) 'Music', (2) Art, Love and Wonder', (3) 'Theurgia', (4) 'The Dweller of the Threshold', (5) 'The Effects of the Elixir', (6) 'Superstition Deserting Faith', and (7) 'The Reign of Terror'. In other words, what we are tracking is a progress via Plato's manias toward failed 'initiation' in a fallen and predominantly evil – or at least very unideal – 'real' world.

The venality of the world and mankind at large is offered as an explanation for the secrecy of Mejnour's and Zanoni's order and a rationale for its elitism. The old alchemist's argument rehearsed in chapter 2 is repeated throughout by both figures. Why should the enlightened deign to share knowledge with those not prepared to work for and respect it? Indeed, are not the dangers of half-digested 'magical' truths in the wrong minds dramatically revealed by the Terror? No arguments are raised about the self-defeating nature of hierarchy and exclusivity in a democratic world, though some criticism may be implicit in the picture of Mejnour with his clinical aspiration to produce supermen –

> a mighty and numerous race with a force and power sufficient to permit them to acknowledge to mankind their majestic conquests and dominion – to become the true lords of this planet – invaders, perchance of others – masters of the inimical and malignant tribes by which at this moment we are surrounded – a race that may proceed, in their deathless destinies, from stage to stage of celestial glory, and rank at last amongst the nearest ministrants and agents gathered round the Throne of Thrones. (p. 181)

Indeed, on his way to his death Zanoni has a last vision of his *confrère* which reinforces this ambivalence:

> Alone, in the distance, the lonely man beheld his Magian brother. There, at work with his numbers and cabala, amidst the wrecks of Rome, passionless and calm, sat in his cell the mystic Mejnour; living on, living ever while the world lasts, indifferent whether his knowledge produces weal or woe. (p. 382)

But in the end, such doubts raised about the 'order' overall are obscured by the dark charm of Zanoni himself. He is a kind of Christ to Mejnour's Old Testament persona; and his idealism justifies the latter's dogma – as does his self-sacrifice.

Such things are what carried away the impressionable young Helena Hahn, as she set out to impress herself on the big world and gain adulation. Nor were persona and message all she took from *Zanoni*. The great, all-embracing sweep of her *magna opera* is prefigured in Lytton's outpourings, notably this from the hero as he nears his *finis*, which previews her contribution of 'hidden masters' to modern 'orthodox heresy':

> In ages far remote – of a civilisation far different from that which now merges the individual in the state, there existed men of ardent minds, and an intense desire of knowledge. In the mighty and solemn kingdoms in which they dwelt, there were no turbulent and earthly channels to work off the fever of their minds. Set in the antique mould of castes through which no intellect could pierce, no valour could force its way, the thirst for wisdom, alone, reigned in the hearts of those who received its study as a heritage from sire to son. Hence, even in your imperfect records of the progress of human knowledge, you find that, in the earliest ages, Philosophy descended not to the business and homes of men. It dwelt amidst the wonders of the loftier creation; it sought to analyse the formation of matter – the essentials of the prevailing soul: to read the mysteries of the starry orbs; to dive into those depths of Nature in which Zoroaster is said, by the schoolmen, first to have discovered the art which your ignorance classes under the name of magic. In such an age, then, arose some men, who, amidst the vanities and delusions of their class, imagined that they detected gleams of

a brighter and steadier lore. They fancied an affinity existing among all the works of Nature, and that in the lowest lay the secret attraction that might conduct them upwards to the loftiest. Centuries passed, and lives were wasted in these discoveries; but step after step was chronicled and marked, and became the guide to the few who alone had the hereditary privilege to track their path. At last from this dimness upon some eyes the light broke; but think not, young visionary, that to those who nursed unholy thoughts, over whom the Origin of Evil held a sway, that the dawning was vouchsafed. It could be given then, as now, only to the purest ecstasies of imagination and intellect, undistracted by the cares of vulgar life, or the appetites of the common clay. Far from descending to the assistance of a fiend, theirs was but the august ambition to approach nearer to the Fount of Good; the more they emancipated themselves from this limbo of the planets, the more they were penetrated by the splendour and beneficence of God. And if they sought, and at last discovered, how to the eye of the Spirit all the subtler modifications of being, and of matter might be made apparent; if they discovered how, for the wings of the Spirit, all space might be annihilated; and while the body stood heavy and solid here, as a deserted tomb, the freed *Idea* might wander from star to star; if such discoveries became in truth their own, the sublimest luxury of their knowledge was but this – to wonder, to venerate, and adore! For, as one not unlearned in these high matters has expressed it, 'There is a principle of the soul superior to all external nature, and through this principle we are capable of surpassing the order and systems of the world, and participating [in] the immortal life and the energy of the Sublime Celestials. When the soul is elevated to natures above itself, it deserts the order to which it is awhile compelled, and by a religious magnetism is attracted to another, and a loftier, with which it blends and mingles.'[13] Grant, then, that such beings found at last the secret to arrest death – to fascinate danger and the foe – to walk the revolutions of the earth unharmed; think you that this life could teach them other desire than to yearn the more for the Immortal, and to fit their intellect the better for the higher being to which they might, when Time and Death exist no longer, be transferred? Away with your gloomy phantasies of sorcerer and demon! – the soul can aspire only to the light; and even the error of our lofty knowledge was but the forgetfulness of the weakness, the passions, and the bonds, which the death we so vainly conquered only can purge away! (pp. 361–3)

II CHARISMATIC CHARLATANESS

Zanoni comes to believe that true immortality lies in 'the life beyond life': what one writer on Theosophy calls 'after-death states'.[14] This prefigures the Theosophical faith in transcendence of this world into 'higher levels': the trajectory of the soul upwards and out of man's 'dense' and 'etheric' bodies toward the 'astral' plane, then the 'mental' and so on, until at last it reaches 'Deva-chan', or heaven, there to dwell in 'bliss', fulfilling all its earthly aspirations, until perhaps a millennium or fifteen hundred years later, when it begins to desire for a new and different kind of experience and thus to descend toward reincarnation.[15] The Buddhist and Hindu ideas and nomenclature which would eventually overlay the basic Western Hermetic philosophy of *Isis Unveiled* – the so-called 'secret doctrine' which animates Blavatsky's final tome – is not yet developed in Bulwer-Lytton. American transcendentalists were an origin of that.[16] But what is present and comes through loud and clear in the passage quoted above is the sense of a massive tradition beyond present metaphysical yearnings: an 'ancient wisdom', to use the term Annie Besant would apply to her Theosophical great book, and an evolution of it from 'dimness' toward 'light'. This quasi-Darwinian view of the development of a spiritual elite would burst forth in full colours in Theosophy's view of the purpose of successive reincarnations: to bring the soul finally to a state where it would inhabit the body of a 'Mahatma' and thus complete a full cycle of progress in this universe.

The personal evolution of man's soul – or inner being, or 'Thinker' – in this way is called by *The Secret Doctrine* 'Anthropogenesis'. The development of the universe which runs parallel to it (indeed, both levels of progress are strictly analogous: a massive case of Léviesque 'correspondence') is called 'Cosmogenesis'.[17] This second, rather complicated, pseudo-scientific doctrine is one of the many areas where Theosophy ceases to be a reasonable and somewhat appealing programme for ethical maturation and wings off into purest speculation. The universe, we are told, is a great hierarchy, with the Absolute behind all manifested in the *Logos*, or solar principle, of each 'planetary chain'. Each chain is divided into seven 'planetary spirits', in which one planet is visible and six are not (just as a man's 'dense' body is visible but his 'etheric', 'astral', 'mental' and so forth are not, except to a 'magical' eyes). Throughout the infinity and timelessness of space there exist vast orders of angels, or 'devas', and forces which affect the whole in an eternally pre-ordained manner. Humans, as in Zoroastrianism, are 'sparks of the Divine fire'. Their purpose, as said, is the Hermetic one of returning toward the light. Historically speaking, progress is conducted through a succession of 'root-races', seven in all, including the fourth or 'Atlantean', followed by the fifth or 'Aryan'. Each 'root race' is divided into seven 'sub-races', of which in our 'Aryan' period, for instance, the Anglo-Saxon constitutes the fifth. At present, man is on the verge of developing a sixth sub-race. Latter-day Theosophists have already seen it emerging in one of their chosen world-centres, California.[18]

The doctrines are clearly a hodge-podge. This is the bad result of the idealistic purpose of the sect from the first: to create one sythetic world religion. Like Lévi, Blavatsky saw an identity between Hermetic 'magic', Cabalism, the Tarot, Gnosticism, 'true' Christianity and Freemasonry. Indeed, she went further, not just summing up in exhaustive detail the oneness between all Western religio-occult systems but delivering them to the door of a new *prisca theologia*, her 'philosophy of the East'. As Lévi, in harmony with his *nom de plume*, made his great contribution to 'magic' in his period by bringing Jewish mysticism to the forefront, so HPB, true to the Asiatic element in her Russian background, made hers by 'discovering' Tibet.[19] Aryanism as an idea was both informed and inspired by her insistence that her great works were written at the direction of 'Mahatmas'. These great lama figures she actually claimed to have met during an obscure period of her career between early journalistic success in St Petersburg and vogue as a 'medium and magician' in Colonel Olcott's America. In fact, the 'Mahatmas', like much else in Blavatsky's saga, have been proved to be a fraud.[20] There is no evidence that she ever went to Tibet, and considerable reason to believe that references to the place in her writing may be traced to a standard travel book of her youth, *Recollections of Travel in Tartary, Thibet and China* by Abbé Huc.[21] The question arises, however, whether such fraud and plagiarism really matter. Great makers of religions steal, they don't borrow, to paraphrase Eliot. Moreover, as John Symonds affectionately remarks, HPB's shams must qualify her as 'one of the world's great jokers'.[22]

What do we know about the woman's career? An inextricable mixture of legend and fact. In middle age she was described as 'a powerful dynamo'; and her youth seems to have been as wild as that of any young 'hippy' free spirit of the 1960s. She probably started by being quite attractive, though more for personality and (one suspects) sexual allure than conventional beauty. Later she would grow fat and dowdy, however dandiacally so. 'From her photograph,' Symonds remarks, 'she looks as if the sitting-room curtains had fallen on her; but this was just one of the Victorian styles. It was more the accessories which distinguished her – the cigarette papers in one pocket, the tobacco in another, the fifteen or so rings on her fingers, and so forth.'[23] She was once accused of smoking 200 cigarettes a day, but, as Symonds reflects, this is 'an impossible number, even if she chain-smoked'. Whatever the number, Blavatsky appeared as if veiled in a nimbus (or 'etheric body') of smoke and incense, the clink of bracelets and chime of tiny bells. Out of this would gaze eyes described as 'huge', 'blue', 'popping' and – in later years – like 'two round, faded turquoises'.[24] Her hair was thick and tightly curled, 'like lamb's wool': a fact which may have contributed to Yeats's impression of her as 'a sort of old Irish peasant woman'.[25] The 'air of humour' and 'audacious power' which Yeats also speaks of were no doubt amplified (like the airy all-embracingness of her prose) by what may have been her most telling habit: 'Hasheesh multiplies one's life a thousandfold. My experiences are as real as if they were ordinary events in actual life. Ah! I have the explanation. It is a recollection of my former existences, my previous incarnations. It is a wonderful drug and it clears up a profound mystery.'[26]

The habit was apparently picked up early on, during the young woman's first flight from Mother Russia. She married a man years her senior in order to escape her father, we are told.[27] She thereupon abandoned the husband, never to return to him, yet to turn him into the victim of bigamy for a brief period twenty years on. The tales of Helena's early exploits may be in part the inventions of her own hasheesh visions and in part those of chroniclers determined to paint her as an inveterate charlataness.[28] We are told that she was at different times an equestrienne in a Turkish circus and a gifted pianist who studied under Ignaz Moscheles and played with Clara Schumann; that she lived with one of the great opera singers of the day, who died romantically in her arms; that she once ran an ink factory and later an artificial-flower shop; that she was one of the sole survivors of a shipwreck of Egypt, dressed like an Arab boy and learned the 'magic' of snake-charmers, spent a night in a tomb in the pyramid of Cheops, became a disciple of the occultist Paulos Metamon and found that the real secret of alchemy was to extort money from the credulous;[29] that in Paris she was the 'right-hand man' of D. D. Home[30] and knew Eliphas Lévi, whom she remembered as 'a glutton' with 'dirty habits';[31] that she was nevertheless the true inheritor of Lévi's 'mantle'; that (as indicated) she spent seven years – or maybe two, or four – as an 'initiate' in Tibet; and that, finally, she was the mother of an illegitimate child (perhaps the fruit of a liaison with one Baron Meyerdorff), who died through neglect or the irregularity of Mama's lifestyle when in Italy fighting for Garibaldi.

Some of this saga is probably true; and it is touching to think that the death of a child might have been one reason why Blavatsky left for a 'new life' in America and threw herself with such energy into communication with spirits and transcendental religion. Be that as it may, America of the 1870s was no place for a single woman 'with a past'. Moreover, as Symonds reminds us,[32] virgins are supposed to have superior 'magical' (or at least 'mediumistic') powers. Thus it was in Blavatsky's interest to cast a veil over her previous life. The matter of the child may have been too painful in any case. When confronted about it in later years, she claimed that motherhood had always been an impossibility for her and invited a gynaecologist to confirm that she had a 'deformed' womb. This inventive defence was probably another demi-fiction. Whatever the truth, the evidence suggests that her youthful amours had been of a kind with her peripeteia and equal in intensity to her later calls for repression. 'To Hades with this sex love! It is a beastly appetite that should be starved into submission.'[33] Renunciation was designed to confer authority. What had she to lose? She was no alluring young *gamine* anymore. Besides, 'Spiritualism' in America had become mixed up with 'free love' in the public mind, and she was not about to let her activities be depicted as a species of witches' sabbathry. Spiritualism at large, which she had come to America to advance, she realised it would be more politic to oppose. Too many séances were being exposed as frauds. Thus, after a flamboyant début had collected sufficient admirers, she moved toward the high ground staked out by Lévi,

leaving behind illusionsim *à la* Home, in whose mouth Browning
had put the self-damning lines,

> Why should I set so fine a gloss on things?
> What need I care? I cheat in self-defence,
> And there's my answer to a world of cheats!
> Cheat? To be sure, sir! What's the world worth else?
> Who takes it as he finds, and thanks his stars?
> Don't it want trimming, tuning, furbishing up
> And polishing over? Your self-styled great men,
> Do they accept one truth as truth is found,
> Or try their skill at tinkering?[34]

'Tinker' Blavatsky certainly did. With Olcott and a handful of
other Masons and Cabalists she founded in 1875 in New York the
Theosophical Society. Its original commission was to follow up the
kind of 'ancient mysteries' suggested in a lecture, 'The Lost Canon
of Proportion of the Egyptians'. Its name, meaning in Greek
'knowledge of God', was taken at random from the dictionary
after rejection of 'Rosicrucian', 'Hermetic' and similar labels,
including one borrowed from Lévi and Bulwer-Lytton, 'The
Miracle Club'.[35] Its original 'bible' was Blavatsky's own compendium of Léviesque scholarship, the famous *Isis*. This appeared in
1877 and was supposed to be the result of two years 'in the astral
light', where Blavatsky had envisioned *grimoires* floating in the
ether before her mind's eye. She wrote in rapture and trance, aided
by 'elementals' and sometimes even 'the Masters' themselves. Or
so it was put out. In fact, she was helped by one Alexander Wilder,
a home-made scholar of the occult who had once produced his
own *magnum opus*, entitled *Eleusian and Bacchic Mysteries, Serpent
and Siva Worship, or a Translation of the Theurgian of Iamblichos;* also
by Olcott, who organised her scrawlings while simultaneously
continuing to proselytise for her 'genuis' in his own *People from
Another World*. On publication, *Isis* sold out several editions. It has
been called an exhumation of the 'wisdom of Atlantis'[36] and a gross
plagiarism. The second description was lent life by Orientalist W.
E. Coleman, who spent three years studying Blavatsky's text
before concluding that it contained 107 unacknowledged borrow-
ings from Ennemoser's *History of Magic*, two or three hundred from
works by Dunlap and Des Mousseaux, thirty-six from MacKenzie's
Masonic Cyclopedia, and so on.[37] Clearly, in following the Léviesque

path, Blavatsky was no freer of Home-like deception than Browning's 'Mr Sludge'. Indeed, her erstwhile friend and compatriot Solov'yov quotes her as demanding,

> What is one to do when, in order to rule men, you must deceive them, when, to catch them and make them pursue whatever it may be, it is necessary to promise and show them toys? Suppose my books and *The Theosophist* [a magazine she published in India in the 1880s] were a thousand times more interesting and serious, do you think that I would have anywhere to live and any degree of success unless behind all there stood 'phenomena'? I should have achieved absolutely nothing, and would long ago have pegged out from hunger. They would have crushed me, and no one would have begun to consider that I, too, am a living creature, that I, too, must eat and drink.[38]

Such self-justification may be true in its way. It is also the thin end of the wedge. Sweeping rationalisations of a similar kind would lead Hitler and Manson to historic brutalities.[39] In Blavatsky's case, they led to a continuation of increasingly unnecessary deceptions. *Isis* was a triumph; she and Olcott took off for diciple-gathering in India; an organisation began to take root. She had it made; yet we find her forging 'Mahatma letters' to impress the Anglo-Indian A. P. Sinnett, constructing a false wall in a shrine in order to fabricate 'miracles' for superstitious natives, and producing lost teacups at garden parties for the colonial gentry. Alerted to her tricks by a disillusioned former associate,[40] the Society for Psychical Research did a study of her activities and decided that Blavatsky had 'achieved a title to permanent remembrance as one of the most accomplished, ingenious, and interesting imposters of history'. She had achieved permanent damage to the credibility of her movement as well, and perhaps to 'magic' at large in her time. Of Olcott, whom she is said to have treated as 'nothing more than a pawn in her game',[41] the same report said, '[He] is a fool of extraordinary credulity.' Outraged but undaunted, Theosophy carried on. Olcott travelled to Ceylon, revived the native religion there and developed one of the most appealing strands in the movement's ideology in his *Buddhist Catechism* (1882). Sinnett, who joined up in spite of the flack, developed this strand as well in his *Esoteric Buddhism* (1883) and *The Occult World* (1881). Madame herself went into 'magical retirement' in

London and fixed the Eastern bent of Theosophy for once and all by producing *The Secret Doctrine*, *The Key to Theosophy* and *The Voice of the Silence* (both 1889), before passing on to higher planes and, presumably, her own 'Devachan', on 'White Lotus Day': her death day, still sacred to devout Theosphists,[42] 8 May 1891.

III   AMONG THE LITERATI

Her last years in London were a kind of 'arrival'. They confirmed her as the 'Mme. Sosostris' of her times. Literary and *beau mondes* took to her as 'the flavour of the season', and the extent to which she revelled in the attention suggests that it may have been a motive in the first place. Of her reception in higher social circles in India she had gushed,

> My graceful, stately person, clad in half-Tibetan, half-nightdress fashion, sitting in all the glory of her Calmuck beauty at the Governor's dinner parties; H. P. B. positively courted by aide-de-camps. Old Upasika hanging like a gigantic nightmare on the gracefully rounded elbows of members of the council, in pumps and swallow-tail evening dress and silk stockings, smelling brandy and soda enough to kill a Tibetan yak![43]

By London, she was ill, a 'ruin', only helped over the Channel to her new abode by the attentions of Dr Ashton Ellis – also known as the head of the London Wagner Society. Sedentary once ensconced, she was described by Yeats as a sort of 'female Dr Johnson',[44] holding court. Fascinated, the Irish poet brought his friends to see her. Ernest Rhys was 'disappointed with the air of bourgeois prosperity'. He had been led to envision a 'sort of temple of Oriental mysticism' and was put off by the faces of the young men at Blavatsky's feet: 'They looked as if the diet and discipline they were subjected to were affecting their health.'[45] Maud Gonne was not much more impressed. When she complained of the criticism she was receiving for her political activities from the Dublin Theosophists, Blavatsky remarked that her Dublin followers were 'flapdoodles' and Theosophy had nothing to do with politics anyway.[46] So much would not remain the case after the appearance of Annie Besant. This socialist activist who took over the Society after Madame's death was smitten like

Saul on the road to Damascus. That filled HPB with confidence for the future. Meanwhile, however, her main concern was repute. In this respect, literary London was less exacting than the fellows of the Society for Psychical Research. 'She is a person of genius,' W. H. Henley is said to have told Yeats, 'but a person of genius must do something – Sarah Bernhardt sleeps in her coffin.'[47]

Yeats of course was the great catch. He became a member of the 'Blavatsky Lodge', went on to join its 'Esoteric Section' and only left in 1889 on request because of apparent conflict with his more strictly Hermetic activities associated with the Golden Dawn. Evidence suggests that HPB knew a rising star when she saw one and, realising Yeats's publicity value,[48] courted him with as much political acumen as Yeats himself would use in his career. At one time, she told him not to shave his beard, as it gave him stronger 'mesmeric' power.[49] At another, she 'materialised' a cigar-case in his overcoat pocket.[50] Attuned to his worship of previous writers, she regaled him with vignettes of those she had known in Paris: Alfred de Musset, whom she claimed to have disliked; Balzac, whom she confessed to only ever having met once (unlikely considering that he died when she was nineteen and before she is known to have set foot in Paris); and Georges Sand, with whom she claimed to have 'dabbled' in magic even though 'neither of us knew anything about it'.[51] All was amusing to the young poet: a willing Parsifal bewitched by a comic Kundry. For Blavatsky, it was part of the necessary 'glamour' her position required.[52] Perhaps she expected Yeats to take her seriously. Perhaps she intuited that, in any case, he would regard her inventions as creative forays. 'Once', she told him, to illustrate the 'witchcraft' of her 'Mahatmas', 'my knee was very bad and the doctor said I would be lame for life. But in the middle of the night the Master came in with a live dog split open in his hands and he put the dog over my knee so that the entrails covered it and in the morning I was well.' Yeats decided that Blavatsky was 'dreaming awake'.[53] Even so, he saw that 'her philosophy had independent, inherent value' and found her Tibetan folklorism fascinating enough to carry some over into his early predominantly Celtic myth-based poetry:

> *Anashuya:* Swear by the parents of the gods,
>   Dread oath, who dwell on saced Himalay,
>   On the far Golden Peak; enormous shapes,

Who were still old when the great sea was young,
In their vast faces mysteries and dreams. . . . [54]

More influenced still was Yeats's friend and fellow poet of the
Irish literary renaissance, George Russell. 'AE' (for 'aeon'), as he
came to be called, had joined Yeats in reading Sinnett's *The Occult
World* and *Esoteric Buddhism* in Dublin in 1885 and went along with
him and others to form an amateurish 'Hermetic Society'. Not
being a congenital 'joiner' like Yeats, Russell did not go on to
sign up with the by-now professionally organised Theosophical
Society. He believed in 'theosophy', he averred, but found the
Society 'representative only of itself – a gathering of many earnest
seekers after truth, many powerful intellects, many saints and
many sinners and lovers of curiosity'.[55] To friends, he argued that
'the formation of the Society was a mistake' and that the problem
was less motive than leadership: 'As the speed of the slowest ship
measures a fleet's progress, so the weak ones of the Society mark
its position in the world.'[56] This eminently sensible *aperçu* would
resurface twenty-five years later in Rudolf Steiner's objections to
Annie Besant's attempt to build a new organization around her
'messiah', Krishnamurti, and Krishnamurti's own later rejection
of his status among 46,000 fawning admirers. Russell, however,
had not yet read *The Secret Doctrine*. Arguably, it was the great
intellectual experience of his life; and it won him over. 'It did not
matter if *The Secret Doctrine* was merely a romantic compendium',
Meade tells us; 'it still contained the grandest cosmogony ever
conceived and would always remain to him one of the most
provocative books ever written.' Indeed, AE is quoted as saying
toward the end of his life, 'My own writing is trivial, and whatever
merit is to be found in it is due to its having been written in a
spiritual atmosphere generated by study of H. P. B. and the sacred
books of the East.'[57]

Other lesser figures of the Irish literary movement profited from
The Secret Doctrine and influential Dublin Lodge of the Theosophical Society. Meanwhile, the greats proved sceptical. Bernard Shaw
did not follow his erstwhile Fabian beloved, Besant, to her spiritual
'true Penelope'. Oscar Wilde apparently attended the first meeting
of the 'Hermetic' Lodge of the Society in London in 1886 in
company with his mother, who 'dabbled in Spiritualism'; his
brother Willie, who was a journalist for the *Telegraph* and 'did his
best to see that nothing derogatory about H. P. B. appeared in

that paper's columns'; and his wife Constance, for whom, we are told, 'just being around Madame gave a second-hand importance' and 'provided an interesting talking-point for those dreary receptions [she] was obliged to attend [in the interests of Oscar's status]'.[58] There may be some truth in this. It is on record that Constance did go on to become an early member of the Golden Dawn,[59] which (as we shall see) grew in part out of the Hermetic as opposed to Eastern faction of the Theosophical Society, the faction particularly aggregating around another powerful female occultist, Anna Kingsford. But there is no evidence in Oscar's writing of anything but passing amusement over such voyages of exploration – unless of course one wishes to see an ennobled and trivialised Blavatsky type in the imperial Lady Bracknell.

Amusement as well was the reaction, for the most part, of the great writer of the period who has most in common with Theosophy's urge toward universalism, James Joyce. 'He joined the rest of intellectual Dublin in taking an interest in occultism', Richard Ellmann tells us; 'his copy of H. S. Olcott's *A Buddhist Catechism* is dated May 7, 1901. His brother Stanislaus thought James was looking for a substitute religion, but it is probable that he, like Yeats and unlike George Russell, was attracted more by the symbology than the pious generalisations of theosophy.'[60] This seems on the mark. Ellmann explores the matter further in describing an unnannounced nocturnal visit the unknown young author made to AE in 1902. They talked of poetry, Yeats's and Russell's; then Joyce read a verse or two of his own. Then,

> they took up theosophical subjects as well, although Joyce was skeptical of Theosophy as being a recourse for disaffected Protestants. He had remarked to his brother that the Dublin mystics had left the churches only to become latter-day saints. 'As such they do not compare either for consistence, holiness, or charity with a fifth-rate saint of the Catholic Church.' Nevertheless, he was genuinely interested in such theosophical themes as cycles, reincarnation, the succession of gods, and the eternal mother-faith that underlies all transitory religions. *Finnegans Wake* gathers all these up into a half-'secret doctrine'.[61]

Ellmann, alas, does not go on to explain what that 'doctrine' might amount to;[62] nor is there space here to speculate on the infinite possibilities suggested by Joyce's 'book to replace all other books'.[63] Suffice it to say that the attempt in *Finnegan* to merge the archetypal night thoughts of the human race is analogous to that in *The Secret Doctrine* to synthesise the great spiritual myths. Ideas of transcendence and cyclic development are common to both, as to *Ulysses*, a book which includes a large number of Theosophy-related recurrent motifs – the phrase 'That Blavatsky woman started it' (page 140.line 30, 185.41); the title *Isis Unveiled* (191.37, 412.32, 553.28); the word 'Theosophy' itself (140.30, 185.14, 185.29, 191.37, 301.13, 398.05, 411.21, 416.26, 420.41, 510.14, 521.25); the concept of 'metempsychosis', which Annie Besant tells us[64] is a Hebrew varient of reincarnation and thus a Theosophical idea (50.13, 64.14, 64.32, 109.01, 110.24, 154.07, 182.31, 269.13, 284.41, 288.18, 377.30, 382.15, 408.36, 414.29, 473.10, 490.16, 653.35, 686.31, 754.01); related phrases such as 'Formless spiritual essences' and 'Oriental and Immortal, Standing from Everlasting to Everlasting'; references via references to AE; and so on.[65]

The above list is the work of a recent beavering scholar who no doubt had use of a computer. A similar job might be done on the texts of HPB herself, in specific to emphasise the wealth of literary quotation and epigraph throughout. Shakespeare is only the most prominent in the vast number of authors invoked. Indeed, the need to invoke great authors reaches a point of neurotic name-dropping; and this is telling. Blavatsky's interest in Yeats and her literary posturings were part of a motive drive of her career. We have already touched on this in reference to Bulwer-Lytton and *Zanoni*. Young Helena Hahn left her father's home first to become a writer and lived out her twenties as if the heroine of a popular adventure novel. So much was inbred. Her mother had been a best-selling authoress, the 'George Sand of Russia', who wrote novels about 'the confining social position of women' under the extraordinary pseudonym 'Zenaïda R-Va'.[66] That Madame Hahn was only seventeen when she gave birth to her daughter and died when the girl was only eleven must have had an effect. But, leaving that for concerned psychologists, we might note the forays the mature HPB periodically tried to make back into serious litera-ture. In 1881, for instance, she translated several passages of Dostoyevsky's *Brothers Karamazov* and published them in *The Theo-sophist*.[67] Some years earlier, down on her luck, she had tried to interest a Russian journal in a translation of the end of Dickens' unfinished *Mystery of Edwin Drood*, which she claimed that the dead author had dictated from the spirit world.[68] Rather closer to her own death, she contributed an article to *Lucifer* (the Theosoph-ical magazine in London) called 'The Sign of the Times', which lays claim to predominant trends in the literature of the day, specifically citing R. L. Stevenson's best-selling *Dr Jekyll and Mr Hyde*, Rider Haggard's *King Solomon's Mines* and 'the thrice famous' *She*, and works by Marion Crawford and Marie Corelli.[69] Having 'colonized' English letters in this way, she finishes by saying, 'We have also to note the fact that theosophy has now crossed the Channel, and is making its way into French literature.'

Where did it take root in the 'decadent' Gallic milieu? We have seen Huysmans noting and disparaging the activities of Theosoph-ists in Paris of the 1890s.[70] No doubt enthusiasts would claim that Symbolism and its offshoots owed much to them. Certainly to the extent that Mallarmé actually believed that 'anything less than the all-embracing would be a pretension', he exhibits the Blavatsky disease;[71] and the Theosophist Edouard Schuré, author of *The Great Initiates*, is a typical example of the kind of literary man of the *fin-de-siècle* who mixed enthusiasm for the new-found East with ancient Western 'magical' traditions and a modish Wagernism. Maeterlinck was another, more directly involved in pure literature. Of *The Secret Doctrine*, which he read and pondered when it came out, he would write years later,

[It is] a stupendous and ill-balanced monument [which combines] speculation which must rank with the most impressive ever conceived with a colossal junkyard into which the highest wisdom, the widest and most exceptional scholar-ship, the most dubious odds and ends of science, legend and history, the most impressive and most unfounded hypotheses, the most precise and most improbable statements of fact, the most implausible and chimerical ideas, the noblest dreams and the most incoherent fancies are poured pell-mell by inexhaust-ible truckloads.[72]

indeed. Blavatsky's most recent biographer goes on to tell us how Maeterlinck 'mused sadly' that, 'if Madame had only seen fit to give the world more information about *The Book of Dzyan* [alleged source of the "secret doctrine"]; if it were truly an authentic prehis-toric document [as was claimed], her explanation of the world and of human life would be truly sensational.'[73] Again: indeed. However, she did not. She *could* not. And fraud continued (and continues) to be charged against her and her work, in spite of the 'back to Blavatsky' and 'defence of Blavatsky' movements of the 1920s and 1930s.[74] Nevertheless, the woman did achieve some of the notice from the literary world she was apparently always after – even a kind of honorary status in it, as a lovable eccentric discussed more than read and remembered for having lent 'magic' to the scene.

IV THE ORGANISATIONAL PHASE

So much might have contented the 'P. T. Barnum'[75] persona for ever in HPB. It would not, however, be sufficient for the apparatchiks and weirdos who came to routinise her hasheesh visions and loose-bound structure into a strict organization. Besant and C. W. Leadbeater, an erstwhile Anglican churchman, were these: she the prime apparatchik, he the 'weirdo' who eventually brought Theosophy its worst scent of scandal when it was revealed that he sometimes used 'indicative' action to help young boys relieve themselves of distracting sexual tensions which he could 'read' in their 'thought-forms'.[76] This odd couple to some extent reproduced the equally odd Blavatsky–Olcott alliance which had got the movement off the ground in the first place. We have noted that HPB was fat and in her mid forties before she began to proclaim the way. Olcott was at least as advanced in age when he abandoned wife and children to live in an asexual relation with Blavatsky and help in her 'mediumish' discoveries. Besant was likewise in her mid forties when ravished by the light. She too had had an irregular career up to then, including an unhappy marriage to a vicar, a bout of single-parenthood, loss of a child through court action and later death, notoriety as a campaigner for birth-control, an affair with Edward Aveling in which she was thrown over for the daughter of Karl Marx, and so forth, to say nothing of her celebrated activities as leader of the match-girls' strike.[77] By the time she was fighting for control of the Theosophical Society in the mid 1890s, she was well enough advanced in age and jaundiced by misadventures to be earnest, if for some hypocritical, about the need for 'chastity'. Leadbeater, her great visionary associate and companion, had every reason to go along with this, being of a like age and 'closet' pederast as said. Thus again, as with HPB in America in the 1870s preaching purity while hiding the truth o her past, we observe increasingly less physically attractive middle-aged types sublimating their never-satisfied longings to exalt 'powers' beyond sexuality.

It is only one of many aspects of Theosophy in this phase which seems meretricious. Of course it is irrefutable that 'transcending' sex may open the being to wider spiritual possibilities: Catholic nuns and monks have been practising as much for the best part of two millennia. Equally it seems self-evident that it would only contribute to the authority of leaders beyond their sexual prime to put a low value of *that* kind of energy and attraction. This is a matter we shall return to in discussing the insurgent 'sex-magician' Aleister Crowley. Meanwhile, it can be said that – between Olcott's guilt over having left his family, Besant's mania for organisational 'displacement' activity, Leadbeater's 'hole-in-the-corner' antics and Blavatsky's opportunistic piety – Theosophy grew up in its formative decades without the important matter of sex being worked out honestly. In dogma, it sidestepped the issue by preaching against sex, a solution which invited scandal in not only the matter of Leadbeater but also the earlier heterosexual escapades of the supposedly 'pure' Hindu *chela* (novice) Mohini among Theosophist women in Paris.[78] More provocatively, one might argue that – in spite of Blavatsky's reading of Hargrave Jennings' pre-'sex-magical' book on the subject[79] – the cult lacked 'phallicism'. The configuration of grand aging female leaders surrounded by fawning, fey followers reinforced this organisationally for a half-century – and not only in the Blavatsky/Besant groupings, but in the 'utopian' Theosophical community of Katherine Tingley in Point Loma, California.[80] Taking this further, one might speculate whether absence of what could be called a 'phallic' dimension – or at least strong and relatively youthful male 'magical' input such as Mathers would supply for the Golden Dawn – might account for what seems lacking in Theosophy overall: acknowledgement of the power and importance of the dark side of experience.

Here the reader might think of the line in Eliot's *Waste Land*, a poem which ransacks the occult for religious direction and has plenty of Theosophical allusion, what with its 'Mme. Sosostris' and '*Shantih Shantih Shantih*'. I mean the line about 'Looking into the heart of light, the silence'.[81] There is, it seems, too much light in Theosophy: too much divine nothingness from the 'voice of the silence'; too little recognition of the active workings of evil – or

even pranksterish wickedness – which animate Western religious
and 'magical' traditions and are in no short supply either amid
the Krishnas, Sivas and other 'destroyer' gods of the East.[82] The
absence is part of what leads to fatal hypocrisies. Blavatsky and
Besant had little capacity for admitting the 'fallen' element within
themselves, as within the rest of the race. Moreover, the vitalising
element of personal moral struggle, so essential to Christian or
even Masonic endeavour, is buried under an avalanche of rhetoric
about how to ascend to 'higher spheres'. Indeed, even this 'how
to' aspect, which comes out particularly in Besant's writings and
may be the great legacy of Theosophy to 'positive thinking' cults
of later decades, is in a sense irrelevant; for, like the Calvinism of
'Boston Brahmins' from which it took motifs, Theosophy posits a
predestined cosmic plan. The individual soul (or 'inner man' or
'Thinker'[83]) will 'evolve' through incarnations inevitably, carrying
its baggage of karma on and on, until, at the end of an infinity of
'working out' imperfections, it arrives at a state of grace (to
become, as we have seen – if it chooses – a 'Mahatma'). As in
Calvinism one is supposed to try to accomplish worldly success
in order to reflect one's status as part of 'the elect', so in Theosophy
one is encouraged to increase the supply of 'good karma' in order
to assist proper evolution. But, though man may contribute to his
destiny in this way, it hardly constitutes a robust doctrine of 'free
will'. On the contrary, the purpose of Theosophical meditation
and action is not the 'magical' one of trying to bring beneficent
'powers' down from heaven onto man, but to eliminate lowly,
earthly man as far as possible and replace his 'powers' with obedience to a dogma of ultimate dispersion into a great mothering
(vaginal?) void.

One does injustice to lay this all at the door of Besant. Blavatsky
herself came to put an overwelming value on obedience in her
final years. The impulse to organisational regimentation and abne-
gation of personality is already there in her twelve rules of 'Practical Occultism'.

1 The place of instruction must be 'right': filled with proper
  'magentic objects' and colours.
2 The student must have undergone preliminary indoctrination
  with other disciples.
3 The teacher should make sure that the student is 'at peace with
  [his] other selves' before instruction.

4 All students must be 'at one' with each other.

5 Students must be 'tuned' to voice their differing aspects of 'Knowledge' in harmony.

6 Those wanting 'siddhis' (occult powers) must renounce all vanities of the world.

7 Students must feel non-separateness from Nature.

8 Students must watch out for influences from external beings (i.e. non-students).

9 The 'heart must be blunt to all but the universal truths in nature'.

10 No animal food, wine, spirits or opium may be ingested.

11 Meditation, abstinence, doing moral good and oblivion of self are the desirable activities.

12 Gradual becoming One with the Universal All is the goal.[84]

In sum we are told, with no sense of implicit contradiction, the law must be, 'MAN KNOW THYSELF.' Now if this were 'MAN KNOW THYSELF' in the most obvious sense and Theosophy were simply a means of leading individuals to more potent 'selfhood', we might recognise it as in the tradition of Faustian 'magic' and looking forward to Jungian psychology. Both in fact may be part of 'true' theosophy – Rudolf Steiner, who led the German Theosophical Society out of the mother organisation, would claim Goethe as a prime precursor; and Jung's parallel Eastern, Hermetic and 'alchemical' interests are well known.[85] But Blavatsky's above rules, unlike Jung's practice or the experimentations of Goethe's hero(es), exude an aura of Victorian schoolmarmishness: an implicit authoritarian relation between 'us' and 'them', old 'org'[86] members and newcomers, 'teachers' and 'students'. This belies the elitism at the base of the cult. Questions of right behaviour are all on the one side (the students), while knowledge and 'powers' on the other. 'MAN KNOW THYSELF' is not so much 'Man search for your own answers within' as 'Kid, shape up and get in step with your betters.'

Here Theosophy separates itself from 'magic' as we have defined it. The learning of 'magic' of a sort may be its goal; and, if manipulation of 'the astral light' is the measure of a 'magician', then Blavatsky qualifies for the title. But a crucial distinction must be made between a practice and a cult. The latter may be run by 'magic', but it is not 'magic' itself: rather, what has brought 'magic' into disrepute in our time, shoddy authoritarianism. This is a matter we did not encounter much in Lévi, as he was, like his Renaissance precursors, a scholar and theorist, not the leader of a cult. The only association in his career which may be relevant is with the Masonic 'Lodge of Perfect Silence'; and indeed Freemasonry, with its fixed scheme from on high, its hierarchy and vows of obedience and silence, is where we find – in spite of the lauded ecumenism and tolerance – the first slithering of this serpent in the garden of modern 'magic'. Masonry's type of organisation and dogma is what all these 'magical' groupings would imitate, whether consciously or because it seemed the logical way to develop a doctrine after it had passed through the 'charismatic' phase of sudden birth.[87] Here is the problem which links 'magic' in our era with Nazism, which indeed (as I argue in *Art, Messianism and Crime* and others have pointed out before[88]) constituted a 'black' freemasonry. Elements of Theosophy were present in the Hitler phenomenon, as were motifs from the Golden Dawn, and from Crowley's Order of Oriental Templars and Steiner's Anthroposophy, both of which were German-based and suppressed by the intolerant *Führer*. Theories of Aryan destiny, racial evolution and great successive historical ages are among many motifs common to the Theosophical Society and the German aberration. Blavatsky's dependence on 'Mahatmas' when challenged had an echo in Hitler's reference to 'hidden masters'.[89] Nor can their mixtures of charismatic leadership with strict, non-democratic organisation be mistaken: both came from the same witch's brew.

Annie Besant, who drove the organisational aspect of Theosophy to its extreme, thereby provoking the departure of Steiner among others, had her initiation into power through the Esoteric Section: an inner circle of loyalists Blavatsky drew around her in her last years. This group practised forms of 'magical' suggestion like those being taken up in the Golden Dawn. Unlike the Theosophical Society in the outer, it had strict rules of secrecy. Designed as a kind of SS to protect Blavatsky-as-*Führer*, it was hardly destined to get Mrs Besant off on other than a Himmlerish foot. But the former socialist, who knew a good deal about the need for tight organisation, strong will and secrecy from her rabble-rousing days, appears to have had a constitutional propensity for this kind of administration. Initiated into a lodge of 'Co-masonry' for women in Paris in the 1890s, she quickly ascended to the thirty-third degree and became head of the organisation in England.[90] Later, having gone to India to consolidate the Theosophical

Society's bridgehead there, she became a founder of the Congress Party and predecessor of 'Mahatma' Gandhi (who, incidentally, credited Theosophy with helping him realise his cultural heritage[91]) in the fight to build a national state. These are the acts less of a 'magician' than of a political agitator; and Besant, we are told (convincingly), was, as head of the 'religion', always dependent on others, not the least Leadbeater, to whom she remained loyal even after segments of the American movement – outraged at his indiscretions and righteous in their prudery – demanded his expulsion.[92]

The 'Bishop' for his part introduced three principal innovations into the movement. One was a process of directed meditation known as 'reading the Akashic Record'. The Akasha is defined as 'the memory of nature where everything is found which has occurred in the history of the globe'. To 'read' this, Besant and Leadbeater would lie out under the Indian sun, chelas surrounding them taking notes. Thus they would discover 'occult biographies' – that is, histories of 'past lives'. Thus Besant realised that she was a reincarnation of Giordano Bruno, which brought her much comfort during the 'martyrdom' of battles in the organisation, which she was for ever going through. Thus too they would explore realms of 'occult chemistry', learning from the inside the 'true nature' of such elements as hydrogen, oxygen and nitrogen;[93] which practice led to an area of quasi-scientific 'knowledge' that some successors in this century would claim allowed them to presage developments in nuclear physics.[94] Clearly there is a kind of occultist eager to inflate his status by pretending to be in on all kinds of transcendental 'secrets', however destructive; thus some latter-day Theosophists would rival Aleister Crowley in maintaining that they helped train minds which created 'the Bomb'.[95] Clearly there is a kind of disciple who gains vicarious self-importance by supposed association with world-shaking 'powers'; others, more preoccupied with morals, may be less readily impressed. These were the target of Leadbeater's second great innovation. During the First World War, he brought into the Theosophical ambit a breakaway sect called the 'Old Catholic Church', later the 'Liberal Catholic Church' and – as such – still extant. This was meant to 'provide a vehicle' for the Theosophical Society's new messiah among those still tied to Europe's 'ancient wisdom'. Unfortunately, the Liberal Church had several members who had been thrown out of orthodox churches for oddities like Leadbea-

ter's own. Thus the whole enterprise degenerated into charges of
pederasty, libel suits, outrage among the Theosophical Society's
pious, and fulminations against their 'prurience' among the Leadbeater core.[96]

The matter smouldered for years, furthering schisms already
rife. Meanwhile, Besant threw her energy into the third of Leadbeater's prime innovations: the matter of this new 'messiah'. The
young Hindu 'Parsifal', Jiddu Krishnamurti, was first spied by
Leadbeater bathing in a river, aged nine. Immediately, the 'Bishop'
recognised an incarnation for the coming sixth 'sub-race' of the
eternal Lord Maitreya, whose last appearance on earth had been
in the form of Christ. Taken from his Theosophist parents to be
educated by the group's leaders, Jiddu soon found his status being
argued out before the law: his parents, getting wind of Leadbeater's reputation, filed suit to get their son back; the Indian High
Court ruled in their favour, but Besant used her influence with
the Privy Council in London and got the decision overturned.
Eventually, Jiddu was whisked off to England, where – proving
'too indolent' to get into Oxford[97] – he was handed over to a group
of genteel ladies whose commission was to 'make a gentleman' of
him. This they succeeded at – so much so that the 'messiah' came
to put charming personality over organisation in his scheme of
earthly values. At a Theosophical 'summer school' in 1929, he
astonished his mentors by dissolving the 'Order of the Star in the
East', which they had set up to advance his cult. Ringing down
the curtain on the Besant–Leadbeater phase of leadership, Krishnamurti declared that 'Truth is a pathless land' and that those
searching for 'real happiness and liberation' must do away with
all conditioning, jargon, systems, philosophies, empty ceremonies
and forms. So much became his theme for the next half-century,
set down in numerous books and lectures. The 'drop-out' element
in it resurrected the 'charismatic' message of HPB when in rebellion against the organisation-building of Olcutt – 'Each man is his
own absolute lawgiver; the dispenser of glory or gloom to himself,
the decreer of his life, his reward, his punishment.'[98] Like Theosophy's founder, Krishnamurti became an inveterate wanderer – a
fact no doubt contributing to his appeal to well-bred 'New Age
consciousness' types in the decades following the Second World
War. Having resigned from the Theosophical Society in the 1930s,
he nevertheless remained an important 'teacher' for those related
to it. Even Besant in her last years refused to 'deny' him, traitor

to her though he may have seemed; and, when he died recently, at the age of ninety-one, he appeared for many to be less a rebel against the Cause then a 'true fulfilment of theosophical ideas'.[99]

V DOCTRINES EXALTING AND DUBIOUS

The reader may have noted that in this chapter I take a predominantly 'historicist' approach[100] – that is, discuss the development of Theosophy as organisation 'in the outer' more than the inner meaning of its doctrines. In general, this kind of approach deserves to be regarded with suspicion. It is easier to regurgitate facts and tell tales of eccentricity than to analyse what a 'magician' truly believes, and why, and what may be the value of it. Moreover, 'historicism' all too often leads to a facile, pontifical sort of attitudinizing (customarily sub-Freudian in type), which ends by approaching character-assassination. The effect is to undermine the credibility of even those ideas which are genuinely new and valuable (which may be the point of much 'historicism' in the first place).[101] Such a problem we hardly encountered with Lévi, as he was a theorist rather than active leader. Theosophy, however, became a 'mass movement'; thus its history and methods may appear more important to many than its myriad – and sometimes protean – ideas. Moreover, to the extent to which these ideas are enshrined in *Isis Unveiled* and *The Secret Doctrine*, students of Theosophy have a second reason to be encouraged to the 'historicist' approach. Both books are even more voluminous, circuitous and repetitive than the *grimoires* of Lévi. To the 'uninitiated', they must appear virtually unreadable. To those already familiar with the occult, they seem for the most part adumbrations of what was already known. In either case, whatever Blavatsky may have surveyed from the top of her 'magic mountain', there is some distance between it and what the novitiate Theosophist has generally believed. For the spirit of this, the key work may be Annie Besant's digest *The Ancient Wisdom*, written in the years following HPB's death and dedicated to her 'with profound gratitude'.

Besant's book tracks the voyages of the soul through all possible manifestations. It is a fairytale of sorts, marked by passages filled with pastel colours and the wafty beauties of imaginary 'higher realms'. (Similar motifs Rudolf Steiner would happily take off with

him for use in Anthroposophy.[102]) Its lore is claimed to have come
from the 'Brotherhood of the White Lodge', or hierarchy of holy
adepts whose teachings have been responsible for great spiritual
developments in all ages. Its message is that all religions are one,
thus that 'no antagonism' should exist between them. The 'basic
verities of universal religion' are (1) 'One eternal, infinite incogniz-
able real Existence'; (2) God unfolds 'from duality to trinity'; (3)
the 'trinity' manifests itself in 'many spiritual intelligences' whose
purpose is to guide 'kosmic order'; (4) man as a reflection of God
is divided into his 'trinity' of body, soul and mind; (5) evolution
is propelled by reincarnations, which the soul is drawn into by
'desire', as we have seen, and set free from by 'knowledge and
sacrifice'. These 'verities' may be found equally though in differing
forms in Taoism, the Upanishads, Hebrew, Egyptian, Zoroastrian,
Orphic Greek and Christian religions. All have a common ethical
teaching of purity, earnestness, virtue, no anger, obedience and
no selfish desires. All partake to one degree or another of the neo-
Platonic aspiration 'to be God', through practical, cathartic and
intellectual steps. Brotherhood with God and other like-minded
souls is the (hermetic) object: 'bliss' otherwise defined as 'no separation from the other'. The ultimate method of achieving this is
couched in Masonic terms: 'The two pillars of [the Brotherhood's]
lodge gateway are Love and Wisdom, and through its straight
portal can pass only those [free] of desire and selfishness.'[103]

The reader will recognize how much such teachings reflect
precepts already encountered in Lévi and *Zanoni*. Besant goes on
to describe the various planes of existence, dividing all after the
standard[104] (and arbitrary) 'magical' fashion into seven parts. Space
does not permit us to explore her descriptions in detail, or their
derivation from the Tibetan Book of the Dead and elsewhere. But
one technique Besant uses is to compare how three different types
of person might experience a given plane. Thus, on the 'astral',
undeveloped man's 'body' is 'murky', recognizable only in response
to passions or appetites. Violent sensations are necessary to evoke
a response from him and 'the more the better'(!). Meanwhile,
average man's 'body' is fully discernible, has its own characteristics
and is active as well as acted upon. In it, the 'wheels' of the higher
centres (what in Indian nomenclature are called chakras) are
apparent, if not yet fully operative. Finally, *spiritual man*'s 'body' is
a 'vehicle of consciousness' which allows him to 'move anywhere
within the astral sphere with immense rapidity . . . no longer

bound to terrestrial conditions'. His 'wheels' are in motion, making him a superbly energised specimen, giving out constant 'vibrations': 'The whole body vibrates only in answer to the higher emotions, his love has grown to devotion, his energy is curbed by patience. Gentle, calm, serene, full of power, but with no trace of restlessness, such a man all the *siddhis* stand ready to serve.'[105]

This is appealing enough – attractive in the way of contemporary French and Wagnerian dreams of the Paraclete – and from it one may see Besant's mind already preparing itself for the cult of Krishnamurti ten years on. Less attractive is evidence of tripartite 'class' distinction. This may grow from the prejudices of Besant's English background, which could merge all too easily with the Indian caste system, and no doubt indicates one of the reasons for the instinctive lack of sympathy between Theosophy's dictatress and the 'untouchable' Gandhi. We keep circling back to elitism. In Theosophy *chez* Besant, this is ineradicable. From it derives the emphasis in this form of 'magic' on education and – ultimately – politics. If 'magic', as Lévi suggests, is above all about 'power', then it will naturally find expression in methods of moulding minds. One of the significant creations of the Theosophical Society in the Besant–Leadbeater years was its 'World University'. Theosophical 'summer schools' for adults and 'pathfinder' groups for adolescents, Anthroposophical 'Waldorf Schools' and lecture courses from Krishnamurti remain among the enduring legacies of Theosophy. High-minded and 'enlightened', they nevertheless provide models not only for imitative 'magical' regiments such as Scientology but also for political disciplinarians. Mass power may rest on 'indoctrination' *à la* Hitler-Jugend. If all the teachers in Texas are required to hammer the virtues of 'free enterprise', then the Sunbelt may be made safe for 'rugged individualism' for ever. Which brings us to the matter of the value of a cult such as Theosophy as a kind of think-tank for methods of 'suggestibility'.[106] Its success at 'manipulating the astral light' would make it of interest to propagandists, just as the secrecy of its international elite would do for their *confrères*, the political spies.

We overleap somewhat here, as the similarities in worldview between 'magical' cults and organisations such as MI6 are more relevant in connection with the Golden Dawn, a far tighter and more secret cadre (at least initially) and Crowley, who played at the 'secret agent' game from time to time.[107] Still, it deserves to be mentioned, if only to remark that Olcott was an undercover detective for the US Army during the American Civil War and that Blavatsky was watched by the British in India as a suspected Russian spy. Even a hundred years ago, it was apparent that this kind of oddball international 'movement' had potential for penetration by covert political forces. So much is worth keeping in mind through the following chapters. Meanwhile, having now to assess the contribution of Theosophy to this tradition of 'magic' overall, we might concentrate, finally, on two principal recurring motifs: (1) the massive infusion of the 'Wisdom of the East', set for the first time in an equivalent (even superior) status to Western occult ideas; (2) the myth of 'Mahatmas' from whom all inspiration and authority derives and toward the condition of whom all human effort should aspire. These ideas had been around in a variety of forms before – we have seen their antecedents in *Zanoni* – as had the fundamental Theosophical objectives of merging science with theology,[108] establishing one universal synthetic religion and impressing upon the individual the anagogical worth of holistic purity. But in the Theosophical Society they received new primary emphasis, undisrupted by any Lévi-like admonition to 'equilibrate', to attend also to the 'shadow': the dark side or devil or 'black magical' forces ever apparent, at least in Western ideology.

And so Theosophy carried on: a religion perhaps more suited to the sunny climes where it prospered, India and California; a loosening organisation once the English ascendency of Besant and Leadbeater had passed, more of a kind with less rigidly dialectical, 'everything is everything' cultures, and subject to the disintegrative influences inherent in them. According to Annie Besant, the Theosophical Society would 'stand or fall on the Mahatmas'.[109] This may be so, strictly speaking; and, if so, it meant (means) the Society's fall. For, however appealing, the 'Mahatmas' remain a fiction, created out of the brain of a novelist-*manqué*, the ambitious young Helena Hahn. As an expression of her *animus*, they are fascinating. Even as ideal *Doppelgänger*[110] or 'astral projections' proposed for the age, they have a value: certainly as much as Crowley's 'guardian angel' Aiwaz, a version of the same idea. But to maintain that they actually exist(ed) somewhere in Kashmir or Ladakh is surely the last bastion of baffled religious wish-fulfilment; and any doctrine built on such imaginative flights must end by seeming fantastic. Perhaps then it is better to build on established *prisci theologi*, as T. S. Eliot would argue.[111] The old myths may have no more truth than the new, but at least they have the weight of 'tradition' behind them to lend authority when challenged. Or did HPB realize something the academic critic is ill-suited to judge: an eternal, archetypal attraction to the type of figure she managed to make appear before Olcott in his study one night in the period before the Colonel had finally thrown in his lot with her amazing confidence-trickery?

I saw towering above me in his great stature an Oriental clad in white garments, and wearing a head-cloth or turban of amber-striped fabric, hand-embroidered in yellow floss-silk. Long raven hair hung from under his turban to the shoulders; his black beard, parted vertically on the chin in the Rajput fashion, was twisted up at the ends and carried over the ears; his eyes were alive with soul-fire; eyes which were at once benignant and piercing in glance; the eyes of a mentor and a judge, but softened by the love of a father who gazes on a son needing counsel. He was so grand a man, so imbued with the majesty of moral strength, so luminously spiritual, so evidently above average humanity, that I felt abashed in his presence, and bowed my head and bent my knee as one does before a god or god-like personage. A hand was lightly laid on my head, a sweet though strong voice bade me be seated, and when I raised my eyes, the Presence was seated in the other chair beyond the table. . . .[112]

5

The Golden Dawn

I ORIGINS AND CHARACTER

Eastern theories of the soul and its reincarnations have an undeniable beauty. Moreover, they can and do give considerable
comfort to individuals preoccupied with death, their own or
others'. The Theosophical Society, with its transcendental paraphernalia, offered mental balm for these. Nor should such a contribution be dismissed: even one of HPB's least impressed
biographers credits it as a true achievement.[1] Cults such as the
Theosophical Society have operated in the void left by breakdown
of traditional belief-systems. This void necessitates alternative
'religion' and, as Lévi predicted,[2] will continue to do so. Some
explanation for the origin and purpose of life is needed; and the
'big bang' theory of modern science seems cruelly minimal in the
face of elaborate, poetic speculations of earlier times. The problem,
however, is that 'teachers' providing 'answers' for more timid,
frightened souls are often – as Solov'yov's attribution to Blavatsky
and Browning's to Home indicate[3] – primarily interested in
promoting themselves. Moreover, the answers provided can rarely
be other than lies, however 'beautiful' at that. Not only is there
no earthly reason to believe in Blavatsky's 'Mahatmas', there is no
reason, either, to believe in her Devachan or 'astral bodies' or
histories of 'root races', though the last may have some quasi-
Darwinian basis. In the end, 'magic' built on such myths drifts
into never-never land, condemning its adherents to the role of
eccentrics tittered over by maiden aunts at tea.[4] Better the methods
of training the self to understand its 'true will' and gain, or at least
recognize, the uses of 'power' in this world. This has some relation
to the fact. It also is an area where 'magic' may provide practical
results, if only by providing various plans for development of a
richer inner life.

The methods of the Theosophical Society, as well as its overarching dogma, were carried on and refined most successfully by Steiner, whom we shall deal with in a later chapter. Meanwhile, the urge to para-religious organisation, the 'cult' aspect of Theosophy and its various Western interests were carried on simultaneously by its rival in England, the Hermetic Order of the Golden Dawn. I say 'rival': several founder members of the Golden Dawn were members of the Theosophical Society as well. One of the three original chiefs, Wynn Westcott, delivered some of his most important lectures before the Blavatsky Lodge after its 'beloved leader's' death.[5] Yeats, as stated, had been a member of the Esoteric Section of the Society; and that section may have been set up specifically to compete with the 'esoteric' attractions of the newly formed rival group. MacGregor Mathers, acknowledged *Führer* of the Golden Dawn in its prime, dedicated his most important book to Anna Kingsford, head of the Hermetic Lodge of the Theosophical Society; and some see Kingsford's death in 1886, thus the eclipse of Hermetic as opposed to Eastern interests in the greater Blavatsky grouping, as a probable immediate reason for the setting-up of the Golden Dawn a year later.[6] Scholars have been sifting documentary evidence for some time now; and, for the last word on the facts, the reader is recommended to consult works by Francis King, Ellic Howe, Ithell Colquhoun and R. A. Gilbert, and the 'Roots of the Golden Dawn' series currently being published by Aquarian Books.[7] Meanwhile, for our purposes, it is important to add that, besides these connections to the Theosophical Society, the Golden Dawn was founded by men who were all Master Masons and high-ranking initiates in the Societas Rosicruciana in Anglia (SRIA). The latter group claimed descent from the original German Rosicrucians and had as 'honorary members' in the previous generation Bulwer-Lytton and Eliphas Lévi.[8]

In fact, the SRIA probably had more to do with the Romantic imaginings of its founders, R. W. Little and Kenneth Mackenzie, than with traceable 'apostolic succession' to Christian Rosenkreuz, or even to the authors of *Zanoni* and *Dogme et rituel*. Still, it was important to the Golden Dawn. It provided the new order not only an overarching 'Rosicrucian' idea and cadre of enthusiasts but also a system of grades and perhaps even the notorious 'cipher manuscripts' from which it developed its principal rituals. I say 'notorious': these manuscripts were unmasked in due course as a fraud.[9] They were supposed to have been sent to Westcott by a high Rosicrucian in Germany. In fact, they were most likely forged by this one of the Golden Dawn's co-founders. Mathers, himself another of the founders, would intimate as much a dozen years later when he revealed that Westcott had never been in contact with any 'secret chiefs' in Germany or anywhere else – a charge which let loose doubts about the Order's authority and purpose which would tear it apart eventually.[10] Responsible students of these questions are obliged to accept that the Golden Dawn was built thus on credulity and lies. Romanticists wishing to maintain a 'Rosicrucian' continuity suggest that debunking scholars have been moved by their own *ingenium*.[11] The rest of us must simply read charge and countercharge and wonder if (1) the forthright tone of Westcott's writing really suggests the deviousness his alleged forgery would have required;[12] (2) Mathers' attack on Westcott was not principally motivated by a desire to establish his primacy as the cult's creator; and (3) some initial German connection is so unlikely given that, when the Golden Dawn was in turmoil after the turn of the century, the chief of its main splinter group went to Germany and discovered evidence of a sister organization there – with contemporary activity again associated with Steiner, himself a 'Rosicrucian'.[13]

These matters are most important in respect of how they helped fracture the group. Before they did, the Golden Dawn prospered. In the words of Gerald Yorke, it was 'the crowning glory of the occult revival in the nineteenth century' and 'synthesised into a coherent whole a vast body of disconnected and widely scattered material and welded it into a practical and effective system, which cannot be said of any other occult Order of which we know at that time or since'.[14] This may be true, at least in England. Certainly the Golden Dawn was more serious in pursuit of 'magic' than the 'Rosicrucian' groupings of Guiata or Peladan in Paris. On the other hand, there may have been stronger groups of the kind in Germany – thus the reference to German authority at the outset and German guidance after breakdown. Reading the principal accounts of the Golden Dawn, one is sometimes struck by an Anglocentric bias. This was not so typical of the group's premier figures. Mathers left England shortly after having set up the Second (or Inner) Order of the Red Rose and Gold Cross, and lived in Paris for the rest of his life. Yeats was always something of a 'tourist' member of the essentially 'British middle class' organisation,[15] since he spent much of his time in Ireland. And Aleister

Crowley, who played a starring role in the group's ructions (though not before he had received a 'magical' education from it), was an embodiment of peripeteia, as we shall see. Geographical dispersion also marked the Golden Dawn lore. If it drew its form from the *Fama fraternitas*, it took its typical methods from the Cabala. Among its colourful attributions, Egyptian gods were prominent; but Christian motifs were present as well – a central feature of the most important grade ritual was symbolic crucifixion. Astrological knowledge was a continuing study, especially for the group's wealthiest and most troublesome member, Annie Horniman, whom literary students will know as patron of the Abbey and Gaiety (Manchester) theatres. Nor were the Tarot, as developed from Lévi, and Enochian systems of Elizabethan 'magicians'[16] neglected in the general pursuit of all methods which might lead men and women 'from darkness into the light'.[17]

The Golden Dawn has been described as an occult 'university',[18] and it had a somewhat academic aura. Mathers, Yeats, Horniman, Mathers' wife Moina (sister of French philosopher Henri Bergson), Lévi translator and eventual Golden Dawn insurgent A.E. Waite all met one another initially in what Waite calls the 'melancholy sanctuary' of the British Museum Reading Rooms.[19] One doubts that the 'sanctuary' could have been that 'melancholy' in an era when George Bernard Shaw might be seen poring over the text of *Das Kapital* while humming the score of *Tristan und Isolde*.[20] Still, it is true that Mathers in particular spent much of his maturity inhabiting libraries (Nodier's Bibliothèque de l'Arsenal would be his 'sanctuary' in Paris); and the framework he set up in the Golden Dawn required lengthy study of old texts and passing of examinations before introduction to 'practical' techniques. Here we might see one of the features which attracted Yeats to this organisation over the Theosophical Society. The Golden Dawn was permeated by an atmosphere of intellectual ardour. Faust in his tower poring over *grimoires* is the appropriate emblem. These 'initiates' were not like Blavatsky before or Crowley after: always seeming to prefer to be out in sunny climes performing 'phenomena' for the credulous and luring them into their charlatanish orbits. Yeats had 'Rosicrucian' fantasies of a 'journey to the East', as we shall note; but he never got so far as Christian Rosenkreuz's first destination of Damcar in Arabia, let alone Blavatsky's Tibet. And, when another high initiate of the Order, the actress and one-time beloved of Shaw, Florence Farr, made her journey to Ceylon, it appears to have been motivated less by a wish for 'magical' discovery (or 'retirement'[21]) than by a part-Christian, part-socialist instinct to end her days teaching the underprivileged.

Maud Gonne's description of the Golden Dawn as 'the very essence of British middle class dullness' fits in with these 'swottish' and moralistic attributes.[22] It also equates with a sexual puritanism such as we saw in the Theosophical Society. Mathers and his wife protested that they had never consummated their marriage, he because of a 'vow of chastity' to pursue higher things, she because of a lifelong repugnance.[23] Horniman, who may have had a more-than-sisterly affection for Moina and supported the Matherses for years, caused a terrific disruption in the order when one of the male members suggested that the sexual 'pneumatism' of Thomas Lake Harris might provide a radical new method for apprehending 'secret wisdom'. Crowley, who would develop Harris-like techniques in his 'sex magick', was castigated for his dubious doings, not least by Yeats, who declared, 'The order is not a reformatory.'[24] Only Farr of the principals seems to have exercised this aspect of her 'whole being' in a way we of the later twentieth century might call 'normal' (though, if she had an affair with Crowley, as one chronicler suspects, she may have fancied a bit of the abnormal as well[25]). Yeats was a sexual 'coward',[26] as the world knows from his relations with Maud Gonne; and from this may come some of what Crowley would deride as 'Weary Willie's . . . drifting, drifting'.[27] Crowley's rising contempt for his *confrères* grew in part out of his relative youth. The emergent twentieth century was determined to shake off vestiges of Victorian prudery. Occult organisations, Freudians would argue, drew strength and perhaps even existence out of 'sublimation'. This is partly demonstrable in the Golden Dawn's case; and, as with the Theosophical Society, an overweening emphasis on sexual purity may have encouraged neurotic and sometimes hypocritical preoccupation with purity overall, leading to fascistic constriction.[28] On the other hand, some spiritual ideas and techniques developed by the Golden Dawn would also appeal to D. H. Lawrence and Jung, neither of whom was known for sexual repression.

II MATHERS AS LEADER

Unfortunately, there is not a great deal known about Mathers.[29] The Scottish addition to his name was an affectation, adopted out of enthusiasm for all things Celtic, such as promoted by Yeats. Identity with a Jacobite clan which had been all but exterminated by the English appealed to Mathers's 'underdog' prejudice, also to a penchant for things of the past now ploughed under by a more prosaic world. At one time, he claimed to be a reincarnation of James IV of Scotland, a king supposed to have discovered the 'elixir'. Frequently, he could be seen going around Paris in a kilt, which garb made him 'feel like a walking flame'. Flame-like seems to have been his personality, though he was born under the sign of the goat. He drank too much brandy, sometimes dined on no more than a plate of radishes, and occasionaly spat blood after energetic evocations. Fierce in defence of his primacy over the Golden Dawn, he could be gentle – tender even – and sensible in his 'teachings', as here in one of the Order's 'Flying Scrolls':

Never attempt any of these Divine processes when at all influenced by Passion or Anger or Fear – leave off if desire of sleep approach, never force a mind disinclined. You must do all these things alone. Do not try to make, or take, others.

This rule is open to some alteration when, passing from Mystic studies, you refer to the worldly guidance of childhood – a parent is in a special position and has a natural duty incumbent upon him or her to train, guide, and protect a child.

Still, even here, do protect and lead, but don't obsess a child, don't override by your peculiar personal predilections all the personal aims of the offspring. A man's ideal of true propriety is often himself, and his idea of doing good to a child is to make it like himself. Now, although this father may be a good man, his form of goodness is not to be made a universal type, and there are many other forms equally existing, and equally fit to exist, and any attempt to dictate too closely a child's 'thought life' may, while failing of success, yet warp aside from the truth what would otherwise pass into a Good Path, through its own peculiar avenue.[30]

This gentleness must have intensified Mathers' feeling of betrayal when Horniman cut off his funds in 1896 and most of the rest of the London Golden Dawn broke with him four years later. Mathers felt with some justice that the Order was his 'baby'; that all that its members knew of 'magic' had come from him; and that their behaviour violated a fundamental precept of all 'Rosicrucian' groups – that is *fraternity*.[31]

Most commentators see Mathers' personality as the original wrecking-force in the Golden Dawn,[32] but evidence does not always bear this out. Though his needs, especially financial, were great, his demands were rarely 'tyrannical'; nor was he ever less than generous in laying open his home to English *fratres* and *sorores* pleased to have a break in Paris.[33] What Mathers was up against was not a dispersed mass of mental and spiritual semi-cripples such as populated the outskirts of the Theosophical Society, but a small cadre (never much more than a hundred in number) of educated and talented individuals, with egos as prone to 'inflation' as his own. Intelligences such as Horniman and Yeats were destined ever to become critical of their teachers. Furthermore, while it was easy to accept titular primacy in an innocuous old buffer such as Westcott, Mathers' apparent youthfulness and vigour may themselves have invited challenge. In her attempt to forge a biography out of the scattered facts of the 'chief's' life, Ithell Colquhoun points out that the 'consonantal skeleton' of Mathers' name is the same as that for 'Mithras';[34] and there may also be an element of wilful, semi-conscious 'sacrifice' of the anthropomorphized bull – the Mithraic christ – in the Golden Dawn's revolt against its *primus inter pares*. Perhaps in this vein we might also allude to Moses; because, after the 'sacrifice', guilt appears to have surfaced, rather in the manner Freud speculates happened among the Jews after they murdered (as he posits) their own leader in Sinai.[35] So much is apparent in various writings Yeats devoted to Mathers, both after their falling-out and after the latter's death in 1918. One of these – the depiction of the 'chief' as a leading light of the 'tragic generation' in *Autobiographies* – is looked to as a principal source on Mathers' character; but it may be distorted. Mathers' widow complained as much when the piece first appeared. Yeats admitted that he had not seen his subject in over a decade and agreed to changes. No substantial alterations, however, were made.[36]

Mathers suffers from Yeats the fate of all early idols later discovered to have feet of clay. From being overadmired, he plummets to being pitied; and Moina Mathers was surely justified in challenging the poet's second-hand assertion (perhaps after all a kind of projection) that her husband's later years were 'melancholy'.[37] There is no firmer evidence for this than for the claim of another erstwhile admirer, Crowley (alias 'Count MacGregor'), that Mathers became a double agent and sometimes resorted to prostituting his wife.[38] The facts suggest no more than that Mathers carried on in the decade and a half after the loss of his English disciples in much the way he had before. As with Farr and Crowley (though not Yeats), Egyptian 'magic' appears to have become the next phase for him after Rosicrucian, Hermetic and Cabalistic techniques more orthodox in the Golden Dawn had been explored. Thus Mathers and Moina gave theatrical performances of a 'rite of Isis' in Paris, to some *demi-monde* acclaim;[39] and he spent time translating the Egyptian *Book of the Dead*. Perhaps Mathers 'tapped' a Typhon–Set strain of 'black magic' in these pursuits, as Colquhoun reminds us Crowley did.[40] Little is certain beyond the fact that one of the manuscripts he worked on was about Egyptian symbolism. This has been lost, as have several of the scripts which the ertswhile 'chief' lent to F. L. Gardner or Crowley, only to have some published by the latter under his own name and as his own work.[41] Ungenerosity to fellow students was not one of Mathers' vices, Colquhoun remarks. We might add that, unlike with Blavatsky, there is no reason to suppose that this 'magician' was ever less than genuine in his dedication to search for and disseminate 'the light'.

His faults were of a different kind. Like Annie Besant, he had an inflated idea of his movement's influence and ascribed the outbreak of the First World War to forces he had helped set loose. In line with his Scottish aristocratic pretensions, summed up in his Gaelic motto for the SRIA ('*S rioghail mo dhream* – 'Royal is my race'), he dabbled in racist, royalist and pre-fascist politics. One observer accused him of 'fanatical' anti-semitism,[42] which would be ironic considering that he was married to the daughter of a well-known Jew, spent years promoting the Cabala, expressed near-mystical faith in the judgement of the Rothschilds when trying to support himself through investment 'tips',[43] and eventually was accused of having set up the Golden Dawn in the first place as part of a worldwide Jewish plot.[44] Mathers did have a militaristic streak – his first publication was a translation of a handbook on infantry manoeuvres, his second a volume of martial verse entitled *The Fall of Granada and Other Poems* – and this is reflected in his motto for the Golden Dawn, *Deo duce comite ferro* ('With God as my leader and the sword as my companion'), which suggests a Mohammedesque aspiration.[45] Like Nietzsche, he was given to apocalyptic statements about the salutary effects of a bloodbath engulfing European civilisation. Like Baudelaire, he rarely missed a chance to *épater le bourgeois*. Like many 'decadents' in his adopted city at the time, his extreme rhetoric may have been exacerbated by poverty, difficulty in getting published properly, and frustration at not always being viewed as the *voyant* he believed himself to be. Thus, in general, Mathers ends by having much in common with such a writer as Villiers de l'Isle-Adam, another 'fallen aristocrat', whose hero Axël shuts himself up in a 'Rosicrucian' castle with his beloved and his visions in an ecstatic attempt to attach to 'higher' realms where he may come into full knowledge of God, the Absolute or his 'genius' – which goal, Crowley wrote in publishing materials which Mathers went to court to try to keep from appearing, was the point of Golden Dawn lore in the first place.[46]

Thus for all his sabre-rattling, the emblem of Mathers' career remains Yeats's tower-bound Faust. That he was ever a 'man of thought' rather than a 'man of action' is evident from the *grimoires* of his that survived to be published under his own name (though even one of these was lost and had to be rewritten[47]). They include his translation of Knorr von Rosenroth's *Kabbala denudata* (1887), which Mathers claimed incorporated materials from Chaldean and Hebrew sources and contains much commentary of his own;[48] also his rendering of *The Book of the Sacred Magic of Abra-Melin the Mage* (1898) from a seventeenth-century French manuscript discovered in the Bibliothèque de l'Arsenal. Though in style no great joy to read, these volumes have been regarded as among 'the most powerful handbooks of practical magic' of modern times.[49] Another such is a third Mathers translation, *The Key of Solomon* (1889), which Colquhoun cites as the source of 'planetary attributions, angelology and talismanic magic' in the rituals of the Golden Dawn. In his Preface to this work, Mathers expresses an aversion to animal sacrifices such as were practised in medieval times.[50] This alerts one to the anti-vivisection and vegetarian enthusiasms he shared with many 'progressive' spirits in Europe of his era, including Wagner, the un-'magical' Shaw, and later the 'black magician' (or magician-*manqué*) Hitler. Regarding 'black magic', the same Preface sets out the relevant view, which Mathers

shared with Lévi among others: that this was to be avoided principally because 'the current will return on the operator'. Whether
the 'current' was released by Mathers on his former colleagues
and returned to 'zap' him has long been a matter of debate.[51]
Under attack, he did not hesitate to warn, 'I shall formulate my
request to the Highest Chiefs for the Punitive Current to be
prepared.'[52] It would seem to be falling prey to the sort of
'inflation' which Yorke cites as Mathers' tragic flaw to believe
that, whatever his knowledge and followers' receptivity, Mathers
actually possessed such 'powers' or used them. On the other
hand, Golden Dawn members would not have discounted the
notion that such a thing was possible, however incompatible with
'bourgeois' rationality.

III   THE PROBLEM OF YEATS

Yeats's most extensive 'treatment' of Mathers comes in his unpub-
lished novel *The Speckled Bird*. A *Bildungsroman* intended to reflect
on the religious and occult ideas Yeats had explored since early
adulthood, the 'final version' of this work was written in the
period after the Golden Dawn had broken with Mathers, thus
when Yeats was trying to present himself as 'statesman'[53] for the
divided group. Fellow adepts reacted with hostility; one remarked
that he had not worked to get rid of one 'tyrant' in order to replace
him with another; Yeats would describe the period as 'the worst'
in his life, and the novel betrays a disillusioned mood. Michael
Hearne is a young Irish aesthete modelled on the author and, like
him, full of yearning for the Great Love and to found a mystical
Celtic order. Taken by his father to Paris, he meets Samuel
Maclagan, a 'travelling Englishman' based on Mathers, who 'might
have been any age from thirty to fifty'. Maclagan talks 'in a deep
voice' and has 'a certain air of mystery that either repelled or
attracted'.[54] He fulminates against French Martinists (who held
views similar to Lévi's about the need to merge 'magic' with Catholicism) and hates the rich. Contending that, 'if all the people who
think so much of themselves' were to vanish he and his kind could
begin to reshape the world, he expresses vigorous enthusiasm
about all current antinomian socio-political movements, including
anarchism, socialism and 'Bohemianism'. Michael is impressed, in
spite of the man's tendency to 'speak of everybody as either angel

or devil in a contest he seemed to see everywhere'; also in spite of his simultaneous attraction to the daughter of the house where the encounter takes place. Her name is Margaret. From this, one might construe a Goethean structure, with the Mathers persona taking a Mephistophelean role in relation to Michael's Faust.

Back in Ireland, Michael recalls Maclagan's suggestion that one should train oneself to 'see things in the mind's eye'; thus he sets out to have 'visions' (pp. 29–31). Sometimes he fasts in order to induce these. At other times, on the point of fainting, he wonders whether he has induced his visions or they have come to 'inhabit' him. His body becomes 'in some strange way impersonal and magical', i.e. medium-like: a state not approved of in the Golden Dawn except under extraordinary circumstances.[55] Practising a form of 'astral projection', he transmits himself to Paris to walk in the Bois with Margaret. When the two actually meet again in the flesh, she is most alarmed by the change in him (p. 46). Michael's opinions are now elitist and apocalyptic. They sound like Maclagan's; and Margaret believes they are 'taking away [his] peace'. This might alert the young Faust to the dangers he is courting. Michael, however, pays no heed. Travelling to London, he chances on Maclagan in the British Museum (a coup of clumsy plotting which the 'travelling Englishman' puts down to 'the will of the gods' – p. 57). Maclagan now haunts the Reading Room writing 'six-penny booklets on fortune-telling, cheiromancy and the language of flowers, for shop-girls'. Invoking Boehme and other post-Renaissance mystics, he complains that in greater eras alchemists were assisted by aristocratic patrons but that he has never been able to discover gold before running out of money. Michael sympathises, setting himself up for the irony in the novel's finale when Maclagan accepts his offer of much-needed funds with 'little thanks', muttering 'something about money being unimportant' (p. 107). Meanwhile, they go on a tour of the Museum, the highlights of which are Maclagan's lecture on the different personalities of the Egyptian gods and his comparison of his physique to Greek statues – a touch inspired by Mathers's Nietzschean belief that the modern 'magician' must above all keep fit.[56]

Michael follows Maclagan back to his mean digs and agrees to found an order with him. Later, the two go to a *soirée* given by the widow of a famous spiritualist (pp. 65–76). She is described as 'the only person who could get all the mystical sections together', which leads Yeats's editor to see her as a version of Madame Blavatsky, but probably she is a compendium of various occult hostesses of the day. In any case, under her roof once gathered the likes of Eliphas Lévi, Kenneth Mackenzie and Frederick Hockley (another member of the SRIA whose papers are now thought a source of the notorious 'cipher manuscripts'[57]). Among those present are an 'indolent' Cockney, whose 'soft voice and languid movements suggested something dim and half-vitalised' yet whom Maclagan's 'strenuous energy seemed to find something peculiarly provocative in';[58] a woman who 'talked incessantly in a disconnected way' and 'had many stories of haunted houses'; a young man 'who lived by astrology'; and others, including an old clergyman who is said to have made the 'elixir' some years before but, failing to summon the courage to drink it at the time, has recently found it evaporated.[59] In general, this retinue strikes Michael as their real-life counterparts had Maud Gonne: 'drab in appearance', 'mediocrities', *et cetera*. He wonders 'what could ever have made them students in magic or astrology of whatever it was'. A friend of the daughter of the house describes them as 'an awful set'. Michael responds Yeatsianly with the theory that 'whatever is the dominant type of thought draws itself up into the better kind of people', offering them 'all kinds of opportunities' while leaving behind to 'the failures and eccentrics' the 'defeated thought – which may really be the better of the two'.

This is a sensible *aperçu*. It is also patronising, however charitable; and, not surprisingly, Maclagan challenges it. 'These are the really brave and vigorous people,' he contends. Michael, chastened, watches in relative silence while the party degenerates into arguments between Swedenborgians, Martinists and American followers of Lake Harris and his rival John Humphrey Noyes. Eventually escaping into the night, he is pursued by an Eliotic advocate of 'tradition' as the only viable solution – Christian tradition at that. Thus this portion of the novel ends like a realist version of *Salomé* (a work Yeats ever admired), in which the incessant bickerings of Jews, Nazarenes and others are finally drowned by Christian apocalypticism from Iokaanan in the crypt. Michael dabbles in Catholicism (pp. 76–9). But even a type of Christianity which turns a blind eye on those who go to church with *The Divine Comedy* secreted in their prayer-books cannot hold this aspirant Parsifal for long.[60] Likened to Wagner's initiate by a traveller just returned from Bayreuth, Michael sets to work devising an order on the model of 'the sacred mountain and castle of the grail'. With an artist friend, he makes symbols, sketches altars and costumes and gathers a group around him (pp. 79–83). This becomes 'filled with a sense of expectancy, with that mysterious feeling that something is going to happen, which gives a leader his opportunity'. Michael's 'new ideas' become more attractive than the 'dark hints' Maclagan retails from his alchemical redoubt in Paris. The group listens to the younger man with 'a tolerance and interest that they did not give to' anyone else. 'He was not yet classified and might therefore be the teacher, the initiate they had long been looking for.'

In this lies an extraordinary revelation of the extent to which Yeats dreamed of being acclaimed as a leader. Needless to say, Michael's ascendancy in the novel leads to conflict with his fellow would-be *Führer*. Maclagan writes from Paris that he must break with his rival: Michael is interested in 'form', while he is interested in 'substance'; Michael is 'some kind of artist', while he is 'a magician'; and Michael will always find 'some charm of colour' or 'charm of words' to be the *summum bonum*, while he will continue to remain committed to the tradition of Rosicrucian 'secret chiefs' and the discoveries of precursors such as Lully and Flamel (pp. 91–5). This strikes one as an apt appraisal of the divergence between Yeats and his one-time mentor. At the same time, Maclagan's criticism hits the nail on the head as regards Yeats's aspiration to inherit leadership of the Golden Dawn. The poet would remain a poet first and always, thus would never have the commitment necessary to reach and hold onto 'magical' power. Something like this is no doubt what Florence Farr had in mind when she responded 'Who are *you* in the order?' to Yeats's attempt to rule his fellow adepts.[61] On another occasion she observed,

This frater did you all great service during the Revolution as you know from your printed documents. Since then he has attended the council meetings at intervals and we all bear him witness that he has talked at greater length than all the other members put together. His position among us is due to his long connection with the Order, the originality of his views on Occult subjects and the ability with which he expresses them rather than the thoroughness of his knowledge of Order work and methods which is somewhat scant. He is however a shining example of the help we may get from Members who have no special talent for passing Examinations.[62]

Readers believing that Yeats's symbols mask deep and consistent occult sub-texts should take note. The fact is that, while for many years he was keen to keep up an association which allowed him to write grandly of 'my Kabbalists', 'my alchemist' and so forth,[63] Yeats's mastery of Golden Dawn 'magic' may have been as *manqué* as his attempt to write satire in a novel he had to abandon as flawed.

George Mills Harper tells us that Yeats looked to the Golden Dawn to fulfil the role of religion for him,[64] even to the degree that T. S. Eliot looked to 'Anglo-Catholicism' years on. But Harper's account of the poet's relations with the order shows Yeats in more than usually ill-fitting masks. Not least is that of would-be politician. Following the break with Mathers, Farr and others began to organise sub-groups to try out new Egyptian rites and the like. Without joining one of these, Yeats declared that their doings would 'desecrate the vault' and conjured up visions of 'black-magical' orgies in which members' 'geniuses' would be possessed.[65] To combat such heresy, he advocated unity and 'tradition'. A 'strict constructionist', he argued that by 'binding loose sticks' the Golden Dawn might yet realise its messianic role. The allusion to *fasces* was no accident. Nor was 'inflation' less apparent than in some of Mathers' apocalyptic flights, though Yeats takes up the tone of a Victorian schoolmaster rather than the commander of an infantry charge. What is absent is appreciation of the demand for eclectic, individual pursuit in matters of spiritual advancement. Mathers recognised this, as is apparent in his remarks on child-rearing quoted above. Elsewhere in the Order's 'Flying Scrolls', his wife had expressed it thus:

> That error of wishing to make another as ourselves is another and a very hurtful form of most subtle egotism. All we can do is to help him to *elevate himself* and to study to 'know himself', in order that by working at that knowledge, he may cross the Threshold of the Portal which leads to Knowledge of the Divine.[66]

Others of Yeats's Golden Dawn related writings betray further evidence of something not quite right in his treatment of the

Order. In the poem 'All Souls' Night' which concludes *A Vision*,
he recalls Mathers, Farr and another dead occult comrade and
suggests that their flaws were not as important as the warmth of
his friendship with them. This was no doubt a comforting sentiment for the author; one wonders, however, how his subjects
might have felt about the facility with which he got in the last
word. Further, what might they have made of his not evidently
more than decorative placement of a secret grade symbol at the
end of 'The Phases of the Moon' earlier in the book? For that
matter, what might they have thought of his pretensions in *A
Vision* overall to provide the world with a complete 'magical' guide,
as dictated by 'secret chiefs' via the 'medium' of his wife?
Mediumship, as said, was frowned on in the Golden Dawn; and
Yeats did not neglect to remind his fellow students of this in his
struggle for power with them.[67] Why, then, did he adopt a mode
which had been under a cloud at least since Madame Blavatasky's
'Mahatmas' had been shown up as a fraud, and certainly since
the 'secret chiefs' controversies had all but destroyed the Golden
Dawn? The answer may be that Yeats after all was mediumistic
himself. That he had always been eager for *visions* is plain from
The Speckled Bird. That this had been a driving force in his pursuit
of occult experience is also confirmed by what may be his finest
accomplishment in prose, the partly Golden Dawn inspired 'Rosa
Alchemica'.[68] This story is about being taken over by an influence,
rather than directing one's actions oneself. In its most transcendent
passages, the narrator is literally swept away by his 'vision'. It
reads like an account of a hashish 'trip' (and may even be one).[69]
Thus it reveals the conflict between need for imposed order and
desire to escape into 'glamour' which Yeats's Gemini nature[70]
never sorted out in itself, and which made him, finally, a divisive
spirit in the group.

IV FRATERNITY, RITUAL AND THE ROSE

At the end of *The Speckled Bird*, Yeats's 'hero' visits Maclagan in
Paris on his way to the East. The object of his journey is to put
his 'old ideas in a new form'. He wants to merge Western Christianity with some Eastern 'lost doctrine of reconciliation'; find the
connection between sexual and divine love as suggested by great
poets, particularly Dante; heal the split between 'religion and

emotions'; and discover a way by which souls divided might meet in 'some country of ideal beauty'. Busy with his Isis working, Maclagan 'does not understand'; but it is unlikely that Mathers would have been so naïve. Yeats's hero is proposing to make his own version of the classic journey which Christian Rosenkreuz was meant to have embarked on at the end of the fourteenth century, leading him to discover the 'secrets' which – along with indigenous Hermeticism and Cabalism – have provided the basis for Western occult lore since. Michael Hearne of *The Speckled Bird* thus becomes a precursor of Yeats's ubiquitous 'magical' persona, Michael Robartes, who 'stars' in 'Rosa Alchemica' and returns in the stories introducing *A Vision* after his own years of wandering the East, where he has learned from the Judwalis tribe the lore which makes up Yeats's *magnum opus*.[71] Unfortunately, there is not space to go into these Yeats matters further here. In any case, I have already been harsh enough not to need to labour the point that, in projecting such 'journeys', the poet was again displaying a kind of fictive Walter Mittyism – unlike, say, Crowley, whose more strictly 'magical' impulse led him to undertake a real 'journey to the East' and gain first-hand knowledge of Taoism, Tantricism and Egyptian lore.[72] But, whether the response was fictive or 'real', what is clear is that the Rosicrucian myth had a pervasive influence in the Golden Dawn milieu. As said, it provided one of the three 'pillars'[73] on which the group's 'religion' was built.

From it, the Golden Dawn took first of all its name. The *Fama fraternitas* (1614), in which Rosicrucianism declared its existence to the outer world, begins with an 'Epistle to the Wise and Under-standing Reader' which predicts an *'aurora* of wisdom' to follow the 'dark night of Saturn' under which Europe has existed for centuries: a 'dawn' which will lead on to 'the blessed Day of Pheobus'.[74] The *Confessio fraternitas* (1618), in which the order first solicited for members,[75] begins with a 'Preface to the Reader who is Desirous of Wisdom' which repeats this vision in yet more ardent, almost flower-child terms: 'What before times hath been seen, heard and smelt, now finally shall be spoken and uttered forth, *viz.* when the world shall awake out of heavy and drowsie sleep, and with an open heart, bare-head and bare-foot, shall merrily and joyfully meet the arising Sun.' We can see here the origin of the idea of moving 'from darkness to light', emphasised in Golden Dawn ritual, particularly that of the Neophyte; also the importance of the compass direction 'East' in arrangement of the

'temple', placement of officials and circumambulations of candi-
dates.[76] More important, we may glimpse an origin of the group's
messianic view of its purpose. 'The Golden Dawn meant to
synthesise a coherent, logical system of practical occultism out of
the scattered remains of a tradition that had been broken up by
fifteen hundred years of religious persecution', Francis King writes
in the finale of his book on the Order.[77] Thus, in its principal
second-order ritual, the group came to incorporate a *précis* of the
Fama fraternitas, also a re-enactment of the opening of the tomb of
Father Rosycross by his disciples a hundred years after the
heretical 'saviour's' death.[78] In this way, it promised to carry on
the subterranean 'religion' which combined Christian piety in
'prais[ing] God' and 'promot[ing] love, help and neighbourliness'
with Hermetic aspirations to 'study Nature', 'combat disease',
'learn', 'correct errors', and 'find out all that is new'.[79]

From Rosicrucianism, the Golden Dawn found encouragement
for its puritanism and took its status as a fraternity and its
condition of secrecy. As the *Fama* relates, the original order was
composed entirely of bachelors and virgins.[80] They created a
dictionary of 'magical' language, studied the Cabala, the *Corpus
Hermeticum* and *Rota mundi* (Tarot?), and spread out to different
countries to find out further 'secrets' and convey their knowledge
to those willing and desirous to receive it. The principles of their
association were (1) to cure the sick, (2) always to take up the
custom of the country where they found themselves, (3) to return
once a year to meet at Corpus Christi, (4) to seek successors, (5)
to use 'RC' as their mark, and (6) to keep their existence as a
fraternity a secret.[81] Thus Golden Dawn initiates would try invocations, astral 'banishments', suggestive and meditative methods
to ward off fevers; establish 'temples' in Scotland, Paris, America,
New Zealand and possibly Australia and South Africa as well as
England; honour the Corpus Christi convocation as the sacred
event of the year; be on the look-out for suitable new members;
identify their grades by special words and gestures; and only
speak of the Order 'in the outer' with circumlocutions such as 'a
group of cabalists', 'some hermeticists' and so on.[82] Many of these
traits may be found in Freemasonry too; and, as said, Masonry
also took inspiration from 'Rosicrucianism'. The corollary – that
the Golden Dawn was 'Masonic' – was determined by Maud
Gonne from its signs and grips; also the fact that it used Mark
Masons' Hall for many of its meeings.[83] Believing Masonry to be

in cahoots with British imperialism, the Irish nationalist quit the Order. But, as has been noted, several members of the Golden Dawn were no less Celtic enthusiasts than she (indeed, where Theosophical Society brought Indian and Lévi Jewish elements into the forefront of Western 'magic' in their times, the Golden Dawn might be described as having brought 'Celtic'); and, finally, the most 'Masonic'. feature of it may be the 'terrible' oath to keep silence which the Neophyte was made to swear.[84]

From later Rosicrucianism such as links with Masonry, the Golden Dawn drew its grade structure. This rose from $0° = 0^\square$ (Neophyte) to $10° = 0^\square$ (Ipsissimus), though no member except the renegade and self-initiator Crowley ever achieved the top three grades,[85] which were reserved for 'secret chiefs' – those spurious higher authorities which, as we have seen, derived from Madame Blavatsky's ill-conceived 'Mahatmas' and beyond them the 'Unknown Supermen' of German 'Strict Observance' Masonry and *supérieurs inconnus* of the French 'Scottish Rite' of the later eighteenth century.[86] The *Fama fraternitas* deals in actual leaders and traditions rather than 'astral travellers', whether out of HPB's 'Devachan' or the Hermetic 'Decan' spheres. The furthest the seventeenth-century document ventured into such fictions is a tale of the classical initiation of Apollonius of Tyana by Brahmins and Magi,[87] fierce mountain-top gurus described as 'never [making] allies when fighting their enemies, but [standing] their ground and [scaring] them off with sparks and fire' – a motif no doubt appealing to the likes of Mathers with his 'Punitive Current' or modern-day Masonic political leaders with their *force de frappe*.[88] Ancient Brahmin/Magian initiation is shown to concentrate on the 'magical' relationship of the elements, particularly fire and water. In a like manner, outer Golden Dawn rituals led the candidate through progressive 'understanding' of elemental powers: Earth for the Zelator, $1° = 10^\square$; Air for the Theoricus, $2° = 9^\square$; Water for the Practicus, $3° = 8^\square$; and Fire for the highest outer grade, Philosophus, $4° = 7^\square$. Elementary attributes give rise to some of the most impressive passages in the rituals' scripts, especially the evocation of Divine Spirit blowing through all things with which the Theoricus rite ends, and the description of the fires of creative ideas pouring down on the earth in great fountains, which dominates the Practicus.[89] Such passages justify Ellic Howe's remark that the Golden Dawn's rituals rank as part of the minor literature of the *fin-de-siècle*.[90] No doubt Yeats was inspired by them when conceiving his plays, always ceremonial and symbolic and rarely much longer than a single ritual. Nor does their eclecticism entirely justify Crowley's charge that 'the rituals . . . are bloated and swollen with much that is silly and pedantic, affected and misplaced . . . wilful obscurity taking place of a lucid simplicity . . . provoking either jeers or a reverence overweening in proportion to the extent it simply cannot understand'.[91]

Crowley goes on to complain about the Golden Dawn invoking 'a hodge-podge of Gods': the 'discarded underwear of Olympus and Sinai'. No one would dispute that the group was committed to 'correspondences'. But whether the mixture of elements (and there are undeniable log-jams in the Order's rituals) made a candidate woozy or impressed him with the universal Oneness behind All was a matter of individual taste. Apparently the minor author Arthur Machen agreed with Crowley and resigned on account of the order's 'syncretism'.[92] Others were inspired by what was surely the most strenuous effort by any cult to that time to forge links between all major Western occult systems. Thus each grade of the Order had its equivalent in the Cabalistic Sephiroth; its specific Tarot paths to master; its principal Hermetic symbols and/or presiding Egyptian dieties. In this, it followed the *axiomata* of the *Fama* that all science, nature and arts should be directed 'like a Globe, or Circle, to the only middle point and *centrum*'.[93] From such a concept may seem to emanate not-so-attractive tendencies to hierarchy and fascism. But also cognate with it are the utopian Rosicrucian aspiration for harmony in *this* world, as in spheres above, and finally the emblem of the rose. About this, which was the central symbol in the Golden Dawn's most important grade ritual, much has been and could be written. Take for example the remarks of Eliphas Lévi in his chapter on the Rosicrucians in *L'Histoire de la magie:*

> The rose, which from all times has been the type of beauty, life, love and pleasure, expressed mystically the secret thought of all protests manifested at the Renaissance. It was the flesh in rebellion against the oppression of the Spirit; it was Nature testifying that, like Grace, she was a daughter of God; it was love refusing to be stifled by the celibate; it was life in revolt against servility; it was humanity aspiring toward natural religion, full of reason and love, founded on revelations of the harmony of being of which the rose, for initiates, was the living floral symbol. It is

in truth a pantacle; the form is circular, its tint offers the most harmonious shades of the primitive colours; its calyx is of purple and gold. We have seen that [Nicholas] Flamel, or rather *The Book of Abraham the Jew*,[94] represents it as the hieroglyphical sign of the fulfilment of the Great Work. Here is the key to the [earliest literary expression of the idea, *Roman de la Rose*]. The conquest of the rose was the problem offered by initiation to science, whilst religion was at work to prepare and to establish the universal, exclusive and final triumph of the Cross.

The problem proposed by high initiation was the union of the Rose and the Cross, and in effect occult philosophy, being the universal synthesis, must take into account all phenomena of being.[95]

Characteristically for an era now in revolt against the ascendancy of science, the attributions had shifted in the Golden Dawn: thus the petals of the rose attach to the spirit, while the wood of the Cross to matter. That apart, the essence of meaning was the same, as can be seen by Yeats's extended footnote on his ubiquitous use of this symbol in his most Golden Dawn related volume of poetry, *The Wind among the Reeds*:

The Rose has been for many centuries a symbol of spiritual love and supreme beauty. The lotus was in some Eastern countries imagined blossoming upon the Tree of Life, as the Flower of Life, and is thus represented in Assyrian bas-reliefs. Because the Rose, the flower sacred to the Virgin Mary, and the flower that Apuleius' adventurer ate, when he was changed out of the ass's shape and received into the fellowship of Isis, is the western Flower of Life, I have imagined it growing upon the Tree of Life. I once stood before a man in Ireland when he saw it growing there in a vision, that seemed to have rapt him out of his body. He saw the Garden of Eden walled about, and on the top of a high mountain, as in certain mediaeval diagrams, and after passing the Tree of Knowledge, on which grew fruit full of troubled faces, and through whose branches flowed, he was told, sap that was human souls, he came to a tall, dark tree, with little bitter fruits, and was shown a kind of stair or ladder going up through the tree, and told to go up; and near the top of the tree, a beautiful woman, like the Goddess of Life, associated with the tree in Assyria, gave him a rose that seemed to have been growing upon the tree.[96]

Here is added, expanding on Lévi, the anagogical power of the rose as beacon at the end of the initiate's path. That the vision should be projected against the backdrop of the Tree of Life, along with its obverse of the Qliphothic tree with 'bitter fruits', is entirely in the spirit of the Golden Dawn's synthesis – especially the break between first– and second-order rituals, in which the Tree collapses into its Qliphothic 'shells' and can only be ascended through the arrival and self-sacrifice of a 'second Adam', Christ, or, in Golden Dawn terms, a combination of Christ and Rosenkreuz.[97] But most of all, in literary terms, Yeats's thoughts here doubtless start from the anagogical framework of Dante. And if he had read Lévi, as is likely,[98] he must have been impressed that that great modern authority on 'magical' symbol should have gone on in the same chapter quoted above,

> The Rosicrucian symbol goes back to the times of the Guelphs and Ghibellines, as we see by the allegories in the poem of Dante . . . His heaven is composed by a series of Kabalistic circles divided by a cross. . . . In the centre of this cross a rose blossoms, thus for the first time manifesting publicly and almost explaining categorically the symbol['s significance]. . . . It will be discovered with a certain astonishment that the *Divine Comedy* is a form of initiation by independence of spirit, satire on all contemporary institutions and an allegorical formula of the grand secrets of the Brotherhood of the Rosy Cross.[99]

V   DEFINING AND RISING TO GOD

The Divine Comedy is a progress toward comprehension of the Absolute. So too, as said, was the practice of the Golden Dawn. This is the theme of both Mathers' main texts: *Kabbalah Unveiled* and *The Sacred Magic*. The first identifies the attributes of God and the Great Man; the second shows how the latter might better approach the former. We have talked about the Cabala in relation to Lévi. The Golden Dawn refined and expanded on the French mage's teachings, adding Hermetic and other motifs of their own. Central for them, as for Lévi, was the overarching ideal of 'equilibrium'.[100] This of course is also embodied in the rose symbol, of which Moina Mathers wrote in her Preface to the second edition of her husband's early work, 'With its mysterious centre, its nucleus, the central Sun, [the rose] is a symbol of the infinite and harmonious separations of nature.'[101] In other words, it is an emblem of the Hermetic world. But, since 'that which is above' is like 'that which is below', it is also an emblem of the ultimate nature of God, which in the Cabala is expressed as *Ain Sof*: the 'Illimitable One' manifest as both 'negative existence' and 'limitless light', expanding through the universe as if in petals.[102] A plate depicting this ambiguous wholeness in roseate form appears prominently in Mathers' text. Yeats would sum up the difficult concept in his phrase 'Where there is God, there is nothing', which he used as title for a story and a play.[103] God is, further, the resolution of all opposites, not least sexual. The complete being is an androgynous combination of masculine 'rigour', which is 'vehement in the beginning' and 'slackening' later, and feminine qualities in which 'the contrary rule obtaineth'.[104] So says the Cabala. So believed medieval Hermeticists, thus their ideal of 'alchemical marriage'. So thus the Golden Dawn practised sexual equality – feminism even – in contrast to Masonic and Rosicrucian forbears. Their interpretation of the Tree of Life reflects this by positing each 'trinity' of spheres as a 'duad' of (sexual) opposites and 'a uniting intelligence which is the result'. Thus Kether unites Chokmah and Binah in the high trinity of 'morality'; Tiphereth, Chesed and Geburah in the middle of 'power'; and Yesod, Netzach and Hod in the low of 'stability'.[105]

The Hermetic Great Man – Adam Kadmon of the Cabala – is a reflection of God. Microprosopus and Macroprosopus are the terms used in *Kabbalah Unveiled*. The initiate makes himself into the former by striving to comprehend the latter. Conversely, he understands the latter in proportion to the degree to which he becomes an embodiment of the former. Both archetypes are described in painstaking detail, with chapters devoted to each part of the body and its deeper significance. Thus there are corresponding passages on the 'dew or moisture of the brain', the skull, the membrane of the brain, the hair, the forehead, the eyes, the nose, the ears, the beard in general, the beard in thirteen particular parts and – in the case of Micro– though not Macroprosopus – the lower parts of the body, including genitals. About these, the reader is in for an irritating, though on reflection not surprising shock. Using the lame excuse that such descriptions are better rendered

in the original language, Mathers fails to translate any phrase
having to do with revealed sex. Thus we must grope to learn that
woman's body is five times more beautiful when naked, or that
man's glory only reaches perfection when he is 'upright' before
God.[106] The extended male member is called 'benignity'; and,
when it is inserted into the female both sexes are 'mitigated' and
'judgment is restored into order'. The Cabala in this view promotes
its own version of the Shiva–Shakti arrangement of Indian 'sex
magic'.[107] Conversely, it warns that, when male and female are not
'associated face to face', demons or spirits which are the 'authors of
disturbance' are more likely to be created. Knorr von Rosenroth's
Latin appears to go on to suggest that anal intercourse is only
permitted to the high priest.[108] Why this might be – and indeed
all the Cabalistic sex lore[109] which Mathers rushes over – would
be left for Crowley and his kind to consider. The Golden Dawn,
as said, was content to struggle on amid its myriad 'authors of
disturbance'.

Besides being the eventual equilibrator of Golden Dawn sex
imbalance, Crowley is also the only member of the group known
to have tried the process set out in Mathers' second *magnum
opus*.[110] *The Sacred Magic* is an elaboration of the Cabalistic–Hermetic desire to rise toward God. As *Kabbalah Unveiled* tells us,

> The petition which a man wisheth to make unto his Lord can
> ordinarily be propounded in nine ways. . . . Either (1) by
> alphabet . . . (2) by commemorating the attributes of God . . .
> (3) by the venerable names of God . . . (4) by the ten
> sephiroth . . . (5) by the commemoration of just men – patri-
> archs, prophets and kings . . . (6) by canticles wherein is the
> true Qabalah . . . (7) by declaring the conformations of his
> Lord . . . (8) by ascending from below to above . . . (9) by
> deriving the influx from on high downward.[111]

Central here is the concept, used widely in Golden Dawn
evocations, of 'vibrating' divine names, particularly Jod-Hé-Vau-
Hé. This is made up of the names of the Hebrew letters (equivalent
to YHWH or JHVH) comprising the divine name Yahweh/Jahveh
('Jehovah'), and has, of course, vast numerological significance.[112]
But in use of all nine techniques, Mathers not unexpectedly adds,
'There is need of very great concentration of attention' – i.e. our
old friend the focused *will*. Discovering one's 'true will' is in fact

the purpose of *The Sacred Magic*. As mentioned in a previous chapter,[113] this is achieved by coming into contact with one's 'Holy Guardian Angel', who then for all time (presumably) becomes guarantor of that will. Here the reader may see the attraction for Crowley, who would raise the concept of will to Hitlerian pitch. But, reading *The Sacred Magic*, he may also see why the nascent 'sex magician' should have abandoned the Abramelin process before reaching completion. Crowley could only grow impatient with any technique which put all emphasis on rising above the physical; and *The Sacred Magic* regards sex, far from being a positive 'mitigating' force, as a prime instigation of Qliphothic distraction.

The practitioner of the process undertakes a six-month-long meditation.[114] He constructs or finds an 'oratory', which must conform to set dimensions and properties, and consecrates vestments and instruments to use in it. His regime requires cleanliness; no sex, drink, drugs, meat-eating, intercourse with 'the ungodly' or sleep in the daytime; consistent and directed spiritual thoughts; two hours a day of reading holy texts; and charity to beggars (p. xvi). The process should begin after Easter, with proper 'banishing' and purification rituals, and end around All Souls' Night. Throughout its course, the practitioner should keep in mind these guiding ideas: that good and light are superior to evil and darkness; that the former should be 'served' by the latter; that all material effects created by the latter should be 'controlled' by the former; that when the latter escape control 'all Hell will break loose'; that escaped evil will try to control man by making him agree to 'pacts'; that it will latch onto whatever obsesses a man and seek to manipulate him through that; that, to maintain control, he must constantly reaffirm his purity of intent; that this is assured by self-abnegation on all planes; that man must emerge as the 'mediator' between all good and evil forces around him; and that to control the 'lower' he must have knowledge of the 'higher'. The ultimate objective beyond gaining contact with the 'guardian angel' is thus to 'obtain the right of *using the Evil spirits for our servants in all material matters*' (p. xiv; emphasis added). At the end of the six months, the successful practitioner will be introduced to Lucifer, Leviathan, Satan and Belial and, through them, the eight 'sub-princes' and their 'armies', in a descending hierarchy through the Qliphoth. As penance for their 'sins', these spirits will pledge to obey the practitioner always and do his bidding (p. 88). Thus we return to the questionable moral area entered with Lévi via his discussion of how to 'manipulate' the elements, or with Goethe via his picture of Faust gaining worldly 'power' through the demonic 'guardian', Mephistopheles.[115] From this perspective, Crowley was dead on the mark when he observed that *The Sacred Magic* represented a more potent and dangerous programme than Mathers had proposed before and may have been his undoing.[116]

The techniques the practitioner calls on to make his way run the gamut of Golden Dawn *praxis*. Though enjoined not to use drink (like Mathers) or sex or drugs (like Crowley), he may fast (like Yeats's Michael Hearne) to get 'visions', or he may use meditation devices: Tarot images, 'tattvas' or particularly Enochian squares.[117] These should help him induce the trance state, or auto-hypnosis, in which he may be better able to 'skry the astral plane' or direct his other body on an 'astral journey'. Essential to the process is to subdue his conscious, worldly personality: to get in touch with his *Doppelgänger*, or counter-self,[118] through whom he may merge more readily into intimacy with the 'guardian'. Here the practitioner is operating in a way not unreminiscent of the Christian ecstatic[119] – St Francis or St Teresa – who actually believed in the possibility of hearing voices from a higher plane; and, like St Anthony, he must engage in a terrible, constant struggle to keep his will focused on the single objective. A recent practitioner tells us in his *Ceremonial Diary* that in the first two months he cried out, 'Oh Faust, I understand and feel for you!' and that he was approached by 'two men, one tall, strong and with a goatee, the other Adolf Hitler', and had to invoke 'Christian knights' to get rid of them (p. 13). Besides these uninvited mental intruders, he is assaulted by irritation from friends and so much opposition from his wife that he is moved to beat her. Days arrive when he is elated, as when he discovers his 'third eye' (p. 18). Other days find him wallowing in fear of vanity, loss of energy or recognition of his status as a 'worm in a dungheap'. With *mantra*-like phrases, he gees himself up: 'All Glory to the One'; 'Grant me O Lord the secret wisdom'. Striving to make himself a 'totally neutral body of energy for use of [the] soul', he reminds himself that 'to be continuously in a state of meditation is the essential key' (p. 40). Eventually, he learns how to affect the human and other forms around him by 'communicating directly with their soul[s]'. Later still, he decides he must 'help' them.

Thus, in proportion to his success in transcending worldly appetites, a messianic urge grows.

Finally, his purpose is revealed as the Hermetic one of raising himself to the ultimate height by imagining what it is to be God.[120] In this, the author of the *Ceremonial Diary* recognises the dangers of 'inflation'. He is of our era and has read of the disasters members of the Golden Dawn brought on themselves by trying to 'develop their latent magical powers without using the protective techniques still taught in all the major religions'.[121] Struggling to keep humility and reason in mind, he continues. Yet, as he reaches higher toward his destination, he does not cease to experience pain and terror like that which Mathers claimed to have suffered in his encounters with his 'secret chiefs':

> My intercourse with them . . . produced [more than] that intense physical exhaustion which follows depletion by magnetism. . . . The sensation was that of being in contact with so terrible a force that I can only compare it to the *continued* effect of that usually experienced momentarily by a person *close* to whom a flash of lightning passes during a violent storm; coupled with a difficulty in respiration similar to the half-strangling effect produced by ether.[122]

This, one might note, Mathers wrote in one of his most autocratic 'manifestoes' for the Golden Dawn, during the period when he was beginning to work on *The Sacred Magic*. Yet in spite of the fearfulness, he carried on. Courage of this kind (at least stubbornness) was one hallmark of the mentality which put such emphasis on will, and was no mean feature of its message. Thus the practitioner of the Abra-Melin process, if he persists, is promised by the end to have learned to circumvent the tedious and plodding ascent of the Sephiroth taught in low, worldly grades of the Order and rise up through the Middle Pillar of the Tree in a manner suggestive of the *Kundalini*, or 'Fire-Snake', energy of Tantric Buddhism.[123] Thus being able to reach his 'guardian angel' at will, to look down on and command legions of fallen spirits below, the 'magician' will have arrived finally. And there he may stand, in the middle of his 'magic' circle.[124] And, if he keeps his eyes open to the full range of possibilities around him and is ever alert to the necessity of beating off adversaries without and exercising

total control within, there is no reason why he should not be able
to continue to enjoy his 'power', for so long as the will may persist.

Magnificent prospect! But, the mere mortal is likely to observe,
if this is what 'high magic' really amounts to, how very tiring and
lonely it must be.[125]

6

Intermediary: *The Magic Mountain*

Writing about 'magic' raises more than ordinary problems of tone. Frances Yates is pious and scholarly about her Renaissance subjects. Francis King, treating characters closer in time, tends to tease and point up the absurd. Others, such as James Webb, are simply exhaustive in attempting to embrace all 'historicist' facts. How a writer approaches this subject – how he deploys 'the Word' – is often the most telling aspect of his message. And few works of literature find questions of tone about 'magic' more pronounced than two of the principal novels of the greatest writer of this century, Thomas Mann.

At the end of chapter 3, I spoke about the 'equilibrating' conscience of the serious novelist, as opposed to 'magical' writer. The former has to take into account everyday life, prosaic morality and by no means just the ideal or ways to attain 'power'. Mann demonstrates this perfectly, in both narrative which achieves 'equilibration' and narrative which shows what may occur when the balance breaks down. Of the first, the great example is *The Magic Mountain*, with its magisterial, humane and all-synthesizing irony; of the second, *Dr Faustus*, with its schizophrenic structure, pairing the ponderous, conventional narrator, Serenus Zeitblom, with his archaic and perverse subject, Adrian Leverkühn.

In these two works, published in 1924 and 1948 respectively, we observe the growth of 'magic' as religion in modern times as it presents itself for good or evil. The first explores the *Zeitgeist* of the nineteenth century up to its breakdown in the First World War; the second shows that breakdown proceeding on toward the Second World War and the grotesqueries created thereby. In the first, Hans Castorp, an unknowing 'initiate', goes through an alchemical 'transmutation' during his seven years on the 'magic mountain' and emerges as an exemplar of liberal self-realisation. In the

125

second, Leverkühn takes derivative self-expression so far that it spills over into the cruel, becoming an abject mockery of the decent, to which Zeitblom on the other hand clings to a point of paralysis of will.

In these respects and others, Mann's two great novels reflect major issues thrown up by this study. There are other books which explore individual points – notably in German those of Hermann Hesse, whose daemonic urge in *Demian* and *Steppenwolf* suggests aspects of Crowley and whose spirituality in *Siddhartha* and *The Journey to the East* reflects impulses driving Theosophy and Anthroposophy.[1] But no works are so comprehensive about 'magic' in relation to civilisation as these two by Mann; and for me they constitute a standard – of both tone and morality – to hold onto in the midst of the illusions, charlatanism and sparks of errant genius ubiquitous in such a study.

Unfortunately, space does not permit discussion of both. It would unbalance the whole to devote so much attention to works of one novelist, however fine. Thus as in the case of Bulwer-Lytton, where I had to choose between *Zanoni* and the equally provocative *A Strange Story*, so here there must be a hard decision. *Dr Faustus* has much to do with the twentieth-century 'magical' impulse to 'equilibrate' in favour of the 'black'; and Leverkühn's evocation in the central chapter of an ambiguously imaginary 'devil' as his 'guardian' suggests the process developed by Mathers and result reached by Crowley.

But in general *Dr Faustus* is less about the pervasive magico-religious reorientation of an age than about a localised (German) and temporal (modernist) aberration. For a picture of what snapped in the *Zeitgeist*, there may be no better choice – though one might raise the criticism that, unlike say Crowley, Mann could only view 'evil' from the outside, as an intellectual problem, rather than evoke it in all its terrifying aspect from within: that is, from the point of view of a psyche which in contemporary psychoanalytical terms was truly 'damaged'. There is, for instance, no early childhood deprivation or 'syndrome' to explain Leverkühn's subsequent 'evil'; thus that 'evil' remains an 'elective affinity' rather than inescapable visceral condition.

Such limitations are less apparent with *The Magic Mountain*. The earlier work is more general and panoramic in its concerns and its focal character more transparently a device – a *tabula rasa* through which these might be explored. This makes it the slightly better choice for our attention (though the reader may find *Dr Faustus* a more exciting and disturbing achievement, as works about 'evil' often are). *The Magic Mountain* also provides a more appropriate pivot from the point of view of time, occupying as it does a more central moment of transition between nineteenth and twentieth century *Zeitgeists*. For these reasons, I devote a single chapter to it, this briefer than the rest, offering a kind of respite and taking an 'intermediary' position between us – the non-adepts – and this arcane and sometimes off-putting subject.

What is Mann's 'mountain' and why is it 'magic'? Literally, the mountain is just that: an alpine redoubt in Switzerland, housing a fashionable sanatorium for tuberculosis sufferers, real and imaginary. Figuratively, it represents the accumulated knowledge and culture of Europe to that point. Thus fancifully, it becomes for Mann's hero 'a variant of the shrine of the initiatory rites, a place of adventurous investigation into the mystery of life'.[2]

In this respect, it is 'magic'; and the 'magic' from the first is described in 'orthodox heretical' terms. 'Chance – call it chance – brought me up to these heights of the spirit', Hans Castorp observes; 'alchemistic pedagogy, transubstantiation from lower to higher, ascending degrees' (p. 596). By the end of seven years (a number with 'a savour of the mythical'), he will look back over a 'hermetic career' (p. 652). 'My Hans Castorp', Mann reflects in an afterword, 'has a very distinguished knightly and mystical ancestry: he is the typical curious neophyte', the 'quester' and 'guileless fool' seeking the 'Grail'. This Mann defines as 'the Highest: knowledge, wisdom, consecration, the philosopher's stone, the *aurum potabile*, the elixir of life' (pp. 725–6).

Among novels, *The Magic Mountain* is as long and full of formulae and suggestion as a medieval *grimoire*. Like *Zanoni*, it is divided deliberately into seven sections. Stylistically, it is held together by what Mann describes as a 'magic system' which links past and future: the *Leitmotiv* (p. 718). By means of this device adapted from Wagner,[3] we are reminded constantly of 'magical' significance behind naturalistic event. Thus 'alchemy', 'hermeticism', 'initiation' and related concepts are not only discussed directly but also referred to continually in connection with apparently mundane thoughts or actions.

For instance, the counter-hierophant[4] Naphta describes the

processes of actual alchemy to Castorp in a disquisition on Strict
Observance Masonry (pp. 510–11). Shortly afterwards, the grave
is described as an alchemical crucible and Castorp meditates on
how his cousin Joachim, who has just died, experienced an
'alchemistical heightening' into goodness and simplicity (p. 542).
Castorp's own progress is described by Mann as an 'alchemical
"keying up" ' (p. 722). Meanwhile, a variety of effects are drawn
into the trope, such as those of music, described with the phrase,
'the alchemical power of this soul enchantment' (p. 653).

Hermeticism appears first in connection with the hierophant
Settembrini. Believer in 'the *Logos*' or power of the Word (p. 113),
he bows down figuratively to Thoth–Trismegistus (p. 524).
Naphta, however, to spite his rival, ridicules Hermes as 'an ape,
moon and soul diety . . . of whom late antiquity made the arch-
enchanter' and thus seeks to transform the 'humanistic orator' into
a 'squatting ape-god'. Use of the term 'hermetic' extends much
further in the novel than this, however. Mann talks of 'the
hermetic, feverish atmosphere of the enchanted mountain' and
'the hermetic enchantment of its young hero within the timeless'
(p. 723). Meanwhile, the guileless seeker associates the term with
its mundane connotation:

> Hermetics – what a lovely word [Castorp observes]. . . . It
> sounds like magicking, and has all sorts of vague and extended
> associations. . . . It reminds me of the conserve jars that our
> housekeeper in Hamburg keeps in her larder. . . . They stand
> there maybe a whole year – you open them as you need them
> and the contents are as fresh as on the day they were put
> up. . . . That isn't alchemy or purification, it is simple
> conserving. . . . The magic part of it lies in the fact that the stuff
> that is conserved is withdrawn from the effects of time. (p. 511)

Here is the process essential to Mann's development and
perhaps 'hermetic magic' overall: to break time and preserve an
essence relatively eternally.[5] Castorp's own self-conservation in
this way is indicated in the chapter 'By the Ocean of Time', which
opens the seventh and last section of the novel. Here we are told
in connection with the fact that he no longer uses a watch or
calendar, 'Thus did he honour to his abiding-everlasting, his walk
by the ocean of time, the hermetic enchantment to which he
had proved so extraordinarily susceptible that it had become the

fundamental adventure of his life, in which all the alchemistical processes of his simple substance had found full play' (p. 708).

This essential relation of 'alchemy' and 'hermetics' to the 'initiation' Castorp goes through is supported by a myriad other 'magical' motifs. The mountain itself is described in metaphysical terms suggesting the 'powers' of Space and Time (pp. 4–5). It is a 'solemn, phantasmagorical world'. The air is such that normal people from the lowlands 'never get used to it' (p. 12). Sunsets are 'luminous'. Then days come when the surrounding peaks and valleys are 'shrouded in vapours'. In the dead of winter, all may gleam with 'diamondlike brilliance in the magic moonlight' (p. 346). Indeed, the natural world here may at its best bring the seeker into 'harmony with the larger, the fundamental facts of nature': the 'cosmic rhythm' (p. 415).

On the other hand, it may at worst be alarming, hostile or simply indifferent. 'Outside was the reeking void, the world enwrapped in grey-white cotton wool' (p. 471). So Castorp discovers to his near-fatal cost in the central chapter entitled 'Snow', in which he flees the inward, intellectual 'hermeticism' of the sanatorium for a nature which changes in an instant from ineffable beauty to stormy terrors worthy of a 'Prince of the Shadows'. 'The unnatural stillness, the monstrous solitude, oppressed his spirit' (p. 479). Yet in the end, having made his way back to home-base in safety, Castorp feels 'proud to have conquered' these elements, thus to have passed another necessary stage in his 'initiation'.

The inner world of the sanatorium is no less varied or eccentric – indeed 'magical' – than outward nature. The patients gathered include an Egyptian princess, a Romanian Jewess, a Moorish eunuch, a red-haired beauty with 'too much Asia' in her (p. 242), a former businessman who takes up 'the negative gospel of anti-semitism' (p. 683) and similar types representing both the conventional *haut bourgeoisie* and exotic fringe of European civilisation of the time. In a general atmosphere of idleness and quest, some dabble in astrology (p. 369). Others gossip at the dining-table about 'astral bodies' and 'doubles', etheric or otherwise (p. 151). There is a vogue at one point for 'spiritualist' sessions, in which a 'medium' conjures up voices from the dead, including Chaldean (p. 664). An ex-lawyer devotes his efforts to 'squaring the circle'

(p. 629). Castorp himself, once a reputable engineer, takes to laying out cards at random 'to have a tussle with abstract chance' (p. 633).

A 'winter carnival' is described in terms of a *Walpurgisnacht* (p. 322; cf. Goethe). Toward the red-haired Russian woman (shades of Madame Blavatsky?[6]), Castorp feels a 'magnetic attraction' (p. 142), in spite of *déclassé* elements in her, even a faint atmosphere of 'evil'. Meanwhile, the populace at large gives itself over to inventions of modern science described in 'magical' terms. Thus there are expeditions to the Bioscope Theatre (cinema), which 'annihilates' all constraints of space and time to create mesmeric illusion (pp. 316–17); also long evenings around the gramophone, which can 'shroud the vulgar horror of actual fact with a veil of beauty' but whose 'vibrations, so surprisingly powerful in the near neighbourhood of the box, soon exhausted themselves, grew weak and eerie with distance, like all magic' (p. 642).

Mann fully intends a genial *reductio ad absurdam* in many of these elements. Quoting Goethe on *Faust*, he describes his novel as 'a very serious jest' (p. 721). Nor is the least matter jested about the treatment these 'pilgrims' have come to their mountaintop shrine for. The sanatorium flies 'a fancy flag, green and white, with the caduceus, the emblem of healing, in the centre' (p. 39). The twined serpents are also a symbol of Hermes; and the taking of temperature – central rite in the overall medical programme – is described time and again in terms of divining 'the whims of Mercurius' (pp. 169, 199, 225, 233, etc.).

The head doctor, Hofrat Behrens, is moved at one point to remark, 'We're not magicians' (p. 177); but the fact that he feels obliged to deny as much indicates the comparison. The X-ray lab, an 'artificially lighted room' full of 'stale ozone', is called 'a technological witches' kitchen' (p. 214). In setting the machine to work, the Hofrat declares, 'The magicking is about to begin' (p. 216). To Castorp's trepidation, he replies, 'Spooky, what? Yes, there's something distinctly spooky about it' (p. 219); and, discussing the finished photo of the man's chest, he reveals his peculiar form of monism. This is a Vitruvian reductionism which considers that – since philology, pedagogy and theology all have to do with man and 'the idea of form lies at the bottom of every sort of humanistic calling' – study of and work at the perfection of individual physical bodies is the great pursuit (pp. 259–64).

Here we have a nice medical equivalent to Blavatsky's doctrine 'MAN KNOW THY SELF';[7] even more to Yeats's idea in 'The Phases of the Moon' in *A Vision* that 'All dreams of the soul end – In a beautiful man's or woman's body'.[8] The self-concern thus played on by the Hofrat links to the narcissism of semi-'sick' types who would gravitate to cults. Similar narcissism is played to by the other principal physician–'magician' in Mann's microcosm. This is the 'devilishly clever' Dr Krokowski (p. 9), who 'psycho-analyses the patients' if they wish and whose 'powers' are so attractive that even Castorp's usually hard-headed cousin proselytises in their favour: 'You ought not to have refused the treatment so brusquely,' Joachim chides, 'at least not the psychical' (p. 17).

Krokowski's 'proper field of study is the night' (p. 64). Like Freud, he naturally concentrates on dreams. Like Jung, he impresses female admirers by lectures on 'the power of love' (p. 126). Inflation in his own personality is revealed when he ends one of these lectures by taking an unconscious posture of Christ on the cross (p. 130). Always obsessed with 'catacombish' interests, he eventually begins exploring the 'frankly supernatural: hypnotism, somnambulism, telepathy, "dreaming true" and second sight' (p. 653). Where Behrens' monism was physiological, Krokowski's is psychical. He comes to believe that 'matter may be influenced by psychic forces' (p. 668). Poltergeists are among various types of 'biopsychical projections of subconscious complexes into the objective' which may appear in this way.

We are in the realm here of Blavatsky's 'phenomena',[9] or of a celebrated 'spirit-photograph' of Yeats which shows the ethereal shadow of a young girl emanating from the poet's skull.[10] In the chapter 'Highly Questionable', Mann shows Krowkowski's lectures leading into the general fascination with 'spiritism'. 'The province of the subconscious, "occult" in the proper sense of the word, very soon shows itself to be occult in the narrower sense as well' (p. 654). Thus Mann identifies the 'revolutionary' medical science of the twentieth century with its medieval 'magical' roots, cutting the former down to size and suggesting more sense to the latter than is commonly ascribed. It is a position typical of great literature: the new is regarded with scepticism, the old with less than conventional temporal prejudice, and both with 'equilibrating' irony.

Modern medicine in this way becomes part of Mann's 'magic'. However, in spite of the medical context of the novel's 'plot' (sickness to health in a sanatorium), it is not finally the centre of interest. More important to true health, thus true 'magic', for Mann are morality and metaphysics. Therefore the principal influences on Hans Castorp are not those who 'treat' him in the received manner of the age, but those who 'proselytise for [his] soul' (p. 513).

The chief hierophant, as said, is Settembrini. This Italian man of letters is introduced in a chapter called 'Satana' (p. 57). Later Mann describes him as 'the protagonist of the protest against the moral perils of the *Liegekur* and the entire unwholesome milieu . . . a sympathetic figure, indeed, with a humourous side' (p. 724). Settembrini's position is indeed ambiguous, as these apparently contrasting descriptions would suggest. His arguments with Naphta are what propel Castorp toward his escape from the 'hermetic' atmosphere and near-death in 'Snow'. No innocent bystander, the Italian has positively encouraged the young man's flight: 'Ah, your good angel must have whispered you the thought. . . . I would be at your side, on winged feet, like Mercury's. . . . By all means pull the wool over the eyes of your Prince of Shadows' (p. 474).

Settembrini's faiths beyond 'Life and Literature' are 'Form and Freedom' (p. 158), *'ragione* and *ribellione'* (p. 478). To him, the 'Word' (p. 113) and *'esprit'* (p. 519) are the great goods. Speech is 'civilisation itself' (p. 518), and civilisation an ideal toward which all good men should strive. He believes in 'illumination' (p. 193) and amelioration (p. 155). The intellect will triumph over super-stition, base nature and the body, which may in some respect be a joy yet is also 'obstructive matter' (p. 251). A kind of all-knowingness may be achieved (p. 151), and from it may come the dawn of universal brotherhood (p. 157). Settembrini talks about the example of Christ and 'individual democracy' (p. 289). At the same time he says to Castorp, 'Let me work on you', and seeks to interest him in the 'great work' of a proliferating, elitist 'Inter-national League for the Organisation of Progress' (pp. 244–6).

Settembrini, in short, is a Freemason; and his character reflects the maddening and appealing qualities of that sect, which Mann presents as a principal (if perhaps decadent) moving-force of the times. Settembrini displays moral arrogance (p. 295). Full of universal geniality, he nevertheless sees himself as superior to ordinary people (pp. 198–9). Mann no doubt expects us to sympathise with his advocacy of Reason over alternative modes of 'magic' ('Engineer! Confide in your God-given power of dear thought and hold in abhorrence these luxations of the brain, these miasmas of the spirit. Delusions? The mystery of life? *Caro mio!* – p. 692). But all is not clear here. In the 'Hysterica Passio' chapter near the end of the novel, we are told, 'Even the unclouded eye of the Freemason was dimmed by the prevailing spleen' (p. 689). Moreover, Settembrini contributes to Naphta's determined (and perversely persuasive) suicide, thus proving that his 'humanistic' ideal is not fully detached from terror, the irrational and blood.

I have called Naphta a 'counter-hierophant'. In every respect, he opposes Settembrini's reforming, protestant *esprit*. Sharp, ugly (p. 372), he is a converted Jew whose father was a rabbi engaged in kosher slaughter of animals. Watching this as a boy has left the man with a sense that piety and cruelty are inextricably linked (p. 443). Naptha believes in Faith above Knowledge and mocks 'Freedom' (p. 400). He is against the literary-critical spirit (p. 411), economics (p. 393) and modern materialism. Paying no lip-service to democracy, he openly enthuses over the aristocracy of the medieval Church or even the socialism of Marx (p. 448). This righteous 'revolutionary' impulse in him derives from his training in the Stella Matutina.[11] There he enjoyed a life both 'monastic' and 'manorial', which formed him into a 'warlike monk': ascetic, secretive, full of contempt for this world and the shameful husk of the mortal body, full too of the 'ghostly lust of power' of the Templars (p. 455).

For the *homo dei* (p. 390), the Unknown Absolute is all (p. 402). God is the proper study of mankind, not man. Nor does the latter necessarily contain any spark of divinity from the former (though a boyhood vision of his father's blue eyes sending out 'gleams like stars' seems to suggest the rays descending from *Ain Sof* in the Cabala – p. 440). God is pure spirit, matter entirely fallen. Naphta would be happy to practise flagellation if it would drive man's concern from the flesh (p. 455). Indeed, he approves of the old habit of burnings at the stake, which destroyed and purified the evil vessel at once (p. 457). Religion has nothing to do with reason, morality or health for him (p. 463). It is of the sphere of Eternity, not Time. There God and the devil fight; life as we know it is only a petty theatre of their operations, and one to which both are opposed. Thus Naphta may welcome earthly chaos (p. 454). Nor does he accept even his own variation of the Hermetic thesis, which sums up the dynamic of sanatorium (and novel) thus: 'Man consciously and voluntarily descended into disease and madness, in search of knowledge which, acquired by fanaticism, would lead back to health' (p. 466).

Where Settembrini's contributions are marked by good humour, Naphta's have a lofty, lacerating radicalism. It is he who, in unmasking Settembrini as a Mason, argues the absurdities and hypocrisies of that cult (pp. 507–18). Essentially, these boil down to vestiges of the irrational among those who assert the power of Reason. Why, Naphta asks, should silence and obedience be required among supposed champions of 'free thought'? Why should oaths be 'sealed in blood'? Why should hierarchy and executive action be practised by partisans of 'democracy', who pretend to be no more than a 'friendly society' or 'charitable' association? Everything about Masonry is politics, Naphta argues. The art of 'master-building' is the art of government; and orthodoxy within the organisation precludes real tolerance without. From the French Revolution at least, Masonry in power has proved to be 'flabby humanitarianism hand in hand with wolfish cruelty', giving birth to bourgeois capitalism and war. Press a Mason (as Naphta's revelations will move Castorp to press Settembrini) and one will discover the opinion that too much tolerance breeds evil – indeed that metaphysics, thus finally even the vaunted pursuit of 'knowledge', distracts from the essential task of 'building the temple of society'.

By circuitous means, Naphta actually proves that Freemasonry is the equivalent in the modern age of the proscriptive Church it fought to supersede. He points out that Adam Weishaupt, head of the *Illuminati*, was an ex-Jesuit; also that it was insurgent Catholics who brought hierarchical ideas and 'strict observance' into the cult in the eighteenth century. To Naphta, the 'mummery' and Cabalism of 'Templar grades' and 'Royal Mysteries' are the most appealing part of Masonry; and he expresses contempt for their decline through the 'philistinism' of Settembrini's era. Initiations involving black halls and dark corridors are not only a source of facile mockery; they are also irrational and link Masonry back to more pristine belief-systems. 'The secrets of the lodge have, in common with certain mysteries of our Church, the clearest connection with the ceremonial mysteries and ritual excesses of primitive man.' Only here where it merges into the true occultism of love feasts, sacrificial and orgiastic rites, metaphoric excursions into realms of death, metamorphosis and resurrection, does Masonry enter the cavern of the religious soul. Only where it thus recalls its origins in rites of Isis and the Eleusinians does it possess 'magic', not in the 'common sense' aspect of its contemporary character – its 20,000 lodges around the world, 150 grand lodges and libertarian 'revolutionary' tradition, attached to bourgeois 'heroes' who were also Masons: Voltaire, Lafayette, Napoleon, Franklin, Washington, Mazzini, Garibaldi.

Naphta thus effectively takes the position of modern 'Rosicrucians' – Yeats, notably, of those discussed so far – against 'Enlightenment' precursors. He too is a romantic in revolt against the new orthodoxy of all-explaining science:

> The modern natural sciences, as dogma, rested upon the metaphysical postulate that time, space and causality, the forms of cognition, in which all phenomenon are enacted, are actual conditions, existing independently of our knowledge of them. This monistic position was an insult to the spirit. . . . Evolution . . . empiricism . . . the atom . . . anybody with a very little logic could make very merry over the theory of the endlessness and the reality of space and time; and could arrive at the result of – nothing. . . . What blasphemous rubbish, to reckon the 'distance' of any star from the earth in terms of trillions of kilometres, or in light years, or to imagine that with such a parade of figures the human spirit was gaining an insight into the essence of infinity and eternity – whereas infinity had absolutely nothing whatever to do with size, nor yet eternity with duration or distance in time; they had nothing in common with natural science, being, as they were, the abrogation of that which we call nature! . . . Naphta's malicious wit lay in ambush, to spy out the weakness of the nature-compelling forces of progress and to convict its standard-bearers and pioneers of human relapses into the irrational.   (p. 691)

To Settembrini, Naphta identifies himself (and his church) with 'the spirit that would deny', which gains significance from being how Goethe described Mephistopheles.[12] Thus, subtly, the 'counter-hierophant' is identified by the author as a second 'Satana' to tempt young Castorp. And, indeed, though Mann puts powerfully persuasive rhetoric into the Jesuit's mouth, he is no more in full agreement with it than is his self-realising hero. In the chapter 'Research' in the middle of the novel, Castorp has already asked himself deep questions on the origin of the universe and nature of the heavens, only to conclude, with semi-Gnostic pessimism, 'Life was nothing but the next step on the reckless path of the spirit dishonoured' (p. 286). But such a conclusion is no prelude to suicide, as a marginally more orthodox one would be for Naphta (or more diabolical one would be for Leverkühn in *Dr Faustus*[13]). No more than his author does Castorp discount entirely that there may be ways through this life which retain positive value, however ridiculous or self-contradictory they may seem in some attributes: 'Not for nothing do Freemasonry and its rites play a role in *The Magic Mountain*, for Freemasonry is the direct descendent of initiatory rites' (p. 726) – themselves the route to a 'Grail' whose importance is neither mocked nor questioned.

Finally, however, there is something something further of value besides self-conscious 'initiation': something more life-spirited and of this world:

> Young man – the simple – the holy. Good – you understand me. A bottle of wine, a steaming dish of eggs, pure grain spirit – let us absorb such things as these, exhaust them, satisfy their claims, before we [speak about disease or death] – Positively, sir. Not a word   (p. 564).

This is the 'philosophy' of Mynheer Peepercorn, last of Castorp's teachers, an 'anti-hierophant' whose 'power' is *personality* and whose 'religion' is the happy satisfaction of appetite:

> Life, young man, is a female. A sprawling female, with swelling breasts close to each other, great soft belly between her haunches, slender arms, bulging thighs, half-closed eyes. She mocks us. She challenges us to expend our manhood to its uttermost span, to stand or fall before her.   (p. 566)

Here is an unconscious advocate of the 'sacred magic': of real, direct and immediate rise to states of 'light', 'power' and bliss. Peepercorn's fearless confrontation of Known and Unknown, and worshipful response to whatever is before him which attracts, constitutes (whether Mann intends us to recognise it as such or not) a version of 'Middle Pillar existence' or the *Kundalini* energy of Tantric yoga.

Indeed, it is yet more direct and transcendental than what the Golden Dawn aspired toward in its second order. For Peepercorn's rise toward ecstatic experience requires no ritual at all, save generous living. He takes a collection of fellow patients out for a picnic by a gorgeous waterfall. There 'they gave themselves over to a blissful *far niente*, enlivened by scraps of conversation in which, out of sheer high spirits, no one hung back. They uttered thoughts that in the thinking had seemed primevally fresh and beautiful, but in the saying somehow turned lame' (pp. 570–1). *Knowledge* here is not a matter of study, degrees, alchemical experimentation, closely weighed good and evil or even self-conscious observation of the dance of a temple girl.[14] It is a question of simple resourcefulness: of being able to produce the perfect bottle of spirits for an occasion, to find a certain type of bark to treat a slight wound or certain type of phrase to charm a beloved out of a temporarily sad mood.

'In making a mystery of personality, you run a risk of idol-worship', Settembrini warns Castorp (p. 584). But, though the latter recognises sense in the Mason's rationale, as well as fundamental truth in Naphta's negations, his favourite 'magic' will remain the natural nobility of the great florid Dutchman, veteran of decades of South Sea trade and *aficionado* of the majestic eagle, highest flyer among the mountain's birds of prey. 'Oh, morality, and that!' Peepercorn in practical ignorance sums up:

> A subject for Naphta and Settembrini to quarrel over. It belongs to the realm of the Great Confusion. Whether one lives for oneself or for the sake of life – one doesn't know oneself, no one can know that precisely and certainly. I mean, the limits are fluid. There is egoistic devotion, and there is devoted egoism. (p. 594)

Here is Mann's most characteristic response to the subject of 'magic'. If driven to choose, he must come down, however reluctantly, in favour of Life – that is, bourgeois reality – over speculative thought, religious system or even art (as *Dr Faustus* shows yet more clearly). The latter are finally more of the realm of ill health, disease and death in Mann's metaphysic; and while they may have essential roles to play in man's long process of 'initiation' into balanced humanity, they must in the end be discarded as preliminary stages. This is the message of Castorp's descent from the mountain at last, after seven years of 'enchantment'. It is a conclusion the twentieth century may now be reaching after seven or more decades of wrestling with 'modern magic'. But that is a matter to consider only after having explored three more manifestations of the *Logos*, prominent since the turn of the century and not completely exhausted of influence today.

7

Rudolf Steiner and Anthroposophy

I PROGRESS OF A PARSIFAL

For the facts of Rudolf Steiner's earthly progress, we must depend largely on the uncompleted *Autobiography* he wrote for his disciples in the period before his death. The source is typical of such efforts by a dying 'master'[1]. History unfolds *ex post facto* as a straight march toward a preordained destiny. Unfortunate episodes are glanced over or omitted; criticism is dismissed loftily. As Geoffrey Ahern remarks, 'What is *not* stated is highly informative. Steiner scarcely mentions the erotic; nor does he publicly examine his microcosmic self for the darkness he attributes to his macrocosmic demons, Ahriman and Lucifer.'[2] While going to great lengths to describe his youthful reading, this dark-eyed, handsome yet diminutive guru maintains that his later domestic career should be 'of no concern to the public'.[3] It is an argument other 'great' men have deployed; and there is of course merit to the idea that the 'song' is more important than the 'singer' – the latter would not be heard of, after all, were it not for the former. Still, the 'song' inevitably partakes of the 'singer's' origins, financial position, loves, hates, ethical choices, success or lack thereof. If T. S. Eliot had not married a neurasthenic as his first wife, would posterity still be reading *The Waste Land*? And, if he had not left her in the way he did, would we be exposed to the strain of guilt in *The Family Reunion*?

This analogy is not entirely extrinsic. In his thirties, Steiner married a widow eight years his senior. A few years later, he left her for a younger, better-off, more worldly-wise woman with connections to theatre and the occult. The first wife provided domestic comfort and motherly support of a kind the impecunious and socially awkward Austrian of peasant stock needed to gain

139

a footing in 'Liszt's' Weimar and *fin-de-siècle* Berlin. The second provided the *nous* and ambition to propel him toward recognition in the creative *demi-monde* of Munich before the First World War. In *California Writers*, I argue that for a surprising number of artists in the modernist period, creation of the *magnum opus* coincides with a wrenching-loose from a more bourgeois first marriage and procession toward a second, more *haut-bohemien* one.[4] As this was true of Jack London, so it was also of his equally upwardly mobile contemporary. Steiner's great time of theoretical production was the first decade of this century. Marie von Sievers appeared near the beginning of it; Anna Eunicke Steiner died abandoned near the end. Steiner then married the former and went on to build his 'Wolf House', the 'Goetheanum' – or, if you prefer a German analogy from the recent past (one which Steiner's milieu would not have failed to note), having buried Minna he went on to marry Cosima and build his personal Bayreuth.

A study of Steiner and his women might be a profitable addition to the apparently endless tomes by and about the man, most of which eschew fact to follow the ethereal style he developed in 6000 lectures delivered in the last two decades of his life. Marie Steiner outlived her husband by twenty years, inherited his copyrights and disaffected many fellow Anthroposophists by the way she chose to publish posthumous materials.[5] This caused the most important schism in an otherwise loose but quite unified movement. Another rift was brought on by the Dutch Anthroposophist Ita Wegman, who contended that Steiner believed that he and she had been connected in a past life as the Assyrian hero Gilgamesh and his beloved Eabani.[6] Whether this tireless eccentric in flowing cravats ever consummated an affair with Wegman or other female followers is not known. Certainly he enjoyed the company of admiring women as much as his contemporary (and in some ways rival) the 'Gnostic' psychologist Jung.[7] But Steiner's character and doctrines suggest chastity along the traditional lines of a Cathar 'pure' more than Jung's brand of genial semi-promiscuity. On the other hand, Steiner's own 'Gnosticism' did lead him to join Theodor Reuss's Order of Oriental Templars (OTO), a Masonic group which practised 'sex magic' (variants of Tantric yoga) and later would be taken over by Aleister Crowley.[8]

This association came in the early years of Steiner's break-out from his first marriage and scholarly shy persona. So too did his membership of the Esoteric Section of the Theosophical Society, which one commentator suggests may have dabbled in 'sex magic' as well.[9] Perhaps sudden 'liberation' from solitude and repression may have led Steiner to 'adventures'. Disaffected associates would later claim as much; also that Anthroposophy's inner circle continued to practise dubious rites.[10] To defuse these charges, Steiner wrote in his *Autobiography* that he only ever joined the OTO to find out what was going on in other occult groupings of the time.[11] This may be true. Like a writer, musician or other 'creative' person, an occultist must be allowed periods of exploration, imitation and theft. Steiner's association with 'magical' Masonry should be seen as analogous to Yeats's with Theosophy, Crowley's with the Golden Dawn, and Ron Hubbard's with Crowleyanity. More substantive, however, was his association with Theosophy, which he became head of in Germany in 1903 (in part through the efforts of Fräulein von Sievers) and left in 1912 after the dispute with Annie Besant over the cult of Krishnamurti.[12]

The Theosophical Society connection had begun in 1900, when Steiner was invited to address the Berlin 'lodge' on the philosophy of Nietzsche. Later he was invited back to talk on the esoteric meaning of Goethe's fairytale 'The Green Snake and the Beautiful Lily'.[13] Nearly forty, he was by that time a fairly well-known academic and writer, having spent the past decade editing the scientific writings of Goethe and the *Magazin für Literatur*. Already, however, he had bemused many by his compulsion to promote 'the spiritual' – 'It was always the same in those days', he lamented. 'I had to come to terms with everything that concerned my spiritual perception entirely alone.'[14] His awareness of a special destiny perhaps emanated from an early 'initiation' he spoke of to Edouard Schuré.[15] This had been at the hand of the mysterious 'M', perhaps related to the 'Book M' of Christian Rosenkreuz or the Mahatmas of Blavatsky, but in any case described as anticlerical, clairvoyant, strong, masculine and an advocate of 'slipping into the skin of the dragon, the spirit of the materialistic modern age, in order to understand and so overcome it'. This advice may explain Steiner's emphasis on what he regarded as a modern, scientific approach when talking about the most medieval, unscientific ideas. ('I was convinced that one must speak about the spirit, but one must have regard for the customary forms of expression in this scientific age.'[16]) It also sheds light on why he sought to challenge Haeckel's Darwinism early and Jung's psychoanalysis later with his 'spiritual science'. This derived in large part from Goethe's preference for 'deductive' over 'inductive' thinking.

How Plato and Goethe had arrived at their ideas was a question which had obsessed Steiner since school days.[17] Both 'great initiates' believed in the existence of archetypal forms independent of human consciousness. To a sceptical Schiller, Goethe had described what he called the *Urpflanze*: the eternal type of the perfect plant toward which all physical plants aspired.[18] How else could one explain the shapes natural matter took but by such a super-natural *idea*? Likewise, how might one explain the entrance of moral concepts into the psyche but by the existence of archetypes of the Good, the Beautiful and the True? Steiner himself had long felt 'intimations of immortality'.[19] This made it impossible for him to accept 'reductive' biology which explained man's morphological development in terms of functional improvements on the ape, or a science of the mind which treated imaginative flights as manifestations of infantile trauma. A hand of destiny was moving behind events. Steiner refers to it in his *Autobiography* ('I cannot but recognise that destiny so guided me that . . .'[20]) with the same sort of regularity as Hitler does in his simultaneously written *Mein Kampf*.[21] All the same, Steiner was also a passionate advocate of 'Freedom'. This concept he refined after meeting the second great literary god of his youth (also an icon of the Nazis, for different reasons), Nietzsche.

Of the 'mad' philosopher Steiner wrote, 'His outlook both attracted and repelled me. . . . I loved his style. I loved his boldness. . . . His disposition of attitude and soul was cultivated as something representing in a certain sense the flower of true and free humanity.'[22] Nietzsche was admirable for having broken through all preconceived dogma. Higher, invisible realms had proved inaccessible for his realistic persona, however; thus the breakthrough had led toward nihilism.[23] Steiner, in no doubt that higher realms existed, felt himself well-placed to lead on where Nietzsche had left off. Though equally alienated from the age as it stood, he would not retreat into an isolated 'Zarathustra' persona. His turning-inward would be to move upward through ever-ascending realms of *idea*, peopled with elemental and daemonic 'guardians'. Through organisation, he would lead like-minded seekers to these realms, which since early childhood had seemed more real to him than mere attributes of the sense world.[24] Thus, instead of just seeing physical bodies, Steiner would teach how to contemplate 'auras'. Instead of just listening to words, his followers would learn to 'read' the 'true spirit' behind speech. Instead of merely fixing dream images into compensatory subconscious formulae, they would follow evanescent shadows on to deeper levels of 'objective' spiritual awareness.

Thus Steiner's brand of 'Freedom'. In many ways, it is typical of an age when the 'inner' and abstract were rebelling against naturalistic fact. Applied to the arts, such ideas have much in common with modernist thinking, from Symbolism to Proust to Expressionism and Kandinsky, who would acknowledge Anthroposophical inspiration.[25]

> The path followed by the true artist [Steiner wrote] is a path to the living spirit. He starts from what is physically perceptible, but he transforms it. And what guides him is not a merely subjective impulse; rather he tries to impart to the sense-perceptible a form that makes it appear as if the spirit itself were visible. I said to myself that the beautiful is not an idea given the form of something sense-perceptible, but the sense-perceptible given the form of something spiritual. . . . At this time I became aware of the interrelation of true knowledge, the spirituality manifest in art, and man's moral will. . . . I saw a centre where man is altogether *at one* with the Absolute Primordial Being of the World.[26]

Compare this, for instance, to Yeats's desire to create a poem which would embody the *Spiritus Mundi;* or Joyce's in *Finnegans Wake* to synthesise the archetypal dream-speech of the race. Steiner's own literary-artistic urge would express itself most in his plays, as we shall see. But Anthroposophy at large was the most dedicated of occultisms to a pervasive 'artistic' approach. This is apparent in the eccentric statuary, murals and architecture of the Goetheanum; also in the free-form cosmic dance (eurythmy) and speech-training Steiner developed in connection with his second wife. Indeed, an 'artistic' approach extends into Anthroposophical science. There the urge to discern an essential spirit behind sense translates into a 'holistic' attempt to discern the *Urpflanze* behind the individual plant in 'biodynamic' gardening, or the essential 'I' behind the handicapped child in remedial Camphill Villages.

This urge to keep the largest context in view with the smallest situation leads to some of the most attractive aspects of Steiner's legacy. Most well-known and widespread are the Waldorf Schools, with their 'organic' belief in educating the 'whole individual', not just his body and routinised sections of his mind but also his transcendent spirit.[27] Less known but highly regarded in the aftermath of the First World War was Steiner's socio-economic programme for a 'threefold commonwealth', in which a 'spiritual—cultural' function for mankind would exist in equality and harmony with a 'rights-body', distinguished by 'independence, impartiality and democracy', and an 'economic function', made up of associations of producers, distributors and consumers, with a currency based on perishable wheat rather than hard ('Ahrimanic') gold.[28] Most influential of all may turn out to be Anthroposophical efforts to de-dogmatise medicine and pay more attention to the head–heart–limbs balance in physical man and possibilities of treatment through 'dynamised' and 'potentised' infusions of a homoeopathic ('like cures like') nature, as well as herbal remedies and even astral influences of a type believed in by Paracelsus and medieval witchcraft.[29] In common with other 'progressives' of his age, Steiner was also a vegetarian, though an undogmatic one ('It is better to eat meat than to *think* meat'[30]). His own recommended diet apparently included 'two litres of emulsion of almonds and fruits that grow in the air'.[31]

As any glance at his bibliography will show,[32] the man was a polymath. Was he also a megalomaniac? The occultist Count Keyserling, whose farm Steiner is said to have rid of rabbits, believed he had a 'tremendous lust for power'.[33] Perhaps Keyserling was envious. By the 1920s, with a cult growing around him and his shrine of the Goetheanum being built, burnt to the ground and rebuilt,[34] Steiner had become the most prominent new messiah in Europe. Originally little more than a mystic, he was now pursued by cranks and true believers as a prophet. Perhaps he responded too readily to too many questions. Kafka consulted him about asthma and was unimpressed by his advice;[35] others have pointed out inaccuracies in his facts.[36] Steiner seems to have put excessive faith in his intuitive 'powers'. Still, he never became authoritarian or gave up essential belief in the need for openness of knowledge and freedom in individual growth. Yet, more than Blavatsky, he sought to bring 'secret doctrine' out of inner temples and into the larger world. Toward the end he did set up an inner 'School of Spiritual Science' for Anthroposophy;[37] but, though structurally analogous to the Esoteric Section of the Theosophical

Society, this was designed less to 'harden' the cult through discipline and dogma than to provide it with a vanguard of minds and methods to continue pursuit of the ever-dissipating and reforming lightness, warmth and motion of *ideas* streaming down on man from higher levels.

II MACROCOSM

Steiner's cosmogony derived from the Theosophical Society but differed in nomenclature, detail and moral thrust. Like Besant and Leadbeater, he claimed to be able to 'read' the Akashic Record.[38] From this, he discovered that universal history began with a 'timeless state' of pure spirit, called 'Crystal Heaven'. Through the aeons, spirit 'densified', creating solar systems. The life of our system would extend through seven epochs, of which we are living in the fourth. The first epoch was 'Old Saturn', in which matter was 'undifferentiated' but began to take physical form through the rotations of two hierarchies of spirits: Love, Harmony and Will (the Seraphim, Cherubim and Thrones of Dionysus the Areopagite); and Wisdom, Movement and Form (the Dominions, Virtues and Powers). After the period of *pralaya* (cosmic repose) which divides all epochs, 'Old Saturn' gave way to 'Old Sun', in which the process of differentiation proceeded as hierarchical rotations created 'etheric' forms of light and warmth. At this time, a third spiritual hierarchy began to make itself felt: the Principalities, Archangels and Angels affecting the lower cosmos. Then another *pralaya* occurred. Then came the epoch of 'Old Moon', in which 'astral' forms emerged and the hierarchical rotations created 'duality', manifesting itself not only in oppositions of night and day, sleep and waking, and so on, but also in the appearance of 'evil' hierarchies presided over by the insurgent spirits Lucifer and Ahriman. Our own epoch of 'Earth' has followed a third *pralaya*. In this epoch, spirit descending reaches its densest incarnation in matter and, having done so, begins to ascend toward pure spirit again.[39]

Like other epochs, ours is subdivided into seven 'cultural' sub-epochs. The first three of these – the Polarian, Hyperborean and Lemurian – recapitulated in Earthly and human terms the cosmic devlopments of Old Saturn, Old Sun and Old Moon. Primeval spiritual instinct gradually eroded as life became defined more densely. This 'hardening' produced rebellion against the original hierarchies. At the end of the Lemurian period, men gave themselves to Luciferic influences of self-aggrandisement, and a great catastrophe like the 'Fall' in the Bible occurred. Similarly, at the end of the next (Atlantean) period, men gave themselves to Ahrimanic forces of material acquisition[40] and, as a consequence, were taken unawares, by what in the Bible appears as the 'Flood'. At present, we are in the Post-Atlantean epoch. Like the rest, this has seven further, 'historical', sub-divisions. The first, centred on India, was illumined by a handful of Sun Oracle initiates who had survived the destruction of Atlantis.[41] The second, in Persia, saw an increase in the use of Nature to serve man.[42] The third, in Egypt and Chaldea, saw yet further immersion in matter and dependence on the senses. The fourth, in Greece and Rome, saw this process of 'materialisation' continue to a point which 'would have led to a final triumph for the Ahrimanic and Luciferic hierarchies, had it not been for the incarnation of Christ, the archetypal "I" '.[43]

According to Steiner (and this is his most notable departure from Theosophical Society lore), the Christ 'event' forms the keystone in a reverse arch of cultural and cosmic evolution.[44] Having been initiated into 'Esoteric Christianity' in Berlin shortly before taking over the German Theosophical Society,[45] Steiner developed a reading of the divine myth similar to that of Lévi, Wagner and other believers in the imminence of an 'age of the Paraclete'.[46] It goes something like this: at the time the boy Jesus visited the temple, a Hebraic 'Wisdom' persona fused with a Buddhistic 'Love' persona to create the biblical character as we know him. In the years not covered by Gospel accounts, this Jesus wandered through India, Persia, Egypt, Babylon, Chaldea and Greece, learning the lore of mystery-cults, becoming a 'great initiate' (perhaps through Essenes[47]) and seeing at first hand the dangers awaiting mankind through his temptation by Satan (Lucifer/Ahriman). At thirty, at the moment of his baptism, Jesus opened himself to Christ: a 'lofty Being of the Sun'[48] whom he intuited to be descending from the upper hierarchies to relieve man's 'spiritual darkness'. Through three years of miracles and messianic acts, this spirit became one with the 'holy grail' of Jesus's body. The union was broken only at the moment of crucifixion, when the dying mortal cried out, 'My God, why has thou forsaken me?' As Jesus died, Christ ascended, having learned at first hand the pain man must undergo at being 'trapped' in finite matter. The message left behind was the ancient one subscribed to by anti-materialist Gnostics: as spirit may descend into matter which dies, so too it must ascend out of matter to 'live'. Thus it is even more important to attend to the spiritual realm 'above' than to attend to the natural (fallen) world 'below'.

In this variation on Hermetic doctrine, Steiner reveals the same bias as Yeats: the twentieth-century 'mage' must propaganise for spirit over 'science', reversing the process of the seventeenth-century. So much is reflected in Steiner's discussion of the fifth, or 'Rosicrucian', cultural epoch, which we are still living through. This period is characterised by the efforts of initiates from previous periods (including since the fourth epoch Orphics, Eleusinians and Pythagoreans) to achieve a rebalance between intuitive awareness and fascination with natural matter. During our part of this period, presided over by the Archangel Michael (the *Zeitgeist*),[49] interest in imaginative arts and 'secret doctrine' increases. This sets the tone for the sixth cultural epoch, in which the process of 'respiritualisation' will accelerate until there is a 'second coming'. By this, Steiner means incorporation of 'knowledge of the Holy Grail' into individuals. So much will establish the 'third age' at last. It will be followed by the seventh and last cultural epoch of our Earth period. This will end in cataclysmic events like those which destroyed Atlantis and Lemuria, taking down with them all who have not experienced the 'Grail' evolution.

A period of *pralaya* will follow; then the three final cosmic epochs – Jupiter, Venus and Vulcan. In these will be recapitulated in reverse order the physical, etheric and astral developments of Old Saturn, Old Sun and Old Moon. Thus physical form will cease to exist in Jupiter, etheric in Venus, and astral in Vulcan. These will be replaced by what Steiner calls the 'Spirit Self', 'Life Spirit' and 'Spirit Man'. Individuals will be repatriated, as it were, to the upper hierarchies – unless of course they exercise their 'free will' and join with Lucifer and Ahriman in opposing evolution, in which case they will drop out of the ascent, like wayward Lemurians, Atlanteans and Earthlings before them. At last, a great 'eternal return'[50] will be accomplished; and the planets – following human, animal and plant life – will be subsumed into vast, swirling hierarchies of spirit, dissipating out into new 'chains of being' (solar systems) throughout 'Crystal Heaven'.

An inspired vision! Of course, it is no more or less true than

Blavatsky/Besant descriptions of 'Devachan', in which Steiner also believed. But, whereas few were surprised by their 'fairytale' excursions into quasi-Eastern myth, many would find such ideas hard to swallow from a man who began his career extolling hard 'scientific' method and broke with the Theosophical Society because it was insufficiently 'Western'. 'Having followed [Steiner] with interest through [writings] which reveal an extremely well-balanced, logical and comprehensive mind,' Maeterlinck wrote, 'we ask ourselves [in coming on Atlantis, Lemuria and the rest] if he has suddenly gone mad or we are dealing with a hoaxer.'[51] The latter is unlikely. Steiner lacked the 'trickster' tendency which enlivened and subverted Blavatsky. To his credit, he lacked the para-fascistic bent of Besant as well. But he did have in common with his most famous occult-minded and organisationally fixated Austrian contemporary (Hitler) what one English reviewer would describe as 'infernal sincerity'.[52] This characteristic, so native to his time and place yet so unleavened by an equally Germanic irony such as redeems 'astral' travels in Hesse,[53] for example, might force us even more than with the original Theosophical Society 'seers' to conclude that Steiner mistook his fantasies for fact.

Defending the man on this score, Francis King argues that 'Steiner's cosmogony and history . . . is a psychic truth in the Jungian sense' and should be neither accepted nor rejected as 'objectively true' but read as sensible contemporary Christians read Genesis: as a splendid metaphor.[54] Steiner spoke 'synecdochically', King adds: he offered 'part for the whole' – a taste of the truth, as it were, rather than the 'real thing', which after all would be impossible to convey. This argument should please modernist minds which, following Kant, believe that reality is ultimately 'unknowable'. But Steiner himself rejected the pessimism flowing from Kant's thesis: 'To speak of limits of knowledge had no sense for me.'[55] Nor does he give any indication that he expected his Akashic 'readings' to be taken as less than explicit.[56] Thus, whatever the comforts of King's defence for those who admire Steiner's achievements in agriculture, education and medicine and want to put faith in his general good sense, it can be no more acceptable to 'strict constructionist' Anthroposophists than Darwin to their 'fundamentalist' Christian cousins.

III MICROCOSM

Regarding individual development, Steiner again recycled much Theosophical Society lore – though, since the break with Besant, his most readable work on the subject has been prefaced by this disclaimer:

At first glance the title of this book [*Theosophy*] may be somewhat misleading. . . . It may suggest associations with Anglo-Indian Theosophy and the Theosophical Society founded by H. P. Blavatsky. . . . Rudolf Steiner, however, used the term independently and with different and much wider connection. In earlier centuries, particularly in Central Europe, 'Theosophy' was a recognised section of Philosophy and even of Theology. Jacob Boehme was known as 'the great theosopher'. In English the term goes back to the seventeenth century [as does 'Anthroposphy', coming from Thomas Vaughan's *Anthroposophia Theomagica* (1650)[57]]. . . . Ultimately it leads back to St. Paul who says (I Cor ii. 6–7): 'Howbeit we speak wisdom among them that are perfect: Yet not the wisdom of this world. . . . But we speak the wisdom of God (Greek 'Theosophia') in a mystery, even the hidden wisdom which God ordained before the world unto our glory.'[58]

In this way, Anthroposophists attach their leader's work to older traditions of Western mysticism, both ortho– and heterodox (the Paulicians and Hermeticists), thus distancing his 'Central European' (pan-Germanic) activities from an 'Anglo-Indian' marriage of opportunism and solipsism which seemed to characterise those he came to rival.[59] Steiner's position was that he arrived at the 'secrets' of Theosophy long before joining the organisation and only joined in order to give this lead battalion of occultism in his time a more 'Rosicrucian' ethos.[60] The argument seems both true and a rationalisation after the fact. At worst, it sounds like Ron Hubbard's argument that he only became involved in Crowleyanity in order to 'break up black magic in America';[61] and one of the least attractive aspects of Steiner is that – more like Hubbard than the others we are discussing – he built his cult on the myth that revelation sprang from his skull like Athena from Zeus, not out of synthesis of others' ideas.

Theosophy is a case in point. Written as Steiner was settling in as head of the German Theosophical Society, it reads in many places like an autodidact's digest of writings of Blavatsky and Besant. To begin with, Steiner divides man into three parts: *body*, which deals through the senses with given facts; *soul*, which deals through desires with whatever has particular meaning to the individual; and *spirit*, which deals through the intellect and other 'supersensible' capacities with the goals toward which the individual strives (p. 18). The purpose of life is for the soul to exert itself so that the 'inner man' may reach the 'supersensible' world (p. 8). The 'inner man' is the true 'I': the 'soul-kernel', 'Ego', or what Besant called 'the Thinker'. This 'I' is the central one of seven constituents through which man as microcosm develops, in analogy to how the macrocosm develops through seven 'epochs'. Thus, roughly equating to Old Saturn, Old Sun and Old Moon are man's physical, etheric and astral bodies. 'I' equates to Earth. Jupiter, Venus and Vulcan find their counterparts in the 'Spirit-self as transmuted astral body', 'Life-spirit as transmuted etheric body' and 'Spirit-man as transmuted physical body' (p. 43).

Placed in the middle, 'I' forms the principal point of tension between forces of the material world working upwards and spiritual working downwards. In striving toward the latter, 'I' may develop through initiation techniques of 'Imagination', having to do with the head and inner self; 'Inspiration', having to do with the heart and afterlife; and 'Intuition', having to do with the limbs and 'spiritual history'.[62] These all lift the soul toward realms of *thought* and *idea*, which are 'the substance out of which Spirit is woven'. Thought and idea manifest themselves as (1) remembrance of individual experiences, feelings and emotions; (2) artistic, scientific or technological 'visions'; and (3) intimations of eternal laws of the Good and the True (p. 51). Aspiration toward increasingly higher forms of thought leads the soul through seven developmental 'regions', which having been mastered may be left behind. These are: (1) Desires, (2) Flowing Susceptibilities, (3) Wishes, (4) Attraction and Repulsion, (5) Soul-Light, (6) Active Soul-Force, and eventually – after many incarnations presumably – (7) Soul-Life proper, which 'frees man from any lingering attachments to the physical world' (p. 79).

Through the lower of these 'regions', the 'I' remains manipulable: potential victim of what Lévi called the 'astral light'. Through the higher, he becomes a potential manipulator. But, in passing through the 'threshold' and overcoming its 'lesser guardians'

Lucifer and Ahriman, man should grow permeated with 'sympathy', making him ever 'more free; illumining and quickening'. By the time he has reached the 'greater guardian' of Christ, thought and idea will have come to direct his activity almost entirely. They will appear to him now in myriad shapes, colours, tastes, sounds, all mixing and/or delineating forces at work in 'the eternal world of forms'. Elementary constituents of these are what medieval magicians described as salamanders, sylphs, undines and gnomes (p. 118). Also present are archetypes of the 'Nation-Spirit' and *Zeitgeist*, governing place and time. Amid such 'beings', man works to establish dynamic balance. If he achieves this, he may become absolutely healthy and absolutely capable of assigning all things to their proper places. Pleasure and displeasure, joy and pain will be revealed to him as ultimately neutral: merely *opportunities* to learn more about the nature of things (p. 137). Death itself will appear as just one more 'portal' to quest and initiation.

As regards death, Steiner taught that the pain of separation from the physical body would last only 'until the soul has learned not to long any more for what can only be satisfied through [that] body' (p. 84). There will be a transitional period before rebirth, in which the 'I' may assess what it needs to perfect itself further. Generally, this will lead on to a new life more pure than the last. But in some cases the urge may appear to develop through hardship: 'The Soul [which] sees, as it were, that an imperfection has clung to it from earlier earth-lives . . . [will] become imbued with the tendency to plunge into a misfortune in the coming earth-life in order, through enduring it, to bring about compensation' (p. 154). Here is one face of the law of *karma*, so central to the Theosophical Society. It and reincarnation in general are equally central to Steiner's doctrine, whatever his protests about the primacy of Western over Eastern ideas. Regarding cultural rise and fall, he clearly drew optimism from Christ's 'intervention', which he saw to promise continued renewal of spiritual awareness. But, as regards personal death, his courage derived less from a sense of God-as-son intervening to propitiate 'sin', or of 'heaven' being arrived at via 'good works', than from this Theosophical Society belief, Hindu in origin, that each mortal life is only one of many stages in a soul's journey on the 'weary wheel of becoming'.[63]

Those who believe in karma must believe in *destiny*, Blavatsky

taught.[64] Those who believe in destiny generally feel free from
doubt that what happens to them is arbitrary or wasteful. This
kind of fatalism is in Steiner, as said. However, it is not used to
justify an attitude of Che sarà, sarà. We have seen, for instance,
that Steiner taught that those who do not take the 'Holy Grail'
into themselves in the sixth Earthly epoch will pass away in the
cataclysms of the seventh. A residue of Protestant 'election'
remains here. But man has the 'free will' to blow it: to 'drop
out' of the eternal ameliorating process. Still, the pattern overall
remains predestined – and optimistic enough to offer converts the
comfort that all will be well in the end. The 'faith' depends heavily
too on the old Hermetic doctrine of analogy: 'that which is above
is like that which is below' – or, in this case, that which is unseen
is bound to reproduce processes quantifiable in scientific fact.
Thus Steiner's most persuasive arguments in favour of multiple,
improving lives for the soul are that, (1) as physical man is born
out of physical parents and produces physical children in whom
traits are carried on, so spiritual man might be expected to do the
same; and, (2) as physical evolution of this sort has raised man
from primitive, animal-like origins, so spiritual evolution must be
progressing as well.

That each man has an independent spiritual ancestry is a precept
again shared with the Theosophical Society. We have mentioned,
for instance, how Besant believed she was a reincarnation of Giordano Bruno and advanced Krishnamurti as the latest in a series
of incarnations of the Christly Lord Maitreya.[65] Being a German
however, and of the generation of Spengler and Mann, Steiner
danced on the head of this pin yet more elaborately. Not only
does he claim that the 'Wisdom' Jesus was the same spiritual entity
as Solomon and Zarathustra, but also he suggests that Novalis was
a reincarnation of the spirit of Raphael, who was a reincarnation of
John the Baptist, who was a reincarnation of Elijah.[66] The Baptist
was also reincarnated as the risen Lazarus and became the author
of the Johannine Gospel and Book of Revelation.[67] Closer in time,
Karl Marx was once 'a warlike Frenchman who often went off
plundering his neighbours'.[68] Nietzsche ended as he did because
in a previous life he had been a self-flagellating Franciscan monk.[69]
And General Helmut von Möltke, whose interest in Steiner caused
the latter much trouble with the Nazis, had in prior form been a
medieval pope who had 'denied' the 'Individual Spirit', thus

helping to inaugurate six centuries of man's descent into the 'abyss' of the material.[70]

The core of the idea here is that at least some 'individualities' persist through time. They are, in Steiner's words, the 'instrumentalities' which ensure the 'onflowing stream of man's evolution'.[71] In them we may 'dimly glimpse the workings of deep spiritual powers': the 'Mahatmas' of Blavatsky, 'secret chiefs' of Mathers, 'Great White Brotherhood' of *Zanoni* or – further back still – guardian angels and 'hierophants' of medieval romance. In succeeding ages, these 'spiritual powers' dress themselves in appropriate physical guise. Thus the myth that the Comte de Saint-Germain was the same being as Christian Rosenkreuz is not incredible, though the two lived (if at all) four centuries apart. 'The living are the dead on holiday', Maeterlinck would write, tongue slipping swiftly toward cheek.[72] 'Death doesn't exist, but the devil does', a young contemporary occultist remarked to me, having just read a book on Lucifer and Ahriman. How is one supposed to respond to such thinking? To many, it must seem paradoxical in the extreme, if not an out-and-out 'hoax': both mildly diverting in a parlour-game manner ('What century would you like to have lived in? Whom do you most identify with in history?') and possibly dangerous (Himmler 'reincarnating' Teutonic Knights in the SS; Hitler as a modern version of the Klingsorian Landulf of Capua[73]).

But Steiner never doubted that there are eternal 'thought forms' or 'spirits', whether for good or evil, which exist independent of their incarnation in matter. That these might be 'invoked' by ritual and 'sympathetic' forces is a standard 'magical' idea, subscribed to by the Golden Dawn and practised not least by Crowley, as we shall see. That a 'magician' should be able to predict (if not influence) the incarnation of personality archetypes is a logical corollary deduction. Jung believed in the existence of such types, if not a chartable pattern for their recurrence.[74] Yeats undertook, via the 'medium' of his wife, to come up with a pattern in *A Vision* and thereby cast light on the waxings and wanings of history. That Yeats should have attempted this at the same time as Steiner was ending his career with an exhaustive series of lectures on 'karmic relationships'[75] may be no coincidence. Many survivors of the Golden Dawn looked to Steiner for direction as their cult declined. These included the head of the Stella Matutina branch, to which both Yeatses belonged.[76] Georgie Yeats was one of eight Golden

Dawn members to join Anthroposophy in England before the First World War.[77] And Steiner himself, following the footsteps of Bruno (whom he, like Besant, identified with),[78] delivered some of his most applicable lectures at Oxford, where the Yeatses were living at the time.

IV　SCHURÉ AND INITIATORY THEATRE

The Golden Dawn pursued enlightenment through meditation exercises, using 'tattvas', Enochian squares, colours, talismans, symbols, invocations and of course rituals, which themselves were elaborated into minor theatrical events. Steiner taught use of 'mental exercises' involving Imagination, Inspiration and Intuition, as mentioned; also eurythmy, speech-training, expressive painting, sculpting and a variety of other 'artistic' pursuits. As Golden Dawn ritual gave birth to public performances of the rites of Isis by Mathers and his wife, so Steiner's techniques led naturally toward ritual drama as a central focus of Anthroposophy. This was in large part the 'child' of Steiner's relationship with his second wife, Marie, who had studied to be an actress in Paris in the 1890s but was blocked from a career by her *haut-bourgeois* Russian family, which thought acting 'bohemian'. In Paris, Marie had been put off by frivolous and naturalistic trends in the arts, much as Steiner would be in Berlin.[79] The one writer whose work she found congenial was Edouard Schuré, the early French Theosophist. Ever an admirer of spiritual women, Schuré took Marie under his wing; and eventually she became translator of his works into German. These included the influential *Great Initiates* (1889); also critical appreciations of Wagner and novels with titles such as *The Angel and the Sphinx*, *The Double* and *The Priestess of Isis*.

Marie introduced Steiner to Schuré at a Theosophical congress in Paris in 1906. Artist-*manqué* that he was, the Austrian polymath was no doubt already impressed by this exuberant Alsatian who held similar attitudes to his yet expressed them in more mellifluous prose. No doubt Steiner had read with interest Schuré's celebrated introduction to *The Great Initiates*, which had identified the 'evil of the times' as 'the hostility between science and religion'; materialism, positivism and scepticism as 'false concepts of truth and progress'; Aryanism, the Vedas, Hermes, the School of Alexandria, Neo-Platonism, Orphic fragments and 'the Pythagorean synthesis' as 'where it all begins'; 'intellectual monism', an 'evolutive and transcendental spiritualism', as the faith; and *gnosis*, or 'the art of finding God in oneself, by developing occult and latent powers', as the goal.[80] No doubt too Steiner would have admired, in reading of the four degrees of initiation of the Pythagoreans, this description of 'the celestial history of Psyche':

> In proportion as the flickering flame of consciousness is lit, the soul becomes more independent of the body, more capable of existing freely. . . . Descending and remounting to the 'dreadful spiral', the humble Psyche at its origin [is] a passing breath, a floating germ, a windswept bird, migrating from life to life. . . . Captive and troubled, [she] struggles between [her] two companions [the physical and spiritual] as between the thousand twining folds of a serpent and an invisible genius calling [her], whose presence, however, can only be felt by passing gleams and the beating of his wings.[81]

Here is the kernel of Steiner's teaching on the microcosm. The development of Schuré's book overall reinforced Steiner's idea of great 'individualities' directing history. Meanwhile, the later chapters, concluding with one on Jesus, provided a wealth of supportive motifs.

An association formed between the two men. This would last several years and bring Schuré into the ambit of Anthroposophy after its break with the Theosophical Society.[82] From the beginning, Steiner emphasised his 'Western' orientation *vis-à-vis* Besant, and Schuré promoted this. The first work of Steiner's published in England includes an introduction by Schuré which is elaborate and praising, just as the preface by Besant which precedes it is curt and patronising.[83] The great mystics, Schuré writes, were Fiore, Boehme and Saint-Martin; the great occultists, Paracelsus, Mesmer and Fabré d'Olivet. The mystic's realm was inner life, while the occultist's was 'descending' Spirit and 'ascending' Nature. The 'weapons' of mysticism were 'concentration' and 'inner vision', while those of the occult 'intuition' and 'synthesis'. When these two types were blended, one discovered the 'adept' or 'higher initiate'. Such a type was Rudolf Steiner. His career to date had been an inspirational progress toward spiritual power, culminating in his new position in the Theosophical Society and alliance with Marie von Sievers. 'Such faith, such devotion must have increased [his] energy a hundredfold and given wings to his words', the Frenchman rhapsodises. 'All his books are of a high quality. He is equally skilled in the deduction of ideas in philosophical order, and in rigorous analysis of scientific facts.'[84]

One might have expected a man of Schuré's literary experience to have been more critical of prose which often takes the consistency of Steiner's favoured emulsion of almonds and fruits. But long immersion in Wagner and a tradition of *grand initiés* had prepared Schuré to look for spiritual heroes. Thus he goes on to extol Steiner's presence, eloquence, serenity, clarity of mind, mysterious vibrations, 'inward and contagious fervour', 'secret music of the soul, which is, as it were, a subtle melody in harmony with the Universal Soul [*Spiritus Mundi*]', and finally concludes in biblical (or Nietzschean) fashion: 'Behold, a master of himself and of life!' Enthusiasm was a hallmark of Schuré's style. Still, one wonders if there were not an ulterior motive here. Perhaps via Marie, Schuré had already gleaned that Steiner might be an influential promoter of his metaphysical dramas. These were not making headway among the Naturalists and humorists of Paris; and elsewhere Schuré echoes the attitudes of Steiner and Marie by complaining that the theatre of the age was dominated by 'materialistic anarchy'.[85]

In due course, Steiner did become his mentor's theatrical 'saviour'. We are told that he had been eager to produce Schuré's *Children of Lucifer* ever since having been introduced to it by Marie early in their relationship.[86] We are told further that, also via Marie, the play may have been instrumental in guiding Steiner toward his destiny: 'Marie perceived that, like a harbinger of light, there shimmered through [*The Children of Lucifer*] . . . a secret impulse of human destiny, and she experienced the significance of [it]. . . . Steiner describes this insight of [hers] as "the portal" through which he was able to lead into anthroposophy.' The play was mounted under Steiner's direction during the annual Theosophical congress at Munich in the summers of 1909 and 1910. It had been preceded at congresses in 1907 and 1908 by productions of Schuré's *Sacred Drama of Eleusis*, text and exegesis of which the Frenchman had not immodestly included as the concluding section of his second *magnum opus*, *The Genesis of Tragedy*. These productions were a marked innovation in the pattern of Theosophical get-togethers. Besant and company had depended mostly on lectures and smaller discussion groups to put their message across.

Steiner and his followers sought to induce an atmosphere of aesthetic spirituality by adorning the congress hall with statues and paintings, pastel-coloured fabrics and appropriate sounds, and ending a day's more academic activities with performances *à la* Bayreuth.[87]

The intent here was to bring souls together by more subliminal means. As Schuré wrote, he hoped that his *Sacred Drama* might provoke audiences to work toward 'a cessation of separate life' and 'consciousness of One Life' and to realise via reincarnations enacted that there is no final death.[88] His *Genesis of Tragedy* was a guidebook to theatre attempting this, from the Greeks to Shakespeare to the 'Third Epoch' and 'Theatre of the Future': a realm of 'legendary and philosophical drama' whose great exponents to date had been Goethe and Wagner. 'Ever since the Renaissance the theatre had strictly confined itself to the things of the Earth', Schuré wrote. '*Faust* is an expression of the passionate desire to include also the astral and divine worlds.'[89] Here was an opinion Steiner also held passionately; and Goethe's great drama became the third work he would mount at Munich and later, on the stage of the purpose-built 'Goetheanum', at Dornach. Wagner he had been familiar with since schooldays in Vienna and debates of Wagnerians and anti-Wagnerians at the 'Megalomania Café'.[90] But, while he admired the 'aristocracy of the Soul', 'supremacy of the Spirit', 'religious atmosphere' and 'certain philosophical discipline' which Schuré extolled in this fellow pan-German, Steiner was tone-deaf, like Yeats, and preferred sparse instrumentation to Wagnerian torrents of sound.[91]

The 'initiatory drama' of the future needed to be positive and uplifting:

> Not then [Schuré writes] with the dark lantern of scepticism with its flickering gleam shall we descend into the dark arcana of tragedy, into the cruel depths of human suffering. We shall take with us the wings of sympathy, and it is the torch of intuition that will help us to return to the luminous heights of initiatory and redemptive drama where – beyond the ephemeral Soul – we shall find the eternal Psyche.[92]

The ideal was indicated by Nietzsche in his *Birth of Tragedy*. But Schuré, like Steiner, finds that 'freedom fighter's' vision ultimately lacking. For all his knowledge of the Greeks, Nietzsche had missed the essential 'drama', that of Eleusis, and fable, that of Persephone (p. 156). Only by combining these with his beloved tale of Dionysus could one gain a complete view of the ancient mysteries. Such a combination would unite psychic (micrcosmic) with cosmogonic (macrocosmic) myth – Persephone's tale being about the journey of a human soul in its birth, death and resurrection on earth, in the underworld and in heaven; Dionysus's being about the origin and end of the world in the faith, love and enthusiasm of a god willing to offer himself to be fragmented in 'a proud holocaust' (p. 260). Schuré's Dionysus exhibits a Wagnerian–Nietzschean joy-in-death of a kind foreign to the contemplative Steiner ('At the height of being and consciousness [to] taste the intoxication of life in the sacrifice of self!') Still, the intent is to convey Steiner-like faith in the ameliorative process of successive incarnations. Thus, when Demeter proves reluctant to give birth to Dionysus a second time, Zeus argues,

> He will be stronger, though not invulnerable . . . and will offer himself to men, to the universe, to the gods. He will do combat in his frenzy and beauty; with shouts of triumph he will see his own blood and tears. On his stainless breast he will bear . . . the radiant star of invincible Love!   (p. 296)

The resurrected god of *The Sacred Drama* combines the beauty, courage and self-will which would characterise Lucifer in Schuré's next play, with an impulse to self-sacrifice belonging to Christ. The latter in *The Sacred Drama* is also prefigured by Triptolemus, a mortal selected to go down to Pluto's domain to find Persephone. Triptolemus is described as 'pure-headed and disinterested', 'motivated by neither ambition nor personal safety' and having a 'sympathy pure and impetuous' (p. 252) – the very qualities of a Paraclete. His nobleness comes from wanting to resurrect the spirit of his father, whom he saw in a dream to say, 'Unless an immortal genius protects us, we dead no longer live except by the love of the living . . . and when they forsake us . . . we pass away like empty vapour. I wander about in darksome terror, a larva haunted by other larvae' (p. 283). Recognizing in Triptolemus the perfect candidate as instrument of divine will, Demeter straightaway offers him 'the bath of fire of enthusiasm which inspires the soul of true heroes with invincible faith, and clothes them, so to speak, with diamond armour' (p. 252). At the end of *The Sacred Drama,* having effected events favourably, the 'generous youth' is initiated by 'courage and pity' and told to reveal nothing of what he has seen to 'the profane' (p. 301). This done, a 'chorus of Invisible Heroes' admonishes the audience, 'We can receive Truth in our inner selves and carry her radiations through the world, but whoever betrays her sublime source will lose her forever.'

V THE MYSTERY PLAYS

Steiner may have seen Schuré as a dramatic precursor: a sort of John the Baptist whose 'initiations' were necessary but preliminary, belonging to the aestheticism of the just-finished century more than the 'science' of his new age. The admonition to silence which ends *The Sacred Drama* is one indication here: Steiner, as said, saw it as his duty to bring esoterica into the light (though not without qualification[93]). Schuré's fascination with the 'lesser guardian' of Lucifer is perhaps another: Steiner would distance himself from the cult of the 'light-bearer' which had fascinated Theosophists, moving Blavatsky to call her house magazine *Lucifer* and he his own German version of the same *Luzifer-Gnosis*. In this connection, we might see Schuré's *Children of Lucifer* standing in the progression of Steiner-sponsored dramas in analogous relation to the position of the spirit of its title in Anthroposophy's trinity of 'guardians of the threshold'. Lucifer is the first an initiate is bound to confront, take knowledge from yet resist mastery by. Ahriman (a version of Mephistopheles) is the second. Christ, however, is the final, 'greater' guardian. Thus, as Schuré's and Goethe's plays took first and second place among Steiner productions, so the 'mage's' own 'mystery dramas' – delivering his ultimate, Christly message – take the last. This incidentally signposts the limit of Steiner's respect for the 'artistic' *vis-à-vis* the metaphysical; because, whatever the merits of his dramas in illuminating a moral scheme, all are repetitive, abstract and static – more tortuous even than *Faust, Part II*, which most dramaturges outside the Goetheanum regard as unplayable[94] – and in structure unworthy to be discussed in the same breath with Schuré's *Children*, which is glamorous in the Yeatsian sense and similar in style and content to symbolist dramas the Irish poet was attempting at the time.[95]

Schuré's play proposes a synthesis of Lucifer and Christ to guide man in the new age (here represented as the fourth century AD). In its final act, Lucifer (invoked as in *Zanoni* by the cry 'Adonai!'[96]) tells the hero–initiate, Phosphoros, that now the world may be Christ's but one day it will belong to the two spirits together, 'He the Messiah come down from Heaven, and I the Archangel, risen again from the Abyss' (p. 119). This is a classic variant of Hermetic doctrine, with Lucifer identified with 'Anthropos' (man) fallen from his high place as 'brother' to God, and Salvation (Christ) identified with 'Sophia' (Wisdom/*gnosis*), aspiration to whom is necessary for Anthropos to reascend the spheres.[97] In Schuré's scheme, the female part of the alchemical unity is taken by Cleonice, daughter of a Coptic priest. Because of his allegiance to the 'fallen angel', Phosphoros is initially hateful to the woman; eventually, however, she comes to love him, because 'Christ is happy in his Heaven but Phosphoros is suffering on earth' (p. 69). Phosphoros's burning desire in this world has been to 'liberate' his city, Dionysia, from the military occupation of Rome and byzantine orthodoxy of the Church. He has inspired a rebellion, but this has failed; and now the people, losing heart, turn on their leader and hound him and his beloved from town as 'the devil's couple'. Taking refuge in the Temple of the Unknown God, where Phosphoros was initiated by his guardian in the first place, the pair determine to offer themselves up in exemplary martyrdom:

Let us die together [Phosphoros proclaims]; but let us die gladly, like true children of Lucifer! The world means to crush us? Let us liberate ourselves. It means to part us? Let us unite forever. Death is pursuing us. Let us go to meet him. God demands a holocaust. Let us offer to him proudly, like a festival, the flower of our two lives and the heroic dream of our souls! Let us pass through the Night of Death towards a nobler day! (p. 130)

Thus Schuré, the arch-romantic, aspiring to fashion a mix of *Tristan, Die Walküre, Götterdämmerung* and prophetic parable. His pair take poison. Over their corpses shines a burning five-pointed star (Lucifer's emblem) superimposed on a cross (Christ's). This strikes awe into the hearts of pursuing Romans and Catholics; and the hierophant of the Temple of the Unknown God concludes, 'They are victorious! For they have loved and struggled to the end. Blessed are they who believe in their dream: they will possess it' (p. 131).

It is a testament to Steiner's earthly passion for Marie that she should have been able to make production of this piece a focal point of his efforts for a decade. Such 'soul' passion seems alien to Steiner's spirit-obsessed theory. However, his own plays – also written out of the von Sievers influence – have a character 'Marie' who stands as the right and constant soul-guide for the young artist–hero in his progress. Ahern suggests that Steiner's second marriage may eventually have become an 'alchemical' model for fellow Anthroposophists rather than vital personal relationship;[98] and, if one chooses to identify Steiner with the young hero of his plays, there is fictive corroboration for the idea that his attraction to women strayed beyond Marie – also that he felt guilty about it. This apart, Steiner's 'mystery dramas' reveal more about the man and his doctrine than most of his theoretical works, and not just that he was a second-rate literary artist. They confirm above all that he came to see himself as a benign and omniscient superior being: guide for mankind-at-large, most of which was woefully deluded by Lucifer and Ahriman – even the 'ancient brotherhood', which is depicted as ignorant of the meaning of its symbols and rites.[99] The extent to which Steiner is judged to have been right in his analysis depends on one's agreement with the relative values he puts on spiritual forces, particularly those of the 'evil' hierarchies. Certainly individuals lose their way through self-obsession and fantasy (Luciferic forces to Steiner) and ambition and materialism (Ahrimanic). But whether the proper antidote to these should be intense concentration on transcendental visions such as proposed in the plays is another matter. Mann prescribes Peepercorn to chase too much Settembrini and Naphta; and even such a spiritually obsessed writer as Eliot would come to see cocktail parties and demotic chat as as essential to life in this world as metaphysical earnestness.[100]

But Steiner is not finally concerned with *this* world. In his plays, the 'well-adjusted' generally appear as philistines who could never understand Goethe's 'fundamental rule of life': 'One must give up one's existence in order to exist.'[101] His plays are for the 'grateful dead', as it were, whose concern is 'the life of the human soul, when it is striving to reach the supersensory'.[102] Like those of Goethe's fairytale from which they derive,[103] Steiner's characters represent 'the powers of the soul which are divided one-sidedly among a number of [forces] yet are nothing but fractions of the human character as a whole'. Thus we observe Johannes the artist,

Capesius the thinker and Strader the technician; also a host of
ephemeral characters who prey on, support or reflect further
aspects of their own and/or the total corporate individuality.
'When in the life of community various human qualities work
together, their mutual influence is simply a picture of the manifold
forces which in their relations to one another compose the entire
being of an individual man.' This is the goal: dynamic integration
of individual and community. The methods of achieving it include
'astral' journeys, 'skryings' of one's own soul-yearnings and
others' 'thought-forms', ordeal-induced revelations and time-
travel back to earlier incarnations, specifically in the Rosicrucian
and Egyptian epochs. All is designed as in Golden Dawn ritual,
to unlock the true will and true self, though Steiner rarely uses
these terms; and unlike in the Golden Dawn, the endpoint is not
individual power so much as truth to essential personality, function and ability to serve.[104]

Love may be the ultimate shimmering behind all; but this love
is not the sometimes sordid type we shall see in Crowley, rather
a refinement of Schiller's 'third force between sensuality and
reason':

> When we are passionately attached to someone who is worthy
> of our contempt, we feel painfully the *compulsion of nature*. If we
> have a hostile relationship to someone who compels our respect,
> we feel painfully the *compulsion of reason*. But when our affection
> is involved and all our respect is won, then both the compulsion
> of feeling and the compulsion of reason disappear, and we begin
> to love.[105]

True love of this kind is a lodestone in the plays, especially as
it relates to Johannes' development through attraction to Marie,
detachment from Marie, misplaced passion for Theodora, whom
Lucifer puts in his path, and ultimate return to a higher, less
dependent love for Marie once more.[106] Such love is also reflected
in the character of Benedictus, a hierophant embodying aspects of
Steiner,[107] and Felix and Felicia Balde, rustics who have reached
'initiation' independently via their close relation to Nature.[108]
These three, with Marie, are the consistently 'free' personalities
throughout the plays and thus the standard by which the others'
progress is measured. They are never tempted to aesthetic irresponsibility, like Johannes through Lucifer; materialistic scepticism,

like Strader through Ahriman; nor solitary retreat into ivory towers of the mind, like Capesius. They are ever open to the songs of gnomes and sylphs, which have formed the outer world, and of Luna, Astrid and Philia, the spirits of human emotion reflecting light, warmth and love.[109] Patience is their hallmark; calm enthusiasm their tone. Mountain landscapes or temples is where they are most likely to appear, generally when the others are in unagitated, reflective moods.[110]

Atmosphere, lighting and scenery are essential at these junctures, as throughout the plays in general. Steiner's stage directions are elaborate, if sometimes vague. They seek to manipulate effects leitmotivally to provide proper correlatives to the 'action' (hardly ever more than speech). Thus the lecture scene which opens *The Portal of Initiation* (play 1) is rose-red; Capesius's study in *The Souls' Probation* (2) is brown; the Hall of the Mystic Brotherhood in *The Guardian of the Threshold* (3) is indigo; and the Spirit Realm in *The Souls' Awakening* (4) is 'a flood of meaningful colours from fiery red above to violet below'.[111] We are told by Steiner's translator–producer that the scripts 'should be called scores' and read aloud as music; also that we should listen for 'the rhythmical flow' and 'thoughts behind words', even though 'English rarely allows a German kind of spiritualisation' and translation fails to do justice to Steiner's 'creation of new words'.[112] Through the 'seals' which open each text, we are told further that we shall be led into 'the secret core of Rosicrucianism'; that there we must unite our 'star-forms' to withstand the 'law of metamorphoses'; that we shall come to a 'crossing' where all will be swept up in a whirlwind until 'no straight line remains'; and that at last we may reach the circle formed by the snake biting its tail, inside which twelve rays form the letters 'ICH ERKENNETS' (roughly 'Self Knows Itself').[113]

Thus arrived, we may begin to intuit the full force of Steiner's message. But in fact this can only be achieved if we allow ourselves to give way to manipulation via what Lévi called the 'astral light'; hear 'speech as tone', as the fairytale spinner Felicia Balde advises;[114] and fall into something perilously close to the medium-like state Blavatsky recommended in *Isis Unveiled*: 'The deeper the trance, the less sign of life the body shows, the clearer become the spiritual perceptions, and the more powerful are the soul's visions.'[115] Thus Steiner's method in the end is revealed as a kind of hypnosis. The experience offered is akin to the 'drop' Jung describes in *Memories, Dreams, Reflections*;[116] nor is the progress promised so far away from what Timothy Leary came to propose via LSD.[117] It is perhaps attractive that Steiner sought to communicate in traditional poetic and philosophic terms, rather than jargon such as Hubbard would concoct for his 'spiritual science' or quasi-Indian afflatus such as dominated the Theosophical Society. But Steiner as poet, if not philosopher, was *manqué*. Thus, if there is permanent value to be gained here, it has less to do with his over-generous production than with an openness of approach and goodness of intent rare among practitioners of modern 'magic'.

8

Aleister Crowley

I THE DARK GOD WITHIN

Before letting go of the Germans, we should pay some attention
to a figure dismissed two chapters ago. While no novelist is more
comprehensive about the relation of 'magic' to civilisation than
Mann, none is more specific about the psychology of the occult-
oriented personality than Hesse. Mann himself recognised the
distinction and identity of impulse: 'Our paths in general take
clearly separate courses through the land of the spirit. . . . And
yet in some sense the course is the same.'[1] Both are concerned
with the sudden, pervasive magico-religious revolution of
consciousness of the first part of this century, experienced with
particular intensity in their country. Both consider this with
'highest' irony at the 'purest' level of literary 'aspiration'.[2] Yet,
where Mann's work has the feel of an overstuffed Victorian sofa,
Hesse's is minimal and shapely, like some neo-Egyptian piece of
Art Deco. Mann remarks on Hesse's 'Chinese character', 'scrupu-
lous refusal to try to please the world' and 'degree of hard-won
spiritual freedom by which he surpassed me'. This is high praise;
but it does not mean that Mann regarded Hesse as *il miglior fabbro*[3]
so far as the novel was concerned. About this, a different kind of
Hesse admirer, Timothy Leary, indicates the difference:

> The critics tell us that Hesse is the master novelist. Well, maybe.
> But the novel is a social form, and the social in Hesse is exoteric.
> At another level Hesse is the master guide to the psychedelic
> experience and its application. Before your LSD session, read
> *Siddhartha* and *Steppenwolf*. The last part of the *Steppenwolf* is a
> priceless manual.[4]

Substitute 'magical' for 'psychedelic' and 'ritual magic' for 'LSD
session' and one may see how Hesse's work on its 'esoteric' level

could hold a pivotal position between 'magic' and literature in the first part of this century. No tapestries of the social fabric, his novels pay scant heed to the requirement of moral 'equilibration'. Like contemporary works of D. H. Lawrence such as we have seen Eliot complaining about,[5] Hesse's books demonstrate an urgent need to break out of old orthodoxies. In a variety of guises, they provide a road map for 'heretical' new 'seekers': a *guide verte* to 'free' personality, 'liberation' or the orthodox 'religion' of the 'new age', *self-realisation*.[6] Thus they poach playfully (and not so playfully) on the territory of what Mann calls 'the erotological "depth psychology" of Vienna';[7] also (and here lies a chief difference from Lawrence, who was interested in myth, symbol and ritual more than traditional 'magic') the fascination for secret societies, transtemporal and spatial elites, altered states of consiousness and transcendence to 'higher planes' which we have seen dominating the un-Freudian (even anti-Freudian) *demi-monde* – all these occult forerunners of Leary and Co., who would attempt to bring on a pervasive cultural alteration of consciousness through self-declaredly 'magical' (often sub-'magical') means, using what in Lévi's terms might be aptly defined as 'manipulation of the astral light'.[8]

I have discussed *Steppenwolf*, Leary and the 1960s in *Art, Messianism and Crime* and do not intend to repeat arguments about their 'antinomianism' here. But, as regards Hesse's opus, it is worth noting that Leary found four works to constitute a theoretical gospel:[9] (1) *Siddhartha* (1922), which contends that the self-realised individual will contain a dynamic unity of multiple personalities, including those of animals, children, murderers, lovers and the Buddha; (2) *Steppenwolf* (1927), which sets out a plan for realising this identity by getting rid of external social personae, using alcohol, drugs, music, ceremony, hetero- and homosexuality and theatrical illusion; (3) *The Journey to the East* (1932), which argues that attachment to a 'mystical group' or 'transpersonal community' may maintain the individual's 'holy sense of unity and revelation' and prevent him from drifting into 'gaseous anarchy, breakdown, confusion, grandiosity, prima donna individualism, disorganised eccentricity, sincere knavery and retreat to conformity'; and finally (4) *The Glass-Bead Game* (1946), which shows how an association of individuals might evolve into a 'society of mystic game players', inhabiting a science-fictive future yet embodying elements of great medieval orders, and developing 'a new language or set of symbols to do justice to the incredible complexity of the human cerebral machinery' while at the same time refining means to make 'direct contact with the regenerative forces of the life processes through meditation or other forms of altering consciousness'.

All these insights and concerns were shared at one time or another by the so-called 'wickedest man in the world',[10] ex-Golden Dawn trickster, Aleister Crowley. He believed in multiple personae and demonstrated as much in his life through myriad assumed names, disguises, shifts of profession, presentation and stated views. He preached self-realisation through use of every kind of drug and sexual act available and brought himself and others to some grief through practice of this, always under the guise of 'religious' rite. He tried repeatedly to form 'mystical groups', but each attempt was deformed at birth by the 'gaseous anarchy' (and so on) of his personality. He believed too that he was creating the 'Brains' of the race,[11] which would direct history for the next 2000 years, during which 'Aeon' the law would be his own 'Do What Thou Wilt', a new 'language' incorporating his 'sex magick' and pseudo-poeticising would be played around with by an 'elite', and much dynamically restorative meditation would be used. There is thus absolute structural similarity between 'Crowleyanity' and Hesse's system as Leary codifies it. But the point of greatest similarity between the opus of the German writer and career of the English Cagliostro may be found in the work of Hesse's which preceded and gave birth to these four Lerary choices: his prototypical novella of 'liberation', *Demian* (1919).

This was written under a pseudonym during the period of personal and cultural stress of the First World War, when Hesse was anathema to his countrymen because he had taken himself off to Switzerland to preach pacifism. (Crowley at the same time went to America and, having failed to interest British intelligence in employing him, wrote pro-German propaganda.[12]) In charting the disillusionment and self-discovery of a youth of the time, the novel focuses on the idea that – if there must be a God at all – He must be the synthetic good-and-evil Gnostic manifestation, Abraxas. It is no coincidence that Carl Jung was also going through a 'dark passage' at this time, leading him to write his eccentric *Seven Sermons of the Dead, from Basilides, a Gnostic of Alexandria, the City where East Toucheth West*, which contains a definition of the same Gnostic diety, written in a pseudo-poetical, 'automatic' style reminiscent of D. H. Lawrence's invocation of his 'dark god' in *The Plumed Serpent*.[13] Hesse took treatment from Jung during the war; moreover, the psychologist of Zurich was making his own contribution to the rise of 'magic' as religion, as touched on earlier and explored by others in detail. But what is most strikingly coincidental for us here is how in its general typological terms Hesse's novel also captures the spirit of rebellion which had led the young Crowley to his own discovery of a version of the Gnostic 'dark god': his 'holy guardian angel', Aiwaz, through whose inspiration the young 'magician' grew bold enough to declare his 'New Aeon' with its 'Thelemic' Law.[14]

Crowley's belief he would later sum up thus: God could hardly be 'good' when he had created men with 'the seeds of evil' in them.[15] This is precisely the point Jung is making when he describes his youthful vision of the Protestant God of his parents tricksterishly dropping a turd through the roof of a cathedral.[16] It is a problem with which *Demian* is concerned through all of its seven principal chapters – the standard number, as we have seen twice, for 'magical' fiction.[17] The book has in addition a 'Prologue', which introduces in the broadest terms the theme of finding the true self; also an end chapter, which marks the expiry of an epoch of self-realisation in the general destruction of world war. The seven chapters between set out essential stages in an archetypal, semi-conscious 'initation'. The first, 'Two Realms', presents the narrator – a middle-class youth, Emil Sinclair – with the first test he must meet and master: how, in breaking out of the fixed shell of his background, to escape falling under the thumb of a lower-class con-man, as he has allowed himself to do through naïveté, vain boastfulness and fear of conventional sanction. The second chapter, 'Cain', introduces the *alter ego* or 'double' of the book's title, Max Demian, a semi-foreigner of vaguely Jewish or Eastern background and apparent great wealth, who has obscure 'powers' emanating both from within and from precocious experience. Demian captures Sinclair's imagination and holds it. He has a magnetic presence; defends the strong and outcast against the weak and timidly conforming (*ergo* the Byronic identification of the chapter's title); displays an uncanny ability to read thoughts and – most important in view of Sinclair's thraldom to the con-man of 'Two Realms' – firmly believes that one must throw off fear by any means, even murder if necessary.

It does not come to that, of course. Demian scares off Sinclair's antagonist with some mysterious words; and chapter 3, 'Among Thieves', allows us to view more of his nature and philosophy through Sinclair's wary yet admiring eyes. In appearance, Max is 'ageless': both highly spiritual and animal at the same time. His strangeness and attraction are enhanced for the other young man by a rumour that he 'knows everything' about sex and perhaps has even been his mother's lover. (Here enters a vague Isis-Osiris-Horus motif which will gain importance later in the novel as Demian's mother takes a lead role in the final stage of Sinclair's 'awakening'.) Max demonstrates how he can manipulate people by subtle suggestion. This apparent 'magic' he reveals to be a matter of close observation of behaviour, followed by concentrated application of energy. 'Do What Thou Wilt' appears to be his law no less than Crowley's. But, also like Crowley and Lévi before him, Demian counsels that, in order to achieve that will, one must first have comprehensive self-knowledge, thus a sure sense of what is and is not essential and what is within one's capabilities. The force of Demian's own will is reflected, like Hitler's and Crowley's[18], through the eyes. These have hypnotic power, and he likes to use them in stare-downs ('Very few people can stand that for long'). His true God would contain the devil, he avers. Sex-drive is a divine impulse, not to be repressed any more than to be enslaved by. Each man must create for himself his own proper law. Trance-like meditation is necessary to restore essential integrity of inner and outer selves.

In chapter 4, 'Beatrice', Sinclair's development proceeds through three necessary and predictable youthful stages: (1) self-degradation through drink and carousing; (2) attachment to a dream woman (*anima*), resulting in chaste, neo-Platonic idealisations; and (3) the taking-up of art – in this case painting. This last leads Sinclair to discover his own image of the inner god: 'my daemon': Demian, but then not Demian: the 'someone within all of us who knows everything' (p. 73) – indeed, something quite close to what Steiner and Theosophists refer to as 'the eternal "I" '. (It is no mistake, incidentally, that this novel, like so many of its time, should be in the first person: discovery of the multiple faces and potentialities of the ego was becoming an essential 'religion' among exoteric intellectuals as well as esotericists.) This leads directly to chapter 5, called 'The Bird Fights its way out of the Egg', a title arising out of an aphorism of Max Demian's redolent of Blavatsky's concept of the 'auric egg':[19] 'The bird fights its way out of the egg. The egg is the world. Who would be born must first destroy a world. The bird flies to God. That God's name is Abraxas' (p. 76). Abraxas's 'symbolic task', we are informed, is 'the uniting of ecstasy and horror, angel and Satan, man and woman in one flesh, man and beast, the highest good and the worst evil' (p. 80). He is a god of chaos and dispersion as well as of creativity. Yet Sinclair (like Crowley with Aiwaz) kneels down before him, worships, blasphemes and projects on him all he passionately adores and hates.

The cult of the amoral diety leads to immersion in traditions of art (here music) and ideas which 'strain toward the miraculous' (p. 83). From an Abraxian organ-master, Pistorious, Sinclair learns about ancient philosophy, the occult and the Vedas. He worships fire and finds hallucinogenic images in it, leading him off on revelatory journeys through the inner psyche. Simultaneously, he studies the other elements and, from their eccentricity, dumb strength and power, gains further insight into 'the individual capacity for everything', thus foolishness of conventional restrictions and harmony of the One with the All. Chapter 6, 'Jacob Wrestling', sees him happily isolated: a 'spirit of solitude'[20] who clearly does not fit in with normal life yet no longer worries over the fact. Pistorius suggests the need for a group or cult; but Sinclair discovers that a young man who has followed more routinised means toward self-realisation (i.e. using 'exercises' and 'continence' such as practised in Theosophy) has been driven to the verge of suicide by the unnaturalness of the regime. As teachers must, Pistorius too descends in Sinclair's estimation: the all-worthy guru ends by seeming an 'antiquarian' incapable of linking 'magical' lore to the 'magical' life. Thus Sinclair leaves him, but not without heeding the man's admonition that – even though a misfit – he should not waste himself as a martyr or revolutionary.[21] The trick of existence is to regard one's career as an 'experiment of Nature': a kind of alchemist's mixing of elements which may either create eternal splendour or end in an explosion which is nevertheless informative to others about what *not* to attempt.

The ultimate explosion of the book will be the schrapnel which hospitalises Sinclair in the First World War and kills Demian, whose spirit the former internalises. But before that is reached comes the final station of Sinclair's upward journey – his Osiran awakening, or rebirth to the Light – chapter 7, entitled 'Eva', about the Isis of the book's initiatory configuration: Demian's charismatic

mother. 'Tall', 'timeless', 'ageless', 'full of inner strength', 'radi-
ating fulfilment' and 'homecoming', *she* might be 'mother',
'beloved' or 'goddess' in Sinclair's estimation; he does not care
which. She is the Earth Spirit, the Universal Generator; and he
goes to her, submitting to the furthest degree he is able to passive
yet vibrant, unobtrusive yet all-touching, authority. Around her
and Max, he finds others who share in the 'enlightenment' of the
time. The old epoch is 'bankrupt'; a 'cataclysm' must come now
to bring on the new. (Thus these 'magicians' claim, like others
noted,[22] prevision of the Great War.) Individuals must live for
'genius', like Jesus or Nietzsche, because Destiny only seeks out
and dignifies those who remake morality for themselves. The rest
of mankind is a sleepwalking mass, perhaps even subhuman.
The elite constitute an 'island of prototypes' for the 'new age':
astrologers, Tolstoyans, Cabalists, Indian ascetics, vegetarians,
'delicate shy creatures' of all types. Their 'great work' is to explore
all myths, religions and ideals of the past and from them
synthesise directing cults for the future. Yet, amid them, an 'inner
circle' retains the ultimate knowledge that all teachings – even
these enlightened new ones – are merely 'metaphor'. The chosen
ones wish for no more than to be ready for whatever comes. Eva
and her kind remain cool amid the others' struggle to arrive. Like
unambiguous Love, she explains to the smitten yet ultimately
diffident Sinclair, they will inevitably attract whatever they wish
because they have *certainty*.

II POET-MANQUÉ

Aleister Crowley had far less certainty than he pretended; thus
the strikingly erratic course of his career. This was indeed an
'experiment of Nature', one that he could neither always control
nor always be content with – though in *de rigueur* 'magical' fashion
he customarily pretended both. The Self, or Inner 'I', was in his
case a shambles; and, to mask essential chaos, he erected his cult
of *will*. This was born out of pain and defiance. No one has done
a proper Freudian analysis of 'the Great Beast's' childhood, but it
seems significant that he had no good word to say about his
mother yet clung to her identification of him as the demon of the
Apocalypse.[23] Here began a habit which would be repeated in
later life, with dismaying results. When Yeats and other members

of the Golden Dawn suggested that Crowley needed a 'reformatory' more than a 'magical university', Frater Perdurabo ('I will endure') proceeded to behave in every way to confirm their prejudice, even stealing their rituals for his renegade Order of the Silver Star and publishing them in his account of his 'magical' progress, *The Temple of Solomon the King*.[24] Then in America during the war, Crowley, penniless and without success in spreading his 'order', fell among prostitutes, petty con-men, pimps and thieves and played up to their camp view of him as a stage Englishman by adopting an increasingly pompous persona as 'a gentleman of the University of Cambridge', top-drawer London clubman and secret emissary on His Majesty's Service – all of which was duly reported to British Intelligence and dismissed as the ranting of an essentially harmless eccentric.[25] Later still, when British and French newspapers and the Italian Government scrutinised Crowley's sex and drug practices at 'Thelma' and concluded that he was not so harmless after all, the 'Beast' grabbed onto the adverse publicity – even whipped it up further by litigations for libel[26] – in hopes that at last notoriety might bring him what honourable talent, hard work and his essential persona had not.

Attention, love, affirmation of his being – these are what young Edward Alexander Crowley seems to have lacked from his self-righteous Plymouth Brethren parents. These were what he sought out of his first and, throughout life, most precious avocation: writing poetry. In *Art, Messianism and Crime*, I rehearse Crowley's career briefly as an example of the artist-*manqué* who – frustrated in attempts to achieve critical recognition – turns toward other, less innocent undertakings which seem to allow increasing scope for 'genius': i.e. ever-accelerating 'inflation of personality'.[27] In fact, Crowley should perhaps have been given more space in that context, because further study deepens one's sense that artistic frustration – maybe more than early Oedipal problems, but in any case building on them with cumulative effect – was a motive force of his career and primary explanation for what in him may appear as megalomaniacal or 'evil'. This we have hinted at in Blavatsky, Steiner and even Lévi. But in Crowley, who worked and worked at his writing throughout his life, churning out Swinburnean epics in verse and sub-Wildean melodramas in prose, the tendency shoves every other consideration aside to confront us first and foremost with the question: to what extent may 'magic' itself be a substitute for artistic expression? – in this case literary expression primarily, though Crowley, like Steiner, also fancied himself a painter, theatrical producer of a kind and even for a time musical impresario.[28] It is a question which will return when we come to that inexhaustible spinner of science-fictive tomes, Ron Hubbard; and the mere asking of it suggests the probable answer and indeed thesis which the sub-title of his study indicates: that literary-artistic and 'magical' impulses in this modern era (since the French Revolution anyway, but clearly in prior romantic eras as well) have been entwined – in some cases intimately, with the result that a very few steps in one direction of the other might make a would-be 'magician' into a great writer (Yeats) or would-be great writer into a 'magician' (Crowley).

The pathos of the matter in Crowley's case becomes plain from a look at his poetical study and production. He believed that Yeats was jealous of him as 'the better maker'.[29] Yeats in return is said to have remarked that Crowley had written about 'six good lines amid much bad rhetoric'. Some suppose that Yeats was being over-generous here. Crowley himself must have been hurt; and the slight from the great writer, who seemed poorly educated by contrast and in other respects not worthy of the attention the literary establishment came to give him, may well explain Crowley's defamations of his Irish rival in *The Equinox*, *Moonchild* and elsewhere.[30] But it was not only Yeats among erstwhile friends who came to snub Crowley. Somerset Maugham used him as the main character in his early novel *The Magician*, but years later in Berlin refused two invitations to supper with the cutting remark that he was too old and busy to be bothered to renew questionable associations of his youth.[31] This is certainly bitchiness of a standard matching Crowley's own embittered jibes and put-downs – of Isadora Duncan, A. E. Waite and others.[32] A more typical and disappointing treatment came from Aldous Huxley, whom Crowley is said to have introduced to mescalin in the 1920s but who refused invitations to see 'The Beast' when in London, generally using excuses of illness.[33] But not all literary characters of the time shunned Crowley. Nancy Cunard solicited her horoscope from him and defended his memory to John Symonds after his death.[34] Frank Harris spent some time in communication with him, apparently hoping that two aging sex rebels of their kind – both of whom had left London for the shores of the Mediterranean – could collaborate on some sort of progressive journal for the 'new age'.[35] Another sex rebel with a preference for the south of

Europe, Norman Douglas, liked to reply to Crowley's greeting in letters 'Do What Thou Wilt Shall Be the Whole of the Law' with the heretical rejoinder 'To Hell with All Laws'.[36] And, among other famous friends, literary of at least a journalistic ilk or artistic, Crowley's correspondence shows long communication with the one-time Communist, later Labour MP Tom Driberg, the painter Augustus John (who did a number of drawings of Crowley, some specifically to illustrate his books) and the director Peter Brook, avid apparently to have the sexagenarian 'magician' speak some of Marlowe's invocations in an experimental production of *Dr Faustus* at Oxford.[37]

So there was some attention. Indeed, there was even some conventional publication of Crowley's literary output: 'Morphia' and other poems and articles in the *English Review* in 1914 and 1922, and *Diary of a Drug Fiend* by Collins in the latter year, *annus mirabilis* of twenties modernism, which saw publication of *Ulysses* (to which *Drug Fiend* was compared for 'lubricity') and *The Waste Land* and the death of Proust.[38] But in general the fate of Crowley's indefatigable literary urge was to be ignored at best or ridiculed. Nor would the opus have seen print much at all were it not for the fact that, going to Cambridge in the 'Yellow Nineties', Crowley developed early on the idea that it was respectable for an educated man to self-publish. In this he imagined himself to be following Shelley, who was sent down from Oxford for producing his tract in favour of atheism. Nor was self-publishing the only motif Crowley imagined in common with the poet of *Alastor*.[39] Believing himself too a 'spirit of solitude', he dropped his given forename and changed his middle name to its Gaelic equivalent in order to identify with the wildest fringes of Britain (in line with the Yeats–Mathers Celtic movement) and with Shelley's mountain-climbing, Eastern-travelling hero. Letting perhaps this new Shelleyan identity be his guide, Crowley left university and spent his first several adult years scaling Alps and Himalayas, searching for 'magical' intimations among Nature's beauties and storms, and furiously scouring all philosophies to justify his 'freedom' and find something in which to believe.[40] He appears never to have developed a jot of the social conscience 'red' Shelley became famous for. Perhaps this is because, unlike his Romantic precursor, he obtained his fortune early, on the death of his father, thus was not subjected to the kind of sadistic upper-middle-class manipulation of means which plagued Shelley and contributed greatly to his Promethean rage against unjust authority.[41] Crowley did, however, self-consciously follow Shelley into a sudden marriage, designed altruistically to 'liberate' a young woman from what he in his 'nobleness' was able to view as an 'intolerable situation'. This in Crowley's case was the beautiful Rose Kelly, sister of a one-time president of the Royal Academy and – if we believe the evidence of Crowley's poetry – the first, most intense and perhaps only true love of the 'magician's' career.[42]

Rose became Crowley's companion in adventure, following him to Egypt, Ceylon and in a walk across China. Together they performed prodigious amorous feats, after which Crowley would write poetry in a characteristically passionate (tumescing/detumescing) flow or wax eloquent about his latest revelations in Egyptian 'magic', Tantric Buddhism or the Way of the Tao. Rose was with him when he made contact with his 'Holy Guardian Angel' in 1904, and this alone qualifies her to be listed among his 'Scarlet Women': chief female disciples with whom he performed 'sex magick' and by this imagined he was initiating himself into ever-deepening levels of *gnosis*.[43] But living like 'a hard, gem-like flame' and constant peripeteia could end in disaster. Rose had a baby who died; she became a dipsomaniac; Crowley, more bent on revelation and licence than human attachments, left her alone to go climbing K2. A pattern of romantic flight, impermanent establishment in faraway places and death of a child suggests the Shelley cenacle in Italy;[44] and Crowley, remaining more messianic than domestic, would repeat another variation of the same with his second most lasting Scarlet Woman, Leah Hirsig, and their daughter nearly twenty years later in Cefalù. It would be wrong to suggest that the man was heartless. Poems such as 'Rosa Mundi', 'Rosa Decidua' and 'Rosa Inferni' show that these experiences tore at his soul.[45] The first is almost pathetic and quite touching in its demonstration of his great need for the emotional reinforcement and ego-boosting which came from the early passion of his wife; and it deepens one's sense that unsatisfied Oedipal longing was a motive force of the man's career and perhaps major explanation for his paradoxical aggression toward and attraction to women. 'Rosa Decidua', on the other hand, shows the bitterness of his sorrow at the one-time beloved's physical and moral decay, and how this might provoke a massive revolt of spirit against flesh: a Promethean – or, perhaps more precisely, Baudelairean – hatred of the human condition whereby beauty, love and youth can in the briefest time be turned to grotesquerie, hate and haggard age.

The rage in Crowley's love poems thus underpins rage in his philosophy overall. The Baudelairean reference is apt: Crowley studied the French *décadent*, published a translation of his *Petits poèmes en prose* in 1908 and was preparing for translation most of *Les Fleurs du mal* as late as his post-Cefalù period.[46] From Baudelaire he took the subject matter of corruption, the attitude of spleen and a self-imposed requirement ever to *épater le bourgeois*. Alas, he did not also take his French model's advice that the modern poem needs to be brief. Swinburne and Browning were his masters in prosody;[47] thus his tendencies to length, traditional metres and rhymes and further modes to get under the skin and shock. Passionate pursuit of yesterday's models left Crowley out of date with the developments of his time, which was a reason he could not understand modernist lauding of Yeats or even countenance the work of Pound or Eliot. It was perhaps not ridiculous for the editor of the *English Review* to claim that Crowley was among the best traditional metrical poets in the language of the day.[48] But equally one must recognise truth in the remark of Mrs Paul Robeson that as a popular piece of drama Crowley's *Mortadello* would have had a better chance in the era of Shakespeare.[49] Here perhaps is a case of the deleterious influence of aspiration to class-highness through fine education in literature and 'tradition'. The 'gentleman of Cambridge', like Bryon, knew more about the popes of the previous age than his form-breaking contemporaries; but, whereas Byron, living though a reactionary era, made many admirers with his fine, neo-classical prosody, Crowley, living through a period of revolution in the arts, was so eccentrically reactionary a prosodist as to be irrelevant.

This is of course not meant to suggest that he was the unacknowledged Byron of his time. Crowley was not a great poet; he was a poetaster and at most no more memorable in this literary genre than, say, the similarly derivative but not nearly so authentic Wilde (whose 'Ballad of Reading Gaol' Crowley roundly and perhaps rightly derided[50]). So much said, his poetry deserves more attention than it has been given. Some of the early work about *place* is remarkably vivid and gives a dramatic picture of the *dolce far niente* attractions of the South and tropics in Crowley's *Weltanschauung*, as against the stormy, spirit-filled, often terrible landscapes of the North, particularly around Cambridge.[51] Poems such as 'Waikiki Beach' and 'Pacific Surf' make one imagine that there might have been a better Crowley – at least a contented one – had he been able to escape his existential daemon to perfect sunsets and restorative physical life. But, whether from the South Seas, Mexico or Sicily, Crowley was always returning to New York, Paris, Germany or (especially) England, where restoration of spirit seemed to require imaginative structures of arcane acts. Like Lawrence and other escapists to the South in the same era, he regarded the Sun as the great god and the phallus his 'vice-regent' on earth.[52] Northern life above all required rites to vitalise these. Clothes covered bodies as clouds covered sky, and the terrible face of Nature was often more manifest than her beauty. Thus Crowley cavorted in poetry, trying to evoke what was not present which seemed most essential. His most famous work, 'Hymn to Pan',[53] which is prominent in his great *grimoire, Magick in Theory and Practice* (1929), and was read out at his funeral in 1947, is a good example of this – and of the extent to which Crowley's poetry, ignored as poetry *per se*, gradually came to subserve his occult interest, reducing itself to the function of invocation. Another potent and telling effort in this regard is 'The Rosicrucian',[54] which sums up perhaps best of all the extent to which Crowley's efforts constituted a quest for the perfectly 'equilibrated', 'magical' *self:* anonymous, stoical, generous, detached, superior, divinely melancholic, fatalistic, pure, omniscient, godly and Godly – in sum, a kind of esoteric Count of Monte Cristo.

III GNOSTICISM

Crowley was not stable enough to become a Mejnour or Zanoni, though from time to time he attracted disciples so strongly that there can be no doubt that he had 'powers'. That these 'powers' came unstuck in every instance suggests that he was better at 'causing spiritual crises', as he once put it,[55] than sustaining a positive new cause. His 'Do What Thou Wilt' motto reveals the anarchic component of his 'magick', though admonitions to discipline pepper his 'sacred' books and his personality was authoritarian. In fact, his 'orders' – the A∴A∴ and later OTO – were more exploratory than creative, more destructive than charitable, more dialectical than fraternal. They were Gnostic more than Rosicrucian, though that is a fine distinction and one which Crowley would no doubt have mocked as sophistical. He was after all proud to declare himself a 33° Mason and took the 'magickal' name Baphomet to emphasise an affinity for the Knights Templar, both of which organisations connect with the Rosicrucians.[56] But, in a general sense, Freemasonry, Rosicrucianism and Templarism were all Gnostic as well: they opposed Catholic hegemony and suggested a higher, Unknown God, ascent to whose level required particular rites, formulae and 'words of power'. 'Gnosticism' can of course mean many things, as Hans Jonas's definitive study of the 'religion' indicates.[57] Hermeticism is a form of it: an 'optimist *gnosis*', to use Frances Yates's phrase. So is Anthroposophy: indeed, according to Geoffrey Ahern, Steiner's faith may be a self-conscious modern adaptation of the Valentinian heresy, which combined early Christianity with Syrian-Egyptian *gnosis* (as opposed to the Manichaean, or Persian-based, kind).[58] The word *gnosis* is Greek, meaning 'knowledge'; and the significance of its umbrella use is that Gnostic sects are those in which *knowledge* is viewed as essential to salvation, not *faith* and/or *good works* such as advocated by St Augustine and most established authority since his day. Unlike orthodox thinkers of pre-Christian, Augustinian or modern rationalist types, Gnostics also believe (though in varying degree) that matter is fallen, thus the material world a prison from which the individual spirit must strive to escape.

In this respect, it is easy to see how Steiner might be viewed as a Gnostic, in spite of his increasing attention to organic matter. But where does Crowley fit in, with his taste for costumes and cigars, fine food and liquor, the whole pharmacopia of drugs and satyricon of carnal possibilities? On the surface, it would seem that he was a devoted sybarite: the farthest thing from a spiritualist ascetic and in no fundamental sense world-rejecting. On balance, this may be true. But so much of his writing suggests rage at material existence that one begins to suspect that some portion of Crowley's apparent voracity for life was a mask held up against despair. His antinomianism, nihilism and libertinism[59] were self-conscious – indeed, routinised into the most unnatural systems, so that 'Do What Thou Wilt Shall Be the Whole of the Law' ends by seeming dogmatic ('*Law*'!) more than 'liberating'. Viewed in this way, the Crowley phenomenon might be seen as symptomatic of a modern outbreak of the most extreme type of Gnosticism, descended from the decadent classical world and further back from the rubble of Zoroastrianism left in the wake of Alexander the Great's conquest of Persia.[60] I have discussed this strain briefly in connection with Hitler in *Art, Messianism and Crime*: also its connection with the Cathars and their supposed 'love feasts' in the thirteenth century. Manifestations of the idea have reappeared through the centuries – perhaps, for instance, among some Anabaptists during the Reformation.[61] In essence, it goes like this: the cosmos is an evil construct of the Demiurge and Archons (a species of angel). God exists above and beyond it and has no direct relation to it, though some sparks in some men have a relation to him as they have descended from the collective of spirit around him known as the *pleroma*. Such sparks make their possessors alien to this world. Revolt is necessary to express their essential separation, disdain for cosmic laws, divine right to 'freedom' and desire to ascend. Moreover, in order to escape this world fully and *never be obliged to return to it in future incarnations*, this elect is compelled to perform every kind of action imaginable – including 'unmentionable deeds' – until all physical powers are exhausted, thus 'rendering to Nature its own'. Sin in this way is the means to Salvation. Jonas reminds us that the Cainites of the early centuries AD blasphemously invoked angels when performing gross carnal acts and dedicated the results to them.[62]

The satanism of Gilles de Rais,[63] the Marquis de Sade and the antagonists of Huysmans's *Là-bas* is motivated by a related rationale. So, on a more attractive level, are the Promethean cults of Shelley, Wagner and the handful of Romantic spirits to whom Crowley gave the only reverence he ever offered anyone.[64] Gnosticism of their sort is not mere satanism; nor is Crowley's, though it often draws close. Consider, for instance, this oath sworn by the 'Scarlet Woman' before collected Crowleyans at 'Thelema':

I will dedicate myself wholly without stint to the Great Work.
I will raise myself in pride.
I will follow Ra-Hoor-Khuit [Horus, of whom Crowley was the
    representative on earth] in His way:
I will work the work of wickedness:
I will kill my heart:
I will be loud and adulterous:
I will be covered with jewels and rich garments:
I will be shameless before all men:
I, for token thereof, will freely prostitute my body to the lusts
    of each and every Living Creature that shall desire it.

I claim the title Mystery of Mysteries, BABALON the Great, and the Number 156, and the Robe of the Woman of Whoredoms and the Cup of Abominations.[65]

This is 'liberating' in terms of conventional morality – a rejection of what is given (the law of the Archons and Demiurge) – but it is by no means a recipe for sheer licence. There is obligation here – a purposeful commitment to experience what in normal life would be considered most shameful, 'evil' – and that obligation is undertaken precisely for the Gnostic reasons of (1) expressing freedom and identity with the transcosmic Unknown, and (2) experiencing every action available in this world so as to exhaust its possibilities. Through the 'path of excess', one proceeds toward the 'palace of wisdom'.[66] Crowley as 'the Beast 666' was in a sense merely the 'guardian of the threshold' leading to the Way: thus his role as a gadfly, the constant mocker and insulter of his neophytes; and thus the ironic appropriateness of the fact that every one of his disciples ended up spurning him and carrying on beyond their experiences with him toward their own destinies. (Leah, for example – the Scarlet Woman for whom the oath above was created – renounced her 'title' in 1928, all relations with Crowley in 1930, and ended her life as what she had been before she had met him: a provincial American schoolmistress.[67])

To be caught up in 'the life whirlwind' is common to radical Gnosticism and Crowleyan 'magick' alike. (One of the few books not written by Crowley to be published by his A∴A∴ was entitled *The Whirlwind*, by Ethel Archer; others in this select company include *The Star in the West* by Captain J. F. C. Fuller and *The Triumph of Pan* by Victor Neuburg, the first a paean to Crowley's poetic skills, the second in large part to his phallic ones.) This element of wildness is what most divides Crowleyanity from the Golden Dawn, with which it otherwise had so much in common. There was little contentment, comfort or fixity *chez* Crowley, nor little sought for this side of the Beyond.[68] A central part of the *praxis* was systematic 'flattening of the ego' – indeed, self-conscious laceration of the psyche, which radical Gnostic tradition believed was as subject to cosmic 'evil' as the physical being.[69] Like Steiner, Crowley was most concerned with *spirit* beyond *soul*. But, whereas Steiner's 'exercises' were meant to locate the spiritual identity in the essential 'I', Crowley's were designed more to open that 'I' to the entry of 'strange gods'. Aiwaz, Chronozon

('Dispersion'), the Egyptian goddess Nuit, Horus and a range of others – possession by these is the object. Scarlet Women were chosen for their receptiveness and ability to get quickly 'out on the astral plane'.[70] Well-integrated personalities were less good than types with distinct oddity; thus Crowley's attraction for what in the 1960s would be called 'freaks'.[71] Drugs were a sacrament for 'opening the doors'; so too sex practices – masturbation, passive homo– or heterosexual acts – which could be extended to a point of 'eroto-comatose lucidity'.[72] Crowley and Crowleyanity in this way were above all mystical. Occult techniques were simply a principal means of reaching the realm of the stars ('Every man and woman is a star'[73] was the favourite Crowley motto after 'Do What Thou Wilt'): of ecstactic sensation and its obverse, agony – all areas where unusual insight might be maximised and, by virtue of it, some link forged with the absolute Other: the 'acosmic' *pleroma* and, beyond, Unknown God.

Crowley's urge in this direction echoes throughout his work:

> Between
> My soul and all its knowledge of
> The universe of light and love,
> Thought, being, nature, time and space,
> The Mother's heart, the Father's face,
> All that was agony or bliss,
> Stretched one infinite abyss.[74]

His cult of strength and will enunciated in *The Book of the Law* was a gauntlet thrown down against the requirements of this-worldly life: a justification for pursuing any means which seemed able to help him overleap that abyss. Cruelty and courage he had to teach himself: only by infliction and endurance of fear and pain could he confront and minimise death, which to his brand of Gnostic had to seem an irrelevance. Thus the sado-masochism of such a poem as 'Kali':

> She breaks me on the wheel of woe!
> . . . to drown my thought,
> To bring my being to naught . . .
> To fill me with the utmost sense
> Of some divine experience . . . [75]

Words and actions express a rage to get out: of this cosmos, this life, this self. Self-disgust surfaces almost as much as self-abuse, both mixed with an inordinate and suspect predilection for self-praise, advertisement and justification. 'Where there is naught – there is naught', the adept declares in a characteristic transformation of his former Golden Dawn brethren's comforting 'Where there is nothing – there is God.'[76] Death, at the end of a battered and burnt-out existence, is where hope may be posited finally. There where total passivity must reign is where spiritual force(s) may be most able to enter and triumph. Dream-filled trance, sex-induced coma or drug-exhaustion have been only shadows of this state; and, if the 'astral' insight gained through them was great, then, by the 'magical' doctrine of analogy, that gained through death might constitute real revelation. Crowley was never a fully doctrinaire Gnostic; his contempt for the cosmos too often turned into gleeful pranksterism for one to believe that he always and only wanted to exhaust himself and go to the Beyond. Still, this impulse was in him; and, like the 'optimist *gnosis*' of the Hermeticists or alchemists' faith that *prima materia* may be turned into gold, it helped him approach the final moment with remarkable calm – even eagerness:

> Out of the night forth flamed a star – mine own!
> Now seventy light-years nearer as I urge
> Constant mine heart through the abyss unknown,
> Its glory my sole guide while spaces surge
> About me. Seventy light-years! As I near
> That gate of light that men call death, its cold
> Pale gleam begins to pulse, a throbbing sphere,
> Systole and diastole of eager gold,
> New life immortal, warmth of passion bleed
> Till night's black velvet burn to crimson. Hark!
> It is Thy voice, Thy word, the secret seed
> Of rapture that admonishes the dark.
> Swift! By necessity most righteous drawn,
> Hermes, authentic augur of the dawn![77]

IV   WESTERN YOGA

Most criticism of Crowley in life was of a low-level, 'yellow journalism' sort. 'The Gnostic and Tantric sources of his philosophy were not even suspected,' John Symonds remarks, 'and the heretical nature of his views, in this age of unbelief, were [*sic*] ignored.'[78] The first element Crowley enshrined in his Gnostic Mass, one of the chief rites performed at his Abbey of Thelema and (according to Francis King[79]) still used with reverence and some beauty by Crowleyans in Switzerland. Crowley's Gnosticism may have had some distant relation to the Gnostic Catholic Church set up by Jules Doinel and 'Papus' in France in the 1890s.[80] His 'Western Tantricism', though largely his own invention, had a rather more demonstrable relation to Taoist techniques, 'left-handed' yoga[81] and sexual theories growing increasingly urgent under the surface of *fin-de-siècle* occultism. We have noted an argument between rival supporters of the American free-love advocates Thomas Lake Harris and John Humphrey Noyes in Yeats's *Speckled Bird*.[82] In passing, we have noted as well that Madame Blavatsky read Hargrave Jennings' *Phallicism*. (She probably had read his *Rosicrucians* too, which proposes the novel theory that the Holy Grail is a metaphysical vagina and glows red because of menstrual blood.[83]) Well before Freud, sexual symbolism was finding its way into swords, cups, wands and similar talismans and objects in a type of occult mind; and Crowley's sexual insurgency in the Golden Dawn and 'charging' of its rituals with latent erotic content was both an effect and a cause of the shift in turn-of-the-century *Zeitgeist* from Queen Victoria to D. H. Lawrence and beyond.[84] This may be the major reason for Crowley's bruising in the popular press, always eager to turn sex to scandal. To an era grown out of the 'sexual revolution', he may seem a sort of martyr in this way. But even by the standards of the 1960s to 1980s, many of Crowley's 'sex-magickal' practices must seem outrageous, even dangerous. Moreover, as Symonds also points out, anyone who persists in signing his name so that the first letter forms an oversized phallus dangling irrelevant testicles can hardly be trying to avoid a bad press.[85]

Taoist sexual techniques are designed to acheive endurance, health and wisdom.[86] Tantric and Sufi practices, derived from them, are about extending sexual energy up through the chakras until it causes a kind of spiritual orgasm behind and above the 'third eye'.[87] Crowley's 'sex magick' incorporated these ideas, adding to them the more typically Western motifs of pleasure, pain and power. Regarding the first: indulgence of every sexual urge was a logical outgrowth of his programme of hedonism and self-determination overall. Regarding the second: over-indulgence and its consequent terrors were justified by Gnostic notions such as described in the previous section. Regarding the third: sexual 'liberation' may give obvious bursts of feelings of potency to men and women suffering from repression and (in Crowleyan cases) inferiority over their 'freakish' natures. But power-through-sex went farther than this *chez* Crowley. Using the 'magical' doctrine of correspondences, he came to believe that, as orgasm represents the supreme ecstasy of physical life, so the spiritual process transpiring with it must produce the maximum psychic energy. Concentrating this energy and directing it may lead to transformational ends. Thus Crowley advocated using sex as a 'sacrament'. Acts were consecrated to pre-planned objectives: control over persons, invocation of spirits, inducement of health, prosperous voyage or even – later in life and rather pathetically – the finding of money.[88] Results of each act were written up in 'magical diaries' and analysed with para-religious zeal, both for quality and quantity. (Quantity was always a concern to Crowley, who was as proud of how long he could keep an erection as he was of the height of a mountain he had climbed, the number of words he had written in a fortnight or grams of cocaine he had ingested.[89]) The whole business might seem a means to enliven what otherwise threatened to become a routine physical function – or, less innocently, to ensure fascination of partners long after baldness and paunchiness had made the 'magician' as much of a 'freak' as any of them.[90] But, if the latter had been Crowley's only (or even principal) motive, he would not have given such high importance to masturbation too. As Symonds remarks, 'He literally wore himself out in acts which had as their object the establishing of the Law of Do What Thou Wilt.'[91]

Crowley played the female to young men but not solely to satisfy Wildean tastes. He presided over the fornication of a Scarlet Woman by a goat but not just to get a bestial, voyeuristic thrill. He called women by animal names as he fucked them, but this was meant to invest them with spirits, not just to abuse. He exhorted the American male to attend to the clitoris and practise delay, but this was meant to encourage spiritual ecstasy, not just the multiple orgasms of the sex manual.[92] 'Polymorphous perversity' was not the goal in itself, though removal of all repression was a *sine qua non* and initiation of the Age of Horus (the 'Crowned and Conquering Child', who exhibits 'innocence and irresponsibility' as well as 'strange modification of the reproductive instinct with a tendency to become bisexual or epicene'[93]) an essential by-product. Androgyny was encouraged, as suggested by Crowley's own identity as the hermaphrodite Baphomet in the OTO; but this too was only a stage. Because, finally, the goal of sex-magick was not really sex for Crowley: sex was merely a means which promised to be most effective, as it used the 'closest parts of man to the Sun and God'.[94] No, the goal of sex, as of all Crowley's *praxis*, was the *Abra-Melin* one of finding the True Self, with its benefits of imaginative insight and will. Thus in the end, as with many who appear obsessed with sex for some portion of life, Crowley's ambition was to be liberated from it:

> Every man should learn to master his passions absolutely. . . . The preliminary condition of success is to obtain a clear view of the subject in every detail, by accurate and intimate analysis. The first step is, obviously, to conquer the fear and fascination which the slightest allusion to the subject arouses in the ordinary man or woman. . . . People [must] acquire a complete intellectual mastery of the subject. When they can contemplate any sexual idea without emotion of any kind, they are well on the way to freedom. It is merely the same principle as that on which we act when we train a medical student to watch operations and dissect corpses, without weeping, fainting, getting cold feet, etc. . . . As long as he is excited about it, he cannot see straight; he becomes confused, and is totally unfit.[95]

Thus Crowley adapts to the most emotive area of personal (soul) life the exacting observational method the alchemist applied to his experiments, and Rosicrucians and Masons grew up to protect during the dawn of the 'new science'.

Crowley's approach to sex was yogic, which means it was about control. But Tantric sex was by no means the only yoga he specialised in. He practised breathing-exercises from early days in Ceylon with Allan Bennett, another one-time member of the Golden Dawn.[96] Stretching-exercises he came to advertise widely through nude photographs of himself.[97] Concentration techniques he refined with Oscar Eckenstein when climbing mountains in Mexico.[98] His particular success with these is related by Israel Regardie, who remembers the sixty-year-old Crowley playing and winning two games of chess simultaneously with eyes closed and mind visualising the moves.[99] This tale, if true, contradicts Symonds' belief that Crowley had damaged his brain by drug-abuse in the 1920s.[100] It also belies the yellow-press assumption that he was only interested in 'wickedness' and 'sin'. The fact is that Crowley wanted to advance all capabilities of the being to their limit – which is why he was always destined to throw away reputability for 'magick'. Regardie tells us that Crowley's chief virtue was his honesty, this especially to his diaries;[101] and there is something genuinely impressive about how the man followed his star come what may. Captain Fuller fell out with him because he, Crowley, would not take a strong stand in defence of homosexual practice in the libel trial of fellow A∴A∴ founder G. C. Jones.[102] But there are many reasons why Crowley should not have courted self-destruction in an era still digesting the fate of Wilde, not least because pederasty alone was not a sufficient cause for martyrdom. No cause save pursuit of the 'Great Work' could be that for Crowley, thus his ambiguous attitude toward his country in wartime and apparently ruthless concern for self above wives, children or anyone. Standard morality may never wholly accept Crowley's kind of behaviour, but it has moved closer toward it in the decades since his death. Nor is it too much to say that for his time Crowley was a kind of hero of the doctrine of 'live naturally', and in the face of opposition much greater than has confronted his successors.

Crowley was a precursor, as I said in *Art, Messianism and Crime*. His life was applied Nietzscheanism, fired by an *Angst* of activity unlike the philosopher's and glimmering with anticipations of 'flower power'. Then, too Crowley was very much a product of his time, which saw the most savage bloodlettings civilisation has known; and some of the brutality in him alien to our day may be put down to this. Mountaintop derring-do, prodigious sex and drug feasts, British bulldog mockery and glorified college-fraternity hazing were all part of this: a regimen of warlike virtues he sought to impress on the bourgeois. Raymond Chandler praised Dashiell Hammett for dropping crime fiction out of the drawing-room into the gutter, where it belonged.[103] Crowley, arch-snob though he was (in this not so different from Chandler), dared to do the same for 'magic': take it out of the teacups of Theosophist ladies and *chiens qui fument* such as Yeats and bring it first to the attention of men of action such as Fuller and later to the hustlers of Americanised 'mean streets'. Following his expulsion from the

Golden Dawn, Crowley grew increasingly disrespectful of high-minded cenacles sharing secrets; thus his publication of Mathers' rituals, lampooning of a typical Home Counties Mason[104] and acquiescence in the yellow-press urge to broadcast the 'truth about Thelema' to the mass. Crowley destroyed 'magic' finally as the bastion of an elite, completing a process Blavatsky had begun. He was ready to deliver it to whomever might use it who was strong, regardless of sex or background. Thus his chief collaborators became women, though he was a misogynist.[105] Nor was he above enlisting Nicaraguan voodooists, Arab catamites or Sicilian peasants into his orders, though at the same time inflating himself as 'Sir Aleister Crowley, Bart.' or 'Count Vladimar Svaroff'.[106] Such slumming, finally, was a two-way education; because from fallen women and hustlers the penniless 'gentleman' learned the most effective lesson for a person of his philosophy in the New Age – how to become a real con-artist.

To pay attention to this part of his persona may seem to avoid his 'magic'. But clearly the character of such a man as Crowley is at least as important as the content of his books – certainly it is more entertaining than his sub-Nietzschean 'holy' ones. Anyway, Crowley's doctrine can be summed up well enough without the Egyptian trappings. 'Be strong,' he wrote in *The Book of the Law*, 'then canst thou bear more joy!'[107] Here is where the essential yoga returns, because yoga in all forms – sexual, respiratory or gymnastic – is about strength: control, as said. 'Statements of feeling are poisonous, feminine things', Crowley wrote to Karl Germer, his successor as head of the OTO, which under Crowley became an active complement to the A∴A∴, which itself was an elaboration of the Golden Dawn. 'Never be weak and amiable: you will be taken advantage of.' And later: 'Personal problems are over in a few hours. Forget them. learn imperturbability. Shrug your shoulders when things don't go your way. Keep people guessing.' Finally: 'Hard work, even with pain, gives pride in manhood.' Lest this seem too male-obsessed or narrow in a power-of-positive-thinking sense, consider what he wrote to another disciple, female, about his orders' purpose and grades. (I paraphrase.[108]) The only way to know more about God is to explore the mind. The Great Work is to make Man God and God Man. As a Probationer, one must learn the nature and powers of one's own being; as a Neophyte, control of the same; as a Zelator, control of foundations; as a Practicus, control of vacillations; as a

Pholosophus, control of attractions and repulsions; as a Dominus Liminus (5° = 6□ in the Golden Dawn), control of aspirations; as an Adeptus Minor, knowledge and conversation with the Holy Guardian Angel. *Samadhi* (the yogic state of enlightenment) will be attained after three months' trance meditation, with diary. What appears the supreme vision will in a year appear as a bar to progress; but falling-away is a natural part of the process; thus, so long as a record is kept, the thread may be picked up again. This will lead on to higher levels – VIII°, IX°, and XI°, of the OTO, for instance, with their ritual counterparts in auto-, hetero– and homosexual acts – thence to the ultimate: completion of the Great Work, which involves passing out through the state of Ipsissimus, where mortal becomes one with his immortal genius and may begin to laugh with the best of transluminaries about the world he has left below.

V   CROWLEY AS *ZEITGEIST*

The ultimate 'magician' may reject 'magic'. Certainly, he is bound to remake it for himself. The remaking is memorable in so far as it captures or anticipates the spirit of the age. This is the case with Crowley and what separates him from his fellow students of the Golden Dawn. They always remained that: students – Mathers with his translations, Waite with his historical tomes, Yeats with his romantic imaginings on partly gleaned facts. Crowley, by contrast, went beyond. Like Joyce in language and Lawrence in sex-content, he was a groundbreaker for the new rather than exhumer of the old. But like Chandler, whom we have also mentioned, he was a spirit hounded by self-contempt; and, like the Dadaists and Surrealists of his Paris of the 1920s, he viewed civilization alternately as an absurdist game or cosmic joke. Regardie says that Crowley should have died in 1914:[109] that all his great thinking had been done by then and, having run through his fortune, he henceforth became a sneerer and sponger, con-man and purveyor of dope. Well, Regardie's point of view has merit for those who believe that civilized life, even for a 'magician', should end up in pipe-smoking, condo-owning and dispensing of post-Freudian analysis from sea-view offices in Pacific Palisades. Krishnamurti could achieve such an apotheosis; the 'Star in the West' neither could nor would. Crowley did become a notorious heroin addict, extort money, engage in unjustified litigation even against old friends[110] and ruin weaker adepts' lives. These were means and by-products implicit in his 'magic' and, finally, what made him familiar to the wild and wide-open 1960s, unlike more tidy spirits discussed. They are also why one publisher who brought out several of his works in the 1970s now claims to be embarrassed to have touched Crowley at all.[111] As an age of excess recedes, its prophets and precursors lose their temporal aura of reputability.

Would Crowley have minded? He wrote to a disciple that personal life does not matter; what is left after death is only the 'Great Work'[112] – the individual's contribution to the great store of human knowledge and achievement. So on this basis is the man forgettable? merely a footnote to our times (the status to which Mario Praz consigned him in his *Romantic Agony* of the 1930s)? Perhaps it is too soon to say, in an era still reverberating from culture-shocks of the 1960s. Perhaps too it depends on what is to be made of the man as *writer*, as well as that more ephemeral designation 'magician'. On this basis, the question boils down to how his books are presented. If readers are confronted with a haphazard smattering of the opus – including so much which is half-baked, embittered or plain bad – they can only conclude that the man was a crank hardly worth mentioning, let alone reading. If on the other hand they are presented with a limited, coherent canon – as say, in the case of Eliot – then some minor literary status may be granted after all. This will seem a heretical view among literary critics, and perhaps even contradictory of what I have already said. But suppose Crowley's opus were consolidated into five or six volumes thus: a selection of poems (though not the one recently put out by Martin Booth, which lacks chronology and annotation at least[113]); a selection of letters, since this is the genre where the personality of a great conversationalist (as Crowley was[114]) is most apparent; the two completed novels, *Moonchild* and *Diary of a Drug Fiend*; an abridged version of *Confessions* (leaving out in particular much of the technical matter about mountain-climbing, which Crowley himself found boring[115]); and perhaps – though not for the 'common reader' – what Symonds calls his 'masterpiece',[116] *Magick in Theory and Practice*.

There is much in these books which is silly, scabrous or inscrutable. At the same time, there are passages of wit, insight and sheer writerly zest – at moments the energy of a Balzac.[117] The so-called 'holy books', by contrast, are pretentious, obscurantist, sub-Nietzschean tracts which shadow the very light they propose to shed and add little to what is available in, say, the last part of *Confessions* or *Magick*. 'Magicians' may object to this assessment. For them, the Cabalistic numbering of *The Book of the Law* or massive system of correspondences indicated in *777* may provide a lifetime of interest. But this is the equivalent of football cards for occultists and looks back toward the spirit of the Golden Dawn and the 1890s more than forward through Freud, Jung and Reich to the mid twentieth century. Out of the buzz and Babel of his 'magical' youth, Crowley refined a philosophy fit for the Nazi upheavals of his last years[118] and 'Do your own thing' era beyond. 'MAGICK is the Science and Art of causing change to occur in conformity with will', he wrote in the introduction to his great *grimoire*.[119] 'Every intentional act is a magical act' and requires for its success:

- understanding conditions
- ability to set in motion the right forces
- belief that 'Every man and woman is a star'
- belief that every man and woman has his own course
- knowledge of one's own will and refusal to let anything block it
- recognition that Nature is a continuous phenomenon
- recognition that Science allows us to know Nature
- recognition that Man is ignorant of his ultimate capabilities
- recognition that Man may subject the whole universe to his will
- recognition that every force may be transformed to a different purpose
- recognition that Man should not separate himself from the universe
- recognition that one should only employ forces for which one is fitted
- recognition that power to use force is limited by mental ability and environment
- recognition that the individual may be self-sufficient but he will only be happy when he is in the right relation to the universe
- recognition that Magick means understanding and applying understanding to action

- recognition that every thought is an action and must be dealt with, as it willy-nilly leads on the the next
- recognition that every man has the right to self-preservation and fulfillment
- recognition that every man has the right to fulfil his own will without being afraid that it may interfere with that of others; for he is in his proper place, and it is the fault of others if they interfere with him. Napoleon is an example. If there is conflict, it means that one party has strayed from his course. Be firm in your course: you will be an example, and not an object of confusion to, others.

We see in this Crowley's emphasis on *the power of thought*. *Reason* in the end is his god, like Lévi's.[120] However, Crowley admires the opposite and equal force of *Unreason* as well. Indeed, the secret of his thought and power, such as it is, depends on the deployment of the one against the other. Consider for instance, this conversation between Crowley's persona Cyril Grey and one of his disciples in *Moonchild*:

'What is the most serious thing in the world?'
'Religion.'
'Exactly. Now what is religion? The consummation of the soul by itself in divine ecstasy. What is life but love, and what is love but laughter? In other words, religion is a joke. There is the spirit of Dionysus and there is the spirit of Pan; but they are twin phases of laughter. Now what is the most absurd thing in the world?'
'Woman.'
'Right again. And therefore she is the only serious island in this ocean of laughter. While we hunt and fish, and fight, and otherwise take our pleasure, she is toiling in the field and cooking, and bearing children. So, all the serious words are jests, and all the jokes are earnest. This, oh my brother, is the key to my light and sparkling conversation.'
'But – '
'I know what you are going to say. You can reverse it again. That is precisely the idea. You keep on reversing it; and it gets funnier and more serious every time, and it spins faster and faster until you cannot follow it, and your brain begins to whirl, and presently you become that Spiral Force which is of the

Quintessence of the Absolute. So it is all a simple and easy method of attaining the summit of perfections, the stone of the Wise, True Wisdom and Perfect Happiness.'[121]

Here we see too how Crowley's essential objective really is the one the Masonic founders of the United States put in their initial Declaration – 'Life, Liberty and *the pursuit of happiness*' – but that the method by which he characteristically tries to achieve this is the one Wilde and British wits always held as ideal: conversation. The latter draws its interest from paradox and authority from precise use of language; and on this Crowley was as much a stickler in his own way as Victorian grammarians had been before him or Scientological neologists would be after.

Crowley's letters are full of lectures about the right use of words. He himself appears to have found his way around in Hebrew, Greek, Latin, French, German, Italian and possibly to some degree Spanish, Portuguese, Hindi and Chinese as well. His use of English can be arch high-Oxbridge or gutter American,[122] as depiction of characters in *Moonchild* shows. He can make language direct and clear or, more subtly, make it appear clear while being obfuscatory, as in the story 'The Stratagem'. He was accused by old friend and biographer C. R. Cammell of resorting to 'James Joyce foolery' when trying to put off creditors.[123] On the other hand, he could hold up the circumlocutory style of A. E. Waite to high comic (perhaps over-the-top) parody.[124] As is obvious from his novels, he lacked facility for plotting and the best stylists' commitment to thorough revision; and he was much given to authorial intrusions, such as boasting, insulting, glorifying self through personae, ham-fisted selling of 'magickal' opinion and sheer exhibitionism. That said, he has few problems with voice or authority. In fact, Crowley seems to have been a born writer, if self-damagingly undisciplined one. Nor was he a one-trick pony in the type of tale he told, either in style or content. *Moonchild* is mannered, third-person, of a pre-First World War era of formalism, and has more in common with *The Picture of Dorian Gray* than just the similarity in heroes' surnames. *Drug Fiend*, on the other hand, is – like *Demian* or *Ulysses* – a book which could not have been written before that great cultural watershed: a book whose first-person narrator loses his manners before our eyes, in a 'confession' which is as chaotic as the title portends – both manically social and anti-social: a super-charged and depleted version of the prototypical tale of an age which in house-broken form made the career of F. Scott Fitzgerald.

It seems significant too that – as in Fitzgerald's last completed novel, *Tender is the Night* – the trajectory of the author's imagination geographically is to the South: specifically the Mediterranean. Here, where he constructed his Abbey of Thelema, is where Crowley came closest to overcoming the terror of being in this cosmos. Here is the antidote to the 'dark night of the soul' of his 'drug fiends': membership in a community organised along those rules set down in *Magick:* to maximise individual happiness and will by application to the 'Great Work' – the specific functional addition an individual can make to the whole – in close relation and harmony with the splendour of Nature. So much had not been possible in the cities of the North; and, like scores of contemporaries, Crowley in life and art manifests European man's urge to break out his prison of place and past into the light and future. Expatriation is necessary for this; but arrival at paradise is premature unless one has gone through the initiation of having been thoroughly damned. Only having done as much may one come – in Crowley's most lyrical and hopeful view, set down near the end of *Drug Fiend* – out the other side, as it were, to a place and order entirely free, utopian, new and yet paradoxically as old as the Eden of all precious dreams of the soul:

'[Take] one glance at the incomparable beauty of the place [the Crowley persona, King Lamus, observes]; a beauty which varies every day and never tires. Look at the sunset every night. It is good for two hours of grand opera. It is almost stupefying to sit in the terrace of the villa and watch the ever-changing glories of night-fall. And the night itself! . . .'

We looked with enthralled attention [the disciple-narrator goes on]. The beauty of the place beat hard upon our brains. It was unbelievable. Patches of cancer like Paris and London were cut ruthlessly out of our consciousness. We had come from the ephemeral pretentiousness of cities to a land of eternal actuality. We were re-born into a world whose every condition was on a totally different scale to anything in our experience. A sense of innocence pervaded us. It was as if we had awakened from a nightmare; our sense of time and space had been destroyed; but we knew that our old standards of reality had been delusions.

Clocks and watches were mechanical toys. In [Thelema], our time-keeper was the Nature of which we were part.[125]

9
L. Ron Hubbard and Scientology

I JACK PARSONS AND 'FRATER H'

Kenneth Grant, present head of the OTO in Britain, tells us that Crowley's most promising disciple of later years was John W. Parsons, second head of the 'Agape Lodge' in California, nuclear-fuel expert and sometime friend of L. Ron Hubbard.[1] John Symonds was sued by Scientology for writing in *The Great Beast* about Hubbard's and Parsons' association;[2] and, in order not to invite a simlar fate, Francis King, in repeating the story, refers to the founder of Scientology as 'Frater H' or 'Frater Scire' ('Scire eventually succeeded . . . in achieving fame in many other fields than magic – inventing an anti-radiation compound, growing gigantic tomatoes, and curing people of lifelong sinus infections, for example'[3]). Having little desire to evoke the wrath of the most litigious of contemporary cults,[4] I will repeat no more than what has been written, synthesising from extant sources and adding the qualification that, just as many of the 'facts' Hubbard told of his life have proved at best demi-fictions, so many of the tales subscribed to by his denigrators may have elements of untruth as well. Evil invites evil; or, in this case – keeping in mind the Scientological doctrine of 'Fair Game'[5] – legend promotes mockery: or, more pointedly still, prevarication produces lies. By proximity in time, Hubbard's life should be the easiest of all our 'magicians" to chronicle. In fact, it is the most difficult. The man was so taken with myth and 'PR', and so mistrustful of received fact in a relativistic world, that he put out what he wanted to be heard and denied what he did not, even when technically accurate.[6] The object from a true-believing Scientological point of view was 'a higher truth'. The result for the rest of us is that Hubbard, on inspection, seems at best a genius of 'flim-flam', or what the

Society for Physical Research called Madame Blavatsky, one of history's great 'imposters'.[7] This may be unfair. The fact of Scientology's size and appeal to people of intelligence as well as psychological cripples suggests that there must be value in it. Moreover, in Hubbard as in Hitler (to whom he is compared by detractors[8]), there was undoubtedly something of 'merit', to use Churchill's word, even if only the captivating detritus of paranoid schizophrenia.[9] Like others discussed here, Hubbard saw himself as a 'liberator', not a destroyer. Successive lawsuits against his cult have testified to opposing opinions. But the man himself appears genuinely to have believed that his 'tech' was made not merely to extort money and power,[10] but to lead individuals toward a higher state of being and ultimately thereby 'clear the planet'.

The Crowley connection illustrates one's problems with facts. In his Philadelphia lectures in 1952, Hubbard is reported to have said, 'The magical cults of the 8th–12th centuries in the Middle East were fascinating; the only modern work that has anything to do with them is a trifle wild in spots but is a fascinating work in itself, and that's written by Aleister Crowley – the late Aleister Crowley – my very good friend.'[11] In fact, Hubbard could not have met Crowley, and what communication there was between them was second-hand via Parsons and hardly 'friendly'. Parsons had written to Crowley in 1946 that he had met a red-haired ex-naval man, writer of science fiction, who had evident 'magical' powers.[12] Crowley, alert to Parsons' guilessness, having preyed on it himself, warned against being taken in by the apparent good faith of interlopers and giving away secret lore. The instinct of the old 'magus' proved justified. The story goes that Parsons first allowed Hubbard to be his 'skryer' (recorder of visions) during acts of VIII° sex-magick (masturbation); then, once Hubbard had fully gained Parsons' confidence and virtually moved into his proto-commune on Pasadena's 'millionaire's row', the guileless young 'magician' invited the interloper to perform the same function in a complicated series of acts of IX° sex-magick (heterosexual) with his wife, these designed to give birth to a 'moonchild'. Such experiments, we know from Crowley's eponymous novel, take months. In the course of theirs, Hubbard and Parsons are said to have set up a company called Allied Enterprises, with a bank-account, and (on Hubbard's suggestion presumably, considering his lifelong naval associations) to have bought a yacht. Eventually, the man whom in letter Crowley had come to refer to as a 'lout'[13] is said to have run off with the yacht, the money from the bank-account *and* Parson's wife, only to be brought to heel some time later in Florida when the yacht ran aground and was impounded. The facts of the bizarre tale may have been knocked askew in retellings, but Hubbard himself did not deny the essence. In a letter to *The Sunday Times* in 1969, he claimed that he had been sent into Parsons' sect by US Naval Intelligence, which was worried about a group of nuclear physicists living together under the same roof.[14] In a recent lawsuit, a British judge poured scorn on this explanation;[15] and it does seem like one of Hubbard's ingratiating fictions. At other times, the Church of Scientology has maintained that Hubbard entered Parsons' cult as an undercover agent working for the Los Angeles Police – not Naval Intelligence, which he may have worked for during the War but probably not after,[16] Nor the Federal Bureau of Investigation, which is the motivating party in some variants of the tale.

What is the truth? *Chez* Hubbard, it is not only difficult but – considering the lawsuits – dangerous to say. Regarding the Crowley link, the other relevant testimony comes from Hubbard's fifty-two-year-old son, Ronald DeWolf, who changed his name out of disgust with his father. DeWolf claims that 'when Crowley died in 1954 [sic], my father thought he should wear the cloak of the beast and become the most powerful being in the universe'.[17] DeWolf is often discounted as a source on the basis that he and his father fell out in the later 1950s and he was entirely disinherited from the multi-million-dollar estate Hubbard amassed via Scientological trademarks and writings.[18] But family animosity does not necessarily always produce lies. Nor does the Crowley identification conflict with DeWolf's claim that when he was a boy Hubbard fed him phenobarbital in his bubble-gum to make him into a 'moonchild', nor with Hubbard's first wife's charge that he was into 'PDH' (pain, drugs and hypnosis) in the 1930s, nor his second wife's claim that he committed bigamy and experimented on her with torture and drugs.[19] The second wife's claim is supposed to have been retracted shortly after it was made. But it seems likely that Hubbard was interested in sex, drugs and 'magic' in this period.[20] He had, moreover, just been released from the pressures of the second World War; and many an ex-sailor in his thirties finds it hard to resist 'adventure' and 'good times'. That Hubbard had long had a taste for the experimental and bizarre is testified to by his early science fiction and fantasy writings.[21]

Finally, intriguingly, he apparently wrote to the Veterans' Administration shortly after the Parsons episode that he felt in need of
psychiatric treatment – a fact which attests to either the kind of
post-combat shakiness which could have led to a period of
dangerous eccentricity, or (as some suggest) an extreme cunning
in trying to get service-related disability payments.[22] (In spite of
claims that he was writing Hollywood screenplays, Hubbard
appears to have been impecunious at the time.) Whatever the
case, the plea for psychiatric help is extremely ironic in light of the
anti-psychiatry, anti-psychology stand Hubbard and Scientology
have taken in succeeding decades.[23] And DeWolf's suggestion of
an intimate, unacknowledged inspiration for Hubbard's 'religion'
in Crowleyanity – or at least what a disturbed Hubbard imagined
Crowleyanity to be during his weird association with Parsons –
deserves to be taken seriously, alongside the theories about its
origins in military programming, sci-fi, Ron's early 'journey to the
East' and so on:

> What a lot of people don't realise is that Scientology is black
> magic . . . spread out over a long time period. To perform black
> magic generally takes a few hours or, at most, few weeks, but
> in Scientology it's stretched over a lifetime and so you don't see
> it. Black magic is the inner core of Scientology – and is probably
> the only part of Scientology that really works.[24]

What is Hubbard likely to have picked up from Parsons?
Symonds says sweepingly that Hubbard stole the lore on which
he would later base his cult;[25] and, if anything justifies Scientology
litigation, it is this kind of speculative overstatement. Still,
Hubbard could have derived significant elements: specifically, the
mesmeric effect of ritual and power of the idea of transcendence.
Such motifs might have been taken as well from Theosophy –
there are some favourable references to the 'Wisdom of the East'
in some Scientology texts,[26] but there is no evidence that Hubbard
had any experience of Blavatsky's cult. On the other hand, he
must have known about one of the older origins of what he
observed *chez* Parsons, because in 1952, in Phoenix, when
searching for a name for his prospective new religion, he fixed for
a time on 'Church of the Golden Dawn'.[27] Parsons evidently had
not tried to disguise where Crowley had stolen *his* lore from.
And what was the nature of Parsons' own mid-twentieth-century,

Californian version of Golden Dawn *praxis*? In a letter to Marjorie Cameron (the 'Scarlet Woman' he took up with after Hubbard had made off with his wife), Parsons lays down the following instructions on 'invoking':

(1) Perform the ritual of the Banishing Pentagram[*sic*]
(2) Open the 'hexagram'.
(3) Perform the main ritual, starting with a preliminary invocation like Crowley's 'Bornless One' and then, if invoking a god (defined as 'superior force' –

    (a) supplicate the force
    (b) describe the force
    (c) identify (causing union) with the force

    –, or, if invoking a spirit, angel, demon or elemental (all defined as 'lesser forces') –

    (a) supplicate a superior force (god)
    (b) describe superior force
    (c) identify (unite) with superior force
    (d) as superior force, invoke and command lesser force.

(4) Close the 'hexagram'.
(5) Reperform the ritual of the Banishing Pentagram.[28]

This of course is essential Macgregor Mathers. Further, Parsons adds these equally Golden Dawn motifs: that the 'magician' must stand in a circle and invoke forces into a triangle; that all perfumes, colours, names, signs and weapons used must be appropriate to the force desired; that the 'magician' should wear a robe and mitre appropriate to the highest force being invoked; that he should carry a sword to use against anyone threatening to break into the circle; that, once started, a ritual should never be interrupted; that a secluded place (temple) should be used; that no non-adept should be allowed to participate.

It would be impossible for Hubbard to have been around Parsons for long and not have absorbed much of this. Fresh from the no-nonsense world of the Navy, he perhaps saw some of it as fanciful, effeminate and foolish. On the other hand, always preoccupied with 'genius', he must have been impressed with the faith an exceptional scientist educated at California Institute of Technology put in such mummery. Nor could he have failed to note the powerful state of 'suggestibility' induced by drawn-out sessions and memorised 'words of power'.[29] Whatever Hubbard's personal feelings about Parsons, some of these 'magical' motifs would eventually find their way into Scientology practice, stripped of their fantastic–poetic elements and reornamented with pseudo-scientific jargon. The latter was better suited to attract an America which knew more about gear-boxes than gods – or, as John Steinbeck remarked in the period,[30] more about the inner workings of a battered Ford than the clitoris, in spite of Crowley's premature 'sex-magickal' efforts. Sex Hubbard also dropped. That he was laughing up his sleeve at Parsons' OTO VIII° and IX° rites seems probable, especially if we believe the story that, while the 'initiate' was occupied with such pastimes, Hubbard made off with his money, yacht and wife. Parsons counselled that invocation of a god was an act of 'art' and 'love' and required 'wooing', while invocation of elements and the like was an act of 'science', requiring 'compelling'.[31] Hubbard threw out the 'wooing' and concentrated on the 'science', where with his background he would naturally imagine true 'power' to lie. In this context, it does not really matter whether he was operating as an undercover agent or simply as a con-man, or both. What would have interested him *chez* Parsons would have been what seemed dynamically *useful*, serving to aggrandise the individual or group and to make others 'suggestible'. Thus he probably paid little attention to Parsons' poetry: the *Songs for the Witch Woman*, for instance, which would so interest another latter-day Crowleyan, Kenneth Anger, that he would spend a sleepless night in the early 1960s smoking marijuana with Parsons' widow[32] and copying out lyrics with titles such as 'Pan', 'Sorcerer', 'Narcissus', 'Sabat', 'Merlin', 'Passion Flowers', 'Neurosis', and 'Lesbians' to send to Crowley archivist Gerald Yorke.[33]

Parsons' poetry concentrates on 'forbidden things'; night-evoked spirits; the 'thaumaturgic tune' which may eventually bring the old gods back. In 'Under the Hill', a goat and girl dance, he wise as a snake, she with 'demon eyes' which lead him down a vaginal byway of flowers to a place where he 'performs stately phallic arabesques in the moonlight'. This is pure 'flower-child' Crowley, full of the 'magician's' transcendental longing for the overarching great goddess: unattainable, star-spangled Nuit.

I remember
When I was a star . . .
I remember
When I was a god . . .
And when a voice cried
Go free, star, go free
Seek the dark home
In the wild sky.

Like Crowley, Parsons would have been at home in the 1960s. As it was, in 1952, at the age or thirty-seven, he was blown up in a mysterious chemical explosion in the lab behind his house.[34] This finis provoked much speculation at the time. Before he died in 1947, Crowley had warned Parsons against the red-haired woman (Cameron) who had appeared in his life at the moment Hubbard absconded with his wife;[35] and, if Cameron were implicated in some way in Parsons' demise (as some suspect), then a fantasist might wish to suggest that Parsons, this young *voyant*, was one of the early victims of Hubbard's Machiavellian pursuit of power.[36] Less fancifully, we can say with reasonable assurance that Hubbard took from his association with Parsons a vicarious relation to the worlds of chemistry, rocket construction, nuclear physics and 'magic'. Moreover, he shared with this fellow free-thinker in the age of the Bomb a fundamental suspicion of the course of the planet's life as it existed and urge to transcend toward something better. Parsons' alienation and elitism in this regard is set down in his succinct posthumous essay *Magick, Gnosticism and the Witchcraft*,[37] which advocates gaining knowledge over man's body, brain, myths and initiatory traditions in order to combat 'the destructive and abortive nightmares of the terminal stage called modern civilisation', and – on the macrocosmic level – calls for study and 'equilibration' of the external force-fields of the universe, which have an analogous relation to what is in man. Both precepts are classical 'orthodox heretical' ones, emphasising *knowledge* above all; and both would have direct successors in the 'dianetic' (clearing the inner self) and 'higher-tech' aspects of Scientology, which Hubbard defined not as 'magic' but as 'religion' – the religion of 'Knowing How to Know'.

II LEGEND OF THE MASTER

One of the 'occult' ideas Hubbard absorbed was of 'past lives'. He never claimed like Crowley to be a reincarnation of specific historical figures; and if he had, he surely would have avoided the likes of Eliphas Lévi, Adam Weishaupt and Cagliostro.[38] Evidence suggests that he saw himself in an exalted tradition of 'white-magical' teachers. A pictorial hagiography of his youth in the 1978 'official' publication *What is Scientology?* is preceded by a synoptic view of man's 'search for wisdom and knowledge', in which the key figures are Zoroaster, Lao-Tse, Gautama Buddha, Socrates, Jesus of Nazareth, Mohammed, heretical opponents of the Catholic Inquisition, the creators of The American *Declaration of Independence* and the founders of modern psychology.[39] The fact that these portraits blend without break into representations of Hubbard's development make the cautious reader pause to think. For the credulous, to whom the book is directed, the impression can hardly be avoided that Ron's life has an intimate relation to the careers of these great ones – indeed, in the light of indications in another 'official' work, *Have You Lived This Life Before?*[40] an implicitly reincarnative one.

Only after such an introduction does the 'official' life unfold. Lafayette[41] Ronald Hubbard was born in Nebraska in 1911. His father was a US Naval commander, his mother a 'thoroughly educated woman' ('a rarity in her time!'[42]). He grew up on 'a large ranch in Montana', where he spent his free days 'breaking broncos, hunting, and taking his first treks as an explorer'. Becoming familiar from an early age with cowboys and Indians, he even became 'blood brother' to a Pikuni medicine man. By the time he was ten, he was 'thoroughly educated', especially by the exemplary mother. By twelve, he had 'read a large number of the world's greatest classics'. As a teenager, he studied Freud under a commander of the US Naval Medical Corps. Then he went to China, where he met the 'last in the line of magicians of Kublai Khan'; then Tibet, where he lived in a lamasary and became friendly with native bandits; then the South Pacific, where he discovered an underground river whose rumblings had been frightening the superstitious Melanesians; then Polynesia, where he ventured intrepidly into ghostly burial grounds, despite warnings of dire consequences. At last, returning to America, he underwent 'intense study' at prep school and finally enrolled in the Engineering College of George Washington University.

Here he took 'one of the first nuclear physics courses ever taught'. But, even while exploring the most *avant-garde* secrets of science, Ron realised that there must be more to man's quest for knowledge: that some higher synthesis of the spititualism of the East and materialism of the West must be sought. Drifting away from academic study, he began to write. Essays, technical articles on sport and aviation, fantasy and science fiction flowed from his pen in a torrent which, by the time of publication of *What Is Scientology?* nearly half a century on, had reached an inundating 15 million words in print. (Alas, by now, with posthumous works plus the 'biggest SF novel ever in terms of length',[43] it must be nearer 20 million – the literary equivalent of the boast over McDonald's hamburger stands of 'Over Four Billion Sold!') Still famished for 'first-hand' knowledge, he travelled to the West Indies to study voodoo and to Alaska to learn of the ways of the Thunderbird from the Tlingit Indians. Then, the book tells us,

> Out of the tremendous body of data he had acquired, he organised and honed many facts. Ron later wrote: 'Workability rather than idealism was consulted.'
>
> The breakthrough came when he found that the basic single thrust of life throughout history was that Man, in common with all species, was striving to *survive* and that 'survival might be defined as an impulse to persist through time, in space, as matter and energy' and that 'by survival is meant everything necessary to survival including honor and morals and other things which make life bearable.'

Following this Buck Rogers youth and prophet-like awakening, the 'facts' begin to get more vague. Ron went to the Phillipines during the second World War. We are told nothing of his combat experience, only that 'he saw enough of war at first hand to be sickened by it' and that he ended up back in Washington in a Naval hospital 'crippled and blinded'. It is implied that the period of convalescence lasted three years – strange when it is remembered that this is the same period when he was supposed to have been writing screenplays in Hollywood and 'breaking up black magic in America'. There is no mention that he was under psychiatric care. Indeed, the care administered is depicted as so ineffi-

cacious that Ron had to develop techniques of his own. Thus out
of personal hardship came the seeds of his future teachings. We
are given the impression that he cured himself and brought hope
to fellow patients. We are told pointedly that his recovery 'shook
the medical and psychiatric officers' of the Navy and delivered 'a
hard blow' to 'their fixed ideas and practices.' Here enters the
motif of antagonism between the self-made genius and powerful
cabal of orthodox medicine and rigid bureaucracy which would
become an increasing hallmark of Hubbard's career, culminating
in a $750-million lawsuit at the time of publication of *What Is
Scientology?* against the US Federal Government for harassment.[44]

What happened? Was Hubbard let out of the Naval hospital
mentally unstable? Had his injury and/or treatment been a kind
to fill him with some smouldering inner rage? Had he in fact
experienced a revulsion (such as later American military personnel
would bring back home from Vietnam) against a kind of authority
which views men as numbers and cannon-fodder? Had he
developed the related neurosis of ex-Intelligence officers bound
by lifetime pledges of secrecy to agencies whose Machiavellianism
they know far too well to trust or believe in any longer? All these
may be so.[45] Then, too, whatever crises Hubbard went through in
the period may have triggered deeper Oedipal aggression against
his Naval father, of whom he hardly speaks. (Education is ascribed
to the mother, money for travel to a wealthy grandparent; nor are
there the typical American boy memories of riding with Dad over
the mountains or going to sporting-events.) The facts are obscure
now. *What is Scientology?*, like other 'official' sources, simply tells
us that Hubbard began to develop a vast theory based on 'the
vital discovery that you can always get function or thought to
monitor structure' – in other words, the old Hermetic–Gnostic idea
that mind is superior to matter.

From this evolved 'Dianetics', which Hubbard derives wrongly
from the Greek (*Dianous*) to mean 'through the soul'.[46] This 'mind-
technology' was soon believed to be able to cure 'such psychosomatic ills as hypertension, combat fatigue, apathy, rage, myopic
astigmatism and chronic skin rash'. Letters 'began to pour in',
soliciting Ron's advice. In 1950 he wrote what would become
Scientology's bible, *Dianetics: The Modern Science of Mental Health*.[47]
This 'surged' to the top of the *New York Times* bestseller list; and
the rest, as they say, is history. Indeed, in terms of Scientology
PR, it is history to such a degree that the rest of the pictorial

section of *What is Scientology?* leaves the career of Ron Hubbard as abruptly as the story of his youth obliterated the preceding saga of man's 'search for wisdom and knowledge'. This second shift is perhaps even more jarring than the first, because the cult of Hubbard has been Scientology's basis since its inception; nor did it wane for three decades 'AD' – that is, after the epoch-making 'discovery' of Dianetics. From 1950 to 1980, the story of Hubbard and his cult are essentially one. Successive books poured forth – *A History of Man, The Science of Survival* and *Advanced Axioms and Procedures* (all 1951), *How to Live through an Executive* (1953), *The Creation of Human Ability* (1955), *The Fundamentals of Thought* (1967) and so forth – as well as a weight of lectures and directives worthy of the workaholic Rudolf Steiner on every conceivable subject of interest to his followers.

From the release of *Dianetics*, a cult grew. In the early 1950s, Gloria Swanson and Dave Brubeck were among celebrities said to be fascinated; a relation of DeMille's was able to get the phrase 'Dianetic processing' into a film in place of 'psychoanalysis'.[48] Always keen on Hollywood, Hubbard no doubt was gratified by this attention. (Later years would see him setting up a 'Celebrity Center' to attract musicians and actors of a younger generation[49]) But more important early supporters were his old science-fiction - writing pals from New York, John W. Campbell, Jr, and A. E. Van Vogt.[50] The former is said to have encouraged Hubbard's move from straight sci-fi to the writing of psychological tracts, while the latter was important in setting up the original Dianetics organis- ation with the help of Mid-Western oil man Don Purcell. Deter- mined to be *primus* and too convinced of his own genius to enjoy being limited by *pares*, Hubbard left Diantics-as-organisation and in 1952 in Phoenix, after searching for a time for a name, launched the Church of Scientology. The 'religious' aspect was assumed from the first to be a ruse to enable administration of psychological treatment tax-free as part of a 'non-profit' enterprise. Scientology went on to make countless millions in this guise. But in defence of Hubbard's contention that he was truly forming a 'religion' is the fact that the major *doctrinal* reason he broke with his early Dianetic comrades is that they wanted to transform his discoveries into widely accepted medical practice, whereas he refused to give up the distinctly mystical idea that the ultimate goal should be to liberate the individual spirit or 'thetan' beyond single earthbound lives.

This religious aspect would become increasingly important in later and 'higher' developments of the cult. Meanwhile, in the 1950s, Hubbard kept fairly close to the 'scientific' ideas of Dianetics, even going so far as to introduce an 'Electropsychometer' (a skin-sensitive ersatz lie-detector) into his 'processing'.[51] As his organisation reached a first plateau of development in the mid-1950s, he began travels which would spread the cult to a number of other countries, mostly English-speaking; Australia, New Zealand, South Africa, Great Britain, Rhodesia and so forth. In 1959, flush with new wealth from publishing and franchise fees, he bought St Hill Manor in Sussex from the Maharajah of Jaipur. This and the London office became bases for much of the growth of Scientology in the 1960s. But the same period saw Hubbard starting to experience his most serious opposition to date.[52] Not only did John Kennedy refuse his offer to help train astronauts, but the America Food and Drug Administration raided the Washington DC office of the Church and confiscated its E-meters, declaring them to be unreliable and potentially dangerous. Shortly afterwards, a court in Australia delivered this decision: 'Scientology is evil; its techniques evil; its practice a serious threat to the community . . . [and] its founder's claims of academic and other distinctions a fraud.' The Rhodesian Government, in spite of its own outcast status among Commonwealth nations after 'UDI', revoked Hubbard's visa. Then, in 1968, Scientology came under serious attack in Britain: 'It is a hollow cult which thrives on a climate of ignorance and indifference', the Minister of Health said in Parliament; 'it directs itself toward the weak, the unbalanced, the immature, the rootless and emotionally unstable.' Foreign Scientologists had their rights to enter Britain restricted, and Hubbard himself was effectively banned.

The 'chief' reacted in the manner which has led enemies to brand him a 'paranoid schizophrenic'. Declaring that Scientology was 'victim of a concerted attempt to squash it by a small group of intensely powerful and evil men', he enunciated the doctrine of 'Fair Game', by which enemies were to be combated by whatever method of deception, cheating or set-up necessary.[53] Hubbard himself avoided hostile governments by living at sea on a succession of yachts. To help and protect him in this new period of adventure, he created the 'Sea Org', which quickly evolved into an 'elite ethical police force' with wide powers to go after 'suppressive persons' both in and out of the Church. Decked out in semi-military, semi-country-club 'uniforms' of grey flannel trousers and blue blazers, Sea Org cadres would descend on 'land Orgs' guilty of 'down stats' from 'out admin' or 'out tech', interrogate, rate and 'declare' members according to a fixed system of 'ethics levels'.[54] Thus came into being vast caches of information on Scientologists and anti-Scientologists. These exist to this day, providing the organisation means to defend itself against subversion, apostasy and extortionate lawsuits. In the 1970s, Hubbard thus became the *eminence grise* of his own secret service – first the 'Sea Orgs' and then, once on land again, the notorious 'Guardians' Office', which attempted to infiltrate the principal US Government agencies perceived to be 'out for' Scientology – the Internal Revenue Service and FBI – and lesser state and municipal entities, such as the office of the Mayor of Clearwater, Florida, a medium-sized town which Scientology effectively took over and is still seeking to make into a 'company town'.[55]

A chain-smoker and insomniac, Hubbard apparently suffered one stroke in the mid 1970s and another around 1980. Having technically resigned as head of the Church,[56] he continued to lay down directives and tape lectures. But ill health and lawsuits drove him towards the status of a recluse. Like Howard Hughes, he sequestered himself somewhere in the South-Western desert. From 1983, there was doubt that he was still alive, and his fingerprints and signatures on documents were questioned.[57] Power-struggles within the Church attested to his weakening grip; also to the ruthlessness inherent in the creed of 'survival' and 'power' he had let loose. It was said that he had gone into retirement to pursue again his first love, the writing of science fiction; and groaning tomes of pulp are appearing still under his name.[58] It is perhaps fantastic to speculate that in his last years he became a hostage of such 'guardians' as he had positioned around him. Still, there are stories of vicious outbursts of temper which suggest creeping awareness of his own impotence and decrepitude. An intelligent Scientologist has speculated to me that Hubbard may have become disillusioned with the people and antics he had promoted.[59] Blavatsky, Steiner and Hitler also were displeased at times with their cults. But, once a 'magician' pins his status on collecting masses of disciples, independence of being has already escaped. Hubbard 'dropped the body' – or so the present spokesmen of his 'church' tell us – at the beginning of 1986;[60] and the cult carries on in the hands of a mix of ex-1960s 'counterculturalists', 'yuppies' and classic American 'new religionists' of the Mary Baker Eddy or Elmer Gantry type.[61]

III BECOMING 'CLEAR'

Hubbard's 'magic' divides logically into two parts: Dianetics, which has to do with psychological processing; and Scientology proper, the religion of spiritual transcendence. The two of course overlap, and Scientology as term has come to mean both; but the 'Church' itself recognises the distinction and indicates it by use of two separate symbols: a triangle crossed by three equidistant, parallel, horizontal lines for Dianetics; and a large scripted 'S' linking two upward-pointing, diagonally placed triangles for Scientology.[62] These symbols are interesting both in themselves and for the fact that the 'Church' should have felt moved to create them at all. The triangle crossed with lines could be a two-dimensional representation of a stair-step pyramid and might bring to mind for anyone acquainted with symbols the 'eye in the triangle' and Egyptological predecessors in Crowleyanity, Masonry and so forth. Like these, it suggests a 'ladder', or hierarchy – all the more so because of the 'stair-step' lines. The Scientology symbol is both more original and more subtle. Disconcertingly, on first glance it may look like an 'SS', which seems unfortunate given enemies' penchant for likening the cult to the Nazis;[63] and one must assume this to be unintended. On second take, the two triangles might bring to mind the classical 'magical' symbol associated with Judaism; but here the triangles are not linked sufficiently to form a six-pointed star, and one is not pointing to 'that which is above' while the other to 'that which is below'. The tip of the lower triangle just bissects the base of the upper, and both point upwards to a 45° angle to the left. What esoteric message may be inferred from this? Perhaps none. Perhaps these are just symbols designed to identify, such as the star of NATO or hexagon of Chase Manhattan Bank, and by no means carry a swastika-like baggage of lore and significance. On the other hand, taken in contrast to the upwards–downwards relation of the triangles of the Jewish star, the upwards–upwards trajectory here might emphasise the importance the cult puts on improvement and optimism[64] – a sort of relentless Reaganite 'up-beatness' typical of American 'power of positive thinking', or (less attractively) a contemporary revival of Nazi-like 'strength through joy.'

There is in Scientology resistance to acknowledging the inevitable claims of the 'black' in human experience. This bias is similar to the one mentioned in relation to Theosophy,[65] and has similar disturbing results. There seems at times too much emphasis on perfection – 'whiteness', if you will – for the cult to remain in adjustment with the real world. 'Aberees'[66] and 'suppressive persons' are outside the pale: they become 'them', opposed to 'us'; and a Manichaean antagonism, entirely counter to Scientology's overall rhetoric of peace, is set up. This seems a fatal flaw. Steiner posits inimical 'Ahrimanic' and 'Luciferic' forces, but he also suggests that these are inherent in each individual and must be worked through for the residual advantages they may confer. Lévi appears to have believed that there were times when a 'magician' might deploy Qliphothic forces legitimately and suggests that the effective restraint on abuse of such 'powers' is the extent to which they might rebound on the 'magus' himself. Mathers taught mastery of demonic forces in context of ascent to the Holy Guardian Angel. Crowley in his 'Every man and woman is a star' implied that there should be no moral proscription in the universe at all, only a natural opposition of 'stars' determined on conflicting trajectories. Such practical recognition of relativity is lacking in Scientological doctrine, in spite of the rhetoric about helping the individual find himself. There is a way, and it is *one* way. Truth is not 'a pathless land', as for Krishnamurti. Indeed, in later years, Hubbard – perhaps influenced by the Christian fundamentalist revival in America under Carter and Reagan – apparently took to enunciating ethical commandments:

'Be temperate', 'Do not take harmful drugs', . . . 'Do not take alcohol to excess' . . . 'Don't be promiscuous; be faithful to your sexual partner'. . . . 'Love and help children',. . . . 'Honour and help your parents.' . . . 'Set a good example for others', 'Seek to live with the truth', 'Don't do anything illegal', 'Be worthy of trust', 'Fulfill your obligations'. . . .[67]

While the most of these sentiments may be perfectly admirable, the sanctimony jars against the spirit of basic Hubbard (though, as said, there is always an emphasis on self-improvement). Basic Hubbard, we have noted, posits that human action, thus faith, grows out of a transmoral – perhaps even 'Nietzschean' – *will-to-survival*. This expresses itself through eight 'dynamics':[68] (1) survival via self-preservation, (2) survival via procreation and sexual relations, (3) survival via family or race, (4) survival via identity with all mankind; (5) survival as a life organism, (6) survival as part of the physical universe of Matter, Energy, Space and Time (MEST), (7) survival as a thetan (variously defined as 'thought, life-force, *élan vital*, spirit or soul'), and (8) survival as part of the Supreme Being. Like Gnostics and Cabalists, Scientologists credit the last as unknowable (unless of course his identity may be reflected in the highest levels of 'Operating Thetan', lore of which grades is 'confidential'[69]). The list as a whole demonstrates the organisation's trajectory for the individual: of opening out toward increasingly higher awareness. This is entirely Hermetic, with the ultimate destination to 'know' God and the practice to reach such macrocosmic awareness by attention to the micro (man). There is also an apparent relation here to the grades of the Golden Dawn, with Scientology's break between man and the transhuman after dynamic 4 equating with the Golden Dawn's break between 'outer' and 'inner' orders.[70] Unlike Golden Dawn, however, Hubbard gives a utilitarian twist to how one should view the dynamics in the aggregate: the optimum solution to any problem, he avers (with comfortingly unesoteric simplicity), is the one which 'brings the greatest benefit to the greatest number of dynamics'.[71]

Such homilies give Scientology a tinge of the spirit animating 'green' movements, with their concern for animals, plants[72] and the ozone, as well as (sometimes to a lesser extent) for individual man, and suggest how the cult might view itself as 'clearing the planet' (also perhaps why it has had particular success in environmentally aware areas such as California and Germany[73]). But, like the 'anti-war' Greens, Scientologists see 'clearing' as a kind of combat for survival. This is waged first of all in the individual, between his 'analytical' and 'reactive' minds.[74] These sometimes have been compared to Freud's *Ego* and *Id*; and, though the analogy is hardly exact, the 'analytical' mind is definitely of the waking world and discursive thinking, while the 'reactive' is aswarm with emotions of pain and pleasure which may arise suddenly to inhibit the effectiveness of the individual as a whole. These unpredictable emotional blocks are called 'engrams'. If not checked, they can create 'aberrated' behaviour, even insanity. The purpose of 'Dianetic processing' is to locate and remove 'engrams'. The result should be to render the individual 'clear'; also to confer on him 'power'. The process consists mainly of quasi-psychoana- lytical therapy, called 'auditing'. The nomenclature – even the word 'clear' – comes from the realm of computers, clerical work and pseudo-science:[75] and there is a real sense, especially in the apparent uninterest in eccentricity such as Crowley might have regarded as a virtue, that the ultimate goal is to make flawed humans into perfectly mind-controlled machines.

Hubbard may have sought to litigate against such a statement, but he appears to have been more eager to transcend the vagaries of the soul than any 'magician' discussed here. The clearest evidence of this is his eschewal of poetic thought and language and substitution of jargon.[76] This has been mentioned already; but, in a study whose counterpoint is literature, it can hardly be emphasised enough. Hubbard purposefully and exhaustively disenchants language. There is something almost vengeful in the way he goes about this, inventing neologisms, writing his own dictionary and demanding that disciples learn scores of terms which have little if any meaning outside the cult.[77] Why Hubbard should have crushed the flower and seed of beautiful archaism under the tractors of newspeak is anyone's guess. Perhaps it was indeed to cover the 'magical' origins of his thought: to cloak it, as Steiner did, in the guise of 'objective' science and thus make it seem all the more to have sprung unassisted from his skull. Hubbard's reluctance to credit inspirers supports this.[78]. But, further, there is (as hinted earlier) a disturbingly macho streak in Scientology, probably emanating from Hubbard's naval back- ground but no more exclusively male in practice than the bully- boy persona sometimes ascribed to Margaret Thatcher. Sure of its 'truth' and preoccupied with 'power', Scientology is permeated by a hectoring tone. There is not a little of the Victorian schoolmarm here (Hubbard's 'educated' mother?), albeit transformed into the 'little Hitlers' of a 'brave new world'.[79] There seems also to be subconscious fear of or embarrassment about subjective passion, source of all authentic romantic creation yet anathema in the no- nonsense milieu of Hubbard's father and no doubt most of the male authority figures young Ron had been fated to encounter.

'Auditing' appears to be about drawing out the individual, but in fact it reflects the regimenting impulse as well. The 'auditor' is a Scientologist from a higher grade level who acts in a role anal-

ogous to that of a psychoanalyst.[80]. An 'auditing-session' generally
lasts about two hours, though in higher levels it may be extended
for most of a day. The 'auditee' in these sessions is hooked up to
an 'E-meter', which measures his tension as the auditor leads him
back along the 'time-track' to locate engrams. The E-meter indicates for the auditor engrams that the auditee attempts to hide
from himself, this by sudden jerks of its needle called 'rock slams'.
('Theta bops' and 'floating needles') are among other elements of
jargon for how an E-meter registers. When an engram is located,
the auditee is asked to describe the experience and 'Go over it
again' repeatedly, until it has been exorcised. The progress is
normally in reverse time, so that an engram deriving principally
from puberty is removed before dealing with the traumas of early
childhood. Theoretically, engrams exist from the moment of birth
back through being in the womb, even to pre-conception as sperm
and ovum. Nor do they stop at these 'basic–basic' physical stages.
Auditing is ultimately about finding one's 'thetan', which – being
quite similar to the 'Thinker' of Theosophy or eternal 'I' of Steiner –
has past lives, themselves full of engrams which must be removed
before the thetan may reach the ultimate state of 'MEST clear'.

On a this-earthly level, Dianetics maintains that a person has
reached basic 'clear' once he has mastered all engrams back
through the pre-natal period. In early practice, a common method
of 'auditing' was to induce 'Dianetic reverie', a sort of trance
entered into after counting from one to seven and broken off in
the end by use of a 'canceler'. Such techniques led to charges of
covert hypnosis; and, whether that charge is accepted, auditing –
far from being just 'listening' in a passive psychoanalytic mode –
has continued to depend on mind-bending tricks. One of these is
the forcing of 'flash answers': a sort of mental Rohrschach meant
to get around verbal cover-ups and defences and reveal to the
auditee what he is really feeling. More imaginative may be 'holding
anchor point' and 'Waterloo Station', techniques designed respectively to force the auditee to take up unusual points of perspective
and to interact with imaginary strangers in a crowd. Such mental
exercises may have derived from Hubbard's experience as a writer
of fiction. 'Bull-baiting' seems more likely to have grown out of
service interrogation. This is not an auditing-process so much as
a situation in which the auditee is confronted by fellow Scientologists intent on finding his 'buttons' and 'flattening' them. (The
word 'flattening' makes me wonder if Hubbard might not have

been inspired by Crowley here as well: the intent is precisely to 'flatten the ego', and an example recorded about bull-baiting a Jew out of neurosis about his Jewishness sounds reminiscent of Crowley's abuse of Victor Neuburg on this score.[81]) Similar techniques are used to gain access to 'overts' and 'withholds' – that is, illegal or immoral acts an auditee is hiding in his past or deceptions he is harbouring in the present. As with a lawyer or psychoanalyst, the seeker of aid is made to feel that he will only benefit if he opens himself fully, giving the whole of the truth of his case as he knows it and putting faith in the outer agency's guidance.

There is thus a way here that an auditor may come to serve as an objective correlative for the individual's 'Holy Guardian Angel'. But a 'Holy Guardian Angel' is an imaginary protector who does not charge a fee; and, whatever he may 'cost' in time and effort to evoke, he has no vested interest in whether the 'conversation' continues – that is up to the practitioner of the 'sacred magic'. With a psychoanalyst, this may be less true, as there are future fees to consider. Still, the psychoanalyst may be disinterested beyond fees: it does not matter so much how the patient uses him to find peace of mind; it is movement out of neurosis which is important. The auditor, however, cannot be so disinterested. Having had to pay large fees himself to reach his supervisory position, he can hardly be indifferent about whether the auditee sticks with it and pays more. Nor would it be possible for him, as a good Scientologist, to accept it as reasonable that an auditee might find some route out of his engrams other than the ladder provided by the Church. Thus the 'clearing' which Dianetic processing offers can not be seen simply as altruistic. It may give direction to the aimless and help able people become more aware of 'present time' and 'at cause' over their destinies; moreover, it employs minor techniques such as 'touch assist' which have a gentle charm in their way and may indeed show sufferers from psychosomatic ailments that they are not ill so much as alienated from parts of their physical beings. But such 'holistic' achievements are only part of the story. 'Becoming clear' in Scientology means above all becoming enmeshed in highly structured group thinking and development of 'powers' in the context of it.

IV TOWARD 'OT VIII'

Scientology is replete with ladders and degrees. A frequently referred-to one is the 'tone scale', by which the state of the 'reactive mind' may be measured. This rises from 0 to 4 in uneven increments which include Apathy, Grief, Despair, Fear, Covert Hostility, Hate, Pain, Boredom, Mild Interest, Strong Interest, Cheerfulness, Enthusiasm and Exhilaration.[82] A common exercise is for a group-leader to conduct a roomful of 'pre-clears' up the tone scale, making them respond with the proper sounds of grief, boredom and so forth in sequence. This kind of catechism reinforces the relentless pursuit of upbeat attitudes and serves to ostracise doubt, confusion and other dissenting emotions such as might intrude otherwise. It also suggests the strongly expressionistic emphasis for pre-clears. Silence, reserve, understatement, subtlety and wit are encouraged no more than intellectual scepticism; indeed, they may be viewed as potentially 'suppressive', though the placement of 'Boredom' rather high on the scale suggests that a modicum of 'laid-back' observation might be allowed, so long as it does not become an unbreakable distancing-device. Clint Eastwood would have a hard time as a 'pre-clear', one supposes; Ronald Reagan on a good day might reach the top of the class. (The political implication here is not much less relevant than the show-biz aside. Preoccupied with the latter, Hubbard also had attitudes on the former: liberalism is higher-tone than fascism, he averred; fascism than communism. Like other spirits spawned by the Cold War, Scientology's founder had a simplistic fear of anything 'pink' and is reported to have warned the FBI repeatedly in the early 1950s that 'subversives' were trying to undermine him.[83] That the FBI took little notice may be one reason why twenty years later it and the Internal Revenue Service had become the 'subversives' he most feared.)

The tone scale is a simple standard of measure, convenient for users to judge pre-clears and non-Scientologists alike. A more elaborate 'Classification Gradation and Awareness' scale attaches to the 'levels and certificates' enrollers may receive through 'Dianetic and Scientology processing'.[84] Here one begins with these 'Levels below need of change – from human to materiality':

−34	Unexistence	−19	Detachment
−33	Disconnection	−18	Oblivion

−32	Uncausing	−17	Catatonia
−31	Criminality	−16	Shock
−30	Disassociation	−15	Hysteria
−29	Dispersal	−14	Delusion
−28	Erosion	−13	Inactuality
−27	Fixity	−12	Disaster
−26	Glee	−11	Introversion
−25	Elation	−10	Numbness
−24	Masochism	−9	Suffering
−23	Sadism	−8	Despair
−22	Hallucination	−7	Ruin
−21	Secrecy	−6	Effect
−20	Duality	−5	Fear of worsening

There are too many of these to dwell on. However, one may be surprised to find 'Oblivion', 'Hysteria' and 'Disaster' higher than 'Glee' and 'Elation' and can only suppose eccentric definitions for these; otherwise, there would appear to be contradiction with the tone-scale, which ranks 'Exhilaration' (surely close to 'Elation' and 'Glee') above all. Further, one might be surprised slightly by the placement of 'Criminality' and 'Sadism' so far down the scale: however wrong-headed such activities may be, they generally show an individual 'at cause' over aspects of his outer, if not inner, life. 'Catatonia', 'Despair' and 'Ruin' would seem on the face of it lower in tone: self-effacing rather than expressionistic and close to, if not below, 'Apathy'.

But to continue: the chart now reaches 'awareness characteristics'. These relate to 'pre-clear grades or states of being' and appropriate processes thus:

−4 Need of change	Group processes	
−3 Demand for improvement	Co-auditing	(tone raising)
−2 Hope	Livingness Repair	(ability to change)
	New Era Dianetics Objectives	(achieving present time)
	Drugs Rundown	(freedom from drugs, alcohol, medicines)
−1 Help	New Era Dianetics Completion	(freedom from pain and unwanted emotions)
	ARC [Affinity-Reality-Communication] Straightwire	(freedom from fear of worsening)
	Expanded ARC Straightwire	

		Grade 0 Release	(ability to communicate with anyone on any subject)
1	Recognition	Expanded Grade 0 Release	
2	Communication	Grade I Release	(making problems vanish)
3	Perception	Expanded Grade I Release Grade II Release	(relief from hostilities and sufferings)
4	Orientation	Expanded Grade II Release	
5	Understanding		
6	Enlightenment	Grade III Release	(freedom from past, facing the future)
7	Energy	Expanded Grade III Release	
8	Adjustment		
9	Body	Grade IV Release	(ability to do new things)
10	Prediction	Expanded Grade IV Release	
11	Activity		
12	Production	Expanded New Era Dianetics Completion	(freedom from cruelty and bad impulse)
13	Result	Grade V Release	(ability to handle power)
14	Correction		
15	Ability	Grade VA Release	(freedom from detested parts of the track)
16	Purposes	Solo Setups	(prep for solo auditing)
17	Clearing	Solo Auditor	(practice of auditing)

Let us pause to draw breath, though the progress is by no means finished. 'Power' has been achieved (Grade V), also the right to 'audit', which is tangible expression of it. The person who entered Dianetics to relieve neuroses and combat lack of confidence has now become a fully-fledged Scientologist, able to judge and control others in the way he has been judged and controlled since entering the organisation – or, perhaps, throughout his life. A feeling of acomplishment can hardly help but suffuse him: he has completed undergraduate studies, as it were, and now may pass on to higher degrees, gaining at the same time rights to instruct as a Teaching Assistant.[85] Further, as said, having paid countless thousands to achieve this position, he is like the gambler so far 'in the hole' that he can no longer afford to cash out of the game.

Nor would he be likely to want to by now, as higher 'powers' are at hand:

18	Realisation	Grade VI Release	(powers to act on own determinism)
19	Conditions	Clear	(at cause over Matter, Energy, Space and Time as regards first dynamic)
20	Existence	Operating Thetan I	(extroversion of being, awareness of self as thetan)

	Operating Thetan II	(ability to project intention)
21 Source	Operating Thetan III	(full self-determinism)
	New Era Dianetics for OTs	(at cause over life)
	Operating Thetan III Expanded	(freedom from overwhelm)
	Operating Thetan IV	(certainty of self as being)
	Operating Thetan V	(exteriorisation of thetan, freedom from MEST)
	Operating Thetan VI	(pan-determination in universe of others)
Power on all 8 dynamics	Operating Thetan VII	(handle all enviroments effortlessly)
	Operating Thetan VIII	

What is Scientology? also lists 'OT IX and above' with characteristics 'to be released'. Statements elsewhere[86] suggest an open-ended number of grades further into 'the beyond', but there is no description of what they might involve; nor could there be. For, in spite of the – 21 rating given to 'Secrecy', Scientology follows the Masonic disciplines from which it derives in absolutely forbidding publication of its higher esoterica. This is reserved for an accredited, paid-up elite; and anyone who gives it out to people not prepared by having passed through the lower grades is liable to be 'declared' as a 'suppressive person'.[87] What is Scientology?, a book of PR, in fact does not describe any of the Operating Thetan conditions; and the parenthetical explanations above come from a more rarefied text, Scientology 0–8, one of Hubbard's numerous works of exegesis which are generally so high-priced that no member of the public would be likely to buy one, if they were available to him at all.

Another of these is Mission into Time, a slim volume Hubbard wrote in the late 1960s in the first flush of enthusiasm for life on his yacht. In general, the book is a precious account of Ron's travels in the Mediterranean and fatuous attempt to affirm his importance as an 'explorer' (an appellation as dear to him as 'mountaineer' was to Crowley but, on the evidence, somewhat less justified).[88] Metaphysically, however, it provided him with an opportunity to reveal that in Roman times he was a Carthaginian sailor and open out from this to say,

I'm not in a position at the present moment to give you a complete history [of my life then] but I know quite a bit about it. I know with certainty where I was and who I was in the last 80 trillion years. The small details of it like what I ate for breakfast two trillion years ago are liable to go astray here and there, but otherwise it's no mystery to me.[89]

Thus with charming jokiness and in everyday parlance,[90] 'Ron' enunciates for his faithful the proposterous – or at best entirely unprovable – sort of notion which permeates the higher grades of his cult. The 'thetan' can rediscover his or her timelessness and relearn how to treat life as a 'game'.[91] He (or she or it) is immortal, omniscient and omnipotent; and it is only to relieve the boredom inherent in MEST that he has allowed limitation on his abilities in the first place. These limitations have left their own engrams through successive lives, as said; but, once they are audited out, the thetan may travel to any point on the 'time-track' – including the pre-human evolutionary states which Hubbard describes in another brief, eccentric work, *A History of Man*, which caused much trouble with early Dianetic *confrères*.[92] According to this, the thetan once inhabited a clam, then another type of mollusc called a weeper, then a sloth, then ape, then Piltdown Man, then Caveman and so on.

The point of recalling such incarnations is to reinitiate awareness of an evolutionary process in which man himself is but a stage. (A debt may be owed here to the Social Darwinist Herbert Spencer, one of the few previous thinkers Hubbard mentions favourably.[93]) The educated thetan will then realise that, just as he was once subhuman, so he may become a superman. In fact, so long as he has become a fully aware thetan, he has already advanced up the evolutionary chain to be more than merely human. He has become a Scientological version of a 'Mahatma' or 'secret chief': one of the icy 'Immortals' who laugh at the Steppenwolf in Hesse's novel of that name[94] and, like them, beyond earthly morality. For like them – and the Indian mystics from whom Hubbard, like Hesse, took inspiration[95] – the thetan knows that the 'illusion' of this world is essentially meaningless: part of an infinitely larger context where 'winning' and 'losing', birth and death and suchlike reduce to minuscule importance. Thus in his travels he may watch Jews being burnt at Dachau or the armies of Pope and King exterminating Albigensians, but he will not lift a finger to prevent these things. Nor is it of much use to ask him to concern himself with the plight of blacks in South Africa, where among whites his cult has been strong, or – some years back – the behaviour of America toward Vietnam.[96] Social conscience of this sort belongs to the realm of Christian good works; and these, as noted, have little place in *gnosis*-oriented 'orthodox heresies'.

Scientology has taken public stands against various brutal techniques of psychiatry (lobotomy, for instance) and recently against widespread abuse of drugs. But there are spurious elements in both these expressions of social concern. The first grows out of a consistent jealousy and suspicion of a profession which Dianetics was set up to supplant; the second provides an apparently innocuous way to get hold of suggestible, addictive personalities and – by 'curing' them of their 'habits' – claim their souls for inclusion among Scientology's suggestible, addictive numbers. Both also are used as self-aggrandising PR exercises, reflecting the Church's awareness in the face of many enemies of the need to project an upright, socially useful image. Furthermore, the *Zeitgeist* has changed. The countercultural 1960s with their Nietzschean expressionism have given way to the yuppie, Reaganite 1980s; and a code of fundamentalist ethics seems a useful appendage to a doctrine essentially about self-promotion. Scientology in this way may appear to be becoming more 'mainstream', even 'establishment'. But there remains a long way to go; and its leaders post-Hubbard must be conscious that the organisation's status as an outcast combating government bureaucracy, the medical profession, orthodox intellectual life and journalism was a significant factor in its appeal during an era of mass antinomianism. Nor should this be dispensed with lightly as the 'charismatic' phase gives way to the 'organisational' one. After all, the continuing martyrdom of Christians during the decay of the Roman Empire only strengthened them to impose their new orthodoxy once the temporal power was in full collapse.[97]

V   BATTLEFIELD CIVILISATION

Prime among doctrinal inconsistencies of Scientology is this matter of martyrdom. When a court in Oregon approved enormous damages against the Church, members of the Celebrity Centre were flown up from Hollywood to protest against a 'witch-hunt' against their 'religion'.[98] Like early Christianity, the cult does seem to draw vitality from 'persecution'. It may even invite it, by litigating against all critics while screaming blue murder over litigation against it. Struggle for survival is the motif here – even more, struggle for dominance against an outer order which is seen as unenlightened at best.[99] What is contradictory is that, while struggle lies at the heart of Church practice, beatitude continues to be the goal in its preaching. This is apparent in Hubbard's 'discoveries of the basic rules underlying all forms of art', which are claimed to constitute 'a full codification of the philosophy of art itself, written in simple language and containing the essential elements upon which any and all forms of art are created'.[100] ('Such an ambitious undertaking had never been attempted before', we are told further, in a statement which either seeks to obliterate two millennia of aesthetic theory or is in woeful ignorance of it.) And what is the crux of these epoch-making 'discoveries'?

> Mr Hubbard [exploded] the age-old idea that the more neurotic an artist is, the more creative he can be. . . . He also exploded the myth than an artist's own mental condition can be judged by his creations. A truly great artist, he found, is not limited by his own subjective reality, but can communicate the full range of human emotion and aesthetics through his artistic creations. . . . Any able composer or author can write in many aesthetic forms. . . . A good poet can cheerfully write a poem gruesome enough to make strong men cringe, or he can write verses happy enough to make the weeping laugh. . . . Through his writings in the field of aesthetics, Mr Hubbard gave artists freedom from the arbitrary constraints which had been forced on them by others for centuries.

The reader will be delighted to learn from this that the fury and grandeur of Beethoven's later symphonies had nothing to do with deafness or his existential *Angst* over it, and that he might just as well have written a novel. Or perhaps we are to construe that Wagner's bathetic prose tale, 'An End in Paris', is as distinguished as his *Lohengrin* prelude, since 'any able composer or author can write in many aesthetic forms'.[101]

These are the reductive prejudices of an autodidactic polymath. There of course does not have to be a relationship between great suffering and great art: Richard Strauss is an example of the confluence of happiness with creativity. But to propose that neurosis is not related to creativity in genius, and that the idea is a concoction which has been shoved down our collective throat, conflicts even with the example of Hubbard's own work. *Dianetics*, which must rank as his *magnum opus*, grew out of ghastly experience and represents surely the author's attempt to throw off paralysing neuroses.[102] And *Battlefield Earth*, one of the big books of imagination Hubbard went into final retirement to pen, is animated (especially in its first quarter) by a sprightly vitality of schizophrenia and paranoia[103] such as we have seen its author being accused of. It is reasonable that the type of 'artist' Hubbard aspired to be (or perhaps was, depending on one's view of the quality of his science fiction[104]) should have wanted to throw off the stricture of ivory-tower-bound, post-Freudian critics[105] that all art should aspire to the condition of, say, Kafka. No doubt it is necessary for types to whom such pained expression seems unnatural. But to turn the process into a general challenge against what is presented as a uniform mindlessness of orthodox aesthetics throughout history is to betray the truly neurotic streak in the mentality making the charge. In his 'discoveries' about art, as in much else in his doctrine, Hubbard again sets up the opposition between 'us' (or even 'me') and 'them', claiming 'us' as freethinkers of the new, the ideal and high-spirited, while 'they' are closed minds of the old, false reality and negation. Here is his anti-intellectualism once more; also an animosity against civilisation – the finally debilitating and destructive twist of mind which may come from a youth of remoteness to centres of culture,[106] or some complex about having to prove that he had been right to drop out of standard higher education, or over-sensitive reaction to an ignoring of his work by most reputable critics.

Wherever it originated, the attitude infects his work, giving it is unique flavour and, ironically, main interest. 'All great writing comes from irritability', Jack London wrote,[107] and Chandler demonstrated; and Hubbard will stand or fall on the extent to which he may have expressed a pervasive, subterranean attitude in our culture of disgust at civilisation as it exists, and man's condition in it, and the need to struggle tooth-and-claw in a neo-Darwinian way for something better. The crucible of his imagination appears to have been the Second World War, by all measures a horrific event for the rational intellect to digest. The context of the world for which he was producing was (and remains) fear of nuclear war, spying, secret police and orthodox suppression. These things are real. To pretend that mankind can get free of them and that suffering is not inherently an inevitable and noble condition is to imagine history to be somehow discontinuous,

moving toward some millennium. To strive for a better world may
be admirable. To react with shock, surprise and rage at the evils
in this one is unstable and adolescent at best. Hubbard and his
cult have had mass appeal among the young, disturbed at the
world they have come of age in and ardent to produce a 'brave
new' one. But, like Hitler promising a disturbed nation a thousand-
year *Reich* or Reagan promising America that it would never have
to go through the humiliation of an Iran hostage crisis again,
Hubbard and Co. lead their needy followers toward the uplands
of fantasy. *Battlefield Earth* and the sci-fi 'dekalogy', last statements
of the 'chief's' career, sum up in a figurative way the trajectory of
Scientology overall – back into the 'astral light' of unreal imaginings: a world where a harried remnant of good humanity, led by
a handsome youth of Promethean courage, does battle with the
wicked, mind-bending 'Psychlos' who have come to rule the
planet and have no motivation other than to drink 'kerbango',
fornicate, embezzle funds, steal equipment, smuggle gold and
otherwise slake selfish, individual lusts while appearing to be in
service of 'The Company'.[108] With the simplicity of the most alienated Manichaean, Hubbard creates a world where one group – the
dominators – is purely venal, while the other – poor, plucky little
men – shows the way out of 'racial'[109] victimisation.

This might as well be the Christians and other cultists of the
second century AD fighting against the 'suppressive' Romans,
or successive heresies of the Middle Ages rebelling against the
proscriptive Church. The spirit is identical. But, projecting the
scenario onto the world as we know it, there are curious inconsistencies. The hero of *Battlefield Earth* is a native of the American
Rocky Mountains, and he uses US military equipment spared
destruction in the holocaust which wiped out that nation and most
of the rest of the world a thousand years before.[110] But the villains
of the piece are a great colonising empire, whose qualities are a
caricature of capitalist greed such as is associated by radicals with
a predominantly American military–industrial–financial establishment. The great sufferers from the latter in our world are the
populations of less-developed countries: victims of the Bhopal
disaster in India, refugees of guerrilla war in Central America, the
urban poor labouring under crushing debt in Mexico City and São
Paulo. For such types, Scientology appears to have cared little to
date (though the organisation has been pleased to 'donate' mass
shipments of its literature described as 'textbooks' to Ghana – a
move very beneficial for tax reasons[111]). Hubbard himself is on

record as regarding 'primitive' peoples to be exponentially more 'aberrated';[112] and the 'Brigante' humans who inhabit darkest Africa in *Battlefield Earth* have made themselves into the lowest of the low by interracial breeding, cannibalism and slave-trade with the Psychlos. But in general the most 'aberrated' behaviour in the novel belongs to the apparently 'civilised' Psychlos, while the 'clear' vision belongs to a handful of 'primitives' surviving in Western America and a few other locales, notably Scotland.[113] What are we to make of this spiralling vortex of seeming contradiction? That Hubbard himself was a 'madman' and did not understand the significance of what he was writing? That would be rash. More reasonable would be to see in his novel and opus as a whole a schizophrenia apparent in part of the culture of his country in the 1980s, from the President down to his beloved Hollywood.[114]

While representing the establishment and its law, Reagan won his campaigns in part by inveighing against intellectuals and bureaucrats; and, as chief executive, he subtly subverted the law he represented by allowing a 'hero', Lieutenant-Colonel Oliver North – a 'gut' thinker and 'primitive' in the world of Washington/New York sophisticates – to run guns and money to the Contra 'revolutionaries' in Nicaragua. Both President and hero then became paranoid (with good reason) that the establishment (of which, by some narcissistic/individualistic twist of mind, they regarded themselves as not part) was 'out to get' them. So much has become all too familiar in the post-Vietnam, post-Watergate American 'mind-set'. The movie *Invasion USA* posits a harassed yet courageous essential American single-handedly beating off a world of demented terrorists, which an effete establishment has done little to curb. *Aliens* shows a female counterpart to the hero of *Battlefield Earth* fighting off swarms of psychotic mother creatures (Hubbard's obsession with 'engrams' of the womb?) on a distant planet, which the establishment's greed has provoked to frenzy in the first place. *Cocoon*, on a slightly different but no less Scientology-related theme, shows a group of 'thetan'-like beings inhabiting human bodies being harassed by bone-headed people when it tries to set up a station for rescue of some of its members near a retirement community in Florida (Clearwater?). And so on. To 'understand' Hubbard requires digesting the rationale, if one may call it that, of a particular *Zeitgeist* and 'Nation-Spirit': one which is in love with computers and the possibilities of 'high tech' but essentially scornful of orthodox traditions of science and education which have produced these in the first place:[115] one which is unprepared to believe that it may not be able to fathom the secrets of human life, as of the universe, and make the former eternal and the latter its 'oyster'; one which is above all self-obsessed, seeing its enemies in organised, suppressive batallions of its own kind, and generally sceptical that helpful answers might come from other times or places in the earthly sphere (though, as in Theosophy, there is sporadic belief that indications may be given by immortal 'wise men' of the past or other-planetary 'gods' looking down on human activity[116]); one which finally is persuaded that it and it alone can 'cure' the 'disease' of civilisation as it has been, and even of its enemies as they exist now, if it merely continues to conjure the power and will to play its messianic role to the hilt.

10

Concluding: 'Magic' and the Moral Continuum

I   REPRISE

To the probable irritation of many, 'magic' and related terms have been put in inverted commas throughout this study. If this has suggested uneasiness between author and subject, then the truth has been served. 'Magic' is not just an ancient gene-pool of ideas which vanished into 'Religion' and 'Science' as mankind matured;[1] it is an ever-metamorphosing, reappearing shadow – the 'astral body' of rational thought, as it were – and to pursue and try to define it is to risk 'dissociation of sensibility', such as all immersion in 'unreason' threatens. Thus an observer from the 'real' world might conclude about this subject, as Bernard Shaw did about passionate love, '[It is] an experience which it is much better, like the vast majority of us, never to have passed through, than to allow it to play more than a recreative holiday part in our lives.'[2]

Inasmuch as it belongs to the semi-conscious, 'magic' involves what Samuel Beckett calls 'the decay of perception':[3] a sort of *Finnegans Wake* rubble of actuality conveyed via symbol, dream image, surreal pastiche, Dadaist whimsy or less obvious languages of breakdown. 'Magicians', forging forth, strain 'the Word' to its limits, creating often whole new structures of their own. Mad in pursuit of 'knowledge' and 'powers', they over-write, over-control and fling themselves over the borders of exhaustion, where, as James Webb writes in concluding *The Occult Establishment*,

Most become trapped in their private worlds and produce sadly little evidence of the power of imagination. There are too many attempts to destroy reason rather than to extend it. . . . [These] may contain the potential for expanding the limits of human existence. It is more likely that [they] will, instead – as has

225

happened in the past – shipwreck many on a desert island separated from all that is humanly satisfying by an ocean of illusion.[4]

This danger is the dark side of the first and most attractive object of 'magic' as considered in this study: to find one's essential identity, maximise energy and 'power', and live with the optimum intensity in one's capacity. Such objectives may be as close to the *good* as modern morality comes, but they are not without limit. At the same time as extolling individual quest, Krishnamurti, for instance, attacks making a cult of the self.[5] The 'Holy Grail' is a poisoned chalice if it holds life as in a stagnant pool; true individuality flows with the river of All. There must be equilibration with the Outer, in both Space and Time; otherwise, self-realisation may lead to rejection of life or – worse – an urge to impose one's own messianic vision onto the cosmos at large.

Transcendence of earthly ego thus becomes a second object. Man is rewarded for this by elimination of his primary fear: death. If one accepts that the whole human contains a detachable 'double', then one may become *parfait* in more leisurely intervals than a single lifetime – or, if an extreme Gnostic, escape from the 'weary wheel' by living out every possibility at once, thus removing the need to return to this 'vale of tears'. Either way, 'magic' posits an answer which science is unable to confirm or deny: reincarnation. This Krishnamurti 'proves' by an analogy with Nature: as it 'dies' in the autumn and is 'reborn' in the spring, so might man be expected to do.[6] Steiner, as we have seen, takes the correspondence further for those eager to 'discover' spiritual ancestries: as the physical body has biological parents who bequeath it its unique genes, so the spiritual ought to have its own precursors who bequeath it its native 'genius' as well.[7]

Thus believers are given access to eternal life. Nor are they denied contact with the beloved present as it recedes into the 'other world'. Spiritualism allowed Bulwer-Lytton to communicate with his dead daughter and Blavatsky to receive from Dickens the final chapters of *Edwin Drood*;[8] and, though its methods fell into disrepute 'in the outer', Besant continued to 'read' the Akasha, the Golden Dawn to teach 'skrying', Steiner to relive 'karmic relationships' and Hubbard to lead his 'thetans' back along their 'time-tracks' – all of which are related. Thus, along with immortality, omniscience is offered. A 'Hermetic' breaking of Time allows

Blavatsky to exhume 'secret doctrine', Lévi to find 'the key' and Crowley to converse with Horus and Aiwaz. Authority is based on such access to the past: to 'mysteries' beyond 'the veil' of conventional wisdom – that 'defeated thought' left to 'failures and eccentrics' which finally is 'better' than what is called 'orthodox' by 'the best kind of people'.[9]

Here 'magic' consorts with not only the occult, but also witch-craft: that animistic 'science' where man is in tune not with some God-given morality, but with the rhythms of the sensible world – the Earth-Spirit, Great Mother, Isis of Apuleius or Hesse's Eva, who knows the arcane lore of drugs, herbs and cycles; whose instinctive doctrine of equilibration is the basis of 'holistic' mind-body balance; and whose spiritual emanations have human correlatives in *Walpurgisnacht* creatures or 'flower children' dancing under the moon. Though anti-Judaeo-Christian in eschewing paternal providence, witchcraft may be 'white magic' inasmuch as it reveals the beneficial to man: the curative 'powers' of sun, sea, mountain air, grasses, sex and so on. Here it underpins modern medicine, prime sub-set of 'magic' as Mann depicts it. At the same time, being fundamentally pre-moral, it is concerned not so much with spiritual transcendence as with return to a pristine state, where Life once again becomes *the* wonder.

Believers in Nature and individual spiritual destiny are both suspect to the forces of civilisation, as they remain unbound by the latter's gods, whether Jupiter, Yahweh, Jabulon or the Bomb. Thus 'magic' is consigned to the realm of rebellion: Prometheus, Lucifer, the antinomian 'tradition' described in *Art, Messianism and Crime*, and heresies of all types, which – as the abbot in Umberto Eco's *Name of the Rose* contends – should not be differentiated finally, as whatever heresy becomes dominant in an age will attract to it all disaffected whatever they believe, as they have a natural instinct to gravitate to the single cult which has the best chance of overthrowing a hated orthodoxy.[10] Thus Christianity became the 'orthodox heresy' against Rome, Masonry against Christianity, and socialist anarchism against bourgeois capitalism. 'Magic', rejected, embraces this spirit of opposition as essential, especially in its 'charismatic' phase. On the individual level, total rejection of parental, state and religious authority is necessary for self-realisation, Krishnamurti counsels.[11] Likewise, Steiner and Crowley preached identification with the Luciferic as preparatory to revised appreciation for authority at higher levels of 'initiation'.

Thus 'magic' becomes a kind of spiritual Bonapartism, with new hierarchies being erected as old ones are pulled down. 'Heresy' progresses to the 'organisational' phase. Individual expression gives way to the group. Messianic purpose galvanises multiple personality into one will: to build 'the City of the Sun' or 'restore the temple'; bring on a 'new age' or fire mankind with the spirit of the Paraclete through some 'League for International Progress'.[12] If successful now, a cult may absorb the properties of old rivals – thus Christianity taking on the empire of Rome, or Masonry in the Lévi–Steiner period making peace with the idea of Christ. Also, with 'power', intolerance may develop toward those on the outside and elite 'esoteric sections' build up within. Finally, what was once vague 'magic' manifests itself on the historical continuum as a new would-be 'orthodoxy': fanaticism of 'us' *versus* 'them', depicted perhaps even as a struggle of incipient 'supermen' against the forces of apathy, envy and negation which wish to prevent progress of the 'race'. Here, as indicated many times in this study, is where 'magic' as it relates to psychic/physical improvement ends and political manipulation begins.

In the charismatic phase, the 'magician' is a prophet; in the organisational, he becomes a priest. The former is 'a revolutionist', we are told by Nietzsche's 'initiator' Guyau,[13] the latter 'a conservative'. Moreover, as 'religions create miracles out of their need for them',[14] so the 'magician' comes to depend on illusion. Astral light, trance states, the gaining of 'visions' – these he encourages, though perhaps giving them up himself. Atmospheres, lighting, scenery, costumes, tricks, talismans, the theatrical – such properties of ritual become his sphere, whether he is Cagliostro or the brains behind the Grateful Dead. Cinema, TV, advertising-media – all partake of analogous manipulation, attempting to 'push people's buttons'. Here there is room for cunning, conning and the sideshow 'magician's' habit of deflecting attention from what is really taking place. As Blavatsky practised fraud to gain attention and Scientology defends itself by 'Fair Game', so the 'magician' reaching 'power' must be a Machiavel. Spies and undercover agencies may be deployed against 'jealous' forces opposing him. Supporters to stay loyal must be kept relative primitives: too credulous and needy to become disenchanted or – worse – adopt his 'magic' and rival him.

For those out of power, 'evil' may be the dominant orthodoxy; for those in, it becomes heretics and apostates. Masons combating an 'evil' Church were not above associating with *enragé* elements which later gave birth to the terrorists posed against their new order.[15] Gnostics regard 'evil' to be 'the cosmos', while Theosophists and Scientologists avoid acknowledging it at all; but Crowley enjoyed the 'sins of the flesh' when on top, and Blavatsky promoted conspiracy theories involving the Jesuits,[16] while Scientology complains about 'witch-hunts' against it by those 'evil' institutions the FBI and Internal Revenue Service. To have tyrants or terrorists to rage against is useful. The 'magician' must be able, even in Steiner's relatively benign scheme, to arise with Lucifer or descend with Christ. The true function of 'evil', Guyau says,[17] is to set off the *good*: i.e. one's own programme in contrast to others'. But to go 'beyond good and evil' is the general goal; and the main obstruction to it is capacity, not morality, which – Guyau also points out – only draws force finally from man's innate anxiety over what may happen to his incorporeal part (soul includes reputation) after death.

The 'mage's' authority rises out of hodge-podge. Confusion breeds him, thus he must breed it, calling it godliness, 'relativity' or the eternal either/or. He can, as said, promote the sublimities of spirit or base instincts of Nature. Always he should 'slip into the skin of the Age', even if he despises it – unless, of course, that despite is so widely shared that he can make a 'new age' by proclaiming it. Essential to him is the trope of 'building', also the 'secret' which may not be revealed (not least because he does not know it himself). In these things, he claims both divine inspiration ('secret chiefs') and the authority of an apostolic succession of mages which link him and him alone back to a *prisca theologia*. He is at once the earthly representative of the Ancient of Days and the humane martyr: great giver of self so that mankind may gain comfort and enlightenment at last. In his state of guardian of the inner and gadfly of the outer, he may be compelled to unleash hostile currents, these justified by the philistine mindlessness of the mass and including the implication of total destructive power such as to bring on an apocalypse.

Having his own prehistory of infinite imaginative pursuit, the 'magician' has 'learned' that there are no limits to man's evolutionary potential this side of becoming God and ordering the universe. He has gained this knowledge through fasting, drugs, tattvas or more recondite means; and now it helps him pursue 'power' untrammelled for his followers to be preoccupied with the same. He counsels concentration on a fixed 'spiritual' goal and discipline of will. As the 'Holy Guardian' is really an exalted 'double', technique and doctrine are in part the equivalent of gazing into a 'magic mirror'. To become 'magicians' themselves is the principal incentive for disciples. Study is their practice, 'knowledge' their lust. Faith is put in the power of thought, in contrast to the heart-oriented Church. Creativity and imagination come out of self-contemplation and rebellion, Krishnamurti tells us.[18] But, we might ask in this epoch of university education and the 'powers' of science, can narcissistic pursuit of thought/knowledge bring final happiness any better than the blind faith of medieval times?

Happiness? Final answers? These are longings of the soul, which is the realm of emotions: feelings manipulable, if not irretrievably fallen into the material abyss. The 'magician' exalts spirit, that higher intelligence capable of non-subjective apprehension, thus of raising man back toward his 'high original place'. Life may be 'a progression of the spirit dishonoured'[19] if unreversed by 'magic'. In any case, emphasis on spirit adds to the 'magician's' power; because, once illusionistic 'spiritualism' is dismissed, nothing asserted here may be falsified. 'Knowledge', being infinite unlike the human body, is where 'power' may be exercised indefinitely – and jealously, as Eco demonstrates in his evocation of the monopoly on it sought by medieval scholar monks. Thus, while cherished as the means of 'liberation' by Hermeticists, Gnostics and their modern successors, 'knowledge' for the orthodox must be controlled – even to the point of being debunked: made the domain of Mephistopheles by *ancien régimes*, of 'disease' by Mann's Jesuit, of 'ivory-tower' self-indulgence by bourgeois philistines, of censorable or even book-burnable *ideas* by fundamentalists and fascists.

But, even when restricted or monopolised by others, 'knowledge' remains apprehensible through 'magic'. Mysticism, made of ardour, connects the devotee to the divine. Eternal forms and *ideas* lie beyond the confines of books and tradition; thus, even in prison or mocked by academe, the 'magician' may reach superior 'truth'. Deprived of material power or success, his intensity of inner commitment need not wane. 'A grain of incense burns in every heart, and when the perfume of it can no longer be given to earth we let it mount to heaven.'[20] Stripped of all externals – possessions, acknowledgement of outer authority – the spirit may pursue yet more fanatically gods and 'voices' within, thus becoming suffused with inspiration and giving way to absolute, triumphant solipsism; which in literary terms leads to Proust's self-vanishing act into the teacup of his imagination and for Huysmans began to seem like the modern equivalent of possession by incubi and succubi.

All is in service of achievement of 'power': of holding God, the devil and other deities in the self and deploying them as indicated. Mantras, incantations or Egyptian rites may be used. Mockery and destruction of the weak mortal ego is required, as is mobilisation of all techniques of 'seeing', whether by ancient 'games' such as astrology and the Tarot or concentration 'exercises'. Dominance over Time becomes a factor – the alchemist's willingness to devote a whole life to creation of one flask of 'the elixir'. Looking for the whole in the part or the part in the whole are alternative methods, each desirable in its proper phase. 'Magnetism' may be necessary, even to the point of hypnosis, of both the self and all others essential to the 'great work'. Finally, simple intensity of *insistence* is the secret: insistence on the sincerity of one's purpose and ideas, whether true or false (all men are sincere at some level, says Guyau,[21] and motivated by self-interest at another). For, in the last resort, if the world is an illusion – which seems the inevitable *a priori* assumption behind all – then it is simply what we insist most successfully on making of it which is what it will become.

Following the second century AD and Renaissance, the epoch culminating in the aftermath of the Second World War [22] may have seen the most extensive moral, religious and aesthetic transform-ation of any time in Western history. As Christianity liberated the individual from Rome and Protestantism from Catholic hegemony, so 'magic' discussed here has sought to detach him from the 'orthodox heresy' of modern times. This we have identified for convenience with Masonry, with its needs for brotherhood, hier-archy, authority, explanations, 'powers' and finally secrecy. Post-Masonic 'magic', joining with or replacing conventional artistic–literary expression, has called for more radical spiritual change. Why should man need even such order as idealistic free-thinkers devised for communication and protection back in the seventeenth century? Why should he not become entirely free at last from the neurotic, historical urge to 'know', belong and be right? Has not the new order of the last 300 years ended by creating a reign of materialism (Steiner's Ahriman), manipulation (Hubbard's Psychlos) or at least stultification (Mathers' bourgeois) in its own ways as oppressive as what went before?

These are questions the 'new age' came to pose. Could not initiation finally become the aware life fully lived, not just a metaphor for it? Might not the process of being 'reborn to the light' involve instead of some ritual a study of self in its detail and relation to the whole? To view all acts as 'magic', as Crowley proposed; to achieve and maintain a pristine sense of wonder – might not these require non-attachment to cults, as Krishnamurti argued? healthy scepticism, recognition of one's own ignorance, humility in the face of all explanations? Heresy may be a 'triumph of doubt over faith', as Guyau defines it,[23] orthodoxy a means of fixing faith against doubt; but, though each may be useful in temporal phases, neither is finally adequate over time. The alive intelligence will resist trying to prove the unprovable and trying to disprove the undisprovable as well. Speculation may replace religion, as Renan predicted.[24] Man may appreciate all gods of prior creation, while happily creating new ones of his own, yet finally believing in none.

The great 'secret' may be laughter, as *The Name of the Rose* implies.[25] Meanwhile, heroes of the 'new age' may become versions of what the Greeks first called 'seekers' (*zētētikoi*)[26] and Grail romances epitomised as Parzival: not believers in one 'ism' or another, but questers through all experience. Against them still stand cult, manipulative 'magic' and state. To gain 'equilibrium' remains precarious. Love of risk and a certain amount of *amor fati* seem required; but these threaten inflation of personality as much as destruction from the outside; and, to the extent that the individual becomes his own law, a degree of paranoid schizophrenia seems assured. The 'seeker' then must avoid the 'religion' of narcissism as much as the dogma of 'chiefs'. The several 'gods' within, ever effective to deploy, must ever be 'crystallising'[27] into new unity: opposites balancing in evolving dynamism – anarchy and order, the old and the new, regard for Nature as well as technology in an era when neo-pagan sex and the nuclear bomb have grown up side by side.

'Death doesn't exist but the devil does'? On the historical continuum, this may have some truth. But individual man is primarily a living organism, likely to remain unnoticed – or at best a footnote – in the ongoing sweep. Thus he might relax with Mann's Peepercorn as well as throw himself forward with Goethe's 'In the beginning was the deed!' An unmessianic version of the 'magician', the 'seeker' embodies passivity as well as action. He does not have to exercise 'power': that is a principal justification for his freedom. He does not feel compelled to become a total master of 'knowledge'; for 'the further one goes, the more one sees that one does not in the least understand'.[28] He recognises instinctively that 'the beliefs of one's neighbour are a compliment to one's own'. On the other hand, he is not simply a *tabula rasa* ('When one venerates and admires everything, it is generally what one simply does not understand'[29]), because *understanding* ('sympathy made wise') is his attitudinal goal.

He may believe that 'Every man and woman is a star' and that truth lies somewhere 'beyond good and evil', but he does not parlay these into divine right to do anything he pleases, including harm. Though 'power' in the twentieth century may have replaced 'reason' and Chandler remarks that we live by 'pressures' not 'principles',[30] the 'seeker' – like Chandler's 'knight of the mean streets' – does not give himself up to utter ruthlessness. In the first place, he knows that 'the current' may return on him; in the second, that – despite 'magic's' contentions – individual 'powers' are limited. Finally, then, he must believe in 'common sense'. This is the ultimate basis of all thought, just as reality is of all art; but that need not mean that life will become wholly prosaic, anymore than that art will always be naturalistic. Because just as, the more an artist looks at Nature, the more abstract it becomes, so, the more the individual deals in common sense, the more it may reveal itself as the true 'magic'.[31]

Activity of thought is the basic condition for existence, Renan said;[32] thus the 'seeker' must be more than just a sensualist on the equivalent of a drug 'trip'. 'Credulity is intellectual original sin'; thus scepticism may be a higher attainment than faith, and philosophy based on reason a higher attainment than either. As for 'power': inasmuch as it is dynamic rather than reflective, it belongs to the realm of action; and, as any action may involve dislocation of another, it should only be undertaken with care. Creativity and terror may seem the identity of God (Abraxas); but man is man, and his actions (indeed, free will overall) must be ruled by watching and waiting. 'Workability', Hubbard argues, may be preferrable to idealism. On the other hand, 'mobility Machiavel-lianism', being action to power, ever threatens to bring the indi-vidual into collision with other 'stars'. Moreover, the 'seeker' tempted to become a 'magician' ('auditor' in the Scientology case) may wake up one morning to find himself, like Hubbard, in thrall to the daemon of his cult.

Still, common sense does not mean retreat into orthodoxy; because, as Guyau says, orthodoxy 'either kills the [entity] in which it entirely stifles freedom of thought, or it kills itself.'[33] No person or group may 'know' the cosmic system. Words and time collapse in the face of the Absolute. Life may be a 'whirlwind' as Gnostics believed, God a 'spiral force' swirling through all. He may well be Abraxas – mirror of the amoral, divided self, fundamentally reflective of Nature – or be 'known' through a constant zigzagging, as in the Cabala, toward higher dis- and re-equilibration. God in this way may be defined by the devil; but, if so, one may agree with Guyau that, as fear of Satan continues to vanish, so belief in Yahweh dies as well.[34] Finally, God, being unknowable, may become a fruitless question. Common sense needs philosophy more than religion. Not just morality, economic reason and appreciation of art and science, but all these categories and more constitute full initiation: that is, life lived as well as possible, and as fully understood.

Believers in the whirlwind try to fire themselves with the spark of divine enthusiasm. This may be 'magic'; but, as Mann says, it is 'all too soon exhausted, growing weak and eerie'[35]. Sparks go out; whirlwinds pass. Whatever unknown possibilities may exist beyond, there is finite energy on the mortal plane. (Exceptional longevity was not even common to the 'magicians' we have discussed: all died in their early to mid sixties except Crowley and Hubbard, who just passed a 'biblical' three-score years and ten.) 'True moral perfection is often the precise opposite of heroic par-oxysm', Guyau concludes;[36] and this applies surely to our 'magic-ians'' paroxysms of over-production. Mind–body balance: yoga, breathing-control, exercise, diet – such techniques, promoted extensively only by Steiner and Crowley of those discussed, may prove the most substantial 'magic' in the long run. By maximising the flow of oxygen to the brain, they allow the spirit to set off on its 'astral journeys' out of healthy impulse, not pathology.

Finally, will 'magic' be found to be 'white' or 'black'? The 'seeker', reflecting, must consider to what end it is used: to benefit the 'magician' or his 'initiate'? If it is to make the latter 'suggestible' in order to inflate the former's 'power', then it is of the sphere of propaganda by governments, subliminal persuasion by advertising or other 'mesmeric' activities designed to coerce and perhaps do harm. If it is pursuit of the Qliphoth to feed basic lusts rather than the Sephiroth to gain higher knowledge, then it may indeed become 'black' to that horrific degree where the 'magician', Sadeanly, tries to make others 'evil' in order to command them (turn them into sub-demons, to use *Abra-Melin* terminology) or at least find the 'evil' in them ('overts' and 'withholds' to Scientologists) in order to blackmail them into doing his will. Tyrannical orders have ever specialised in this – inquisitions, secret police – and 'white' democracies are not above adopting 'black' means to achieve 'the common good'.[37]

What does the 'seeker' do when confronted with such 'evil'? He tries to avoid it, remembering that to concentrate on it may be to encourage its existence. But, if he cannot, he may agonise over it until he is sure it *is* 'evil'; sympathise with those possessed by it as well as suffering from it (for no one commits harm to others unless somewhere, however far back, some harm has been done to him[38]); and finally oppose it, but only with the maximum reluctance and minimum vindictiveness possible. Thus Parsifal may be forced to bring down the 'magician' Klingsor finally, and exorcise his disciple Kundry. But he may be advised to break up the Grail Order as extant at the same time; because an excessive impression of *good* may be as dangerous in the ever-shifting realm of 'magic'-as-morals as a self-righteous, paranoid, carping insistence that 'evil' is ubiquitous and must be combated perpetually.

II 'MAGICAL' REALISM

Existentialism partook of this cult of the 'seeker'; only, in strict Existentialist form, he refused to engage in moral questions directly, preferring to act and be acted upon like a sleep-walker – Camus's 'stranger', or Kerouac's 'lonesome traveller' with the 'Bodhisattvic heart'.[39] The existential hero only begins to think about acting morally when his back is 'against the wall', like Randall McMurphy in *One Flew over the Cuckoo's Nest*; but here a neo-romanticism intrudes, making the tardy fight-back ineffective. Instead of using 'magic' (in this case vindictive cunning) with the persistence and will of the 'Psychlo'-type establishment he is enchained by, McMurphy gives way at crucial moments to fellow feeling, thus assuring his martyrdom. Martyrdom may be 'magic', as the example of that 'great initiate' Christ shows; but only if one believes in a 'second coming', which for Kesey's hero will only take place in the imagination of the narrator, Chief Brom. Brechtian survivors may finally be more congenial to the contemporary mind (to a degree Kesey's second novel, *Sometimes a Great Notion*, indicates this); but the cult of 'survival', as seen, may lead to empire-building *à la* Scientology.

Reference to Kerouac and Kesey is appropriate here, in terms of one of the trajectories of the relationship between literature and the 'orthodox heresy' discussed. Webb devotes the penultimate chapter of his *Occult Establishment* to 'The Great Liberation', by which he means the 1960s, whose origins he finds in the Surrealism and Dadaism of the 1920s – Bréton and Artaud – and the Symbolist–irrationalist revolt against Naturalism in the 1890s. A development quite similar is described in *Art, Messianism and Crime* and need not be gone into again. In any case, too much emphasis on the *Zeitgeist* of the 1960s would confine the significance of what amounts to a pervasive magico-religious change. In literature, the symptoms of this are by no means restricted to pot-smoking apostles of 'new age' consciousness. Preoccupation with 'power', cults, the summoning of 'dark forces', battles between good and evil, unusual spiritual and psychic phenomena, and most of all the quest for self-realisation, are so widespread in the contemporary novel as to suggest that 'magic' may have become its principal topic.

Social realism retains some life, and generational sagas of gentr-ification (or its reverse) fill airport news-stands as well as TV screens. But even these genres are not without their penetration by 'magic'; and the 'thriller' has been full of it since at least the time Dashiell Hammett evoked a Crowleyan cult of the Grail in *The Dain Curse*.[40] At the top end of recent writing, Iris Murdoch is ever concerned about 'power' and playing 'black' against 'white', as in *A Fairly Honourable Defeat*, where the diabolical Julius King vies with the Christly Tallis Browne over the 'soul' of a failed female 'seeker'. Similar struggles and their relation to ortho-heterodox tradition occupy Anthony Burgess in various of his books, not least *Earthly Powers*, which follows the struggle of good and evil to the cult of God Manning in California, a Jim Jones figure not above sending his disciples to their death, against whom the counterforce is the sybaritic Cardinal Carlo Campanati, who (by ironic contrivance) allowed Manning to be born in the first place. These are hardly cult novels or novelists: they are the mainstream of contemporary British letters. Nor, slightly down the scale, has the preoccupation been much less, as evidenced by John Fowles' *The Magus* and works by Colin Wilson.

In continental Europe, fascination with 'magic' has perhaps been more muted since the Second World War. Certainly the Russians and Germans, who did so much to 'illuminate' politics (as well as art) in the century,[41] have either restricted themselves to a materialist outlook (the former) or felt chastened by their excesses (the latter) and thus have resisted too much return to the literature of amoral 'liberation' and free-flying speculation. In Italy and France, this may be less so; still, at the upper levels of culture, some of the greatest and most 'magically' interested books have approached their concerns through projection back into the last major epoch of dislocation, the late Middle Ages. Into this category fall Eco's *Name of the Rose*, already mentioned, and Marguerite Yourcenar's *The Abyss*, which charts the progress of a Renaissance 'seeker' through struggles such as produced Giordano Bruno and later engulfed him in flames. In both these books, as in *Earthly Powers*, novelist and hero are by no means wholly opposed to the Church. It may have seen unspeakable evil done in its name, but it remains the source from which moral good is still most likely to come.

So much, not surprisingly, is less apparent in American novels of the period. Norman Mailer quotes at length from Yeats's essay 'Magic' in the epigraph to his journey into Egyptian *prisca theologia*, *Ancient Evenings;* and Saul Bellow's hero in *Humboldt's Gift* pokes around the precincts of Rudolf Steiner's ideas to see if real answers may be found there. 'Magic' is not regarded with quite such suspicion in a culture where Protestant, Masonic and Jewish traditions have not been overshadowed by Catholic orthodoxy. One has to move south, toward Latin America, to find that element prominent in the struggle again, along with something entirely foreign to Western culture elsewhere – a taciturn, long-suffering, perhaps noble, perhaps savage but at any rate Nature-related primitivism, deriving from American Indian origins but over the past century having become entwined with elements of emigrant peasant culture from Europe and ex-slaves from Africa.

Out of the literature of the strange, sad yet sometimes ebullient
continent of South America, the term 'magical realism' has
emerged, in a tradition whose principal language is Spanish but
whose purview is a phantasmagoric – sometimes pandaemonic –
mixing and merging of all.

As with the often 'magical' genre of science fiction, it is beyond
the scope and competence of this study to go into 'magical realism'
in detail, or its origins in works of Borges and Marquez. But, since
the term has implanted itself into contemporary culture, bringing
methods and inspiration to writers beyond its original
geographical sphere, and since the literature of Latin America in
general has become an increasingly fascinating force in the world
(not least because it is a principal graveyard for Western ideas in
religion, politics and personal morality), it seems appropriate to
attempt a few generalisations about it before disengaging from
this study.

A most charming example of the genre is Isabel Allende's *House
of the Spirits*. A generational saga, this depicts 'magic' as once
having been a benign and organic part of civilised South American
life. The author's persona, Alba Trueba, is great-granddaughter of
a Mason and early member of her Catholic nation's liberal party.
This man's brother was a fortune-teller, illusionist and general
eccentric who kept a trunkful of *grimoires*, which remains in the
family until being burnt by the agents of a present-day dictatorship. These *grimoires* and their collector inspire the imagination of
the Mason's daughter, Clara, who herself proves to be clairvoyant
following a traumatic experience at the age of six. Alba's grandmother, Clara, emerges as the central, cohesive character of the
book. Ethereal and angelic, she evokes affection from all in the
disparate society around her: her patriarchal, land-owning
husband, embodiment of the macho *patrón*; his devout Catholic
sister, who has repressed lesbian tendencies; peasant workers, a
trio of spiritualist sisters, Rosicrucians, astrologers, visionary
artists and a host of unusual 'spirits' (thus the book's title) similar
to those Hesse draws around his Frau Eva in a proximate historical
period.[42]

Clara sometimes levitates through the house. At other times,
she gives up speech entirely. Such eccentricities lend character to
what otherwise might be a somewhat conventional *haut-bourgeois*

regime; and Clara's divinations at a three-legged table invariably predict exactly what will happen to the members of her family. Of her twin sons (both educated, ironically, at a rationalist, English-type boarding-school), Jaime buries himself in a cavern of 'magical' books, whence he emerges to become a physician to the poor. Meanwhile, Nicolas follows a failed attempt to sell advertising-by-balloon with a journey to India, where he becomes a fakir. On returning home, he writes a treatise on yoga, parades around naked and collects a 'cult of nothingness' around him – all of which leads his father to throw him out, whereupon he goes to North America and promptly becomes rich. Blanca, the twins' sister, is no less romantic. She becomes pregnant by the peasant she has adored since girlhood and is rushed into marriage with a homosexual French 'count'; but, discovering evidence of one of his gay soirées, she leaves him and supports herself and her child by making increasingly bizarre ceramic figures to set around Christmas crèches.

Alba, Blanca's daughter, is the sole representative of a present (and perhaps final) generation. She witnesses the passing of the old agrarian–liberal order and democracy which went with it. Coming of age in an era of socialist–fascist struggle, she soon discovers that her grandmother's 'spirits' are insufficient to protect her friends from military terror. Thus the events which take up the last quarter of the novel (a veiled representation of Pinochet's Chile) seem to define 'magic' as a light-hearted eccentricity of a past which may have been pleasant but was culpable. Alba is politicised: i.e. she comes to believe that 'answers' may be found in the material world. Drawn into helping the guerrillas (of which her boyfiend and father are both leaders), she is eventually arrested herself and thrown into solitary confinement. Here she is only able to keep herself from madness by intense acts of imagination and memory. Finally, these make her realise that on a personal level the best 'answer' to tragic division and spiritual frisson in her times may be to resurrect her family's history through her grandmother's diaries.

Thus Clara's 'magic' is redeemed, for both its light and serious qualities: to decorate, amuse, surprise, assist in self-realisation, predict the future and unearth the past, break time and at least fleetingly achieve some oneness with 'spirits' beyond the grave. This is 'magic' of a transcendental type, free of the cults of 'will' and 'power', which remain the obsession of military men, *políticos*,

capitalist *patrones* and the odd primitive hero whose energies are
concentrated by passion, necessity or – in less attractive cases –
the spirit of revenge. 'Magic' in Allende's scheme is associated
with delicacy, innocence and a certain careless impotence in
relation to things of this world. It is not, significantly, at odds
with the church; indeed, the two exist side-by-side in a kind of
harmonic counterpoint, as they have seemed to always. Meanwhile, though having nothing to do with wordly power as such,
'magic' – especially in the person of Clara – becomes a source of
inspiration and confidence for the most powerful figure in the
book, her land-owning husband.

In the political sphere, the reason given by conservatives for the
downfall of democracy and socialism is that they lack 'magic' – a
diagnosis not contradicted elsewhere in the text, where 'magic' is
always associated with the dramatic and transcendental, thus finds
its most natural place in situations of chaos or earthly despair,
where only apparent 'miracles' can give joy and hope in an all-
too-swift journey to the grave. Social cohesion – always a perilous
business amid Latin divisions of wealth and privilege – vanishes
quickly after the death of Clara, suggesting that, without belief in
'other worlds', compassion becomes a mere matter of poulticing
a material ulcer (the function of Jaime as physician), thus implicitly
political and subject to the prejudices of 'power'. Without faith in
a potential to communicate with the Unknown also comes deterio-
ration of will to communicate with the strange, even if strangeness
is only a matter of difference of class or opinion. What once could
be respected, or at least tolerated, across natural cultural divides
now comes all too quickly to seem hostile and incapable of being
resolved with elements of the familiar into a sense of wider
community.

Thus breakdown in communication between essential 'spirits'
hastens society to the abyss of civil strife. This process is reflected
too in Mario Vargas Llosa's *War of the End of the World*, a less
charming and 'magical' book which none the less demonstrates
the degree to which Latin America has been crucified by 'magico'-
moral chaos. Llosa presents a struggle for the political soul of
Brazil after the fall of the Portuguese monarchy at the end of the
nineteenth century. The villains here are 'Freemasons': republicans
whose interests are mercantile and means military. The victims
are an alliance of peasants, Indians, 'heretics', Catholic apostates
and revolutionary romantics, all brought together against the

'Antichrist' by a Christly 'magician' called the Counsellor. After years of bloody war which exterminates soldier and peasant alike, the Counsellor and his cult are defeated. Their numbers, faith in their rightness and will-to-die have proved unequal to the techno- logical 'magic' of the 'Freemasons'. Yet they threaten to live on as martyrs, with a romantic cachet like the Cathars of twelfth-century France. Thus their moment of spiritual vindication (the novel itself, for instance) may be still to come.

Thus is demonstrated a truth which plagues Latin America and similar Third World situations to this day. Without a 'magic' of 'power' and technology – the *force de frappe* mentioned in connec- tion with the *Fama fraternitas*[43] – the 'magic' of spirituality and witchcraft of the natural world are doomed to lose all influence, save that of martyrdom. The upper plateaux of La Plata and rain- forests of the Amazon no longer hold preserves of pristine Indian culture, or even the missions of eighteenth-century Jesuits, which – if we are to believe a contemporary film on the subject[44] – were devoted principally to agriculture, music and the making of violins. Forces of state, 'progress' and greed have long since invaded, turning noble savage and unsophisticated Christian into essential allies – not necessarily members of a single Counsellor's cult, but together in belief that some 'spirit' must transcend the terrors of an all-too-material world; that love and fellow-feeling are imperative; that life must be lived with intensity and resistence in this 'vale of tears'; and that the reign of the Antichrist may indeed be at hand, in the form of a military–industrial–commercial *novus ordo seculorum*.[45]

Communism is an 'unmagical' answer for those wishing to combat this. Others may give up what seems a fruitless struggle to decide, in essence, 'If you can't beat 'em, join 'em', or 'The best way to fight fire is with fire.' Members of this second group are often drawn to the 'magic' of individual survival and 'power', thus may pass through cults such as Scientology. In the context of Latin America and 'magical realism', a codification of the type of thinking which attracts them may be found in the works of Carlos Castaneda. These are not a happy place to end this study from a literary point of view, because, as literature, Castaneda must rate as at best sub-Hesse. (In fact, having become increasingly plotless, his books appear more and more like attempts to put the philosophy of Hubbard-types into pop-Socratic dialogue.) But it is easy to be dismissive from a high armchair of European tradition, and another matter what one might read – where one might turn for the 'magic' to survive and succeed – if, say, a youth on the run from death-squads in El Salvador who had recently scrambled through miles of rat-infested sewage pipeline to 'freedom' in the United States.[46]

Castaneda comes from the largest Spanish-speaking city outside a Spanish-speaking country – Los Angeles – and his 'anthropological' studies of the 'sorcery' of a Yaqui Indian read like a synthesis of old Western (Masonic) 'magic' with the indigenous 'genius' of the Mexican-American Southwest. His style is matter-of-fact and deceptively simple, as we have noted Hubbard's to be.[47] His mode is to guide the reader through the eyes of himself as narrator, depicting himself with a coyness and timidity which ever allows the 'sorcerer' Don Juan to appear more formidable. The structure is of Faust to Mephistopheles; only Castaneda is no heroically God-defying scholar, and Don Juan is a weasel-like Brechtian survivor rather than dauntless opponent of the Lord. This is High Magic reduced to the level of everyman. Don Juan teaches reason over passion like Lévi, spirit over soul like Steiner, and experiment over tradition like Crowley. He attempts to initiate his neophyte into a 'brave new world', like Demian with Sinclair, rather than show up the vanity of new ideas, like the 'magicians' of Hans Castorp's mountain. Here are 'how to' books for malcontents of the 'new age' rather than celebrations of life in the aggregate, as in fine literary accomplishments such as *The House of the Spirits*.

The lore of the Don Juan books is too extensive to go into here; in any case, I have touched on it in *Art, Messianism and Crime* in connection with the *Zeitgeist* which produced Charles Manson.[48] At the simplest level, it is a matter of 'seeing' and 'will'. There is some good sense in it, such as how to endure and overcome a 'petty tyrant';[49] also much illusionistic 'magic', initially (as with the generation Castaneda writes for) having to do with visions from drugs but later with alteration of 'assemblage points' through meditation, surprise and other non-chemical means of 'destabilisation'.[50] Intimacy with the spirit of Nature is important: recognition of and connection to the 'Eagle's emanations', which are in some ways Don Juan's versions of the rays of the Sephiroth.[51] God, however, is, as such, absent. Nor is there any morality of good and evil – what is powerful and effective is what counts. From this follows that there is little sense of civilisation: no aspiration to build a new and better community. Under the intense sun of the Southwestern desert and in hard towns of the Mexican hinterland, man's relation with the elements seems the first important study, his control over himself the second, and his ability to invoke allies and beat off enemies the third. Survival thus again is the law, love and charity accidental at best.

Knowledge and will supplant faith and good works – this is true with Don Juan as with all the figures we have discussed, except perhaps Zanoni, Clara Trueba and one or two other 'magical' types encountered in literature. That such 'magic' should have become the dominant 'religion' in our age may be disquieting to many, not least orthodox and/or essential Christians. If so, they might consider the degree to which Christian authority and hierarchy in its ascendancy served to undermine the ethics of Christ and thus persuade man to construct new orders based on what he saw as fact over fiction, truth over hypocrisy. In a world visibly ruled by power and will, this could not help but have bred doctrines of the same. That they should emphasise spirit and matter over soul may be sad – perhaps even 'evil' in Christian terms. But one has merely to look at literature to discover that man has not yet been transformed into a 'thetan' or robot; that his soul still exists, if perhaps (as the proliferation of psycho-disciplines indicates) in a somewhat more 'diseased' state; and that, in the human aggregate, love and charity have not vanished.

One might also, however late in this study, make a sexual distinction such as the one Don Juan hints at thus: 'Men have sobriety and purpose, but very little talent; that is the reason why a nagual [sorcerer] must have eight women seers in his party. Women give the impulse to cross the immeasurable vastness of the unknown'.[52] The point of 'magic' for the male is characteristically 'knowledge' and 'will'; for the female it is often the mysteries of another world. This is a generalisation with permanent exceptions; but even in this study it may be seen to have truth. Lévi, Mathers, Crowley – for all of them 'will' was the principal matter; Madame Blavatsky, on the other hand, was ever wafting out into the spirit world, as was Annie Besant with her descriptions of 'Devachan', Florence Farr with her 'skryings', and George Yeats with her transcriptions for her husband's A Vision. Some male 'magicians', notably Steiner, have spent large periods of their careers intuiting unknown (and unknowable) 'facts'; but, as with so much in the case of Steiner, this was done first by Blavatsky and probably imitated from her. Pursuing the distinction to 'magical realism', one may be impressed by the way Isabel Allende melds the tragedy of South America with the supernatural, whereas Vargas Llosa seems stuck in Hemingwayesque evocations of gore. *This* world evokes the macho in man (*animus* in women as well). A feminine instinct ('Das Ewig-Weibliche') seems better able to suspend disbelief and entertain possibilities for transcendence to other, perhaps better, worlds to come.

III APOLOGY

But I have now said enough about 'magic' – perhaps too much, though it seems unlikely that, as Yeats feared,[53] adepts are going to emerge to chastise me for having revealed too many 'secrets', Such criticism as this book may receive will probably suggest that (1) it has discovered and revealed too little to justify so many words, and (2) it has failed to subject its material to a constantly rationalist scrutiny, preferring at times to let impressionistic trance take over, perhaps out of some misguided attempt to let the character of the subject be revealed as it were more 'magically'. If the reader has been put off, I apologise. I myself have been put off many times in this study, by not only the bulk and seeming nonsense of so-called 'magic' but also the difficulty of defining and conveying it at all.[54] Thus, if I have learned one thing from the effort, it is that a writer tackling such a subject had better be prepared for an 'honourable failure' at best – which is all that even the greatest genius might expect from the Unknown, though few of the 'magicians' encountered here would have been eager to admit such a humbling truth.

Notes

CHAPTER 1. INTRODUCTORY: 'MAGIC' AS WORD AND IDEA

1. An indication as to why I have put this and related terms into inverted commas throughout this book may be found in Ch. 10, section I.
2. Eliot, *The Waste Land*, l. 430.
3. On witchcraft, one might consult among other works Francis King's *Sex, Magic and Perversion* (London: Neville Spearman 1971); also Ch. 10 below.
4. 'Cabala' will be spelled in this manner unless appearing otherwise in direct quotation. See Ch. 3, section IV, and Ch. 5, section V, for discussion.
5. Grillot de Givry, *Witchcraft, Magic and Alchemy*, tr. J. C. Locke (London: Harrap, 1931) p. 205.
6. According to the *Shorter Oxford*. But of course 'black magic' in spirit if not name has been around since time immemorial.
7. Some say the Egyptian was older. But the Egyptian magical strain which is described by Frances Yates in *Giordano Bruno and the Hermetic Tradition* (London: Routledge, 1964) seems to have blended Zoroaster with its own supposed *priscus theologus*, Trismegistus. See p. 416 and elswhere.
8. Theodore Ziolkowski, *Disenchanted Images: A Literary Iconology* (Princeton, NJ: Princeton University Press, 1977). See ch. 1.
9. Notably Aleister Crowley and his disciple Kenneth Grant, who refers to the pair as 'Fraud and Junk' in *Cults of the Shadow* (London: Muller, 1975) ch. 6. The close relation of psychoanalysis to the occult is explored by James Webb in *The Occult Establishment* (Glasgow: Richard Drew, 1981) ch. 6.
10. The preceding represent titles of major chapters in Givry's *Witchcraft, Magic and Alchemy*.
11. Obviously Catholic cardinals are not beeing condemned to the stake by nuclear physicists. On the other hand, the fate of the religious in totalitarian states, combined with benign neglect in much of the West, gives such an assertion some credibility.
12. Aleister Crowley (pseud. The Master Therion), *Magick in Theory and Practice* (Paris: published for subscribers, 1929) p. 114.
13. Such tautologies are by no means the exclusive provenance of the joky Joyce. Kibbo Kift founder John Hargrave advocated a 'yoga meditation exercise teaching everything is everything' (see Webb,

Occult Establishment, p. 90); and Crowley quite seriously uses the phrase 'Nothing was Everything' in his contemporary 'Aceldama', *Selected Poems*, ed. Martin Booth (London: Crucible, 1986) p. 153.

14. Crowley, *Magick in Theory and Practice*, p. 121.
15. Ibid., p. 144.
16. Ibid., p. 107.
17. This is Crowley's *Logos*, 'the Word of the New Aeon' and 'Law of Thelema' (the name of his 'abbey' in Sicily), and, as such, reappears throughout his opus, notably in *The Book of the Law* (1904) and as an epigraph on the frontispiece of *Magick in Theory and Practice*.
18. This is a principal lesson in the self-initiation an aspirant 'magician' must go through, according to *The Sacred Magic of Abra-Melin the Mage*, a medieval text on the subject influential since its rediscovery by MacGregor Mathers at the end of the last century. See also Ch. 5, section v.
19. See Grant, *Cults of the Shadow*, p. 124 and elsewhere.
20. This is an essential in the seminal doctrine of Bruno as Yates argues it, particularly in his essay on infinity *De immenso, innumerabilibus et infigurabilibus*.
21. The 'magical' background of Hitler is discussed in my *Art, Messianism and Crime* (London: Macmillan, 1986) ch. 7. See also Louis Pauwels and Jacques Bergier, *The Morning of the Magicians*, tr. Rollo Myers (London: Mayflower, 1971) pt II, ch. VIII; also Webb, *The Occult Establishment*, ch. 5.
22. Again, a point of Bruno's, especially in his attack on humanist 'pedants'. See Yates, *Bruno and the Hermetic Tradition*, pp. 159–68; also ch. XII.
23. In his essay 'Magic' in *Ideas of Good and Evil* (London: Bullen, 1903) p. 29. FURTHER REFERENCES IN TEXT.
24. See the essay on Yeats and Jung in *Yeats and the Occult*, ed. George Mills Harper, Yeats Studies 1976.
25. In Givry's *Witchcraft, Magic and Alchemy*. See note 5 above.
26. In this Yeats shows himself to be more in the camp of medieval and Celtic than of Renaissance magic, with its strongly Italian flavour: i.e. a more backward-gazing, apocalyptic and romantic tradition.
27. He may be using this word in a specifically Theosophical sense. According to G. M. Williams in her biography of Annie Besant, *The Passionate Pilgrim* (New York: Coward-McCann, 1929) 139, the Theosophists (of which group Yeats was a part, as we shall see) regarded the term beyond its normal connation to cover 'every sort of illusion from hypnotism to the black magic of the spirits of darkness'.
28. Certainly with many of the figures I mention in *Wagner to the Waste Land* (London: Macmillan, 1982). See also Ch. 3, section II.
29. The phrase is, of course, from Baudelaire: 'Au lecteur' at the beginning of *Les Fleurs du mal*.
30. Trismegistus's City of Adocentyn, for instance, and derivatives from it as Frances Yates describes: Campanella's City of the Sun, *et cetera*. Yeats's image also suggests the fifteenth-century miniature of Eden reproduced by Carl Jung in his *Man and his Symbols* (London: Aldus,

1964) p. 86. Memory systems too play an essential role in the 'magical reforms' envisioned by Pico della Mirandola and other Renaissance 'magi', according to Yates, who takes the matter up in her *Art of Memory*; also Jonathan Spence, who deals with it in his *The Memory Palace of Matteo Ricci* (New York: Viking, 1984).

31. Yeats, *Ideas of Good and Evil*, p. 308.
32. This antithesis is also reminiscent of the Renaissance 'magus' *versus* Christian humanist, as described by Yates. See note 22 above.
33. T. S. Eliot, *After Strange Gods* (London: Faber, 1934) p. 29. FURTHER REFERENCES IN TEXT.
34. Extensive discussion of Blake, Swedenborg, their relation to each other, to Masonic and Rosicrucian ideas and to Yeats may be found in Martha Schuchard's thesis 'Freemasonry, Secret Societies, and the Continuity of the Occult Traditions in English Literature' (University of Texas, 1975), esp. pp. 232–53.
35. It is characteristic of Hermetic magic that the only way one can know God, or the driving force of the universe, is to expand until one can imagine oneself to be God:

> Unless you make yourself equal to God, you cannot understand God: for the like is not intelligible save to the like. Make yourself grow to a greatness beyond measure, by a bound free yourself from the body; raise yourself above all time, become Eternity; then you will understand God. Believe that nothing is impossible for you, thinking yourself immortal and capable of understanding all, all arts, all sciences, the nature of every living being. Mount higher than the highest height; descend lower that the lowest depth. Draw into yourself all sensations of everything created, fire and water, dry and moist, imagining that you are everywhere, on earth, in the sea, in the sky, that you are not yet born, in the maternal womb, adolescent, old, dead, beyond death. If you embrace in your thought all things at once, times, places, substances, qualities, quantities, you may understand God.
> (*Corpus Hermeticum XI*, 'Egyptian Reflection on the Universe of the Mind', as rendered in Yates, *Bruno and the Hermetic Tradition*, pp. 32 and 198)

This sort of attitude of course represented extreme heresy to the Church, though something not dissimilar was practised by the Jesuits in their 'exercises'. More recently, it provided a disturbing spectacle to many when hippies began practising their variation on a theme under the influence of LSD (see *Art, Messianism and Crime*, esp. ch. 8, on R. C. Zaehner and Timothy Leary). Still, it remains a goal implicit in most doctrines of 'self-realisation'.
36. I am thinking, of course, of *Dallas*, *Dynasty* and their spin-offs.
37. 'Chameleon' was the title of a recent 'smash' hit by the androgynous pop-star Boy George; and a tradition of identification with this deceptively innocent, curiously Machiavellian type goes back at least as

far as Shakespeare, whose early 'black magician' Richard III says of himself,

> I can add colours to the chameleon;
> Change shapes with Proteus, for advantages,
> And set the murtherous Machiavel to school.
> (*Henry VI, Part III*, iii.ii)

Shakespeare of course was deeply influenced by Renaissance magic in general and Bruno in specific. See Yates, *Bruno and the Hermetic Tradition*, p. 357.

38. The phrase is Nietzsche's and can be found throughout his works, notably the later ones such as *The Antichrist*. And Nietzsche's works (which I deal with at some length in chapters 1 and 9 of *Wagner to the Waste Land* and ch. 6 of *Art, Messianism and Crime*) should be of some interest here as the great philosophical expression of man lost and groping after new spiritual vision. In particular, one might find similarities between them and the 'magical' thought of the Occidental Gnostic tradition which runs through Lévi, the Golden Dawn and Crowley. To Nietzsche, however, the paraphernalia of cults was odious: anarchic, glorious individualism was the great goal; and, when Wagner superseded the raw heroism of *Siegfried* with the quasi-Catholic, quasi-Masonic 'initiation' of *Parsifal* (see next chapter, first paragraphs), Nietzsche was revolted. See also Ch. 5, note 125, and Ch. 7, note 93.

CHAPTER 2. FROM EGYPT TO FREEMASONRY

1. See Joseph Henderson's essay in Jung, *Man and his Symbols*, pp. 110–48.
2. 'Durch Mitleid wissend' is the echoing refrain which identifies Parsifal's destiny as the 'great initiate' in Wagner's drama of that name.
3. He starts his opening essay in *Man and his Symbols* with images of Egyptian gods. See pp. 20–2.
4. On this, see ch. 2, 'Solomon's Temple and the Ancient Mysteries', of Gareth Knight's *History of White Magic* (London and Oxford: Mowbrays, 1978).
5. Aleister Crowley, *Diary of a Drug Fiend* (1922; York Beach, Maine: Weiser, 1970). See especially the final chapters, which describe the regimen at Crowley's 'Abbey of Thelma', here transparently fictionalised as 'Telepylus'. On p. 325, for instance, one adept tells the book's main character, 'Big Lion [Crowley] puts us through [initiation] without our knowing what he's doing. Though I've been through it myself. I didn't know in this clear way what had really happened until I tried to explain it to you.'
6. Yates, *Bruno and the Hermetic Tradition*, p. 9.
7. I quote from the Aldington translation: Lucius Apuleius, *The Golden*

Asse (1566), in *The Golden Asse, Satyricon, Daphnis and Chloe* (London: Simpkin Marshall, 1933) p. 225.

8. Ibid., p. 219.

9. Ibid., pp. 230–1.

10. See especially the chapter 'Love under Will' and pp. 355–6, which describe the result of the dual initiation in terms of the 'alchemical marriage': 'Our honeymoon had begun; and – this time – it was no spasmodic exaltation depending on the transitory excitement of passion, or stimulants, but on the fact of our true spiritual marriage, in which we were essentially united to each other not for the sake of either, but to form one bride whose bridegroom was the Work which could never be satiated so long as we lived, and so could never lead to weariness and boredom' (*Diary of a Drug Fiend*).

11. See Yates, *Bruno and the Hermetic Tradition*, pp. 9–10.

12. Yates makes this linguistic distinction to emphasise the powers Hermetic Man may have *over* the stars, rather than *vice versa*. See ibid., p. 60.

13. Notably the Renaissance, as Yates shows, and the end of the nineteenth and beginning of this century.

14. The epithet arises out of his importance in all three ancient religions: Egyptian as Thoth, Greek as Hermes and Roman as Mercurius.

15. On the authorship of these books see, among others, Knight's *History of White Magic*, ch. 3, 'The Coming of Chritianity and the Hermetic Synthesis'.

16. In this and the following description, I draw heavily on Yates's *Bruno and the Hermetic Tradition*, esp. ch. i-iii.

17. Ibid., p. 24.

18. Ibid., p. 10.

19. See ibid., ch. vii.

20. On the relation of Grail romance with Hermetica and the occult, see Knight, *History of White Magic*, ch. 4, 'Medieval Magic, Alchemy and Visions of the Quest'.

21. We shall discuss Rosicrucianism more in Ch. 4, section i, and Ch. 5, section iv. Meanwhile, the reader might refer to Eliphas Lévi's description of the movement in his *History of Magic* (1960), tr. A. E. Waite (London: Rider, 1913) pp. 351–9; also to Waite's own study, *The Brotherhood of the Rosy Cross* (London: Rider, 1924), and of course Frances Yates's distinguished *The Rosicrucian Enlightenment* (London: Paladin, 1975).

22. On the relation of Brunian ideas to Freemasonry, Yates writes,

> Where is there such a combination as this of religious toleration, emotional linkage with the mediaeval past, emphasis on good works for others, and imaginative attachment to the religion and the symbolism of the Egyptians? The only answer to this question that I can think of is – in Freemasonry, with its mythical link with the mediaeval masons, its toleration, its philanthropy, and its Egyptian symbolism. Freemasonry does not appear in England as a recognisable institution until the early seventeenth century, but

it certainly had predecessors, antecedents, traditions of some kind going back earlier though this is a most obscure subject. We are fumbling in the dark here, among strange mysteries, but one cannot help wondering whether it might have been among the spiritually dissatisfied in England, who perhaps heard in Bruno's 'Egyptian' message some hint of relief, that the strains of the Magic Flute were first breathed upon the air. (*Bruno and the Hermetic Tradition*, p. 274)

23. See Lévi's chapter on Freemasonry in *History of Magic*, pp. 381–9.
24. Pauwels discusses the Rosicrucians in Paris in *Morning of the Magicians*. Yates devotes one of her concluding chapters in *Bruno and the Hermetic Tradition* to the so-called Fludd Controversies between the Hermetic 'magical' worldview and the 'new science'. Another exhaustive source on these connections is offered by Schuchard in 'Freemasonry, Secret Societies' (see esp. pp. 94–189). In the words of the scholar to whom I am indebted for drawing this work to my attention, Schuchard is an 'enthusiast' who tends to see the 'invisible hand' of the Masons in places many might not expect. Among sixteenth-century English precursors, she identifies the 'magician' John Dee as a Rosicrucian; also perhaps Sir Philip Sidney. She sees the wedding of James I's daughter to the Elector Palatine's son as a great Rosicrucian event and therefore ascribes 'Rosicrucian' inspiration to the masques written for the occasion by Francis Bacon and Inigo Jones, also Shakespeare's *The Tempest*. Jones was possibly the first English Grand Master, she avers (p. 127). Fludd has 'long been viewed as the bridge between' the Rosy Cross and Freemasonry (p. 120). There is a probable Rosicrucian connection with Milton (p. 144) and a 'Cabalistic' inspiration in *Paradise Lost* (p. 147). The Stuart dynasty had an association with Masonry, among other ways via the Order of the Garter, on which the Mason Elias Ashmole published a book (p. 138). At the same time, Cromwell was careful never to 'persecute' the 'invisible college' (p. 160). Robert Boyle's chemistry arose out of 'Hermetic' pursuits (p. 157) and Sir Christopher Wren is 'often cited as a Grand Master of Freemasonry' (p. 158). As the eighteenth century opened, many literary men became taken up with Masonry, including Jonathan Swift, who 'wrote parodies of Masonic rituals' (p. 175), and Alexander Pope, who included Rosicrucian paraphernalia in *The Rape of the Lock* (p. 170) but later protested his orthodoxy (Catholic) in the *Essay on Man* (p. 189).
25. See discussion by Kenneth Grant in *Cults of the Shadow*, esp. ch. 2, 'The Draconian Cult of Ancient Khem'.
26. Pauwels and Bergier, in *Morning of the Magicians*, p. 66, claim that there are some 100,000 titles on the subject.
27. See, for instance, his story 'The Sandman'.
28. The following description comes from Pauwels and Bergier, *Morning of the Magicians*, pp. 82–9. The reader may also wish to consult the writings of the English 'alchemist' W. A. Ayton, which have recently been published by Aquarian Books in their 'Roots of the Golden Dawn' series.

29. Such as, in the case of Paracelsus's homunculus, for instance, a human embryo; which is, of course, the 'magical' precursor of our test-tube babies.

30. See Pauwels and Bergier, *Morning of the Magicians*, p. 29.

31. See, for instance, the works of Douglas Knoop and G. P. Jones, *An Introduction to Freemasonry* and *The Genesis of Freemasonry* (Manchester: University of Manchester Press, 1937 and 1947 respectively).

32. This is the received opinion of many today and is reflected in Stephen Knight's best-selling, hostile *exposé*, *The Brotherhood* (London: Granada, 1983). Mr Knight, who died recently and unexpectedly at the age of thirty-three, had antagonised many English Masons by adding fuel to the current flare-up of anti-Masonic sentiment, evidenced for instance by some Labour councils' demands for disclosure of Masonic affiliation among their members.

33. The problem of 'The Theology of the Masons' was discussed by Clifford Longley in an article of that title in *The Times*, 27 May 1985. Mr Longley believes that the cult could have avoided some of its recent difficulties by 'coming out of the closet' and admitting its status as a religion.

34. The relationship of Masonry to these epoch-making events is discussed by André Bouton in his *Francs-maçons et la Revolution fran-çaise, 1741–1815* (Le Mans, 1958); also by Schuchard in 'Freemasonry, Secret Societies' (esp. pp. 191–5). Among French *philosophes* whose ideas contributed to their country's revolution, Diderot, Montesquieu and Voltaire were all Masons, Schuchard tells us. Voltaire was actually initiated into a Parisian Lodge of which the American revolutionary Benjamin Franklin was Grand Master, and which also included the pirate John Paul Jones and the literary aristocrat the Comte de Gebelin, whose study of the Tarot would influence Eliphas Lévi and his followers (see next chapter, section v). Franklin had been initiated in the 1730s in Pennsylvania ('The Keystone State'); George Washington in the 1750s. Fifty-three of the fifty-six signers of the *Declaration of Independence* were Masons, as was their French supporter the Marquis de Lafayette, who would go on to be influential in the events in the Estates-General in Paris in 1789 and made the famous comment that 'an invisible hand' was guiding what followed. The irony here is that Louis XVI was also a Mason, as were the leaders of the most forceful opposition to the expansion of the French Revolution, Pitt and Burke in England.

35. See Knoop and Jones, *An Introduction to Freemasonry*; also Schuchard, who finds the origins of the Abiff legend in I Kings 7:13 and II Chronicles 2:17 ('Freemasonry, Secret Societies', p. 125).

36. See note 23 above.

37. And in literature. See for instance Marie Robert's study *British Poets and Secret Societies* (London: Croom Helm, 1986), esp. end of first chapter.

38. See Knoop and Jones, *Genesis of Freemasonry*, ch. IV, 'The Ms. Constitutions'.

39. Ibid., ch. V, 'The Mason Word'. See also *The Brotherhood*, pp. 236–7,

in which Knight quotes from the nineteenth-century American occultist and anti-Mason, the Revd Albert Pike.

40. On the pervasive influence of these cults on deist thinkers of the later eighteenth century, see 'Magic in the 18th Century: Freemasonry, Mesmerism and Secret Societies' in Gareth Knight's *History of White Magic;* on Goethe in particular, p. 140. See also Schuchard, who tells us that Goethe and Herder both joined Adam Weishaupt's radical, anti-tyrannical sect in the 1770s ('Freemasonry, Secret Societies', p. 204) and that Goethe was later brought into Masonry by his patron the Grand Duke of Weimar (p. 222). In sympathy with the revolutionary politics and anti-Jesuitical bent of Weishaupt's grouping, Goethe grew disenchanted with high Masonry as it became obsessed with Egyptianised rites under the influence of Cagliostro. According to Schuchard (p. 225), Goethe abandoned a projected 'sequel' to Mozart's *Magic Flute* because of this, and concentrated on Hermetic, Cabalistic and Swedenborgian systems in his rendering of the spiritworld in *Faust*. 'Die Geheimnisse', she goes on (p. 227), is 'an unfinished poem on Rosicrucianism'; 'The Grand Cophta' an attack on Cagliostro and other 'charlatan occultists' of the era.

41. In conversation, British Library, 9 May 1985. Felicity Baker was also present and pointed out the Masonic interests of Mozart's librettist Da Ponte and Masonic symbolism in Joseph Losey's movie version of *Don Giovanni*.

42. It is also Cabalistic. See Ch. 1, note A.

43. See *Faust* in 'Books that Have Changed Man's Thinking' edition (London: Heron, 1969) pp. 15–16.

44. See Ch. 1, note 18.

45. See, for instance, the speeches of the Archbishop at the end of *Faust, Part II*, Act IV.

46. Lévi, *History of Magic*, p. 388.

47. As described in particular by Grant in *Cults of the Shadow*, ch. 6, 'The Cult of the Beast – I (Aleister Crowley)'.

48. See ibid.; also references to Set throughout, as indexed. See also M.-L. Franz's essay in Jung, *Man and his Symbols*, esp. p. 225, where she discusses the fourth party found in modern trinitarian thinking:

> In the manifestations of the unconscious found in our modern Christian culture, whether Protestant or Catholic, Dr. Jung often observed that there is an unconscious tendency at work to round off our trinitarian formula of the Godhead with a fourth element, which tends to be feminine, dark, and even evil. Actually this fourth element has always existed in the realm of our religious representations, but it was separated from the image of God and became his counterpart, in the form of matter itself (or the lord of matter – i.e., the devil). Now the unconscious seems to want to reunite these extremes, the light having become too bright and the darkness too somber. Naturally it is the central symbol of religion, the image of the Godhead, that is most exposed to unconscious tendencies toward transformation.

49. Ours is an age presided over by Saturn, according to Pauwels and Bergier, *Morning of the Magicians* (p. 89 and elsewhere), the most baleful yet contemplation-inducing of cosmic influences.
50. This is also a Cabalistic concept, as 'man' in Hebrew (like 'Mensch' in German) also means 'mankind' and the 'Adam' of Genesis is also 'Adam Kadmon' of the 'Tree of Life'. (See also Ch. 5, section v.)
51. This trope appealed to Crowley, who claimed that he was training people to become the 'brains' of the human race. See my *Art, Messianism and Crime*, p. 76.
52. In her *Sword of Wisdom* (London: Neville Spearman, 1975) p. 36, Ithell Colquhoun speculates that there may be an identity between Goethe's 'Mothers' and what in the Golden Dawn would be called the three 'secret chiefs'. Another correlative to these oracular, subterranean movers-and-shakers may be Wagner's three Norns at the beginning of *Götterdämmerung*.

CHAPTER 3. ELIPHAS LÉVI

1. *Ezra Pound and Dorothy Shakespear: Their Letters, 1909–14*, ed. A. W. Litz and Omar Pound (New York: New Directions, 1984) p. 302.
2. The term is a standard one and means 'grammar' or 'cookbook' of 'magical' recipes and formulae.
3. In *Yeats Annual no. 4*, ed. Warwick Gould (London: Macmillan, 1986).
4. In Ch. 1, section II.
5. In 'The New Sculpture', *The Egoist*, 16 Feb 1914.
6. The 'novel' was first published in 1670 and numerous editions are available. For our purposes, the relevant version is Olivia Shakespear's (*The Egoist*, 16 Mar to 1 June 1914, inclusive).
7. First published 1841. A recent reprint of this most relevant book is the Steinerbooks paperback (Blauvelt, NY, 1971).
8. In Ch. 2, section III.
9. See Ch. 2, section II.
10. See Yates, *Bruno and the Hermetic Tradition*, ch. II.
11. This concept is most extensively explored in Crowley's novel *Moonchild* (1929).
12. The formulation comes from Catulle Mendès in an essay he wrote commending the ideas and methods of Wagner to his Symbolist contemporaries but warning them to adopt a French rather than German style. See my *Wagner to the Waste Land*, pp. 4 and 242, note 9.
13. Schuchard mentions Dürer in connection with Rosicrucian ideas about art as 'talismanic magic', incorporating Ficinan 'memory systems' and 'alchemical, erotic and suggestive' motifs. See 'Freemasonry, Secret Societies', pp. 99–102.
14. Of the many books which include studies of these two fascinating figures and their contribution to modern occultism, one might refer to the voluminous contemporary *grimoire* by Manly P. Hall, *An Encyclopedic Outline of Masonic, Hermetic, Kabbalistic and Rosicrucian Symbolical*

Philosophy (1929, Pasadena, Calif.: Society for Philosophical Research, 1971). Whether Mr Hall actually exists or represents a pseudonym for a collection of occult scholars like 'Gareth Knight' might be cleared up helpfully by some Californian scholar. Bruce Campbell in *Ancient Wisdom Revived* (Berkeley, Calif.: University of California Press, 1980) suggests that Hall is a single individual. If so, he has no doubt benefited by the concentration of Theosophical and 'magical' sects around Pasadena since the 1920s; also the emergence of an implicit 'orthodoxy' on high occult matters in the relevant communities of southern California, evident from a tour of its 'New Age' bookstores.

As to the development of French Masonry before the Revolution, another source is Schuchard. She discusses the appearance of *Acacia* (mistranslated *Écossais*, thus 'Scottish Rite') Masonry, with its anti-Pentateuch and pro-Cabalistic bias, and its contribution to the proliferation of degrees, thus autocratic hierarchy over egalitarianism, and of the idea of 'secret' grand masters or *supérieurs inconnus* (cf. Blavatsky's 'Mahatmas' and the Golden Dawn's 'secret chiefs' in the next two chapters), and of 'strict observance' ('Freemasonry, Secret Societies', pp. 187–200); of Anton Mesmer and his mixing of theories of 'animal magnetism' with contemporary Masonic and quasi-Masonic ideas (pp. 267–83); and of Cagliostro and his use of 'techniques of applied psychology and of religious and optimistic auto-suggestion' (pp. 292–306). About the influence of Cagliostro in France, Schuchard writes, 'It has been suggested that Cagliostro's mission, financed by the German Illuminati, was to unify the discordant lodges of French Freemasonry into one grand Egyptian rite' (p. 300). Thus we see an early association of Masonry and the occult with the shadowy world of spying and political subterfuge (see also next chapter, section v).

On the related development of French 'Martinism' – that is, occultism with Roman Catholic sympathies – and its influence on Lévi's particular mixture, see Christopher McIntosh's *Eliphas Lévi and the French Occult Tradition* (London: Rider, 1972), especially the initial chapters. Schuchard discusses Martinez de Pasqually, his 'Order of Elect Cohens' and 'his most famous disciple' Louis-Claude de Saint-Martin in relation to the Swedenborgian influences on French Masonry, particularly among the Avignon Illuminés ('Freemasonry, Secret Societies', p. 207 and *passim*).

15. Nodier may be a seminal figure. He is cited by the authors of *The Holy Blood and the Holy Grail* (London: Jonathan Cape, 1982) as is Hugo, as one of the leaders of the ultra-covert, quasi-Masonic group the Priors of the Elders of Sion, and as such is claimed as one of the moulders of the *Zeitgeist* of the nineteenth century. His indirect influence on literature is seen customarily as more important than his accomplishments as a writer. Even so, some of his works have held continuing interest for writers with eccentric and occult tastes, notably *Le Roi de Bohême et ses sept châteaux*. A recent indication of Nodier's importance comes from Francis King, who quotes the Frenchman thus in concluding his *Rebirth of Magic* (London: Corgi, 1982):

It is impossible to deny or affirm things which do not fit in with the little rules of our little minds. The occult sciences have their root too far in the past, and they have aroused too much interest throughout the history of mankind, for them to be meaningless. . . . Here is a pathway to be explored leading back into the darkness of time. Madness may be at the end, or perhaps the supreme wisdom; it is a dangerous way, but triumph would not be without its reward. . . . If a man can recapture in tbe mirror of memory the fugitive images of the past, he may well be able, either through some evolution in his being, or through forgotten science, to create or rediscover some means to illuminate the future, the other face of the eternal Janus.

16. Hugo's bizarre evocations, related to his personal cult of grandeur, are described in McIntosh's *Lévi and the French Occult Tradition*, pp. 198–200.

17. Specifically, Dumas published several poems. In addition Lévi was commissioned to do illustrations for editions of Dumas's *Louis XIV et son siècle* and *Le Comte de Monte Cristo*. See McIntosh, *Lévi and the French Occult Tradition*, pp. 91, 110.

18. 'Séraphita', which includes a long resume of Swedenborg's life and doctrine, was perhaps influenced by the activities of the Avignon Illuminés (see note 14 above) and was no doubt assisted by the appearance in France in 1820 of a translation of the Scandinavian mystic's complete works. A second translation, which Lévi would be more likely to have read, appeared in 1840. 'Le Réquisitionnaire', one of Balzac's 'philosophical tales', tells the story of a mother who dies at precisely the same moment that her son is shot by a firing-squad 500 kilometres away. It would be most intriguing to those interested in the field of 'sympathetic magic', which is central to 'white' witch-craft but less immediately germane to our line of discussion here.

19. Balzac, *The Wild Ass's Skin*, tr. Herbert Hunt (London: Penguin, 1977) p. 124. Ideas of Mesmerism are apparent here, as in Lévi's theory of the 'astral light', which we shall take up in section v. On Mesmer, see note 14 above.

20. Balzac, *Wild Ass's Skin*, p. 52. In orthodox 'magical' terminology, this kind of old man advising a young initiate is called a 'hierophant'. See, for instance, Madame Blavatsky's glossary at the end of her introductory chapter to *Isis Unveiled* (New York: Bouton, 1877).

21. See Ch. 4, section i, and Ch. 5, section iv.

22. See Eliphas Lévi, *Transcendental Magic*, tr. A. E. Waite (1896, London: Rider, 1984) p. 202; also T. A. Williams, *Eliphas Lévi: Master of Occultism* (Montgomery: University of Albama Press, 1975) p. 3.

23. Among other factors which may be involved here is a conflict between the radicalism of the Illuminati, in which Goethe was interested, and more establishmentarian forms of Masonry. For discussion see Schuchard, 'Freemasonry, Secret Societies', p. 202; also Robert, *British Poets and Secret Societies*, esp. on Shelley.

24. Also involved here may be the collapse of the Illuminati (cf. previous note).

25. The idea of a Christianised Napoleon is advanced most notably in Lévi's *The Key of the Mysteries*, tr. Aleister Crowley (1959; London: Rider, 1984). p. 54. A cult of the Paraclete was prevalent throughout Europe during the waning decades of the nineteenth century and is reflected in such works as Wagner's *Parsifal* and Huysmans's *Là-bas*. See the latter, tr. Keene Wallace as *Down There* (New York: Dover, 1972) pp. 262–7.

    On this matter of the French Revolution as a 'magical' watershed: something of the sort may be being reflected in *Zanoni*, which is set in large part in France at the time of the Reign of Terror and was written by the English 'initiate' who was arguably the greatest living influence on Lévi's mature trajectory. On Bulwer-Lytton's further influences, see the beginning of the next chapter.

26. This book animadverts on the lifestyle and 'magic' of a favoured precursor of both Lévi and Balzac, Rabelais, and in due course would provide Crowley with the name of his cult (Thelema) and its 'law' ('Do What Thou Wilt', etc.). See Ch. 1, note 17.

27. Williams pays close attention to Lévi's poetry in ch. IV of *Lévi: Master of Occultism*. Leví's most important volume, *Les Trois harmonies* 1845), is pre-Symbolist in style. It contains the poem 'Les Correspondances', which was written a year before Baudelaire's widely anthologised sonnet of the same title. Among other things, the poem makes a distinction which prefigures Lévi's subsequent, extra-poetic development:

    > Le sentiment des harmonies extérieures
    >   fait les poètes.
    > L'intelligence des harmonies intérieures
    >   fait les prophètes.

    On Baudelaire, Schuchard reminds us that he too was a 'student of occultism' (see 'Freemasonry, Secret Societies', p. 609). She cites in particular his 'famous critical act of bringing Poe into the tradition of French literary history'. Baudelaire 'rightfully saw the American as part of the "Illuminist", Swedenborgian, and "magnetic" philosophical tradition'.

28. As, for instance, in Lévi's remark in *Key to the Mysteries* (p. 100) about Dumas being author of *The Wandering Jew*, a book in fact written by Eugène Sue.

29. An intriguing speculation: might not Villiers and Mendès have also mentioned Lévi's work, or at least some of its ideas, to their idol Wagner during their 'pilgrimage' to him at Treibschen in 1869? I should think it likely. However, I have not been able to turn up any reference to Lévi in the most exhaustive source for Wagner's interests at this time: his wife's diaries.

30. Huysmans, *Down There*, p. 77.

31. Among Encausse's interests was homoeopathy, which is also an

important topic in the 'magical' discussions between the focal character of *Là-bas* and his scholar friend, aptly named Des Hermies. Encausse went on to tutor the royal family of Russia. He is said to have evoked the spirit of Alexander III and enjoyed status as a sort of pre-Rasputin. Later, back in Paris, he associated with MacGregor Mathers during the period when that 'magician' of the Golden Dawn was holding public theatrical séances for the invocation of Isis. See also Webb, *The Occult Establishment*, ch. 3.

32. The influence of this exotic reappearance of 'Rosicrucianism' is most apparent in the arts. Peladan's 'Salons of the Rose-Croix' were a major source of exposure for French Symbolist painters of the 1890s, from Gustave Moreau to a host of obscure yet talented figures. (See Philippe Julian's introduction to the catalogue of the 1972 Arts Council exhibition of these painters at the Royal Academy.) On a larger canvas, the elitist, 'gnostic catholic', life-decrying atmosphere of this movement may have helped pave the way for Hitlerism, as I argue at the end of my chapter on that German 'anti-christ' in *Art, Messianism and Crime*.

33. Huysmans, *Down There*, p. 236.

34. Lévi's own account of his early years may be found in his introduction to *L'Assomption de la femme* (Paris: Le Gallois, 1841). On biographical matters, I have found the relevant chapters of McIntosh's *Lévi and the French Occult Tradition* most useful.

35. Compare these to Crowleyan view of the 'three ages' mentioned in the previous chapter, section v.

36. See Ch. 2, section III.

37. See Williams, *Lévi: Master of Occultism*, p. 11.

38. See Lévi, *Transcendental Magic*, pp. 132, 140 and remarks on women in general.

39. Like Williams. See 'Women, Wisdom, Famine' in *Lévi: Master of Occultism*.

40. See for example Lévi, *Key to the Mysteries*, pp. 52–3.

41. See passages from Lévi's *History of Magic* quoted in the previous chapter.

42. Home's contacts with English literati were many: Elizabeth Barrett Browning admired him; Dickens thought him 'a rogue and scoundrel' but may have had him in mind when composing *Edwin Drood;* and Bulwer-Lytton consulted him (see note 74 below, and Ch. 4, notes 30 and 34). Lévi's account of his dealings with his rival and others is contained in *Key to the Mysteries*, 'Spooks in Paris' section.

43. This first appeared in *The Rosicrucian and Red Cross* (London), May 1873, and was reprinted in *The Occult Review*, Dec 1921. On Mackenzie's relation to the Golden Dawn, see Ch. 5, section I.

44. From a letter to Baron Speladieri, quoted in McIntosh, *Lévi and the French Occult Tradition*, p. 125.

45. See note 21 above; also McIntosh's chapter 'The Holy King' in *Lévi and the French Occult Tradition*.

46. See Lévi, *Transcendental Magic*, 'Dogma', ch. XIII, 'Necromancy'; also

Williams, *Lévi: Master of Occultism*, 90–3, and McIntosh, *Lévi and the French Occult Tradition*, pp. 101– 4.

47. On Apollonius, see I. G. Edmonds, *The Kings of Black Magic* (New York: Holt, Rinehart and Winston, 1981) ch. 3.

48. Mathers's most extensive statement to this effect comes in a letter written to London members of the Golden Dawn during the controversy over the fraudulence of the 'secret chiefs' which effectively destroyed that organisation. See Ellic Howe, *The Magicians of the Golden Dawn* (York Beach, Maine: Weiser, 1971) pp. 127–33. Crowley's statements may be found in various of his works. In his own career, the most critical evocation was the notorious 'Paris Working', which apparently resulted in death for one of the participants and left Crowley deranged for some months after. See Dennis Wheatley's introduction to his edition of Crowley's *Moonchild* (London: Sphere, 1972). The main point here, I think, is that evocations of this kind, if undertaken with full 'religious' commitment, demand a degree of mental concentration (not to mention moral 'transvaluation') which is liable to stretch a man's faculties to their limit. Chevalier's *The Sacred Magician: A Ceremonial Diary* (London: Hart-Davis, 1976) shows how this might occur. In short, self-induced maniacal derangement is the likely physiological explanation for what might otherwise be seen as 'possession' by demons or 'punishment' by spirits angry at having their other-worldly slumbers interrupted.

49. This may be one reason why Lévi's books are 'turgid, confused and naive', as Christopher McIntosh at one point complains (*Lévi and the French Occult Tradition*, p. 143). The problem is not reduced in English by the translations of A. E. Waite, a latter-day member of the Golden Dawn whom Crowley describes as 'the most platitudinous and priggishly prosaic of pretentious pompous pork-butchers of the language'. See *The Spirit of Solitude: subsequently re-antichristened The Confessions of Aleister Crowley* (London: Mandrake, 1929) vol. I, p. 163.

50. Lévi actually supported himself from time to time by drawing. Besides editions of Dumas and magazine illustrations, he earned money by painting for the Church. (See McIntosh, *Lévi and the French Occult Tradition*, ch. 8, 'The Radical'.) On Bruno's drawings see Yates, *Bruno and the Hermetic Tradition*, ch. XVII.

51. Schuchard suggests many of the points which might be taken up in such a study. She discusses Blake's Swedeborgian, Masonic and general occult links throughout her 700-page work. She even proposes that Blake may have been a member of a previous version of Yeats's Golden Dawn, run by the mysterious Cabalist Dr Falk. See 'Freemasonry, Secret Societies', p. 445.

52. In Williams' very helpful ch. VI, 'Correspondences and Cabala' (*Lévi Master of Occultism*). I say 'Lévi's Cabala' in order to underline the fact that interpretations of this arcane system are almost as numerous as the number of practising Cabalists since the beginning of its history. For further discussion, the reader might consult *Main Currents of Jewish Mysticism* and *The Cabala and its Symbolism* by the great post-war Jewish mystical scholar, G. S. Scholem.

53. In Crowley, *The Spirit of Solitude*, vol. II, p. 21.
54. See also Williams' helpful chapter x, 'The Language of Number' (*Lévi: Master of Occultism*).
55. And whom Kenneth Grant discusses in his *Cults of the Shadow*.
56. See Eliphas Lévi, *The Mysteries of the Qabalah*, tr. by transcription (Wellingborough: Aquarian, 1974), from p. 57.
57. This method is in part an innovation of contemporary 'magician' Michael Bertiaux (See Grant, *Cults of the Shadow*, 'The Cult of the Black Snake, I & II'). However, something similar is implicit in the belief of the Golden Dawn that Daath inserted itself into the Tree of Life at the time of the Fall and constitutes the 'head of the dragon', or serpent, which leads on to the many 'dragons' heads', or 'shells' (as opposed to 'spheres'), of the fallen Sephiroth, or Qliphoth. See Israel Regardie, *The Golden Dawn* (River Falls Minn.: Hazel Hills Corp., 1970), II, 'Ritual of the Philosophus'.
58. See his Introduction to *L'Assomption de la femme*; also Williams, *Lévi: Master of Occultism*, p. 15: 'Constant's answer to the problem of evil had been to refuse to admit its existence except in a relative, contingent way.' See also, among other things, Lévi's remarks on 'The Senary' in *Key to the Mysteries* (pp. 53–4): 'Evil is the disordered appetite of good, the unfruitful attempt of an unskilful will'; and 'It is because of the shadow that we are able to see light; because of cold that we feel heat; because of pain that we are sensible to pleasure. Evil is then for us the occasion and the beginning of the good.'
59. See the second part of *Mysteries of the Qabalah*.
60. See the last chapter of *Transcendental Magic*, devoted to the Tarot; also Williams' ch. XI, 'The Tarot and its Mysteries' (*Lévi: Master of Occultism*), which is particularly helpful in explaining the relation of the twenty-two trumps to their corresponding Hebrew letters and Cabalistic significances.
61. See Manly P. Hall, *The Secret Teachings of All Ages* (Pasadena, Calif.: Society for Philosophical Research, 1971) p. CXXIX, for discussion of the inconsistencies between different decks. Two versions used extensively in this century have been associated with Lévi's two most influential translators, Waite and Crowley.
62. See Ch. 2, note 34.
63. Huysmans is particularly attracted to the moral character of this period. For him, the mass-murderer of Brittany and the Maid of Orleans represent two sides of one phenomenon of high spiritual aspiration and awareness. 'From lofty mysticism to base satanism there is but one step', he says (*Down There*, p. 52). 'In the Beyond all things touch.' And later (p. 108): 'Anybody but a medical theorist can see that the desire for good and the desire for evil simply form two opposing poles of the soul. In the fifteenth century these extremes were represented by Jeanne d'Arc and the Marshal de Rais.' See his remarks too on 'the white splendour of the soul of the Middle Ages' (p. 232 and elsewhere).
64. In *Transcendental Magic* (p. 197), Lévi 'calls upon the eastern Magi to come forward and recognise once again that Divine Master Whose

cradle they saluted, the Great Initiator of all the ages'. This underlines the dominance of the Christian idea in his work. But interestingly it looks to 'eastern Magi' to regenerate the idea. These we might identify narrowly to be Masons, or more broadly to be a growing body of proponents of some synthetic Indo-European religion (see next chapter). More obscurely, the phrase may resonate of Rosicrucianism, with its basis in the legend of a magus who wandered for decades learning his lore in the East before returning to Europe to resurrect spirituality through a humanist, synthetic and 'magical' brotherhood (see Ch. 5, section IV).

65. In *Mysteries of the Qabalah*.
66. Ch. IX of the *Ritual*, 'The Ceremony of the Initiate'.
67. In his introduction to Lévi's *Letters to a Disciple* (i.e. Baron Spedalieri) (Wellingborough: Aquarian, 1980) p. 7.
68. See ch. VI, 'Magical Equilibrium', in the *Dogme*.
69. Particularly Williams' section on the subject in his chapter 'Dogma and Ritual' (*Lévi: Master of Occultism*, pp. 100–3).
70. See my discussion in the 'Shaw' and 'Lawrence' chapters of *Wagner to the Waste Land*; also in the 'Sade' chapter of *Art, Messianism and Crime*.
71. The phrase is John Symonds', used to describe the imaginary assistants Madame Blavatsky claimed to have helped her write *Isis Unveiled*. See *Madame Blavatsky: Medium and Magician* (London: Odhams, 1959) pp. 86–90.
72. Thus a nuclear physicist may be in effect an 'elemental' to the politicians who use him, or a chemist to a *parfumier* who turns his discoveries into best-selling scents. Ariel, who helps Prospero, is an equivalent in Shakespeare, as is Loge, who helps (and mocks) Wotan, in Wagner.
73. About eternal life, the 'elixir', and so on, see Ch. 2, section III.
74. According to Schuchard, *A Strange Story* was inspired by an evocation Lytton conducted with Lévi; also an attempt via D. D. Home to contact the English peer's dead daughter. See 'Freemasonry, Secret Societies', pp. 566–71.
75. Huysmans wonders, among other things, whether his own solipsistic imaginings might not represent a modern equivalent of possession by these inimical spiritual forces (see *Down There*, pp. 87, 134–5, 180 and elsewhere). Would it follow from this that the extremely inward literature of the next generation, particularly Proust's extended development of the Huysmanesque novel, represents a case of cultural demonic possession? I can imagine some critic of the future looking back on the first part of the twentieth century and arguing as much. Meanwhile, it may be interesting in this connection that the more recent and quite different American 'decadent' William Burroughs apparently believes something similar to Huysmans about the persistence of succubi and incubi in modern life. See his remarks in 'On Psychic Sex' in *From the Bunker: Conversations with William Burroughs by Victor Bokriss* (London: Vermillion, 1982).

76. Nietzsche's moniker for his former idol in his famous attack, *The Case of Wagner*. See *Wagner to the Waste Land*, 'Wagner and the French'.
77. Lévi, *Key to the Mysteries*, pp. 83–4.

CHAPTER 4.   MADAME BLAVATSKY AND THE THEOSOPHISTS

1. According to Bruce Campbell in *Ancient Wisdom Revived*, p. 26.
2. His wife called him 'Zan'. See Colquhoun's *Sword of Wisdom*, p. 51.
3. See Marion Meade, *Madame Blavatsky: The Woman Behind the Myth* (New York: Putnam, 1980) p. 28.
4. *Ibid.*, p. 170.
5. No doubt she was also inspired by *The Last Days of Pompeii* (1834), which portrays a cult of Isis. See Robert, *British Poets and Secret Societies*, p. 129.
6. Lytton's text merely ascribes him an aura of having come from 'the East'.
7. Quoted in Symonds, *Blavatsky: Medium and Magician*, p. 51.
8. See Ch. 2, notes 23 and 45.
9. Bulwer–Lytton, *Zanoni*, p. 127. (Details of edition used can be found in previous chapter, note 7.) FURTHER REFERENCES IN TEXT.
10. See last section, 'The Reign of Terror', esp. pp. 319 and 404, where Lytton declares that Robespierre is 'the real Sorcerer', 'not the starry Magian'.
11. See also the chapter on Shelley in Robert's *British Poets and Secrets Societies*.
12. This word is used extensively by Annie Besant in her *Ancient Wisdom* (London: Theosophical Publications Society, 1897) and clearly had cult currency long before it was taken up by the mass during the 'flower-power' period of the 1960s.
13. Lytton footnotes this quote, 'From Iamblich, on the Mysteries, c. 7, sect. 7.' The whole speech suggests in style, mood and placement in context, if not content, Lohengrin's 'In fernem Land' at the end of Wagner's opera of that name. Zanoni, who came from the Brotherhood to help mankind, is now preparing to return to 'higher places,' just as Lohengrin tells Brabant he must do. The similarity would not be worth noting were it not for the facts of Wagner's enthusiasm for Lytton's work and the vogue for *Zanoni* in particular during the 1840s, when Wagner was conceiving his early 'Grail' work.
14. Campbell in *Ancient Wisdom Revived* (p. 62) says, 'The core of Theosophical teachings consists of four sets of ideas: evolution, man's constitution, karma and reincarnation, and after-death states.'
15. The great exposition of this process is Besant's *Ancient Wisdom*.
16. Campbell describes the contribution of indigenous American ideas to Theosophy in *Ancient Wisdom Revived*, pp. 8–20; on Transcendentalism, see esp. p. 9.
17. 'Cosmogenesis' and 'Anthropogensis' are the names of the two volumes of *The Secret Doctrine* as it was orignally published. Campbell

offers one of the best digests available on these two exceedingly rich concepts in his section on Blavatsky's great book (*Ancient Wisdom Revived*, pp. 40–8).

18. This was Besant's response when she visited the state for a second time, in 1927, and bought several hundred acres of prime real estate in Ojai which passed to Krishnamurti and still belongs to the sect. See G. M. Williams, *The Passionate Pilgrim*, p. 329.

19. Always a semi-mythical place in her scheme, Tibet was 'almost impossible' to get into in Blavatsky's day, Symonds tells us (*Blavatsky: Medium and Magician*, p. 34), and thus had special status as a 'land of priests and magicians'.

20. Campbell gives a list of sources on the 'Mahatma letters' controversy in *Ancient Wisdom Revived*, p. 213, note 8.

21. According to G. M. Williams in her biography of Blavatsky, *Priestess of the Occult* (New York: Knopf, 1946) p. 28.

22. Symonds, *Blavatsky: Medium and Magician*, p. 199.

23. Ibid., p. 80.

24. A description quoted ibid., p. 218, from V. S. Solov'yov in his *Modern Priestess of Isis* (London: Longmans, 1895).

25. See. W. B. Yeats, *Memoirs*, ed. Denis Donoghue (New York: Macmillan, 1973).

26. From a conversation with the American artist and Orientalist A. L. Rawson, who met Blavatsky in Cairo in 1851. See Symonds, *Blavatsky: Medium and Magician*, p. 35.

27. By G. M. Williams, who gives the most lively account of this phase. See *Priestess of the Occult*, from p. 25.

28. Notable sources on Blavatsky's early career include her cousin, the Russian statesman Count Witte; A. P. Sinnett, to whom she told the 'official version' in 1886; Countess Wachtmeister, with whom she lived while beginning *The Secret Doctrine*; Olcott in his *Old Diary Leaves*; and Solov'yov.

29. See Williams, *Priestess of the Occult*, from p. 34.

30. Home denied this. According to Marion Meade (*Woman behind the Myth*, p. 70), the Anglo-American Spiritualist did meet Blavatsky in Paris but 'did not find the earthy [woman] to his taste. . . . "It was most repulsive to me that in order to attract attention she pretended to be a medium." ' Home's own attack on Theosophy can be found in his *Lights and Shadows of Spiritualism* (New York: Carlton, 1877), a book which on a far less grand scale attempts to sum up the origins of occult tradition which Blavatsky would essay in *Isis Unveiled*, published in the same year. Home is particularly scathing about the claims for Madame as a 'medium' conveyed by Olcott in his *People from Another World*, published two years earlier.

31. Blavatsky's relationship with Lévi probably extended no further than her inheritance of the adulation of his one-time tutee, Frau Gebhard. But, as Symonds remarks, 'It would have been a great moment in the history of occultism if the Abbé Constant and the youthful Madame Blavatsky, back from one of her flying visits to Tibet, had been

brought a fact to face in some Parisian drawing-room' (see *Blavatsky: Medium and Magician*, pp. 190–1).

32. Ibid., p. 62.
33. She allegedly said this to Rawson. See ibid., p. 64.
34. Robert Browning, 'Mr Sludge, "The Medium" ', in *Dramatis Personae* (1861), ll. 1345–53. Browning apparently attended a séance of Home's with his wife before her death. Elizabeth found the Spiritualist impressive, and even Robert's characterisation of him conveys considerable sympathy. It must be some measure of Browning's fascination that 'Mr Sludge' is by far the longest inclusion in perhaps his most famous book. Nor was Home entirely put out by Browning's attentions, as his remarks about the poet in *Lights and Shadows* (p. 228) show.
35. All commentators give an account of the founding and decision on the name. Campbell alone mentions the 'Miracle Club' (*Ancient Wisdom Revived*, pp. 27–8).
36. By Symonds (*Blavatsky: Medium and Magician*, p. 90). One suspects that his praise is either tongue-in-cheek or semi-intentionally obfuscatory, however, as there is little evidence that he was willing to wade through either of Madame's great tomes with the alertness, say, which he devotes to Crowley's key texts in his more distinguished occult biography, *The Great Beast*.
37. Coleman's 'The Sources of Madame Blavatsky's Writings' is included as an appendix to Solov'yov's *Modern Priestess of Isis* (pp. 353–66).
38. Ibid., quoted in Symonds, *Blavatsky: Medium and Magician*, p. 220.
39. See the relevant chapters of *Art, Messianism and Crime*.
40. One Madame Coloumb, who with her carpenter husband aided Madame in many ruses. The Society's 'Report of the Committee Appointed to Investigate Phenomena Connected with the Theosophical Society' first appeared in *Proceedings of the Society for Psychical Research*, 3 (Dec 1885) 201–400.
41. According to Symonds. See *Blavatsky: Medium and Magician*, p. 209.
42. According to Williams. See *Priestess of the Occult*, p. 6.
43. Quoted with no reference, alas, by Maurice Leonard in his *Madame Blavatsky* (London: Regency, 1976) p. 91.
44. To George Moore. See *Salve* (New York: Boni and Liveright, 1923) p. 23.
45. Ernest Rhys, *Wales England Wed* (London: Dent, 1940) pp. 105–6.
46. M. G. MacBride, *A Servant of the Queen* (Dublin: Golden Eagle, 1950) pp. 246–7.
47. Yeats, *Memoirs*, p. 24.
48. Publicity was not something Madame was ashamed to court. Williams suggests that Olcott's influence as a journalist was what attracted her to him initially (*Priestess of the Occult*, p. 5); and before her death she wrote an article, 'The Blessings of Publicity' for *Lucifer* which suggested that conveying 'the message of Love' in the outer was one of the highest duties of the Theosophist and would help the world more than all the guns and munitions of righteous wars. See *Studies in Occultism* (Covina, Calif.: Theosophical University

Press, 1946) essay 3. Among the various motifs of the twentieth century Blavatsky anticipated, we can see from this that propaganda was not the least.

49. See *The Collected Letters of W. B. Yeats*, vol. I: *1865–95*, ed. John Kelly (Oxford: Clarendon Press, 1986) pp. 202–3 (letter to Katherine Tynan).

50. See J. G. Sime and Frank Nicholson, *Brave Spirits* (London: Simpkin Marshall, 1952) pp. 63–4.

51. See Yeats, *Memoirs*, p. 26.

52. See Ch. 1, note 25.

53. Meade, *Woman behind the Myth*, p. 402. 'Dreaming awake', according to Lévi (*Transcendental Magic*, p. 121), is the best way to 'read' the 'astral light'.

54. 'Anashuya and Vijaya' in *Crossways*. Among three poems on Indian themes dating from 1887.

55. See George Russell, *Letters from AE* (London: Abelard-Schuman, 1961) pp. 6–9.

56. See Meade, *Woman behind the Myth*, pp. 403–4.

57. See 'H. P. Blavatsky's Influence on Ireland's Literary Renaissance' by W. Emmett Small in *H. P. Blavatsky and the Secret Doctrine: Commentaries on her Contribution to World Thought* ed. Virginia Hanson (Wheaton, Ill.: Theosophical Publishing House, 1971) pp. 108–23.

58. See Meade, *Woman Behind the Myth*, p. 405.

59. She rose quickly to the 'Philosophus' grade before going 'in abeyance with the sympathy of the Chiefs' (see Howe, *Magicians of the Golden Dawn*, p. 50).

60. Richard Ellmann, *James Joyce*, new and rev. edn (Oxford: Oxford University Press, 1982) p. 75.

61. Ibid., p. 99.

62. However, he does go on to tell us of an escapade later in the same summer, when Joyce and his friend Oliver St John Gogarty (Buck Mulligan of *Ulysses*) broke into the offices of AE's Hermetic Society, 'surveyed the "yogibogeybox" ', with its occult reference books such as Madame Blavatsky's *Isis Unveiled*, and made a flag by tying a pair of women's drawers to a broomstick before they departed. See ibid., p. 174.

63. See my discussion in *Wagner to the Waste Land*, esp. pp. 153, 166.

64. In the Introduction to *The Ancient Wisdom*.

65. See William Schutte, *Index of Recurrent Elements in James Joyce's Ulysses* (Carbondale, Ill.: Southern Illinois University Press, 1982).

66. See Meade, *Woman behind the Myth*, ch. II; also Campbell *Ancient Wisdom Revived*, p. 3.

67. See Meade, *Woman behind the Myth*, 231.

68. See Leonard's *Madame Blavatsky*, p. 58.

69. See *Studies in Occultism*, pp. 58–9.

70. See Ch. 3, note 29.

71. See my *Wagner to the Waste Land*, pp. 10 and 243, note 24.

72. See Maurice Maeterlinck, *The Great Secret*, tr. Bernard Miall (London: Methuen, 1922) pp. 201–3.

73. Meade, *Woman behind the Myth*, p. 418.

74. This second period of controversy over Blavatsky's method and fraud provoked some of the most exotic works in her favour, including one by Modigliani's mistress Beatrice Hastings and another by the actress Elizabeth Robbins; also an attack by Arthur Conan Doyle. See Williams, *Priestess of the Occult*, 12–13; also Campbell, *Ancient Wisdom Revived*, pp. 127–8, 191–2.

75. The comparison is drawn by Williams (*Priestess of the Occult*, p. 10): 'Barnum made a world reputation on the thesis that people liked to be fooled.'

76. Francis King tells the saga of Leadbeater's perversion in 'The Bishop and the Boys' chapter of *Sex, Magic and Perversion*. 'Thought-forms' emanate around men 'like a full-length halo' and are visible to psychic 'sensitives', Leadbeater contended (see Williams, *The Passionate Pilgrim*, p. 240). The concept is similar to that of 'auras', common to Theosophy and present-day trendies.

77. Besant's pre-Theosophical Society history is given in the first half of *The Passionate Pilgrim*.

78. Yeats was also bowled over by Mohini, though not of course sexually. The chela's 1885 visit to Dublin inspired the poet (see Meade, *Woman behind the Myth*, p. 400).

79. When staying with Countess Wachtmeister and writing *The Secret Doctrine*, Blavatsky asked Sinnett to get her a copy of Jennings' *Phallicism* (Meade, *Woman behind the Myth*, p. 380); also 'to beg Mohini to write out the esoteric meaning of some of Shakespeare's plays' (cf. Blavatsky's literary pretensions as described in the previous section). Jennings' writings were of general interest to occultists in the period, especially his *Rosicrucians: Their Rites and Mysteries* (1870), though, as Howe tells us, 'Anyone who supposed that Jennings knew anything about the "Rosicrucians" was capable of believing anything' (*Magicians of the Golden Dawn*, p. 31). See also, King, *Sex, Magic and Perversion*, ch. 8.

80. Tingley's career, which has typological similarities to those of Blavatsky and Besant, is discussed by Campbell in *Ancient Wisdom Revived*, pp. 131–42.

81. Eliot, *The Waste Land*, l. 41.

82. On the basic psychological need, especially in the West, for recognition of the dark force in modern conceptions of 'the godhead', see Ch. 2, note 47. Jung's perception may shed light on the attitude in note 85 below.

83. I have used this phrase twice now. The formulation of 'the Thinker' is Annie Besant's. See *The Ancient Wisdom*, ch. iv, 'The Mental Plane'.

84. 'Practical Occultism' is the first essay in *Studies in Occultism*.

85. A Theosophical criticism of the kindred spirit Jung is included in Small's *Blavatsky and the Secret Doctrine* (p. 19):

> It is unfortunate that C. G. Jung took the attitude he did toward the Orient and the spiritual path in general. The entry to the path opens inward, and for practical purposes can be equated with the

psychological inquiry into the causes of behaviour, emotion and thought. All real spiritual teachers have been wise in the science of the soul. . . . But Jung, who seems to have come nearer to an affirmation of the spirit than any of the other modern psychologists, sows his doubts in the minds of his readers as he leads them to the point beyond which he fears to go, so that, as he turns away, they turn away with him. . . . Unless we are ready to enter the gateway into the subconscious parts of our natures, we never really learn anything about ourselves.

86. I borrow this term from Scientology jargon. It seems applicable here, as a similar sort of authoritarianism masquerading as 'help' becomes apparent in the later cult. See Ch. 9.

87. The 'law' of development of cults from charismatic through organisational phases is described by Max Weber in his famous *Sociology of Religion* (Boston, Mass.: Beacon Press, 1963); see also Campbell, *Ancient Wisdom Revived*, pp. 187–8.

88. For instance, Nicholas Goodrich-Clarke in *The Occult Roots of National Socialism* (Wellingborough: Aquarian, 1985); see also Ch. 1, not 21.

89. According to Jean-Michel Angebert, the secret of Hitler's personality may have been that he was a 'medium'. In any case, he is said to have been haunted by 'hidden masters' and to have imported to Berlin high-ranking lamas from Tibet. See *Art, Messianism and Crime*, p. 86.

90. See Williams, *The Passionate Pilgrim*, p. 303. This book includes a photograph of the octogenarian Besant done up in flowing Indian robes yet full Masonic regalia.

91. See M. K. Gandhi, *Autobiography* (Washington DC: Public Affairs Press, 1948) p. 91.

92. *The Passionate Pilgrim* discusses Leadbeater and his power over Besant at length. As Williams says, the 'Bishop' was Besant's 'key to fairyland' and necessary to her imaginative and psychic experiences – a sort of personal Rasputin.

93. The frontispiece to *The Ancient Wisdom* contains a (to me) inexplicable chart of the innards of the principal chemical elements.

94. This claim would find its most ardent enunciator in L. Ron Hubbard, which is fitting enough when one considers that science fiction and the Bomb are principally American contributions. Crowley, however, had advanced it as early as the 1930s. Nor is it irrelevant in this connection that Hubbard got his start as an occultist by association with Jack Parsons, a Crowleyan and nuclear physicist. See Ch. 9, section I.

95. Campbell tells of the Halcyon Community of Pismo Beach, California, which combined Theosophical philosophy with communalism, provided pioneers in the electronics and X-ray industries, and included 'friends and co-workers of the radical author-politician Upton Sinclair'. See *Ancient Wisdom Revived*, pp. 159–60.

96. See Williams, *The Passionate Pilgrim*, pp. 311–24. As early as 1890,

one disillusioned Theosophist had said of Besant, 'She will die in the odor of sanctity within the pale of the Catholic Church.'

97. See ibid., p. 287.

98. See ibid., pp. 335–8; also Campbell, *Ancient Wisdom Revived*, p. 129. Campbell also quotes a famous passage in which Blavatsky, rather like the young George Russell, declares her allegiance to 'the CAUSE' but not even to her own movement (ibid., p. 188).

99. A brief, complete and perhaps surprisingly sympathetic account of Krishnamurti's career may be found in his obituary in *The Times*, 19 Feb 1986.

100. As the proprietor of the Atlantis Bookshop has pointed out (in a conversation overheard, Jan 1986), 'historicism' has become the fashionable mode in 'magical' writing over the past two decades. This is demonstrated by the vogue for works of John Symonds, Ellic Howe, Francis King, 'Gareth Knight', the exegetes of Yeats's occultism and others. It may also represent a 'decadence' in the 'magical' tradition of our times. In any case, it is plain that a period of consolidation of facts has succeeded the great era of gathering ideas out of the 'astral light'.

101. Paranoid occultists have often believed that 'historicist' criticism is part of an 'establishment' plot against them. Certainly Blavatsky felt something of the kind when the Society for Psychical Research came out against her; and the Nazis were for ever charging that journalistic–literary 'trashing' of their movement was motivated by the 'magical' jealousy of Freemasons and Jews. In this connection, there are no doubt occultists of the present day who feel that the rise of 'historicism' (see above) may be part of a design to undermine their practising groups.

102. Besant's most impassioned evocation of 'colours' comes in her chapter v, 'Devachan'. This describes 'the Shining Land': a 'realm of light and beautiful sound and perfection' which leads on to the 'seventh heaven' of popular myth. See *Ancient Wisdom*, pp. 199–212.

103. See ibid., Introduction, pp. 1–49.

104. Cf. the seven divisions of *Zanoni* described in the first section of this chapter and the definition of the number by Lévi in Ch. 3.

105. See Besant, *Ancient Wisdom* ch. iii, 'The Astral Plane', pp. 73–107.

106. The word comes from Hubbard, who claimed that US Intelligence once approached him for help in finding ways to make the populace more 'suggestible'. See *Art, Messianism and Crime*, pp. 180 and 208, note 27.

107. As is told, for instance, by Maurice Richardson in a review of a reprint of Somerset Maugham's *The Magician*, TLS, no. 577 (1978).

108. The two volumes of *Isis Unveiled* are entitled 'Science' and 'Theology'.

109. See Campbell, *Ancient Wisdom Revived*, 199.

110. A subject Blavatsky wrote on extensively. See *Studies in Occultism*, pp. 185–95.

111. See Ch. 1, section v.

112. From *Old Diary Leaves*, as quoted in Symonds, *Blavatsky: Medium and Magician*, p. 104.

CHAPTER 5. THE GOLDEN DAWN

1. See G. M. Williams, *Priestess of the Occult*, p. 7.
2. See Ch. 3, end of section III.
3. See Ch. 4, end of section II.
4. See Francis King, *Ritual Magic in England* (London: Spearman, 1970) ch. 11, where he quotes Rudolf Steiner's impression that the Theosophical Society in England was for 'women who wanted a little spiritualism with their tea'.
5. See *The Magical Mason*, ed. R. C. Gilbert (Wellingborough: Aquarian, 1983). Westcott goes so far as to describe Blavatsky as a modern Christian Rosenkreuz.
6. On Kingsford, see Howe, *Magicians of the Golden Dawn*, p. 40. On Mathers' relationship with this 'energetic', 'beautiful' and 'good' woman who nevertheless 'dyed her hair' (in the *mots justes* of Blavatsky), see Colquhoun, *Sword of Wisdom*, p. 76; also Moina Mathers' Preface to a reissue of her husband's *Kabbalah Unveiled* (London: Kegan Paul, 1926).
7. I have given details on the Howe and Colquhoun titles and *Ritual Magic in England* already. Another relevant King title is *The Rebirth of Magic*, co-written with Isabel Sutherland (see Ch. 3, note 15). Gilbert's contributions, besides *The Magical Mason*, include an edition of writings of Mathers and J. W. Brodie-Innes (*The Sorcerer and his Apprentice*) and a new, brief history of the Order at large, both recent releases from Aquarian.
8. See Howe, *Magicians of the Golden Dawn*, ch. 2.
9. Ibid., ch. 1.
10. I am thinking in particular of Christina Mary Stoddart's dissolution of her branch of the Order in 1922, following increasingly frenetic and unsuccessful attempts to discover the truth about its origins. See ch. 9 of George Mills Harper's *Yeats's Golden Dawn* (London: Macmillan, 1974); also Stoddart's *Light-bearers in Darkness* (London: Inquire Within, 1930).
11. See Colquhoun, *Sword of Wisdom*, p. 134.
12. See note 5 above.
13. See Howe, *Magicians of the Golden Dawn*, ch. 17, on R. W. Felkin's search for the 'secret chiefs'; also Harper, *Yeats's Golden Dawn*, Appendix U, on Steiner's response to requests for information and assistance. Steiner's own status as a Rosicrucian is claimed, among other places, by the Preface to the Steinerbooks edition of *Zanoni*.
14. See Howe, *Magicians of the Golden Dawn*, Foreword, p. XI.
15. The characterisation is Maud Gonne's (MacBride, *A Servant of the Queen*, pp. 259–60).
16. Specifically, of Elizabeth I's astrologer Dr John Dee and his Mephistophelean companion Edward Kelley, of whom Crowley would regard himself as a reincarnation. See, for instance, Edmonds, *Kings of Black Magic*, ch. 3.
17. On 'the light', see Yorke's Foreword to Howe, *Magicians of the Golden Dawn*, p. IX and *passim*. The prominence of women in the Golden

Dawn was an innovation for Rosicrucian/Masonic sects and was no doubt inspired by the Theosophical Society and the feminism Mathers had been encouraged in by Anna Kingsford.

18. By Howe in his Preface to *Magicians of the Golden Dawn*, p. xxii.
19. In an obituary of Mathers in *The Occult Review*, Apr 1919.
20. As recalled by his theatre *confrère* William Archer. See my *Wagner to the Waste Land*, p. 81.
21. A term favoured by Blavatsky, as we have noted (see Ch. 4, end of section ii); also by Crowley – see Francis King, *The Magical World of Aleister Crowley* (London: Weidenfeld, 1977) p. 119 and elsewhere. Both may have used the term to mask exhaustion or simple lack of imaginative inspiration.
22. See note 15 above.
23. See particularly Moina Mathers' letter to Annie Horniman (Howe, *Magicians of the Golden Dawn*, pp. 117–19) when the latter was in hysteria over the Lake Harris suggestion; also Colquhoun (*Sword of Wisdom*, p. 176 and *passim*), who speculates interestingly on the sexual tendencies through the group at large.
24. *The Letters of W. B. Yeats*, ed. Allan Wade (New York: Macmillan, 1955) p. 340.
25. See Colquhoun *Sword of Wisdom*, pp. 155–6.
26. See Yeats's account in his *Memoirs* of his courtship with Olivia Shakespear, whom it took him two years to kiss.
27. For Crowley's amusing, intemperate yet sometimes accurate attack, see 'The Shadowy Dill-Waters, or Mr. Smudge the Medium' in *The Equinox*, i.iii (1910) 327.
28. In this connection, the Golden Dawn's leaders were ever warning against excessive 'asceticism', which might lead to 'hypocrisy of self-congratulation' and therefore would disequilibrate the 'whole being'. See the Order's 'Flying Rolls', published as *Astral Projection, Ritual Magic and Alchemy* by Francis King (London: Spearman, 1971), p. 104 and elsewhere.
29. The facts are most fully mustered in the first half of Colquhoun's *Sword of Wisdom*.
30. *Astral Projection*, pp. 67–8.
31. As Moina Mathers tells us in her Preface to *Kabbalah Unveiled:* 'Great stress is laid on the ideal of Fraternity. . . . Any breach in the harmony of a circle will permit the entry of an opposing force.'
32. Especially Ellic Howe. It seems to be the driving theme of *Magicians of the Golden Dawn* and suggests an instinct for the 'hatchet job' which Howe may have picked up when in the 'dirty tricks' division of the intelligence services during the Second World War.
33. Indeed, this sometimes reached a point where the Matherses seemed to be running a commune. See ibid., pp. 154–5, for instance.
34. See Colquhoun, *Sword of Wisdom*, p. 41.
35. In *Moses and Monotheism*, tr. Katherine Jones (London: Hogarth Press, 1939).
36. See Harper, *Yeats's Golden Dawn*, pp. 145–8.

37. The origin of this impression on Yeats's part may have been Maud Gonne. See Colquhoun, *Sword of Wisdom*, p. 95.

38. In his novel *Moonchild*, where Mathers is depicted as Douglas.

39. Yeats gives an account of this rite at the end of his final version of *A Speckled Bird*, ed. William O'Donnell, Yeats Studies 1976.

40. See Colquhoun, *Sword of Wisdom*, p. 86.

41. See ibid., p. 111; 'To purloin someone else's work and pass it off as one's own is a poor-spirited plot at best and subserves the lowliest psychological needs; but Crowley was more than an invalid: he was a petty crook, despite his great and varied gifts.'

42. F. A. C. Wilson. See ibid., p. 108.

43. See Howe, *Magicians of the Golden Dawn*, pp. 157, 162–3.

44. In her frenzy to discover the true origins of the Golden Dawn, Christina Stoddart arrived at this conclusion. Surprisingly, Yeats does not seem to have tried to convince her otherwise. See Harper, *Yeats's Golden Dawn*, p. 142: 'She thanked Yeats for some clippings on the Jewish peril.'

45. Mathers may also have identified with Napoleon. Like the great French warrior–leader, his favourite poet was Ossian.

46. See 'The Temple of Solomon the King', *Equinox*, i.i (1910) 159. This extended article included transcriptions of the Golden Dawn grade rituals. Mathers came to London from Paris to try to prevent them from being published. He obtained an injunction but did not have sufficient funds to maintain it. A comic and characteristically spiteful account of the exchanges in court is given by Crowley in *The 'Rosicrucian' Scandal* (privately printed, 1911).

47. The manuscript of *The Sacred Magic* was left on a train and Mathers subsequently had to rewrite it. See Howe, *Magicians of the Golden Dawn*, pp. 170–2.

48. The claim may attach to the *Zanoni* identification, which Mathers shared with Blavatsky. See previous chapter, note 6.

49. See Colquhoun, *Sword of Wisdom*, p. 99.

50. Published by Redway.

51. See, for instance, King, *Ritual Magic in England*, ch. 7.

52. See Howe, *Magicians of the Golden Dawn*, p. 216.

53. See Harper, *Yeats's Golden Dawn*, p. 36.

54. See Yeats, *The Speckled Bird*, pp. 18–23. FURTHER REFERENCES IN TEXT.

55. See, for instance, Westcott's paper 'Man, Miracle, Magic: From the Ancient Rosicrucian Dogmata' (*The Magical Mason*, pp. 66–70), in which he says, 'An Adept of the Rosicrucian ideal is the very opposite to the Medium. He is living trained vital energy illumined by the Spiritual above; the Medium is a negative being, the prey of every evil influence, and of anyone with malign passion: he is deceiving and self-deceived, the catspaw of every elemental force, and baneful misdirected energy.' On the other hand, Mathers seems to have seen nothing amiss in practising mediumistic methods in order to gather Golden Dawn lore: 'Almost the whole of the Second Order knowledge has been obtained by me from [the "secret chiefs"] in various ways; by clairvoyance, by Astral projection on their part

and on mine – by the table, by the ring and disc, at times by a direct
Voice audible to my external ear, and that of Vestigia [his wife], at
times copied from books brought before me, I know not how, and
which disappeared from my vision when the transcription was
finished, at times by appointment *astrally* at a certain place, till then
unknown to me' (Howe, *Magicians of the Golden Dawn*, pp. 130–1).
This of course sounds remarkably like accounts of how Blavatsky
managaed to write *Isis Unveiled*.

56. In *Autobiographies* (London: Macmillan, 1926) p. 226 and elsewhere,
Yeats would write of Mathers' 'athletic' body. Nietzsche's encourage-
ments to 'great health' may be found in, for example, *The Joyful
Wisdom*, vol x of *The Complete Works of Friedrich Nietzsche*, ed. Oscar
Levy (London: T. A. Foulis, 1909–13) p. 351.

57. See *The Rosicrucian Seer: The Magical Work of Frederick Hockley*, ed.
John Hamill, 'Roots of the Golden Dawn' series (Wellingborough:
Aquarian, 1984).

58. What is Yeats up to here? Is he making a homoerotic suggestion
about Mathers? Elsewhere he complains that Mathers always seemed
to need a favoured male disciple around him (see *Letters*, p. 340).
Yeats himself seems to have filled this role in the early 1890s. Later,
for a time at least, he was supplanted by the youthful Aleister
Crowley, a camp version of whom may be behind the 'Cockney'
described here (though some scholars have cited A. E. Waite).

59. This, as a note in O'Donnell's edition of the novel tells us, is a
version of W. A. Ayton, another founder member of the Golden
Dawn, of whom Yeats told a similar vignette in a letter to Lady
Gregory, written about the same time as the 'final version' of the
novel (see *Letters*, p. 365).

60. The original Welsh version of the Parsifal tale, 'Peredur', was Yeats's
favourite story in the *Mabinogion*, which was one of the primary
sources for his projected 'Order of Celtic Heroes' (see, for instance,
The Speckled Bird, 'the flaming tree').

61. See Harper, *Yeats's Golden Dawn*, p. 43.

62. Ibid., pp. 63–4.

63. To Lady Gregory (see Yeats, *Letters*, pp. 339– 40 and 365).

64. See Harper, *Yeats's Golden Dawn*, esp. pp. 55–6: 'To him, membership in the Order represented a symbolic search for membership in
the ideal order of the universe. . . . "This great Order" had become
the religious instrumentality for closing the doors of his imagination
against a pushing world.'

65. In his 'Final Letter to the Adepti of the R. R. et A. C. on the Present
Crisis', partially reproduced and discussed ibid., pp. 56–9.

66. See *Astral Projection*, p. 144.

67. See Harper, *Yeats's Golden Dawn*, p. 58: 'The medium, the mesmerist.
the harmless blunderer or the man who seeks a forbidden pleasure
by symbols that are now better known that they were, may form his
secret "group". . . .' He was evidently most concerned with the
nascent 'sex-magick' of Crowley here. But no one can doubt that

Yeats himself was infinitely more 'mediumistic' than the bully-boy author of 'The Shadowy Dill-Waters' (see note 27 above).

68. Though dedicated to AE, the story is clearly more 'Rosicrucian' than Theosophical and was written during a period of strong Golden Dawn activity.

69. That Yeats smoked hashish with 'some Martinists' in Paris is on record in *Autobiographies*, p. 347. Further discussion of this occurs in 'Discoveries' in *Essays and Introductions* (London: Macmillan, 1961) pp. 281–3.

70. Yeats had his uncle, George Polloxfen ('Festina Lente' in the Golden Dawn), do his chart on several occasions. Polloxfen and Annie Horniman were both serious astrologers, as was Yeats's wife, Georgie Hyde-Lees, and Yeats himself.

71. See W. B. Yeats, *A Vision* (New York: Collier, 1965) pp. 31–57.

72. See Crowley,*The Spirit of Solitude* (*Confessions*), esp. vol. II.

73. On the significance of the actual three pillars in the Golden Dawn's Cabalistic scheme, see Regardie, *The Golden Dawn*, vol. I, pp. 110–17.

74. See *Fame and Confession of the Fraternity of the Rosy Cross*, tr. Eugene Philaethes (London, 1652) p. 3.

75. Indeed, though the *Confessio* admonishes the applicant not to look for the author ('as he is melancholy more than social'), it amounts to a proselytising tract in a tradition which Scientology and other such sects are working today. It promises the reader that he may learn to 'control spirits and influences princes'; live for ever 'and in many places'; and find 'no secrets barred from him'. And, should this fail to persuade, it adds that 'stars and portents' are already auguring a new age in which the order will prosper: an angle which Mathers would use in his remarks on history and the Golden Dawn.

76. See Regardie, *The Golden Dawn*, vol. II, for detailed discussion on all these.

77. King, *Ritual Magic in England*, pp. 151–2.

78. The 'Ceremony of the Grade of Adeptus Minor', in Regardie, *The Golden Dawn*, vol. II, pp. 198–244.

79. *Fame and Confession*, p. 8.

80. Ibid., pp. 12–13.

81. Ibid., pp. 14–15.

82. See for instance Howe, *Magicians of the Golden Dawn*, pp. 46–7.

83. See MacBride, *A Servant of the Queen*, pp. 257–9.

84. For this ritual see Regardie, *The Golden Dawn*, vol. II, pp. 11–43.

85. See, for instance, King, *The Magical World of Crowley*, pp. 60, 113, 136.

86. See Schuchard, 'Freemasonry, Secret Societies', pp. 199–200.

87. *Fame and Confession*. see Preface.

88. Naturally one thinks of President Mitterand, with his well-known Masonic connections. An intriguing detail in this regard is that he should have adopted the rose as the symbol of his 'equilibrating' political movement.

89. See Regardie, *The Golden Dawn*, vol. II, pp. 69–91 and 92–120 for these rituals.

90. Howe, *Magicians of the Golden Dawn*, p. 59.
91. *Equinox*, ii, 288.
92. See Colquhoun, *Sword of Wisdom*, p. 222.
93. *Fame and Confession*, p. 9.
94. Lévi's remark here confirms Howe's suggestion that the *Abra-Melin* lore had a French rather than Jewish 'provenance' (*Magicians of the Golden Dawn*, p. 159).
95. Lévi, *History of Magic*, pp. 351–2.
96. Allen Grossman in his *Poetic Knowledge in the Early Yeats* (Charlottesville: University Press of Virginia, 1969) speculates that there may be a specific Golden Dawn pattern behind *The Wind among the Reeds*. See *The Poems of W. B. Yeats* (London: Bullen, 1909) pp. 148–9.
97. Mathers explained the difficult concept involved here in his 'Flying Roll X', *Astral Projection*, pp. 117–26.
98. We have seen, for instance, Yeats refer to Lévi in the occult-*soirée* section of *The Speckled Bird*.
99. Lévi, *History of Magic*, 346.
100. See, for instance, Mathers' Introduction to *Kabbalah Unveiled*, p. 16.
101. Ibid., pp. ix–x.
102. Ibid., p. 20.
103. Both works were written during the period of Yeats's greatest activity in the Golden Dawn, as was another early play with probable Golden Dawn resonance, *The Shadowy Waters*.
104. See Mathers, *Kabbalah Unveiled*, pp. 85, 27.
105. See ibid., Introduction, pp. 27–8.
106. See ibid., pp. 229–40 and *passim*.
107. See my *Art, Messianism and Crime*, pp. 73, 114.
108. See Mathers, *Kabbalah Unveiled*, 'The Lesser Holy Assembly', xxii, c. 740–60.
109. Schuchard speaks of this in 'Freemasonry, Secret Societies' (p. 26) in relation to the 'influence of Cabalistic "messiahs" on the sexual and political antinomianism of William Blake and the British Israelite movement, with which he was associated'.
110. Crowley discusses his *Abra-Melin* preparations in *The Spirit of Solitude* (*Confessions*), ch. 22.
111. Mathers, *Kabbalah Unveiled*, pp. 88, 4.
112. These four letters are called the 'Tetragrammaton'. One discussion of it may be found in Crowley's *Magick in Theory and Practice*, ch. iii.
113. Ch. 2, section v.
114. I am indebted to Chevalier's *The Sacred Magician: A Ceremonial Diary*, especially its Introduction, for the discussion here. FURTHER REFERENCES IN TEXT.
115. See Ch. 2, section v, and Ch. 3, section v.
116. See Crowley, *The Spirit of Solitude*, ch. 22.
117. Tattvas were cards with geometrical symbols of the elements on them, apparently Hindu in origin. Mathers discusses the making and use of them in 'Flying Roll XXX', *Astral Projection*, p. 77. Enochian squares were more sophisticated variations on the same

idea. Mathers devoted the bulk of the second half of his *Sacred Magic* to reproduction and explanation of them.

118. Again the reader may consult Blavatsky on this. See Ch. 4, note 107.
119. A point made by Gareth Knight in his chapter 'Magic in the Nineteenth Century: From Somnambulism to the Golden Dawn' in *History of White Magic*.
120. See Ch. 1, note 35.
121. See the first sentence of Yorke's Foreword to Howe, *Magicians of the Golden Dawn*.
122. Ibid., p. 130.
123. King makes the point (*Ritual Magic in England*, p. 72) that the concentration on 'Middle Pillar Existence' (the path *Samek*) in the second order of the Golden Dawn is 'analogous' to the raising of the Fire-Snake, though without use of sex.
124. See Nevill Drury, *Inner Visions: Explorations in Magical Consciousness* (London: Routledge, 1979) p. 18, discussing Bardon and the Qabalah.
125. The impression one gains after all is of a Nietzsechean figure: frantically and electrically alone, inspired and dwelling on a mountaintop overlooking the 'edge of the abyss'. Nietzsche's final decade of madness was, of course, precisely the period of the Golden Dawn's flourishing; and Nietczsche's title *Morgenröthe* became the name of the Order after the 'revolution' against Mathers. This may not be coincidental. At the time, Yeats was reading Nietzsche 'until [his] eyes went bad'. In any case, Nietzsche's history has considerable 'correspondence' in spirit to that of the Golden Dawn, which Howe describes as a 'mad chronicle' (*Magicians of the Golden Dawn*, p. XXIII).

CHAPTER 6.   INTERMEDIARY: THE MAGIC MOUNTAIN

1. Hesse supported a socio-political initiative based on Steiner's 'Threefold Commonwealth' after the First World War. He does not mention Steiner specifically in *The Journey to the East*, as he does other contemporary occultists, such as Count Keyserling. However, Anthroposophy was arguably the principal force in the 'Rosicrucian' movement of the 1920s which the book depicts; and a glancing refernece to 'Rudiger's grave' may be a covert acknowledgment of Steiner's central place in it. See *The Journey to the East*, tr. Hilda Rossner (London: Panther, 1972) pp. 36–7.
2. Thomas Mann, *The Magic Mountain*, tr. H. T. Lowe-Porter (New York: Viking, 1972) p. 226. FURTHER REFERENCES IN TEXT.
3. For further discussion of *Leitmotiv*, see my 'Wagner and Literature' (MA thesis, San Francisco State University, 1974).
4. Not only is Naphta the *counter*-force to the self-proclaimed *hierophant*, Settembrini; he is also a latter-day *Counter*-Reformation figure, with the new 'protestant' sect of Masonry being the principal 'heresy' in his sights.

5. Thus the central importance of reincarnation and spiritual transcendence in much of the 'magic' we are discussing.
6. Claudia Chauchat's role of shaking up the Western inhabitants of the mountain – especially the embodiment of Central European naïveté and tradition, Hans Castorp – is an element shared with Blavatsky; and Castorp's fascination for her (and later growing out of fascination) mirrors European response to the Russian adventuress.
7. See Ch. 4, end of section IV.
8. See Yeats, *A Vision*, p. 61.
9. See Ch. 4, section II and note 38.
10. See frontispiece to *Yeats and the Occult* (Yeats Studies 1976).
11. This is not to be confused with the breakaway group from Golden Dawn to which Yeats and other principal members belonged, interesting though the coincidence of names may be. Nietzsche had used the title *Dawn of Day* for one of his celebrated books (see previous chapter, note 125), and there is not a little of the illiberal 'mad' philosopher in Mann's cynical Jesuit (see 13 below).
12. See *Faust*, 'Prologue in Heaven', final speech to the Lord.
13. Leverkühn is a further development of Naphta in several respects. He begins his adult career as a theology student. 'Real life' leaves him cold. He is fascinated by chaos and the grotesque. Cruelty hardly fazes him; and absolute order of an arbitrary kind is his answer to the breakdown of old aesthetic laws. He does not kill himself outright in the end as Naphta does; but his contraction of syphilis through 'Hetaera Esmeralda' is certainly a conscious self-destructive act. In this respect among others, he may be modelled on Nietzsche, the 'self-flagellating monk' whose existential tragedy Rudolf Steiner imagined he had found the 'spiritual' answer to (see Ch. 7, section I). In fact, however, Leverkühn's pandaemonic interests have more in common with those of the self-conscious diabolist and prankster Crowley – though as said, Leverkühn's 'evil' is intellectual, not visceral, and Crowley applied a relatively antiquated order to his 'art', compensating perhaps for chaos in life, whereas with Leverkühn it is the reverse.
14. See Grant, *Cults of the Shadow*, Introduction and ch. 1, on the importance of the temple priestess or 'holy whore' in raising *Kundalini* energy; also R. C. Zaehner, *Drugs, Mysticism and Make-Believe* (London: Collins, 1972) p. 99, on the role of the dancer in 'decadent' Sufi mysticism.

CHAPTER 7. RUDOLF STEINER AND ANTHROPOSOPHY

1. For instance, *Mein Leben*, which Wagner dictated to his second wife at a similarly advanced stage in his career.
2. Geoffrey Ahern, *Sun at Midnight* (Wellingborough: Aquarian, 1984) p. 69.
3. Rudolf Steiner, *Autobiography*, tr. Rita Stebbing (New York: Steinerbooks, 1977) p. 326.

4. See my *California Writers*, esp. pp. 84–5, 140. The comparison to Jack London, whose mother was a Spiritualist, is often striking. See note 34 below.

5. See Ahern, *Sun at Midnight*, p. 92.

6. Ibid. This is one of many indications of Steiner's tendency to ego-inflation, increasingly apparent in later years as he pursued a furious study of 'karmic relationships' throughout history.

7. On Steiner and Jung see Frncis King, *Rudolf Steiner and Holistic Medicine* (London: Rider, 1986) pp. 171–82; also Colin Wilson, *Rudolf Steiner: The Man and his Vision* (Wellingborough: Aquarian, 1985) p. 121 and elsewhere.

8. On the OTO see King, *Sex, Magic and Perversion*, esp. ch. 11. On Steiner's association with the OTO see King, *Steiner and Holistic Medicine*, pp. 26–8.

9. See Ahern, *Sun at Midnight*, pp. 32 and 221, note 26. Ahern apparently heard this from a Scandinavian formerly associated with the Theosophical Society. But another member of the Society dismissed the charge on the basis that too few in the organisation were young or vital enough to practise such rites. I have not come across other references to 'sex magic' in the Theosophical Society, but this may have varied from lodge to lodge and time to time.

10. See King, *Steiner and Holistic Medicine*, pp. 26 and 210, note 8; also the discussion of offshoots of the German Theosophical Society in Ellic Howe's *Urania's Children* (London: Kimber, 1967). Some disaffected associates of Steiner's later became Nazi enthusiasts.

11. See Steiner, *Autobiography*, ch. xxxvi.

12. See Ch. 4, section iv. Steiner's fall from grace in Theosophy of course involved more than the matter of Krishnamurti. Besant and he had been heading for confrontation for years. See, for instance, the discussion by Colin Wilson, who believes that Steiner's 'decision to swallow the doctrines of Theosophy to gain an audience' was his great mistake (*Steiner: Man and Vision*, pp. 144, 166 and *passim*).

13. Steiner credited much of his thought to this obscure work, including inspiration for his mystery dramas. See *Four Mystery Dramas*, tr. Ruth and Hans Pusch (Vancouver: Steiner Book Centre, 1973), *The Portal of Initiation*, synopsis.

14. See Steiner, *Autobiography*, p. 214 and chs. xxiv and xxv on his period as an editor.

15. In an 'Autobiographical Sketch' (reproduced in *The Golden Blade*, 1966).

16. Steiner, *Autobiography*, p. 214.

17. Ibid., p. 178.

18. See *Readings in Goethean Science*, ed. Linda Jolly and Herbert Koepf (Wyoming, RI: Biodynamic Gardening Association, 1978), especially 'Nature: An Essay in Aphorisms'. See also Rudolf Steiner, *Goethe's Conception of the World* (London: Anthroposophical Publishing, 1928).

19. See Wilson, *Steiner: Man and Vision*, pp. 39–40 and 74, for comparison of the 'profoundly *meditative* temperaments' of Steiner and Wordsworth.

20. Steiner, *Autobiography*, p. 174 and elsewhere.
21. Comparisons and contrasts between Steiner and Hitler may be found throughout Trevor Ravenscroft's compulsive but undependable *Spear of Destiny* (London: Neville Spearman, 1972), especially the later chapters, where Steiner is portrayed as a 'white magician' hated and attacked by Hitler's 'black' cadres. In *Urania's Children* (p. 209), Howe also recommends Wolfgang Treher's psychiatric pathology *Hitler, Steiner, Schreber: Beiträge zur Phänomenologie des kranken Geistes* (1966), which explores 'delusions of grandeur frequently demonstrated by schizophrenics and the tendency of those suffering from mental illness to assume a prophetic mantle'. Treher concludes, 'Many astrologers and occultists are undiagnosed schizophrenics. . . . Symptoms include persistent and obsessive belief that they have made outstandingly important scientific, philosophical and cultural discoveries . . . compulsive desire for an audience and for opportunities to communicate their "message" . . . brutality (to their "patients") . . . creation of personal "sects" . . . disproprotionate belief in their own geniuses.'
22. Steiner, *Autobiography*, p. 165 and ch. xviii.
23. This is the argument of *Friedrich Nietzsche: Fighter for Freedom* (New Jersey: Steiner Publications, 1960), the book Steiner wrote after having met the philosopher in the last, catatonic years of his life. See also *Steiner: Man and Vision*, pp. 86–90.
24. See Ahern, *Sun at Midnight*, ch. 4, on how Steiner apparently failed to have complete normal attachment to the sense-world until after the age of forty (i.e. the period of his [erotic?] awakening with Marie).
25. In *On the Spiritual in Man* (1912). See also King, *Steiner and Holistic Medicine*, p. 212, ch. 6, note 1.
26. Steiner, *Autobiography*, p. 128 and elsewhere.
27. For an introduction to Steiner's views on education see the edition of lectures *Human Values in Education* (London: Rudolf Steiner Press, 1971).
28. See Rudolf Steiner, *The Threefold Commonwealth* (London: Anthroposophical Publishing, 1923).
29. King's *Steiner and Holistic Medicine* is exhaustive and up-to-date on this.
30. See Ibid., p. 86.
31. According to the diary of Franz Kafka. See Wilson, *Steiner: Man and Vision*, p. 142.
32. See Ulrich Babbel, *Bibliographical Reference List of Published Works of Rudolf Steiner in English Translation* (London: Steiner Press, 1977).
33. According to Rom Landau, *God is my Adventure* (London: Unwin, 1964) p. 174. The story of Steiner's 'magical' ability to scare off rabbits and how the Nazis wanted to adapt this to rid Europe of Jews is told in Ravenscroft, *Spear of Destiny*, pp. 321–5. Alas, it is probably apocryphal.
34. The burning of the Goetheanum and possible Nazi involvement in it is recounted many places, including again *Spear of Destiny*, which

also tells of a Nazi attempt to assassinate Steiner in a Munich railway station (pp. 170, 288).

35. See note 31 above.
36. For instance, Colin Wilson, who is disturbed by Steiner's belief that he could *see* King Arthur and his knights at Tintagel (*Steiner: Man and Vision*, pp. 114–16) when dating has proved that the historical Arthur died 600 years before that castle was built.
37. See Ahern, *Sun at Midnight*, pp. 31–3.
38. Principal sources here are Steiner's books *Occult Science*, tr. G. and M. Adams (London: Steiner Press, 1972), and *Knowledge of Higher Worlds* (Letchworth: Garden City Press, 1973). Steiner's first writings on these matters were 'From the Akashic Record', which appeared in his Theosophical magazine, *Luzifer-Gnosis* from 1904. Good digests may be found in the three principal secondary texts used here: King's *Steiner and Holistic Medicine* (pp. 159–68), Wilson's *Steiner: Man and Vision* (pp. 107–12, including a comparison to Blavatsky's cosmogony), and Ahern's *Sun at Midnight* (pp. 116–32).
39. See diagram in *The Essential Steiner*, ed. R. A. McDermott (San Francisco: Harper and Row, 1984) p. 173.
40. According to Ahern, Ahriman is identical with Mephistopheles (see *Sun at Midnight*, p. 127).
41. Origin of the 'Mahatmas'? the Great White Brotherhood of *Zanoni*? See also the second section of my chapter on Hitler in *Art, Messianism and Crime*.
42. And this service could be to belligerent ends, as suggested by the *Fama fraternitas* in its comments on the Zoroastrians and their *force de frappe*. (See Ch. 5, section IV and note 88).
43. Ahern, *Sun at Midnight*, pp. 128–9.
44. See note 39 above. According to Steiner, Christ would have intervened in the Atlantean epoch, thus making perfect symmetry out of cosmic history, had not the Luciferic and Ahrimanic spirits been so ascendant at the time.
45. See Ahern, *Sun at Midnight*, p. 83.
46. See Ch. 3, section III.
47. As Edouard Schuré indicates in *The Great Initiates: A Sketch of the Secret History of Religions* (see discussion in section IV of this chapter), tr. Fred Rothwell (London: Rider, 1912).
48. As he is described in Steiner's second mystery drama, *The Souls' Probation*, in *Four Mystery Dramas*, p. 93.
49. Steiner makes much of this in *Rosicrucianism and Modern Initiation* (London: Steiner Press, 1982), esp. lecture 6, 'The Tasks of the Michael Age'. One wonders if the concept were widespread enough in occult circles to have inspired Yeats to use the name for his most prominent 'magical' personae (Robartes and Hearne) or even Dr Goebbels (no stranger in youth to fringe ideas of the time) to have used it for his eponymous *Bildungsroman*.
50. Steiner was of course familiar with Nietzsche's theory on this subject and appears to have absorbed it into his overall scheme in a characteristically ameliorative new guise.

51. See Maeterlinck, *The Great Secret*, pp. 206–11; also discussion in Wilson, *Steiner: Man and Vision*, pp. 136–7, and King, *Steiner and Holistic Medicine*, p. 168.

52. The *Telegraph* reviewer of *Mein Kampf* (see *Art, Messianism and Crime*, ch. 7, note 18).

53. Especially in such a charming tale as 'Life Story Briefly Told' (1925) Hermann Hesse, in *Autobiographical Writings*, tr. Denver Lindley (New York: Farrar, Strauss, 1971).

54. See King, *Steiner and Holistic Medicine*, pp. 161, 180 and *passim*.

55. See Ahern, *Sun at Midnight*, p. 71.

56. Steiner, *Autobiography*, p. 192.

57. See ibid., p. 491; also Ahern, *Sun at Midnight*, p. 17.

58. Rudolf Steiner, *Theosophy* (London: Steiner Press, 1970), 'A Note on the Title'. FURTHER REFERENCES IN TEXT.

59. There seems to have been an undercurrent of nationalism in this. The break between Steiner and Besant came on the eve of the First World War, during which both leaders would remain loyal to their own sides. Since youth in multi-racial Austria, Steiner had taken pride in his Germanness – again like Hitler, but without fanaticism (see Ahern, *Sun at Midnight*, pp. 72–3, on 'West' *versus* 'East').

60. See Steiner, *Autobiography*, chs. xxx, xxxi and esp. p. 362; 'At the time I accepted the invitation to enter the Society it was the only institution that could be taken seriously in its search for spiritual life.'

61. See my *Art, Messianism and Crime*, ch. 6, note 42.

62. See Steiner, *Occult Science*, pp. 233–6 and *passim*; also Ahern, *Sun at Midnight*, pp. 51–4.

63. Somerset Maugham's phrase in his discussion of Eastern ideas in *The Razor's Edge*. For discussion see *Art, Messianism and Crime*, ch. 8.

64. See *Blavatsky and the Secret Doctrine*, pp. 192–7.

65. See Ch. 4, section IV.

66. See Rudolf Steiner, *Occult History* (London: Steiner Press, 1957) lecture 6.

67. See Steiner's lecture series *The Apocalypse of St John* and *The Gospel of St John* (both 1908).

68. So Steiner says in *Karmic Relationships* (see Wilson, *Steiner: Man and Visions*, p. 118).

69. Ibid., p. 119.

70. See Ravenscroft, *Spear of Destiny*, p. 134.

71. See Steiner, *Occult History*, lecture 6.

72. Maurice Maeterlinck, *Before the Great Silence*, tr. Bernard Miall (London: Allen and Unwin, 1935) p. 186.

73. See *Spear of Destiny*, p. 167 and elsewhere. Ravenscroft suggests that Hitler may have borrowed this identification from Crowley. Piquant fantasy!

74. See note 7 above; also Ch. 1, note 8. The identity of Jungian psychology with 'magical' thinking has been summed up thus:

If one obtains an article or a book written by a practising analyst
of any school of depth psychology save the Jungian and goes
through it substituting for the words 'therapy' or 'analysis' the
phrase 'invocation of the gods by means of ritual magic', and,
similarly, substituting the phrase 'spiritual evolution' for the words
'improvement' or 'cure', one ends up with what is clearly a piece of
meaningless nonsense. If one follows a precisely similar procedure
(save that the word 'individuation' is also replaced by 'spiritual
evolution') with almost any lengthy passage from Jung's writings
one ends up with a coherent statement which could have been
written by almost any twentiety-century practitioner of Western
ritual magic. (King, *Steiner and Holistic Medicine*, p. 179)

75. These are collected in eight volumes (London: Steiner Press, 1981).
76. See Ch. 5, note 13.
77. See Richard Ellmann, *Yeats: The Man and the Masks* (Oxford: Oxford University Press, 1979) p. 219; also Ahern, *Sun at Midnight*, p. 91.
78. Steiner's familiarity with Bruno dates from at least his lectures before the Giordano Bruno Union in Berlin in 1899 (see *Autobiography*, pp. 338–9).
79. See ibid., esp. ch. xxiv.
80. See Schuré, *The Great Initiates*, vol. i, pp. ix–xxiii.
81. Ibid., vol. ii, p. 115.
82. See Camille Schneider, *Edouard Schuré: Seine Lebensbegegnungen mit Rudolf Steiner und Richard Wagner* (Freiburg: Kommenden, 1971).
83. See Rudolf Steiner, *The Way of Initiation* (London: Theosophical Society Publishing, 1908) pp. i–iii (Preface) and 1–39 (Introduction).
84. Ibid., p. 37.
85. See Édouard Schuré, *The Genesis of Tragedy and The Sacred Drama of Eleusis*, tr. Fred Rothwell (London: Steiner Publishing, 1936) p. 125 and *passim*.
86. See Marie Savitch, *Marie Steiner–Von Sivers*, tr. Juliet Compton-Burnett (London: Steiner Press, 1967) p. 45.
87. See J. M. Hemleben, *Rudolf Steiner: A Documentary Biography* (London: Goulden, 1975) pp. 101–6.
88. See Schuré, *Genesis of Tragedy*, pp. 267–71.
89. Ibid., p. 83.
90. See Steiner, *Autobiography*, ch. iv.
91. See Ahern, *Sun at Midnight*, p. 218, note 28.
92. Schuré, *Genesis of Tragedy*, p. 153. FURTHER REFERENCES IN TEXT (applies also to references to *The Sacred Drama*, in same edition).
93. Specifically to Schuré, in this letter quoted in *The Essential Steiner* (p. 20):

Within this whole stream [of Christian mystical initiation] the
initiation of Manes, into which Christian Rosenkreuz was also
initiated in 1459, was considered as a 'higher degree': it consists
of a true knowledge of the function of evil. This initiation, with
its background, must remain completely hidden from the masses

for yet a long time to come. For where even the smallest ray of light escaped from it into literature, great harm resulted, as happened, for instance, in the case of the noble Guyau, whose pupil Friedrich Nietzsche became.

This extremely provocative statement suggests not only that Steiner's own moral researches may have been more Crowleyan than he would openly admit but also that some of this sense of mission may have derived from study of the relatively obscure French aesthetician and sociologist Jean-Marie Guyau, whom Nietzsche probably met in the south of France during his final (*Antichrist* and *Ecce Homo*) period. Guyau died young, like Nietzsche, but not before having produced a large opus of radical works, of which the most provocative are *Esquisse d'une morale sans obligation ni sanction* (1884) and the exhaustive *L'Irreligion de l'avenir* (1887). Both books, replete with marginal notes, would have been discovered by Steiner in Nietzsche's library, which the philosopher's sister invited him to arrange. See Steiner, *Autobiography*, ch. xviii; also F. J. W. Harding, *Jean-Marie Guyau* (Geneva: Droz, 1973).

94. See Ahern, *Sun at Midnight*, p. 16: '[The Goetheanum] is said to be the only place in the world where *Faust* Part Two is regularly enacted.'

95. Schuré and Yeats as dramatists were both working out of the same tradition refined by Mallarmé and Maeterlinck after Wagner (see my *Wagner to the Waste Land*, esp. ch. 1, 4 and 7).

96. See *Zanoni*, book iv ('The Dweller of the Threshold'), ch. ix; also pp. 378–81. See also Édouard Schuré, *The Children of Lucifer*, tr. Beresford Kemmis (London: Steiner Publishing, 1935) ii.ii. FURTHER REFERENCES IN TEXT.

97. See in this connection Ahern's informative analysis of the similarities between Theosophical–Anthroposophical 'religion' and the Valentinian strain of Syrian–Egyptian *gnosis* in *Sun at Midnight*, esp. pp. 14–3.

98. Ibid., p. 85.

99. See Steiner, *The Guardian of the Threshold*, esp. scene i, in *Four Mystery Plays*.

100. What did Eliot make of Steiner and Anthroposophy? I am intrigued by his emphasis on 'guardians' in *The Cocktail Party*, especially the middle acts; also the name and origin of 'Marie' in the first part of *The Waste Land*, a poem which depicts the spiritual breakdown making for the rise of Anthroposophy and less attractive cults (see also *Wagner to the Waste Land*, pp. 206–14).

101. See Steiner's article on Goethe's work in *The Fairy-Tale of the Green Snake and the Beautiful Lily*, tr. Thomas Carlyle (Edinburgh: Floris, 1979) p. 62.

102. Ibid., p. 63.

103. According to the synopsis of *Portal of Initiation* (*Four Mystery Plays*).

104. The emphasis on service comes out increasingly toward the end of Steiner's final play, in which Strader becomes crucial to all others'

progress. This harks back to the emphasis on service ('Dienen! Dienen!') at the end of Wagner's *Parsifal* and looks forward to the curious primacy of the servant Leo in Hesse's occult parable *The Journey to the East*.

105. Steiner, in *Fairy-Tale*, p. 53.

106. Steiner in fact discusses Schiller's 'third force' as a starting-point for ideas of Goethe; and the true love of the mystery dramas is strongly redolent of Goethe's ideal of the 'Eternal Feminine'.

107. And aspects of omniscient cult-leaders in general right down to the science-fictive one in Robert Heinlein's *Stranger in a Strange Land* (1964). See also note 21 above.

108. Balde is a representation of an itinerant herbalist (Felix Kogutski), whom Steiner met and was 'initiated' by in youth (see *Autobiography*, p. 62).

109. The songs of these spirits include some of the happier flights of Steiner's 'art'. But, while the effect sought may be that of 'The Kings of Thule' in *Faust* or songs of Ariel in *The Tempest*, the words remain intractably portentous.

110. A note tells us that Steiner wished to convey the atmosphere of Grecian mystery schools in these Arcadian, temple-side colloquies – the Eleusinians or perhaps Pythagoreans as described by Schuré in *Great Initiates*. Undoubtedly much along this line in the dramas represents a vision of what Steiner wished to go on in the temple and on the grounds of the Goetheanum.

111. Scene v of the last play in *Four Mystery Plays*.

112. See Steiner, *Portal of Initiation*. Introduction (ibid.).

113. See 'Thoughts on the Seal' which begin each play (ibid.). The uroborus, or snake biting its tail, is a central emblem of Anthroposophy (see *Sun at Midnight*, frontispiece and *passim*). So was it as well for Goethe and Wagner, appearing prominently in the former's *Fairy-Tale* and (metamorphosed) as the latter's ubiquitous 'ring'.

114. See Steiner, *The Souls' Awakening*, 84 (in *Four Mystery Plays*).

115. Blavatsky, *Isis Unveiled*, p. 181.

116. Carl Jung, *Memories, Dreams, Reflections* (London: Collins, 1963) ch. VI.

117. See Timothy Leary, *The Politics of Ecstasy* (London: MacGibbon and Kee, 1970); also discussion in my *Art, Messianism and Crime*, ch. 8.

CHAPTER 8.   ALEISTER CROWLEY

1. See Introduction to Hermann Hesse, *Demian: The Story of Emil Sinclair's Youth*, tr. Michael Koloff and Michael Lebeck (New York: Bantam, 1965) p. v.

2. The words are Mann's. Ibid., p. ix.

3. As Eliot called Pound in the dedication of *The Waste Land*.

4. See 'Poet of the Interior Journey' in *Politics of Ecstasy*, repr. as an 'introductory chapter' to *Journey to the East*.

5. See Ch. 1, section II.

6. In the second decade of this century, Count Keyserling decided in his *Travel Diary of a Philosopher*, tr. J. H. Reece (London: Cape, 1925) vol. I, pp. 157–8, that 'Theo- and Anthro-posophy, New Thought, Christian Science, the New Gnosis, Vivekananda's Vedanta, the Neo-Persian and Indo-Islamic Esotericism, not to mention those of the Hindus and the Buddhists, the Bahai system, the professed faith of the various spiritualistic and occult circles, and even the Freemasons all start from essentially the same basis, and their movements are certain to have a greater future than official Christianity.' James Webb in *The Occult Establishment*, p. 184, sums up the rest of the argument thus: 'The basis of all [these] religious belief[s], Keyserling decided, was self-realisation.' Note that Keyserling was enunciating this conclusion at precisely the same time that Hesse was writing *Demian*.

7. Hesse, *Demian*, p. viii.

8. See Ch. 3, section v.

9. See Hesse, *Journey to the East*, pp. 11–26.

10. As he was called by the *Express* newspapers in a notorious series of articles following publication of *Diary of a Drug Fiend*.

11. See Ch. 2, note 51.

12. See John Symonds, *The Great Beast* (London: Macdonald, 1971) p. 200; also King, *The Magical World of Crowley*, p. 112. Crowley would contend that he had been 'trying to wreck German propaganda on the root of *reductio ad absurdam*'; but later he admitted that his mind was 'split' and that he was one half a traitor and the other a patriot. See also note 48 below.

13. Some of the relevant passages on Abraxas are quoted by Miguel Serrano in his work of *belles-lettres*, *C. G. Jung and Hermann Hesse: A Record of Two Friendships*, tr. Frank MacShane (London: Routledge, 1966) pp. 94–6:

> There is a god whom ye knew not, for mankind forgot it. We name it by its name ABRAXAS. It is more indefinite still than God and the devil. . . . Abraxas standeth above the sun and above the devil. . . . Had the pleroma [Gnostic realm of highest spirit – see this chapter, section III] a being, Abraxas would be its manifestation. . . .
>
> Abraxas is the sun, and at the same time the eternally sucking gorge of the void, the belittling and dismembering devil. . . .
>
> What the god-sun speaketh is life.
>
> What the devil speaketh is death.
>
> But Abraxas speaketh that hallowed and accursed word which is life and death at the same time. . . .
>
> It is as splendid as the lion in the instant he striketh down his victim.
>
> It is as beautiful as a day of spring.
>
> It is the great Pan himself and also the small one.
>
> It is Priapos.
>
> It is the monster of the underworld. . . .

> To look upon it, is blindness.
> To know it, is sickness.
> To worship it, is death.
> To fear it, is wisdom.
> To resist it not, is redemption. . . .

And so on. Compare these to the speeches of Quetzalcoatl in Lawrence's most occult novel. See also my *Wagner to the Waste Land*, pp. 179–81.

14. I.e. 'Do What Thou Wilt', see Ch. 1, note 17.
15. In a letter to a female disciple. Yorke Collection, Warburg Institute, Accession II, file 12/13 (citation authorised courtesy John Symonds).
16. See Jung, *Memories, Dreams, Reflections*, p. 50; quoted in *Art, Messianism and Crime*, p. 121.
17. In the cases of *Zanoni* (Ch. 4, section I) and *The Magic Mountain*.
18. See *Art, Messianism and Crime*, pp. 78, 101–2.
19. See Blavatsky, *The Secret Doctrine* (London: Theosophical Publishing Company, 1888) vol. II, p. 117.
20. As noted, Crowley used the sub-title of Shelley's *Alastor*, 'The Spirit of Solitude', as the original title of his 'autohagiography', *Confessions* (see Ch. 3, note 49).
21. Most Hesse novels have internal echoes of others. In this case, one is reminded of the departure of Goldmund from the monastic sanctuary of his 'brother' Narziss (Narcissus) in the 1934 work of *Narziss and Goldmund*.
22. Annie Besant and Mathers, for instance (see Ch. 5, section II); also, of course, Crowley (*Art, Messianism and Crime*, p. 103).
23. A partial analysis is offered by Israel Regardie in *The Eye in the Triangle: An Interpretation of Aleister Crowley* (St Paul, Minn.: Llewellyn Publications, 1970) pp. 437–45; but Regardie is hardly a dispassionate observer.
24. In *The Equinox*. See Ch. 5, section II.
25. See note 12 above.
26. See King, *The Magical World of Crowley*, pp. 143–9. Crowley's campaign against the *Express* tried to enlist the support of Bertrand Russell among others known to dislike Beaverbrook (Yorke Collection, I, E21).
27. My small piece on Crowley in that previous volume depended largely on King's amusing biography, which derives largely from Symonds's prodigious work, at present being revised for a final, definitive edition. Future visions of 'the Great Beast' will depend on Symonds as much as those of Dr Johnson depend on Boswell. But there are some – notably Gerald Yorke and Israel Regardie – who have criticised Symonds' work as sensationalising facts and playing fast and loose with matters of occult practice. Without having known Crowley personally, future chroniclers are not going to be able to bring great authority to bear on this dispute. But a reading of Crowleyana in the Warburg tends to suggest a personality at least as frus-

trated as 'beastly' and ever concerned to to pose as a 'gentleman', however caddish.

28. Of Leila Waddell and her 'Ragtime Girls', whom he tried to take on a tour of Moscow in 1913. See Symonds, *The Great Beast*, p. 145; Yorke Collection, II, 12/13.

29. See Crowley, *Selected Poems*, Introduction, p. 14.

30. See Ch. 5, note 27; also Aleister Crowley, *Moonchild*, ed. John Symonds and Kenneth Grant (London: Sphere, 1972) p. 143 and *passim*.

31. Two notes from Maugham may be found in Yorke Collection, I, E21.

32. See Crowley, *Moonchild*, pp. 20–8, 142 and *passim*.

33. See Webb, *The Occult Establishment*, ch. 7, note 39; also Yorke Collection, I, E21.

34. Ibid.; also II, 96. Presentation copies to Crowley of two of Cunard's privately printed poems may be found ibid., II, 49.

35. See Symonds, *The Great Beast*, pp. 326–8; also my *Art, Messianism and Crime*, p. 76. Crowley, in a particularly poverty-stricken and bitter period of his life, absconded with 500 francs Harris had raised for him and later disparaged the other man's *magnum opus, My Life and Loves*, as 'the autobiography of a flea'.

36. Letter in Yorke Collection, I, E21.

37. Ibid..

38. Having set himself up in Paris first in 1899, Crowley would refer to himself in later years as 'the patriarch of Montparnasse'. Maugham depicts him in his early years there in *The Magician*. Hemingway has a picture of him *circa* 1922 in *A Moveable Feast* (London: Jonathan Cape, 1964) pp. 76–80. On Crowley's publication with the *English Review*, see King, *The Magical World of Crowley*, p. 136; also correspondence with Austin Harrison in Yorke Collection, II, 12/13. Crowley's poems were prominent in the issues in which they appeared – often the lead inclusion – and he was invited to contribute not one but three pseudonymous pieces to the July 1922 issue. This was the time of publication of *Drug Fiend*, i.e. just before attacks on him in the press made Collins and the reputable literary world drop him. Thus it might be argued that the acceptance Crowley had wished and worked for was indeed snatched from him at the very moment of its bestowal. He was not James Joyce, but to many he was no less a part of the literary–cultural explosion which followed the First World War.

39. See his piece on the 'satanic' genius of 'the Revolutionary Epoch' in the *English Review* (July 1922), under the pseudonym 'Prometheus'. His tremendous admiration for this fellow poet and mystic is also conveyed by marginalia in his copy of *Shelley's Poetical Works* (Yorke Collection, II, EMH 800), such as on *Adonais*, which he calls (p. 528), 'The most sublime, most equally sustained poem that exists in the world.'

40. This is the subject of much of *Confessions*. The young Crowley's quest also comes through vividly in many of the poems in Martin Booth's

selection, notably 'A Spring Snowstorm in Wastdale', 'A Descent of the Moencii' and 'Night in the Valley'.

41. Crowley did not inherit a great fortune, but he would have had enough to carry on in reasonable comfort had he been less of a Wildean dandy and doctrinaire believer in living for a moment. See Regardie, *Eye in the Triangle*, pp. 420–5.

42. I am thinking in particular of the 'Rosa' poems discussed in the next paragraph. But throughout Crowley's works there are hints that the pain from breakdown of his first marriage was a lash to the beast in him and contributed to the course of his later career. See, for instance, *Magick in Theory and Practice*, ch. xvi(i), 'Of the Oath'.

43. Crowley looked for women who had 'powers'. Like Yeats with his wife, he had a propensity to use women as 'magical' agencies, even 'mediums', and would dispense with them when their use for him seemed to be spent. See also section iii below, esp. note 70.

44. See Isabel Clarke, *Shelley and Byron: A Tragic Friendship* (London: Hutchinson, 1934).

45. See Crowley, *Selected Poems*, pp. 119–43.

46. His copy of the 1896 edition of this book includes pencilled translations in the margins of a selection of Baudelaire's most horrific efforts. Yorke Collection, ii, EBH 1052.

47. Swinburne he was compared to by many, not least Fuller in *The Star in the West* (London: Walter Scott, 1907); and as late as 1942 he was sent a picture of the poet by a female admirer to keep on the desk in front of him to reflect on the amazing eyes and spirit of the 'man youth' who had once so inspired him (Yorke Collection, i, E21). Browning he appears to have gone off in later years, somewhat as he did with Wilde (see note 50 below). A volume of the *Poetical Works* which he bought in 1945 contains the marginal epithets 'Bilge' next to 'Evelyn Hope', 'Ugh!' next to 'By the Fireside' and 'Rot' by 'Bishop Blougham'. Even at seventy, Crowley was full of prickly response to his reading, picking up on incorrect facts and pretensions. Such acerbity against the great might suggest the bitterness of old age were it not for the fact that he had been responding in much the same way since Cambridge. The acuteness of some of his remarks suggests that perhaps he missed a métier as a reviewer; but of course he had no temperament for such a sedentary occupation and lacked sufficient 'equilibrating' ability to be generous about others' talents. Always self-obsessed, he saw in Browning images of himself, such as in cantos clvi-viii of 'Two Poets of Croisic' and stanza x of 'The Mermaid':

> Have you found your life distasteful?
> My life did, and does, smack sweet.
> Was your youth of pleasure wasteful?
> Mine I saved and hold complete.
> Do your joys with age diminish?
> When mine fail me, I'll complain.
> Must in death your daylight finish?

My sun sets to rise again.

48. This description was offered to British Foreign Secretary Sir Edward Grey when Crowley was under investigation during the War (Symonds, *The Great Beast*, p. 199).
49. Crowley had sent her his verse play with an eye to gaining the advocacy of her famous husband (Yorke Collection, I, E21). However, not everyone thought entirely disparagingly of play and author (see *English Review*, Aug 1912).
50. In a copy of Wilde's works which he read in 1942, Crowley pencilled in 'Drivel in Doggerel' as a sub-title for the poem, and he criticises it throughout with such marginalia as 'silly' and 'ass!'. Nor do other Wilde works fare much better. *Dorian Gray* he calls 'all bad Meredith and Henry James'; *The Soul of Man* seems 'the dying Age's dim-lit vision of the New Aeon which was to come 13 years later' (i.e. with his own *Book of Law*); and *Lady Windermere's Fan* is 'insufferable trash' whose 'jests' are 'insipid' and 'often dragged in by the hair'. Yorke Collection, II, EMH 1070.
51. See in particular Crowley, *Selected Poems*, pp. 77–81 and 105–8.
52. See my *Art, Messianism and Crime*, p. 75.
53. See Crowley, *Selected Poems*, pp. 61–2.
54. Ibid., pp. 36–7.
55. Symonds, *The Great Beast*, p. 316.
56. Crowley's status as a Mason is confused. In *The Spirit of Solitude (Confessions)* vol. II, p. 4, he claims to have been initiated and led up the grades in Mexico. However, in letters in the Yorke Collection (II, 12/13), he maintains that he was initiated in the Anglo-Saxon Lodge in Paris in 1904. Questions were apparently raised about the legitimacy of his status in the Grand Chapter of the Royal Arch in Freemasons Hall. In 1913, at the time of his joining the OTO and before his long sojourn in America, he made a particular effort to get on good terms with the Grand Lodge. But, in typical Crowley fashion, he then (June 1914) published a story in the *English Review* which makes a credulous buffoon out of a typical Home Counties Mason (see note 104 below). On Baphomet and the Templars, see King, *Sex, Magic and Perversion*, ch. 9 and 10.
57. Hans Jonas, *The Gnostic Religion: The Message of the Alien God and the Beginnings of Christianity* (Boston, Mass.: Beacon Press, 1958).
58. See previous chapter, note 97.
59. These are traditional modes of Gnostic expression. See Jonas, *Gnostic Religion*, chapter 11(b), 'Gnostic Morality'.
60. See ibid., chapter 1; also my *Art, Messianism and Crime*, ch. 7.
61. See for instance the depiction by Marguerite Yourcenar in *The Abyss*, tr. Grace Frick (London: Black Swan, 1985), chapter called 'Death in Munster'.
62. *Gnostic Religion*, pp. 273–4. Jonas quotes Bishop Irenaeus.
63. Crowley was scheduled to give a lecture on Gilles de Rais at Oxford in 1930, but in the event it was banned – which fact Crowley tried to turn to his advantage in typical fashion by printing 'The Banned

Lecture' in pamphlet form and having it sold on the streets of the university town.

64. See *Moonchild*, ch. 16, for a pantheon of Crowleyan heroes of the past.
65. Quoted in Symonds, *The Great Beast*, p. 334.
66. The phrase comes from Blake, whom Crowley includes as the last and greatest in his procession of spirits (*Moonchild*, ch. 16).
67. See Symonds, *The Great Beast*, pp. 344–50. Other disciples who did not fare so well post-Crowley were Raoul Loveday, who died amid the filth and unhealthiness at Thelema, and Normal Mudd, who died by suicide in water, as Crowley had predicted he would (see ibid., pp. 297–301, 350–1).
68. This view is somewhat disputed by Regardie, who came to know Crowley when the latter had reached relatively sedentary middle age, and who depicts him sitting back quietly in a chair smoking a cigar, sipping Benedictine and playing chess (see *The Eye in the Triangle*, p. 14 and *passim*).
69. See Jonas, *Gnostic Religion*, p. 269.
70. Symonds seems disgusted with Crowley's unattractive choice of women but accepts Kenneth Grant's assertion that they offered the 'magus' unusual potentialities (see *The Great Beast*, pp. 387–8).
71. Crowley's taste for bizarre humanity increased during his years in America, where he once advertised specifically for 'FREAKS' to use as models in his alarming, expressionistic paintings (see ibid., p. 206).
72. See King, *The Magical World of Crowley*, p. 106 and *passim*.
73. This motto expresses Crowley's personalised version of the Theory of Relativity. He believed that, as stars have their fixed courses through the universe, so human souls do through life; thus that *not* to pursue one's destiny with determination would cause an upset of universal balance. This may seem an intriguing rationalisation for high selfishness. Meanwhile, the phrase was also meant to remind one that, via astral projection, one might learn to view oneself as if from a distant star, thus appreciate better one's place and function in the universal scheme of things.
74. Crowley, *Selected Poems*, pp. 22–3.
75. Ibid., pp. 40–1.
76. Ibid., p. 43; see also Ch. 5, section v.
77. Crowley, *Selected Poems*, p. 194, 'Logos'.
78. See Symonds, *The Great Beast*, p. 362.
79. See King, *The Rebirth of Magic*, ch. 12, 'Sex Magic'.
80. See Webb, *The Occult Establishment*, pp. 220–1.
81. For definition see Grant, *Cults of the Shadow*, Introduction.
82. See Ch. 5, section III.
83. See King, *Sex, Magic and Perversion*, ch. 8, 'Priapus Rediscovered'.
84. This is a main point of Regardie's throughout *The Eye in the Triangle*. He sees the Crowley phenomenon good and bad as symptomatic of what Wilhelm Reich called 'the Emotional Plague' of modern times.
85. See Symonds, *The Great Beast*, p. 364.

86. See Jolan Chang, *The Tao of Love and Sex: The Ancient Chinese Way to Ecstasy* (New York: Dutton, 1977).

87. See Kenneth Grant, *Aleister Crowley and the Hidden God* (London: Frederick Muller, 1975) ch. 5, 'The Tantric Element in the OTO'.

88. A chronicle of the ends to which Crowley used 'sex magick' may be found in *The Magickal Record of Aleister Crowley*, ed. John Symonds and Kenneth Grant (London: Duckworth, 1974).

89. He was particularly pleased at having produced 150,000 words during a trip to Moscow in 1913 (Yorke Collection, II, 12/13) and writes in the margin of the introduction of his copy of *Fleurs du mal* (p. 66) that a friend of his once took 40 grams (not grains) of cocaine – this to dispute what he regards as naïveté of Gautier's remarks on Baudelaire's drug-taking.

90. Baldness may have been a particular trauma to Crowley. In the margin of 'Rosalind and Helen' in Shelley's *Works* (p. 224), he writes, 'The only example in all literature of the tragedy of baldness.'

91. Symonds, *The Great Beast*, p. 250.

92. The full chronicle of Crowley's acts is given by Symonds, the apology for them by Regardie.

93. See Aleister Crowley, *The Book of the Law* (London: OTO, 1938) p. 12.

94. See Grant, *Crowley and the Hidden God*, p. 67; also pp. 70–1.

95. See 'Synopsis on Six Articles on Drugs', quoted ibid., p. 68.

96. See Crowley, *The Spirit of Solitude*, vol. II, pp. 67–80.

97. He circulated cards with these photos on them (Yorke Collection, II, 74).

98. See Crowley, *The Spirit of Solitude*, vol. II, pp. 22–4.

99. Regardie, *The Eye in the Triangle*, p. 210.

100. See Symonds, *The Great Beast*, p. 275.

101. Regardie, *The Eye in the Triangle*, p. 434.

102. See Symonds, *The Great Beast*, pp. 125–6.

103. In 'The Simple Art of Murder' in *The Second Raymond Chandler Omnibus* (London: Hamish Hamilton, 1962).

104. In 'The Stratagem'. See note 56 above.

105. This is a general conclusion derived from Crowley's spoiled-public-schoolboy jibes about the inferiority of women. But, as with many who display such male chauvinism, Crowley had a pressing need for feminine love.

106. Tom Driberg spent a year or more addressing letters to Crowley in the first manner (Yorke Collection, I, E21). Russian counts, Chinese princes and other such personae were adopted usually to impress some new Scarlet Woman.

107. Crowley, *The Book of the Law*, p. 37. Regardie, in quoting this, adds, '[Crowley] pretended to be nothing more than a man. But, what a man!' (*The Eye in the Triangle*, 506). Need more be said about Regardie's dispassion? (See note 23 above.)

108. From Yorke Collection, II, 12/13.

109. Regardie, *The Eye in the Triangle*, pp. 419–21, 425–7.

110. For instance, against Nina Hamnett for some relatively innocuous remarks she made about him in her memoir *Laughing Torso*.

111. Colin Haycraft of Duckworth. In conversation, Gloucester Crescent, Nov 1986.
112. Yorke Collection, ii, 12/13.
113. This selection was published without permission from Crowley's executor and may be subject to litigation.
114. Acknowledged by all commentators and attested to by the fact that, disreputable as he had become by the 1930s, Crowley did not lack for lunch- and dinner-companions.
115. He wrote to a subscriber to skip on to the second volume where 'the villain of the piece' enters (Yorke Collection, ii, 12/13).
116. In conversation, Lyncroft Mansions, Oct 1986.
117. An author whom he, like Yeats, admired, though not without disparaging his ignorance, like Gautier's, in drug matters. (See note 89 above).
118. He believed that Hitler may have been influenced by his *Book of the Law* and marked his copy of *Hitler Speaks* to indicate the similarities. (In Yorke Collection, DHD 350.)
119. Crowley, *Magick in Theory and Practice*, p. xvii.
120. See Ch. 3, section v.
121. Crowley, *Moonchild*, pp. 195–6.
122. For the latter, see the characters Butcher and Cremers (ibid., chs 17, 19 and 21, for instance). Crowley, who hated the experience of being the financial inferior to ill-spoken people in America, is typically heavy-handed in these depictions.
123. Yorke Collection, i, E21.
124. See for instance Crowley, *Moonchild*, p. 214, where the teasing of Waite's style reaches its *reductio ad absurdam*.
125. Crowley, *Diary of a Drug Fiend*, p. 308.

CHAPTER 9.   L. RON HUBBARD AND SCIENTOLOGY

1. Grant, *Crowley and the Hidden God*, ch. 5.
2. The suit was settled out of court for an undisclosed, but according to Symonds relatively low, amount of money.
3. See King, *The Magical World of Crowley*, pp. 164–7; also King's *Rebirth of Magic*, ch. 12.
4. An account of their recent and current court battles is given by Stewart Lamont in *Religion, Inc*, (London: Harrap, 1986).
5. This notorious doctrine, by which enemies of Scientology 'may be deprived of property or injured by any means by any Scientologist without any discipline . . . tricked, sued, lied to or destroyed', is described by, for example, Christopher Evans in *Cults of Unreason* (St Albans: Granada, 1974) p. 105. It was abandoned in 1968 after much adverse comment, but shades of the principle linger on in Scientology practice. See Lamont's comments in *Religion, Inc.* about Scientology's treatment of the Mayor of Clearwater, Florida.
6. Some of the misrepresentations may be the fault of promoters around him, but Hubbard did nothing to discourage them. Thus at various

times it was put out that he had grown up on one of the great feudal landholdings in Montana, when in truth he had only spent a period of his youth on a grandparent's ranch; that he had made important discoveries in nuclear physics, when he had only attended a course on the subject as an undergraduate and later hung around with some members of the Jet Propulsion Laboratory (cf. Parsons); that he had fine academic distinctions, when he failed to finish his under-graduate degree and bought a doctorate from the unaccredited Sequoia University. See Evans, *Cults of Unreason*, ch. 1.

7. See Ch. 4, section II.

8. Especially by anti-Scientology class-action lawyer Michael Flynn. See Lamont, *Religion, Inc.*, p. 136.

9. Hubbard was diagnosed from afar as suffering from this by the chairman of the Mental Health Authority of Victoria, Australia. See ibid., p. 55.

10. As many have seen its major purpose to be. See ibid.; also Omar Garrison, *The Hidden Story of Scientology* (London: Arlington, 1974).

11. *Philadelphia Doctorate Course*, lecture 18, as quoted in Lamont, *Religion, Inc.*, p. 21.

12. See Symonds, *The Great Beast*, from p. 392; also note 3 above; also Maurice Burrell, *Scientology: What it is and What it Does* (London: Lakeland, 1970) pp. 15–17.

13. According to Symonds, quoting from Crowley letters in private possession.

14. *The Sunday Times* had published an article on Hubbard and Co. in October of that year. This included some facts 'misreported or misunderstood in some particulars' by the author, and the news-paper later agreed to pay a small settlement to the Church. It also printed a Hubbard press statement to air the 'official' story, but this has since been contradicted in part and cast in doubt. See Roy Wallis, *The Road to Total Freedom: A Sociological Analysis of Scientology* (London: Heinemann, 1974) pp. 112–12.

15. Mr Justice Latey in the Family Division of the Royal Courts of Justice, 23 July 1984: 'He was not [sent by Naval Intelligence to break up black magic]. He was himself a member of that occult group and practised sexual magic in it.' Quoted in Lamont, *Religion, Inc.*, p. 20.

16. See Evans, *Cults of Unreason*, p. 23: 'He worked for a short time in naval intelligence, during which period he took a four week course in military government in Princeton.'

17. In an interview with *Penthouse* magazine, June 1983. Quoted in Lamont, *Religion, Inc.*, p. 21.

18. In 1982, DeWolf, represented by Flynn, filed suit to see if Hubbard, reported to be in voluntary seclusion, was in fact dead. At the time he estimated his father's net worth at $1000 million (see *San Francisco Examiner*, 22 Nov 1982). Scientology's lawyers beat off the suit, arguing that DeWolf's only genuine motivation was greed. By presenting signed and finger-printed affadavits explaining his desire not to break his 'Constitutional right to privacy', they were able to avoid having to produce Hubbard himself in court. One explanation

for his reluctance to be seen is that, having suffered two strokes, he was now a shadow of his once-robust self; and it would be bad PR for the world to know that this great 'healer' could be reduced thus as surely as any other mortal.

19. See Lamont, *Religion, Inc.*, pp. 129–30; also Evans, *Cults of Unreason*, pp. 26–7. Hubbard's first wife became an alcoholic, like Crowley's. That she was imbalanced is clear; but whether this was her fault, Ron's or a result of 'the Bohemian ways and fluctuating professional success' of his early career is now anyone's guess.

20. See Ron Hubbard, *Dianetics: The Modern Science of Mental Health: A Handbook of Dianetics Procedure* (Los Angeles: Bridge Publications, 1985). This book, written following Hubbard's release from hospital and eccentric experiences with Parsons, is full of lurid instances of how people may be made neurotic, psychotic or insane by the actions of others when they are not fully conscious. Extended discussion of how 'engrams' may be inserted into the 'reactive mind' when the subject is under hypnosis or in drug-trance suggest more than academic familiarity with these states. Discussion of sexual perversion, Manichaeanism and the evil power of blasphemy (pp. 140–3) suggest that Hubbard had either experienced or observed such practices. Both could have been learned from Parsons, especially the second. The first may connect as well to Hubbard's treatment in hospital. There is repeated reference to a nurse who deceives a patient into thinking she is his 'ally' by speaking sweetly to him when he is under nitrous oxide and playing with his genitals (pp. 155–7), which results in his making a disastrous marriage with a nurse-like woman once he is 'well'. This and other accounts of difficulties between husbands and wives (for instance, the 'problem in mutual therapy' between R and C, described pp. 495–9) sound not inconsistent with the little we know about Hubbard's first two marriages. But most striking of all preoccupations in this *magnum opus* is how sex by a mother when pregnant may permanently damage the child in the womb. How Hubbard came to believe in this theory, and its possible relation to fears about his own pre-natal experience or surrounding the fathering of DeWolf and other children, is left for the reader to speculate. The sketchiness of facts about the man's life itself leads to lurid supposition.

21. A voluminous list of the whole opus in these genres is given at the beginning of Hubbard's *Battlefield Earth: A Saga of the Year 3000* (Copenhagen: New Era Publications, 1985).

22. See Lamont, *Religion, Inc.*, pp. 131–2.

23. See repeated outbursts against the profession and its practices of lobotomy, leukotomy and so forth in *Dianetics* (pp. 132–3, 147 and *passim*). Was Hubbard threatened with some such treatment during hospitalisation?

24. See note 17 above.

25. See Symonds, *The Great Beast* from p. 392.

26. For instance, *The Scientology Religion* (East Grinstead: Church of Scientology Worldwide, 1974) pt II, ch. II.

27. So I am told by Julie Beard Gerbode Spickler, a high-level Scientologist who has been married to two heads of 'Church' missions in the San Francisco area. Those familiar with the Golden Dawn may also recognise a latter-day version of its Rose-Cross lamen in the Scientology cross.

28. This letter is contained in the Yorke Collection, II, 110.

29. Crowley lectured Parsons on the importance of memorisation and pointed out that his rituals were shorter and easier to learn than many required in higher-degree Masonry. See letter, ibid.

30. In *Cannery Row*. See my *California Writers*, p. 97.

31. In the same letter identified in note 28 above.

32. Parsons eventually made Cameron his second wife as well as high priestess.

33. These are also in the Yorke Collection (II, 85). The poems impressed Anger and Yorke and are sensually evocative and glamorous in a loose-structured, Californian sort of way. It seems a pity that one of the West Coast small presses of the 1960s did not publish them.

34. Not the least startling feature of this incident was that Parsons' mother, immediately on hearing of her son's death, took an overdose of barbituates and died. See the *Los Angeles Mirror* and *Herald-Express*, 19–20 June 1952.

35. In a letter to 'The Beast', Parsons described Cameron as if she were an elemental who had materialised directly as a result of one of his rituals. The Yorke Collection (II, 74) contains clippings about Cameron's bizarre progress post-Parsons, including reviews of her Austin Spare or Steffi Grant-like paintings (see reproductions in Kenneth Grant's *Crowley and the Hidden God*), all of which might belong to a sort of 'school of Crowley'; also news of the suicide of another young man who became bewitched by her.

36. Wallis in *Road to Total Freedom* (pp. 63–5) identifies elements in Scientology with the 'mobility machiavellianism' noted in many modern cults by Thomas Luckmann and Peter Berger in 'Social Mobility and Personal Identity', *European Journal of Sociology*, 5 (1964).

37. This book, published by 93 Publications (Quebec, 1979), shows the Parsons ethos at its toughest, most idealistic, proto-sixties best. The last chapter, 'The Witchcraft', is a marvellous admonition to return to organic healing and fertility rites such as practised perhaps by the Druids and resurrected by many 'flower children'. The spirit of Parsons was certainly to dance under the moonlight in joy on top of the bare Brocken Hill.

38. Whom Crowley claimed as prior identities. See my *Art, Messianism and Crime*, p. 73.

39. See *What is Scientology?* (Church of Scientology Worldwide, 1978), 'Illustration'. The extent to which Hubbard regarded himself among the greatest visionaries may also be inferred from his comparison of the discovery of Dianetics to primitive man's mastering of fire or invention of the wheel.

40. A book about various Scientologists' intimations of past lives (East Grinstead: Department of Publications Worldwide, 1968).

41. An intriguing first name, especially considering the French revolutionary's Masonic associations. One wonders in this connection whether Hubbard might have been exposed to Masonry in youth. It permeated Middle America then, even in rural hamlets, where it still is in evidence today. See, for instance, the finale of Francis Coppola's film *Peggy Sue Got Married*.
42. Probably in an attempt to score a feminist point, the text sounds a bogus note here. There were plenty of educated women in America, and many other places, in the early part of this century. As a matter of fact, in the rural milieu where Hubbard was brought up, it was often typical for the woman to have more education than the man.
43. See Hubbard, *Battlefield Earth*, pp. xiv–xv.
44. See *What is Scientology?*, p. 324.
45. See notes 20 and 23 above.
46. See, for instance, *The Guidebook to Clear and OT* (Tampa, Fla.: Church of Scientology International, 1986) p. 3. To make the mix-up symmetrical, Hubbard mistranslates 'psycho' to mean 'mind' (*Dianetics*, p. 125).
47. See note 20 above.
48. See Evans, *Cults of Unreason*, ch. 3.
49. The Celebrity Center is housed in an old stars' hotel once called Chateau Elycee. Present star members include Chick Corea, Nicky Hopkins, Karen Black, John Travolta and Priscilla Presley. In recent years, this Centre has been the fiefdom of the wife of the present President of the Church.
50. Early histories of the Church are contained in Evans's *Cults of Unreason*, and Wallis, *Road to Total Freedom*. 'Official' versions are usually brief in the extreme.
51. See Evans, *Cults of Unreason*, p. 87. On the E-meter in general, see Wallis, *Road to Total Freedom;* also Hubbard's many works on the subject, such as *Electropsychometric Auditing Operator's Manual, E-Meter Essentials 1961* and *The Book Introducing the E-Meter*.
52. See Evans, *Cults of Unreason*, ch. 6; also the catalogue of the Church's run-ins with the law and their resolution in *What is Scientology?*
53. See note 5 above; also Evans, *Cults of Unreason*, ch. 7.
54. Ethics levels implied their own rewards and punishments: Power, Affluence, Normal Operation, Emergency, Danger, Non-Existence, Liability, Doubt, Enemy, Treason.
55. An account of the Church's activities in Clearwater is given in Lamont, *Religion, Inc.*, esp. ch. 4.
56. Since 1966, or about the time he began his wanderings at sea.
57. See Lamont, *Religion, Inc.*, ch. 8; also appendix C.
58. 'Pulp' is not meant necessarily as a term of denigration. In a promotional blurb on the back of *Battlefield Earth*, A. E. Van Vogt writes, 'Pure science fiction . . . 430,000 words written by a superwriter of the Golden Age of Science Fiction . . . the great pulp music in every line. . . .'
59. Julie Beard Gerbode Spickler. In conversation, Stanford, June, 1986.
60. An extraordinary tribute, *L. Ron Hubbard: The Man and his Work*, was published as an advertising supplement to the *Los Angeles Times* in

June, 1986. This constituted, as it were, an 'official' announcement
of his passing.

61. Evans' Introduction to *Cults of Unreason* discusses Eddy among theosophical and spiritualist precursors (p. 12). The Gantry aspect may
be imagined best by reference to Lamont's *Religion, Inc.*, with its
gaudy cover phot of Hubbard in sateen 'urban cowboy' gear and its
accounts of the glad-handing PR of the present President of the
Church (see esp. pp. 105–14).

62. These may be found on any number of Scientology documents,
including for instance *The Guidebook to Clear and OT*, p. 3.

63. See notes 8 above and 109 below.

64. This is demonstrated nicely by the 'tone-scale' catechism reproduced
in *Religion, Inc.*, pp. 126–7; also the toothpaste-advertisement smiles
on the faces of the girls delegated to guide Lamont around Church
headquarters in Los Angeles (see photo following p. 128).

65. See Ch. 4, section IV.

66. Hubbard's attitude toward what he describes as the 'aberrated' individual has always struck me as crypto-fascist:

> Perhaps at some distant date only the unaberrated person will be
> granted civil rights before law. Perhaps the goal will be reached
> at some future time when only the unaberrated person can attain
> to and benefit from citizenship. These are desirable goals and
> would produce a marked increase in the survival ability and happi-
> ness of man. (*Dianetics*, p. 534)

Hubbard's intention may be admirable: to protect those who have
taken the trouble to 'clear' their beings from those who make no
effort and thus remain psychologically damaged. But this would
involve just as fine an element of judgement as is required in present-
day jurisprudence *and* absolute faith in the ability of Hubbard
processes to 'clear' all people equally. As regards the latter, only a
Scientologist's disbelief is likely to be suspended.

67. See *Hubbard: Man and Work*, p. 18 (quoting *The Way to Happiness*). I
say 'apparently' because such words-to-live-by, typical under the
new President of the Church, may be only of titular Hubbard authorship. This would certainly be the case if one believed the theory,
long held by Ronald DeWolf amongst others, that Hubbard has been
dead since 1980 or 1983, that his signatures have been forged, his
tapes made by manipulation of old voice-prints (see Lamont,
Religion, Inc., p. 157) and so on.

68. See Hubbard, *Dianetics*, bk I, ch. 4, on the first four dynamics, and
Science of Survival (Wichita, Kan.: Hubbard Dianetics Foundation,
1951) vol. I, p. IX, on the completed eight.

69. As we are told, for instance, in *The Guidebook to Clear and OT*, p. 9.

70. See Ch. 5, section IV.

71. See *Notes on the Lectures of L. Ron Hubbard* (East Grinstead: Hubbard
Communications Office, 1962) p. 96; also discussion in *Dianetics*,
pp. 49–51.

72. Around 1959, Hubbard was particularly interested in communicating

with plants and studying plant mutations. So Evans tells us, quoting from the article 'The Sex Life of a Virile Cabbage' which appeared in *Lilliput* at the time (see *Cults of Unreason*, pp. 76–7).

73. 'Stats' confirm Germany as one of the strongest areas for the cult outside the English-speaking world. It is also a country in which Scientology has been relatively unharassed by the law. (See relevant sections of *What is Scientology?*, esp. p. 158.)

74. From here proceeds explication of some of the principal terms and ideas of Dianetics. For further elucidation of these the best in-house sources are *Dianetics* itself and *Science of Survival*, while the fullest external exegesis may be found in Wallis, *Road to Total Freedom*, pp. 24–31 and *passim*.

75. 'Clear' in fact comes from an analogy with a calculating machine (see *Dianetics*, pp. 61–4). 'File clerk' is another of Hubbard's oft-used, office-oriented terms. He revels in the banal language of contemporary 'normalcy' and often mocks the Latinate terms of traditional medicine.

76. Examples of these are so plentiful that the contention need hardly be argued. However, believers that there is something poetic in Scientology may cite such 'sacraments' as 'The Scientology Wedding Ceremony'. Here are two of its most aesthetic verses:

> Rejoice!
> Your line of struggling life
> From aeons gone to now
> For here again your tack is sped
> And winged into a future fate
> By this
> A union of man and bride
> Whose child shall pace
> A further span
> Of Destiny
> And Life.
>
> Forbear!
> For here shall be
> No calumny
> Or whispered word against
> You, Man
> Or Woman thou
> For this union you contract
> does wipe away
> All sorrow
> Of the past.
>   (*Scientology Religion*, p. 65)

77. Admonitions to look up words pepper Hubbard's books. *Dianetics*, for instance, begins with this 'Important Note':

> In reading this book, be very certain you never go past a word
> you do not understand.
> *The only reason a person gives up a study or becomes confused or*
> *unable to learn is because he or she has gone past a word that was not*
> *understood. . . .*

It then explains that, 'as an aid to the reader', footnotes will be
included in the text and a glossary at the end. The glossary contains
the basic Dianetics neologisms. The footnotes include two types of
words: those which Hubbard imagines his readers may be too ill-
educated to understand, and those which come from slang and
therefore may seem bizarre to the normally educated. The process
is stultifying and covertly anti-intellectual. It is also authoritarian in
its promotion of the idea that Hubbard alone has the right to create
and define language.

78. Hubbard occasionally mentions thinkers whom he admires, such as
Francis Bacon, Darwin and Herbert Spencer in his note on 'The
History of Dianetics' (*Dianetics*, p. 530). But such allusions, often
attended with brief, encyclopaedia-like notes, never lead on to
considered discussion of distinguished theories of the past; they are
merely a species of name-dropping.

79. 'Little Hitler' is a phrase used by ex-Scientologist John McMaster,
first person to have reached 'clear' (Lamont, *Religion, Inc.*, p. 58).
On 'brave new world': Hubbard is on record as having admired
Huxley, who in turn is reported to have been interested in Dianetics
in its early stages.

80. See note 74 above.

81. See Jean Overton Fuller, *The Magical Progress of Victor Neuburg*
(London: W. H. Allen, 1965); also Wallis, *Road to Total Freedom*,
p. 119.

82. The 'tone scale' may be found in any number of Scientology texts,
including *Science of Survival*, 1 (loose sheet); see also p. 124 on political
'tones'.

83. See Lamont, *Religion, Inc.*, p. 131.

84. See *What is Scientology?*, pp. 55–65.

85. It has often been remarked that Scientology provides an alternative
higher education for those who did poorly in conventional school
(or, like Hubbard himself, rejected standard higher education as
insufficiently related to the 'real world'). My experience with Ms
Spickler and her first husband (see notes 27 and 59 above) would
suggest that the cult can also provide a continuing educative framework for types who always did well in school and knew hardly any
other environment. She had a BA and MA in Elizabethan literature
from Stanford, he a BS from Stanford, a year in philosophy at
Cambridge and an MD (psychology) from Yale. Both were also
accomplished Renaissance musicians, she on viola da gamba, he on
lute.

86. The present *Guidebook to Clear and OT* list grades up to "OT XV".

Clearly, progression up the ladder becomes too addictive for many to want to stop.

87. See, for instance, *Scientology 8–8008* (Scientology Publications Worldwide, 1967) p. 116. In general, Hubbard took the view that a person who dispensed higher lore out of sequence could be recognised as 'not one of us'.

88. *Hubbard: Man and Work* lists the founder of Scientology's avocations as 'author, philosopher, educator, research pioneer, musician, photographer, cinematographer, horticulturalist, navigator, explorer and humanitarian'.

89. L. Ron Hubbard, *Mission into Time* (Copenhagen: Advanced Org Publications, 1973) p. 69.

90. A persistent technique of Hubbard's which is very disarming, because it always makes him seem to be talking in the language of common sense.

91. See Evans, *Cults of Unreason*, p. 44.

92. See ibid., p. 46.

93. See note 78 above.

94. See my *Art, Messianism and Crime*, p. 137.

95. There are references to 'ancient Hindu wisdom' here and there in Hubbard's works (see, for instance, *Dianetics*, p. 530), and the Chinese and Buddhists are among the most highly regarded humans by the end of *Battlefield Earth*.

96. I had numerous and sometimes fairly heated discussions about such matters when living in the house of Scientologist 'Sarge' Gerbode in Palo Alto in the early 1970s. I was working for the Department of Public Health and Welfare in the East Palo Alto black ghetto at the time but could persuade no 'thetan' to come help my poverty-stricken clients.

97. *Dianetics* makes several remarks on the fall of civilisations (pp. 186, 540); Hubbard clearly expected the Amercian 'empire' to collapse; and Scientologists no doubt dream of replacing its secular order with their 'sacred' one.

98. See *The Sunday Times*, 19 May 1985.

99. 'Dominance' is the key to success for the hero of *Battlefield Earth* in his negotiation with leaders from other planets (see pp. 838–9 and 854–5). Jonnie Goodboy Tyler is given specific training in how to achieve this condition.

100. See *Hubbard: Man and Work*, p. 15. Again, being a PR sheet put out by the present leaders of the Church, this may not precisely reflect 'Mr Hubbard'.

101. Hubbard evidently aspired to the standard of this other creator of *Gesamtkunstwerk* of world-historic proportions and messianic purpose. *Battlefield Earth* contains several advertisements to 'Buy the dynamic music soundtack of the book', composed by him and performed by 'Celebrity' pop-musicians Nicky Hopkins, Chick Corea and others. The music which announces Jonnie's entrance into the conference room at the beginning of part 27 is described in terms which might be used for the entry of the Grail Knights in *Parsifal*:

'It was slow dignified music. Ponderous. Impressive. . . . Fit for regal functions' (p. 853). The idea for it has come from discovery of an old recording of the Cleveland Symphony Orchestra playing *Lohengrin*: 'The music was much like that but deeper, fuller, quite impressive' (p. 830).

102. In this sense, the book may seem heroic, even inspiring.

103. I am thinking here specifically of the relationship between Jonnie as caged 'animal' and his captor, Terl, the demonic Psychlo who at one point is associated with Hitler (p. 620) and another Satan (p. 656), and whose incessant concern is to achieve 'leverage' against others so that they can never speak out against him (a technique Lamont, in *Religion, Inc.*, ascribes to Scientology).

104. Opinions are mixed on this. Hubbard classes himself with the classic writers of the 'Golden Age' of the genre: Asimov, Bradbury, Heinlein – even Huxley (?) and H. P. Lovecraft (also a cult figure among latter-day Crowleyans). I am no judge of science fiction, and can only remark that to read a 'pulp' novel of the length of *Battlefield Earth* (let alone write one) seems like dedication taken to the point of folly.

105. The stereotype may be bogus, but it has had wide currency among anti-academics of the post-war period, including even the civilized Gore Vidal.

106. In this context, it seems ironic that one of the methods by which Jonnie achieves dominance over his Tolnep adversary, Lord Schleim, is by mocking his accent as 'uncouth' and 'provincial' and subtly directing others' attention to his boots, which are 'old', 'rough', 'dirty' and do not go with the rest of his outfit (Hubbard, *Battlefield Earth*, pp. 855–6).

107. See *Letters from Jack London* (London: MacGibbon and Kee, 1966) p. 117.

108. Psychlo 'aberration' is assured from birth by implantation of electronic control mechanisms in the brain – an apt fictive representation for the mind-control Hubbard and others of his period feared was being put into practice by a manipulative establishment. (See *Dianetics*, p. 306: 'Whole populations are handled by their push-button responses.')

109. Hubbard depicts the human 'race' as being in a struggle for survival against greater, unseen forces in the universe (*Dianetics*, pp. 187, 539; *Battlefield Earth*, pp. 669, 715 and elsewhere). At times the urgency of his view that the 'race' must come together to protect itself recalls that of Hitler on the need for Germans to stand together against the Jews and related 'dark forces'. Throughout *Battlefield Earth*, Hubbard mocks the German *Führer* (see esp. pp. 608–9); but this seems ingratiating. His Jonnie is after all merely a more attractive version of the charismatic leader with messianic purpose. A war-lord embodying Darwinian principles of survival-of-the-fittest, Jonnie exterminates the Psychlos, Brigantes and Tolneps, which in his Manichaean world are fairly precise counterparts to Hitler's antagonists; he also subdues an all-powerful and conspiratorial banking-

system – another of the Nazi bugaboos. Above all, he believes that he and he alone can see the way for his kind to achieve a better future (see p. 630), which is what persuades him to allow, as a necessary evil, an organisation to grow up around him. This attitude is not treated as hubris in the novel, but in Hubbard's career it may be the chief 'tragic' flaw.

110. Jonnie wears a US Air Force belt-buckle. Indeed, the whole novel, taken up with war, terror and peace-negotiations as it is, seems on one level an exercise in nostalgia for Hubbard's days in the navy in the Second World War.

111. See *Hubbard: Man and Work*, p. 10.

112. See *Dianetics*, p. 183. As a rule, Hubbard was not charitable about what he saw as inferior cultures. When the Australian province of Victoria banned the Church in the 1960s, he responded that it had been founded and was run by criminals and the riff-raff of England (see Evans, *Cults of Unreason*, p. 87).

113. *Battlefield Earth* shows prejudice in favour of these north Britons, but not their southern neighbours. The invading Hockner allies of the Tolneps speak with upper-class English accents (p. 781), as do many of the emissaries in Part 27. The latter are 'loathed' as 'weak and corrupt and dangerous' by Sir Robert the Fox, Jonnie's chief Scottish lieutenant: 'That had always been his opinion of the breed', we are told (p. 846) in a statement which may reflect Hubbard's ultimate attitude toward another country which banned him.

114. In light of remarks in the following paragraph, it may be significant that Scientology and related 'mind-dynamic' disciplines have concentrated so much attention on the film community, especially since the later 1970s.

115. Consider Steven Spielberg here. *ET*, *Young Sherlock* and *Back to the Future* are all relevant; also George Lucas's *The Explorers*.

116. An example of the 'wise man' or hierophant figure is the mad scientist in *Back to the Future*. 'ET' is an example of the beneficient being from afar.

CHAPTER 10.   CONCLUDING: 'MAGIC' AND THE MORAL
CONTINUUM

1. As Frazer argued in *The Golden Bough*.

2. In *The Perfect Wagnerite*. See my *Wagner to the Waste Land*, p. 84.

3. In *Imagination Dead Imagine*, expanding on ideas of Locke's.

4. Webb, *The Occult Establishment*, p. 514.

5. *The Penguin Krishnaumurti Reader*, comp. Mary Luytens (London: Penguin, 1970), 'The Problems of Living', VIII: 'What Is the Self?'

6. Ibid., pp. 191–2.

7. See Ch. 7, section III.

8. See Ch. 3, note 74, and Ch. 4, note 68.

9. See Ch. 5, section III (Michael Hearne on Maclagan's occultists).

10. Umberto Eco, *The Name of the Rose*, tr. William Weaver (London: Picador, 1984) pp. 150–3.

11. *Krishnamurti Reader*, 'For the Young', pp. 96, 132, 146 and elsewhere.

12. As ascribed to by both the venal 'Brown Limper' in Hubbard's *Battlefield Earth* and Settembrini in *The Magic Mountain*, as we have seen.

13. In *The Non-Religion of the Future: A Sociological Study* (London: Heinemann, 1897) p. 128. On Guyau's identity, see Ch. 7, note 93.

14. Ibid., p. 95.

15. A fictive illustration of this may be found in Mario Vargas Llosa's *War of the End of the World* (London: Faber, 1985), where the anarchist revolutionary Galileo Gall is approached for assistance by the Masonic, republican politician Epaminondas Gonçalves.

16. See Webb, *The Occult Establishment*, 226–8. Anti-semitism was endemic to Theosophy too.

17. In *A Sketch of Morality Independent of Obligation or Sanction*, tr. Gertrude Kapteyn (London: Watts, 1898) p. 13.

18. See note 11 above; also *Krishnamurti Reader*, pp. 164, 176 and elsewhere.

19. See Mann, *The Magic Mountain*, p. 286 (quoted in Ch. 6).

20. Guyau, *The Non-Religion of the Future*, p. 132.

21. Ibid., p. 91.

22. I.e. in general the period covered in this study, with its roots in the French Revolution and most recent shoots in the 1960s and after.

23. Guyau, *The Non-Religion of the Future*, p. 154.

24. To Guyau, who admired him greatly. Quoted ibid., p. 373.

25. In choosing, as the 'forbidden' text which scholar monks commit murder to keep from general consumption, Aristotle's lost (or perhaps never written) treatise on comedy.

26. See Guyau, who discusses 'seekers' in his chapter 'Religious Individualism' (*The Non-Religion of the Future*, p. 375).

27. Word and concept are Stendhal's, in reference to the experience of love. Guyau, however, adapts them to the experience of religion.

28. Guyau, *The Non-Religion of the Future*, p. 150.

29. Ibid., p. 152.

30. See my *California Writers*, pp. 172–3 and 186.

31. I am indebted for this idea to Mrs William Wilkins, speaking in reference to her husband's *pointilliste* paintings.

32. To Guyau (*The Non-Religion of the Future*, p. 374).

33. Ibid., p. 151.

34. Ibid., p. 165.

35. See Mann, *The Magic Mountain*, p. 642 (quoted in Ch. 6).

36. Guyau, *The Non-Religion of the Future*, p. 362.

37. Thus Ronald Reagan's defence in the 'Irangate' scandal (see Ch. 9, section v), which the American public was persuaded to accept.

38. This is one of the concepts in Hubbard's *Dianetics* which seems reasonable.

39. See my *California Writers*, p. 189, and *Art, Messianism and Crime*, pp. 128–30.

40. Interest in occultism by mystery writers of course predated Hammett. Conan Doyle was taken up with it, as was Poe.
41. A major theme in Webb's *Occult Establishment*. See ch. 1, 3 and 5.
42. An interesting connective between Hesse and Allende's Chile may be the ambassador and philosopher Miguel Serrano, whose 'slim volume' on Hesse and Jung is cited in Ch. 8, note 13, and whose persona is precisely the civilised liberal type whose passing *The House of the Spirits* laments.
43. See Ch. 5, section IV and note 88.
44. Roland Joffé's *The Mission*, which won the Palme d'Or at Cannes in 1986.
45. The inscription under the pyramid surmounted by a triangular eye which appears on the back of the US dollar bill.
46. Two recent films, *Salvador* and *El Norte*, evoke this situation admirably.
47. See Ch. 9, note 90.
48. See my *Art, Messianism and Crime*, pp. 176–9.
49. See Castaneda's most recent book, *The Fire from Within* (London: Black Swan, 1985) ch. 2.
50. See ibid., ch. 7–9. 'Destabilisation' is a term emanating from the intelligence services, such as the CIA, and has to do with bringing on a new regime by stirring up and subverting a *status quo*.
51. See Castaneda, *Fire from Within*, ch. 3 and 10.
52. Ibid., p. 156.
53. See Ch. 1, section II.
54. 'To write the history of religions is to write a damaging criticism of them', Guyau remarks. Needless to say, it is also to define the limitations of one's own belief.

Index

Note: certain words and concepts seem too general and pervasive in this study to cite. These include among others 'magic', God, Nature, Man, Love, the devil, knowledge and power.

303

Index